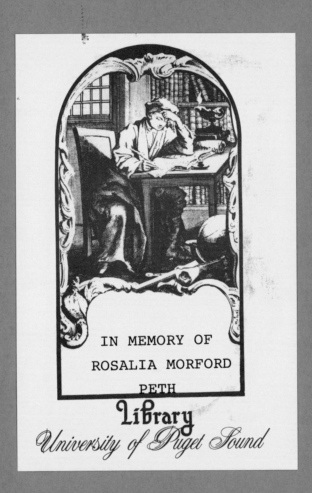

D1706378

CORMAC McCARTHY

CORMAC

McCARTHY

New Directions

Edited by
James D. Lilley

University of
New Mexico Press
Albuquerque

FIRST EDITION

Library of Congress Cataloging-in-Publication Data:
Cormac McCarthy : new directions / edited by James D. Lilley.—1st ed.
    p. cm.
Includes bibliographical references and index.
ISBN 0-8263-2766-4 (cloth : alk. paper)
1. McCarthy, Cormac, 1933—Criticism and interpretation. 2. Mexican-
American Border Region—In literature. 3. Southern States—In literature.
4. Tennessee, East—In literature. I. Lilley, James D.
(James David), 1971–
PS3563.C337 Z63 2002
813'.54—dc21

                                                            2001007154

Dana Phillips' essay, "History and the Ugly Facts of Cormac McCarthy's
Blood Meridian," is reprinted with permission from American Literature,
68:2 (June 1996), 433-60. Copyright 1996, Duke University Press. All
rights reserved.

An earlier version of the essay "The Lay of the Land in Cormac
McCarthy's Appalachia," by K. Wesley Berry, was published in The
Southern Quarterly, vol. 38, no. 4.

An earlier version of the essay "All the Pretty Mexicos: Cormac
McCarthy's Mexican Representations," by Daniel Cooper Alarcón, was
published in Southwestern American Literature, vol. 25, no. 1.

An earlier version of the essay "From Beowulf to Blood Meridian:
Cormac McCarthy's Demystification of the Martial Code," by Rick
Wallach, was published in The Southern Quarterly, vol. 36, no. 4.

CONTENTS

CONTRIBUTORS

Daniel Cooper Alarcón is an associate professor of English at the University of Arizona in Tucson. A creative writer and literary critic, he is the author of *The Aztec Palimpsest: Mexico in the Modern Imagination* (1997), and his scholarship has appeared in *Aztlan, American Literature, MELUS,* and *Southwestern American Literature.* His most recent short fiction has appeared in the anthologies *New Chicana/Chicano Writing 3* and *New World: Young Latino Writers.*

Edwin T. Arnold is professor of English at Appalachian State University. He has written widely on Southern literature and film. He is coeditor, with Dianne C. Luce, of *Perspectives on Cormac McCarthy* (1999) and *A Cormac McCarthy Companion: The Border Trilogy* (2001). He served as guest editor for the "Faulkner and Film" double issue of *The Faulkner Journal* (fall 2000/spring 2001).

K. Wesley Berry is an assistant professor of English at Rockford College in northern Illinois. He teaches creative writing and contemporary literature and has published short stories, creative nonfiction, and critical essays on Walter Inglis Anderson, Wendell Berry, Toni Morrison, and Leslie Marmon Silko. The essay on Cormac McCarthy included in this collection is from a book in progress on ecological literary scholarship entitled *Landscapes of Healing in Contemporary American Prose.*

Timothy P. Caron is an associate professor of English at California State University, Long Beach. He has published essays in *Studies in American Fiction* and the *Southern Quarterly*, and he is the author of *Struggles Over the Word: Race and Religion in O'Connor, Faulkner, Hurston, and Wright* (2000). Caron is currently editing two other projects: a collection of Civil War writings that originally appeared in *Century Magazine* during the 1880s, and a collection of essays on southern literature and literary theory.

Ann Fisher-Wirth is professor of English at the University of Mississippi, where she teaches courses in American literature, creative writing, and literature and environment. She is the author of *William Carlos Williams and Autobiography: The Woods of His Own Nature;* numerous essays on Williams, Willa Cather, Cormac McCarthy, and others; and a forthcoming book of poems, *Blue Window.* A former Fulbright professor at the University of Fribourg, Switzerland, she is also newsletter editor for the Association for the Study of Literature and the Environment.

George Guillemin received a Ph.D. in American literature from the Free University in Berlin. He wrote the first dissertation on Cormac McCarthy in Germany and hosted the first European Conference on Cormac McCarthy in Berlin in 1998. He currently works in the public relations department of a German high-tech corporation.

Matthew R. Horton is a Ph.D. candidate in English at the University of Georgia, where he studies twentieth-century British and American literature. His essay in this collection derives from his master's thesis, "Narrative Structures of Time and Space in Cormac McCarthy's *The Orchard Keeper* and *Outer Dark.*" For his dissertation, he plans to explore the relationship between historical perception and fictional narrative in all of McCarthy's novels.

Robert L. Jarrett is an associate professor of English at University of Houston-Downtown, where he directs the Professional Writing degree. He is the author of *Cormac McCarthy*, a volume in the Twayne

United States Authors series, and has published several other articles on Cormac McCarthy and southwestern literature.

James D. Lilley is the author of essays, reviews, and interviews that have appeared in the *Southern Quarterly, Interdisciplinary Studies in Literature and the Environment, MELUS,* and the *Mississippi Review.* He is working on a Ph.D. dissertation at Princeton University that explores how the literature of the emerging U.S. nation influenced, and was influenced by, the politics of Indian removal and African colonization.

Dianne C. Luce is chair of the English Department at Midlands Technical College in Columbia, South Carolina. She has published several articles on Cormac McCarthy since 1980. Together with Edwin T. Arnold, she is editor of *Perspectives on Cormac McCarthy* (1993, rev. ed. 1999) and *A Cormac McCarthy Companion: The Border Trilogy* (2001). Her other books include *Annotations to William Faulkner's* As I Lay Dying (1990), *William Faulkner's* As I Lay Dying: *A Critical Casebook* (1985), and an edition of William Faulkner's *Elmer* (1983).

Adam Parkes is an associate professor of English at the University of Georgia, where he teaches modern British and American literature. He is the author of *Modernism and the Theater of Censorship* (1996) and *Kazuo Ishiguro's* The Remains of the Day: *A Reader's Guide* (2001), and articles on Radclyffe Hall, Henry James, James Joyce, D. H. Lawrence, George Moore, Ezra Pound, John Ruskin, and Virginia Woolf.

Dana Phillips has taught at the University of Pennsylvania, Princeton, Bryn Mawr, and Brown. His book *The Truth of Ecology: Nature, Culture, and Literature in America* is forthcoming from Oxford University Press, and he is completing work on a second book, tentatively entitled *Whitman and the Politics of Nature.*

Sara Spurgeon received a Ph.D. in literature from the University of Arizona, and is an adjunct lecturer there in the Women's Studies

Department. She is the co-author, with David K. Dunaway, of *Writing the Southwest,* a literary study of contemporary southwestern writers.

Rick Wallach is the editor of *Myth, Legend, Dust: Critical Responses to Cormac McCarthy,* as well as coeditor, with Wade Hall, of *Sacred Violence: A Reader's Companion to Cormac McCarthy.* He teaches literature at the University of Miami.

Linda Townley Woodson is professor of English and chair of the Department of English, Classics, and Philosophy at the University of Texas at San Antonio. Her research interests include contemporary rhetorical theory, theory and practice of teaching composition, and the literature of Texas and the Southwest. She is the author of numerous books and articles on rhetoric and composition and has also published articles on Cormac McCarthy.

"There Was Map Enough for Men to Read"

Storytelling, the Border Trilogy, and *New Directions*

James D. Lilley

I WISH I could tell you that this essay collection was inspired by the closing words of Cormac McCarthy's most recent novel, *Cities of the Plain*. *"The story's told,"* insists the dedication of the final installment of McCarthy's Border Trilogy: *"Turn the page"* (293). These words remind the reader that from the feral Appalachian wilderness of his first four novels—*The Orchard Keeper* (1965), *Outer Dark* (1968), *Child of God* (1973), and *Suttree* (1979)—to the austere southwestern borderlands of his most recent fiction—*Blood Meridian* (1985), *All the Pretty Horses* (1992), *The Crossing* (1994), and *Cities of the Plain* (1998)—the intertextual matrix of Cormac McCarthy's work is held together by an unending faith in the power of storytelling.

Earlier in *Cities of the Plain*, the two protagonists of the Border Trilogy, Billy Parham and John Grady Cole, participate in a hunt for wild dogs. In the frieze of violence that ensues, gesture is more important than discourse. "Goddamn" is all that Billy can manage after "the slack of [his] catchrope hissed along the ground and stopped and the big yellow dog rose suddenly from the ground in headlong flight taut between the two ropes and the ropes resonated a single brief dull note and then the dog exploded" (167). The dance of the dog hunt, with its "dull" report of exploding heads and singing ropes, guides us back toward the central image of the Border Trilogy—the puppets dancing on a string that Alfonsa, the strong-willed great-aunt of John Grady Cole's Mexican lover Alejandra, offers in *All the Pretty Horses* as a reading of Mexican history. "For me," Alfonsa admits, "the world has always been more of a puppet show. But when one looks behind the curtain and traces the strings upward he finds they terminate in the hands of yet other puppets, themselves with their own strings which trace upward in turn, and so on" (231).

Here we observe the existential backdrop to McCarthy's land-scape, the nexus of puppet and string that ties the tapestry of existence together. The central question of McCarthy's fiction has always centered on the possibility of agency—"whether the stuff of creation may be shaped to man's will or whether his own heart is not another kind of clay" (*Blood Meridian* 5)—and in McCarthy's world this possibility is actualized only through a further perpetuation of the dance, a witnessing and retelling of the story, a reweaving of the world. "That man who sets himself the task of singling out the thread of order from the tapestry," insists *Blood Meridian*'s Judge Holden, "will by the decision alone have taken charge of the world and it is only by such taking charge that he will effect a way to dictate the terms of his own fate" (199).

For McCarthy, storytelling is the definitive human activity. Through the story we engage ourselves in the tapestry of creation, single out and witness our own thread in this fabric, and merge our voice with the "desert absolute" for a fleeting, and often violent, moment in history (*Blood Meridian* 295). In *Whales and Men*—a screenplay that McCarthy uses to rehearse the major thematic issues that he will tackle in the Border Trilogy—the Irish aristocrat Peter Gregory writes the fol-lowing comments in his ship's log: "We have no faith in being because we have fractured it into history. And this is the way we live. In archives of our own devising. Among sketches and bones. . . . There is no book where the world is written down. The world is that book" (96).[1] McCarthy's representations of the Appalachian South and the borderlands of the U.S. Southwest are not fractured archives of "sketches and bones." Rather, they are a work in progress, a living and fluid dialog, that exists only at those storied moments of intersection between speaker and witness, traveler and desert absolute. And McCarthy suggests that our agency, our "faith in being," can be realized only to the extent that we accept the roles of storyteller and witness. Otherwise we are left like puppets and dogs on a string, dancing to a distant and stale rhythm. For McCarthy, both history and agency exist dynamically in the interface between word and flesh, story and witness. To refuse to participate in this strange dance of narrative and meaning is, as the judge warns *Blood Meridian*'s nameless kid, to give in to fate, to refuse to "take charge of the world" (199). McCarthy's Border Trilogy is filled with characters that, like Alfonsa in *All the Pretty Horses,* dedicate themselves to this dance by defiantly forcing the hand of fate. "It's not so much that I dont believe in [fate]," Alfonsa avers. "I dont subscribe to its nomination. . . . At some point we cannot escape naming responsibility" (241). Or, as the blind pianist in *Cities of the Plain* puts it, the point is to "press" the world into action and narrative—a task that he admits takes much audacity and dedication. But such is the trajectory of the trilogy.

When Billy, at the close of *Cities of the Plain,* looks at his lined and patterned hands—each segment of flesh marked with its own story, its own witness—he begins to gauge the scope of his involvement in the dance: he begins to take charge of his history, his narrative. No longer alone in an empty and menacing desert ("Well, Mr Parham, I know who you are," insists a friend who has taken him in from the cold weather [292]), the runes and patterns etched onto Billy's hands have become markers that unite him with, rather than alienate him from, the "stuff of creation": "Gnarled, ropescarred, speckled from the sun and the years of it. The ropy veins that bound them to his heart. There was map enough for men to read. There God's plenty of signs and wonders to make a landscape. To make a world" (291). We have seen these same capable, human hands in McCarthy's five-act play *The Stonemason* (1990)—hands "shaped in the image of God. To make the world. To make it again and again. To make it in the very maelstrom of its undoing" (133). In McCarthy's landscape, such hands make their home in the complex borderlands between fate and agency: they press the world into service and witness its stories in the flesh. These are not Alfonsa's "hands of yet other puppets." Rather, they resemble the hands of *The Crossing*'s storyteller God—a God who sits "solely in the light of his own presence. Weaving the world. In his hands it flowed out of nothing and in his hands it vanished into nothing once again. Endlessly. Endlessly" (149).

So when the trilogy closes by urging its readers to *"Turn the page,"* I take this as a challenge to continue the storytelling process, not as a sign that the author wants us to forget about his decade-long textual project. I can think of no better epigraph for the collection that follows—a collection that bears witness to the matrix of McCarthy's fiction by teasing out a variety of different threads from its tapestry.

The truth of the matter, however, is that this book did not begin with the end of *Cities of the Plain*. Rather, the collection started several years ago after the 1994 publication of *The Crossing*. Although a significant number of essays examining McCarthy's work had been published at that time, I felt that this scholarship had failed to address important questions about the author's fiction. Critics have been quick to address McCarthy's indebtedness to southern literature, Christianity, and existential thought; however, the essays in this collection are among the first to tackle issues such as representations of gender and race in McCarthy's fiction. My goal from the outset was to assemble a collection of essays that reflect the astonishingly diverse readership that McCarthy's work continues to attract. I felt, for example, that it was important to solicit essays from scholars working outside of the United States, and I also wanted to include scholarship produced by both established figures in the nascent field of McCarthy studies and academics who had yet to publish on McCarthy's work.

I was helped in this enterprise by an almost overwhelming initial response to my call for papers. The essays you are about to read were selected from nearly fifty completed essays that I have solicited and received over the last five years. I cannot thank the authors enough for their patience and diligence during the editing process. A special thanks is also due to Robert H. Brinkmeyer; his untiring help and generous advice helped to initiate and sustain this collection. At the University of Arizona, I was fortunate enough to join a rich intellectual community of scholars well versed in the literature and culture of the U.S. Southwest. In particular, I want to thank Larry Evers, J. Douglas Canfield, Randy Accetta, Daniel Cooper Alarcón, and Chris Carroll for their fascinating insights into McCarthy's fiction. I also thank my friends at the University of Mississippi, Donald Kartiganer and Jay Watson, for their assistance with my work on McCarthy in general and with this essay collection in particular. For all their help with the editing process, I am indebted to Joan Dayan and Annette Kolodny. Their invaluable counsel and inspiring examples helped me to put the finishing touches on this collection. Finally, I thank my editor at the University of New Mexico Press, Elizabeth Hadas, for her enthusiasm and support, and my copyeditor, Gregory McNamee, for his astute comments and exacting eye for detail.

The first two essays in *Cormac McCarthy*, Dana Phillips's "History and the Ugly Facts of *Blood Meridian*" and K. Wesley Berry's "The Lay of the Land in Cormac McCarthy's Appalachia," approach McCarthy's work from an ecocritical perspective. Such a perspective focuses on McCarthy's representation of the natural world and the relationships established between that world and the human subjects who encounter it. For Dana Phillips, in McCarthy's fiction "the world of nature and the world of men are parts of the same world, and both are equally violent and indifferent to the other." Phillips's essay is an extremely important addition to McCarthy studies. Published in the June 1996 issue of *American Literature*, it immediately caused a stir among McCarthy scholars. Phillips's central contention is that *Blood Meridian* does not "assert the meaninglessness or utter fragmentation of existence or experience as given. Rather, [it suggests] meaning on a scale of time and space which we can only dimly perceive, marked by the scraping of rock upon rock. . . . The meaning of these scrapings is not connected to human value." Phillips's approach to *Blood Meridian* thus signals a radical departure from a critical discourse that had been dominated by existential readings of McCarthy's fiction and approaches that sought to decode the symbolic depth of that fiction.

There is meaning within McCarthy's landscape, Phillips argues, but it is a meaning that transcends and tests the limits of human time and comprehension. Within such a landscape, the search for moral parables or religious epiphanies in McCarthy's work will ultimately miss the mark.

In his essay, K. Wesley Berry looks at "natural resource usage in Appalachia" and argues that, within this context, *The Orchard Keeper* and *Child of God* can be read as "complex" pastoral and agrarian ecological critiques. From deforestation and land erosion to mining and the development of heavy industry, his essay details "real-life economic and ecological conditions" that form the backdrop of these two novels. Although the "apocalyptic tone is overbearing," Berry finds "elements of hope" in what he calls McCarthy's "inhumanist perspective": "'Inhumanism,' as poet Robinson Jeffers defines the term, is 'a shifting of emphasis and significance from man to not-man; [it is] the rejection of human solipsism and recognition of the transhuman magnificence.'" As Berry notes, Jeffers's definition of "inhumanism" is similar to Dana Phillips's discussion of "optical democracy," because they both "question whether humans have a privileged position in the world."

Sara Spurgeon's "The Sacred Hunter and the Eucharist of the Wilderness: Mythic Reconstructions in *Blood Meridian*" continues to explore how McCarthy represents the relationship between the human and the natural world. Whereas Dana Phillips argues that humans "and the natural world are not antagonists" but are instead "parts of the same continuum," Spurgeon observes that in *Blood Meridian* "it is the fundamental change in this relationship, enacted on the level of the mythic and sacred, that McCarthy is interested in uncovering." Like K. Wesley Berry, Spurgeon examines how McCarthy's fiction critiques human participation in the natural world. "It is human will that ultimately shapes myth," Spurgeon argues, "and . . . it is our myths that ultimately shape the world." Drawing on Annette Kolodny's work on North American frontier literature, the essay illustrates how mythmaking—the making of the "Sacred Hunter" myth in particular—helps to hide the "dark spots on the geography" of the emerging nation. The most basic function of myth, the author reminds us, is "to organize and impose order on humans and their worlds, though in McCarthy's antimyth the revelation of the profound disorder at the heart of our myths seems to be the ultimate goal." What began as an ostensibly mutual and reciprocal relationship between the human and the natural world has, by the close of *Blood Meridian,* "shifted to the side of humans. The original covenant has been violated, the sacred myths structuring the relationship of humans to the natural world now perverted to an extent that McCarthy suggests cannot be redeemed, reprieved, or corrected."

Issues of race and gender in McCarthy's fiction remain largely unexplored critical terrain. The next four essays begin to chart this complex topography by discussing the author's representations of Mexico and Mexicans and by exploring gender and gender identity in his work. In "History, Bloodshed, and the Spectacle of American Identity in *Blood Meridian,*" Adam Parkes explores McCarthy's revisionist history of the American Southwest. Instead of looking at how McCarthy rewrites the historical events or mythical material of the West, Parkes focuses on the author's representation of gender and gender difference. "In restaging the history of the Wild West," Parkes contends, McCarthy "emphasizes the performativity of American selfhood." Parkes draws heavily on Judith Butler's work on gender, especially her concept of "performative fluidity"—"a notion that *Blood Meridian* turns into the founding principle of existence." Gender identity in *Blood Meridian* is not fixed in essential and unchanging categories. Rather, Parkes argues, identities are performed through a "mobile theatricality." The resulting gender trouble "subverts the opposition of natural versus unnatural by presenting bodies . . . as costumes that are equally well suited to masculine and feminine roles." Such bodies lay "bare the seams of historical and cultural constructions of American masculinity" and also challenge essentialized notions of racial, as well as gender, identity. McCarthy thus reveals the "concept of American nationhood . . . to be no more fixed or stable than the notions of racial and sexual identity on which it depends." In Parkes's view of *Blood Meridian,* gender, racial, and national identities are redrawn as fluid and protean categories "open to rewriting."

Ann Fisher-Wirth's "Abjection and 'the Feminine' in *Outer Dark*" offers a persuasive and insightful reading of one of McCarthy's most mysterious and haunting novels. Fisher-Wirth's argument is informed by Julia Kristeva's influential *Powers of Horror: An Essay on Abjection*—a book that examines from a neo-Freudian perspective the nature of the feminine and its relationship to the "symbolic order." "For Kristeva," Fisher-Wirth notes, the feminine signifies "that realm of experience or existence that lies outside . . . the symbolic order, and that must be repressed or repudiated if the subject is to retain his illusion of autonomy, identity." Read from this perspective, *Outer Dark* and its central characters—Culla and Rinthy Holme—explore the feminine and the "abject" in rich detail. Although "fully developed female characters do not exist in McCarthy's novels," from Fisher-Wirth's Kristevan viewpoint "McCarthy is a brilliant symbolist of 'the feminine'": "What would in another novelist's work be sensational-ism, even pornography . . . is in McCarthy's fiction apprehended so powerfully at the level of the unconscious that it becomes the stuff of nightmare and beauty."

In "All the Pretty Mexicos: McCarthy's Mexican Representations," Daniel Cooper Alarcón argues that "Mexicanness" in McCarthy's southwestern fiction is informed by a familiar discursive network of tropes of and assumptions about life south of the border. Cooper Alarcón briefly surveys the body of U.S. literature that represents Mexico as what Ronald Walker has called an "Infernal Paradise": "Enchanting/repellent, beautiful/desolate, civilized/cruel, dreamlike/bloody, paradisal/infernal. These are the standard oppositional terms with which Mexico has been consistently represented by Anglo writers." From here, Cooper Alarcón offers two ways to read McCarthy's involvement with this literary tradition. His first reading of *All the Pretty Horses* places McCarthy firmly and uncritically within the "Infernal Paradise" tradition, while his second reading focuses on John Grady Cole's "stubborn adherence" to the chivalric code of the West—a code that, of course, carries its own assumptions about and repre-sentations of "Mexicanness." Here Cooper Alarcón—like Adam Parkes—reads McCarthy's fiction as self-conscious of its own involve-ment in the construction of racial identities. "McCarthy's stereotypical representations are," he notes, "offset by a degree of self-reflexivity that [calls] attention to their discursive origins." Whichever argument you find yourself favoring, it is important to note the differences between this and José Limón's reading of *All the Pretty Horses* in his *American Encounters: Greater Mexico, the United States, and the Erotics of Culture.* For Limón, McCarthy has radically rewritten the "hegemonic western genre and all that it ideologically and materially entails" (204). The author's nuanced (and untranslated) representations of Spanish-speaking communities in the U.S.-Mexico borderlands constitute such a significant shift in the Western genre that Limón concludes his argument by referring to McCarthy as the "Mexican from Tennessee." I hope that dialog between these two very different readings will help to spawn more work on McCarthy's Mexican representations.

Timothy P. Caron shares with Daniel Cooper Alarcón an interest in issues of race and racial identity in McCarthy's fiction. His essay "'Blood is Blood': *All the Pretty Horses* in the Multicultural Literature Class" details his experiences of teaching McCarthy's novel at Biola University—a "small, private, Christian, liberal-arts university in Los Angeles County whose student population is very largely white." Given the increasing interest McCarthy's fiction has gathered in academe, more and more teachers are including his work in their reading lists. From courses on contemporary literature of the American South and the American West to classes that investigate the Western genre or the historical novel, McCarthy's work is a regular feature on many syllabi. And although Cormac McCarthy—a "white male of Anglo-Irish extraction"—might "seem like an odd choice as a subject for . . . an American multicultural literature class," Caron's essay illustrates how *All the Pretty Horses* raises important and interesting questions about racial and ethnic identity. "McCarthy's novel," Caron notes, "provided a solid foundation for the course as we began interrogating John Grady Cole's reasons for traveling to Mexico, his romanticized expectations, and how his lack of knowledge of Mexican history and customs causes so much pain for him." He and his students become aware that as a result of John Grady's "nationalistic attitudes" Mexico "remains an empty space onto which they project their ideas of a cowboy's perfect paradise." Using Héctor Calderón's metaphor of *atravesados*—"border-crossers"—Caron and his students use McCarthy's novel "to understand better the skills necessary to become true atravesados" and ask such questions as "how much historical, contextualizing knowledge must we have before we can understand others and their cultures? . . . [and] what abstract (and often naive) ideals must we as students of literature be willing to move beyond to forge real and lasting literary relationships across cultures?" Throughout Caron's essay, we watch the professor and his students struggle with "McCarthy's statements on humanity's inability to make connections across borders," but we are also reminded of the "cautious optimism" that his students began to craft for themselves by the end of the course.

As with Daniel Cooper Alarcón's essay on McCarthy's Mexican representations, the work of the next three scholars forces us to reconsider McCarthy's position vis-à-vis specific sociocultural and literary traditions. Whereas early McCarthy criticism was preoccupied with tracing the author's southern and Faulknerian roots, current scholarship has moved beyond these admittedly important aspects of McCarthy's literary heritage and has begun to chart a more varied literary terrain of influence. In "The Cave of Oblivion: Platonic Mythology in *Child of God*," Dianne C. Luce argues that McCarthy "engages Platonic philosophy in all of his works." Her essay focuses on *Child of God* and its central character, Lester Ballard, and examines the novel in terms of its Platonic symbolism. In "*Child of God*," Luce argues, "McCarthy employs elements of Platonic myth to define the metaphysical dimensions of Lester Ballard's trials and crimes." Luce reads Ballard's progression through the text as "a descent into materialism rather than transcendence" and illustrates how McCarthy's text plays with images associated with Platonic mythology in order to highlight Ballard's crisis of vision. However, Luce also argues that *Child of God*—"with its implications of the limits of human vision and of humanity's bondage to materiality"— implicates the surrounding "community of similarly blinded men and women" in Lester's necrophilic descent. Because McCarthy insists on representing Lester as a member of the surrounding community—a "child of God, much like yourself perhaps" (4)—he also, Luce contends, "delineates the purgatorial world of Sevier County as one in which human members participate in mutual torture and persecution."

Rick Wallach also argues that McCarthy's fiction exposes the mechanisms through which violence perpetuates and justifies itself. "From *Beowulf* to *Blood Meridian:* Cormac McCarthy's Demystification of the Martial Code" explores the "outlandish violence" of *Blood Meridian* by comparing its representation of "mimetic violence" to *Beowulf*'s martial code. *Blood Meridian,* Wallach argues, "advances beyond the Old English epic in its exposure of the mechanisms behind the martial code." Through a detailed discussion of Judge Holden's role in the perpetuation of mimetic violence in the novel, Wallach uses René Girard's work to illustrate how McCarthy "exposes the mechanism by which the [martial] code perpetuates itself." Wallach's unusual and interesting textual juxtaposition also enables him to illustrate how this code, by the end of *Blood Meridian,* "has been reinscribed in a new commercial guise."

In "McCarthy and the Sacred: A Reading of *The Crossing,*" Edwin T. Arnold illustrates McCarthy's "Christian sensibility" by tracing the influence of "esoteric philosophical and religious . . . thinkers like Jacob Boehme" in *The Crossing.* For Arnold, *The Crossing* and its central metaphor of the "matrix" point toward the "'literal interrelatedness' of man and man, and of man and environment." As such, Arnold's McCarthy is both a Christian writer rooted in the mystical/spiritual tradition of thinkers such as Boehme (who argued that "all human beings are fundamentally one man") and an author who "suggests a biocentric view of nature." Arnold takes us through the complex text and its three enigmatic parables in order to illustrate what the protagonist, Billy Parham, learns in the novel. Billy is warned throughout the text to respect the ecospiritual matrix that ties together "man and man, and . . . man and environment," but it is only at the close of the novel, Arnold insists, that he comes to realize the consequences of extricating his life from that matrix. When Billy witnesses the first nuclear explosion on U.S. soil, at New Mexico's Trinity Site, he finally sees that the "basic structure of the natural matrix has been violently shattered, undone by man in an act of tremendous hubris."

What are the mechanics of McCarthy's storytelling techniques? How do we begin to talk about the experience of reading a McCarthy text? And how can we describe the complex relationship between McCarthy's narrative voices and the events they narrate? These are just some of the questions that the final four critics explore, adopting several approaches and methodologies to investigate McCarthy's use of and attitudes toward language. Some of these strategies make use of involved psychoanalytic and linguistic theories, whereas others rely on close textual readings of McCarthy's fiction. George Guillemin's essay "'See the Child': The Melancholy Subtext of *Blood Meridian*" focuses its attention on McCarthy's first novel to be set in the American Southwest and employs an array of approaches from Jungian psychoanalysis to neo-Freudian psycholinguistics to examine the "melancholy subtext" of the novel. Guillemin's essay offers not only a detailed analysis of McCarthy's narrative style but also a nuanced reading of the novel's ostensible protagonist, the nameless "kid." Given the reticence of this character and McCarthy's reluctance to give his readers access to his thoughts, Guillemin's analysis is indeed daring. He relies on the work of Julia Kristeva and Jacques Lacan to diagnose the kid (and the novel) as suffering from "melancholy psychosis"—"the eruption of 'a mindless violence' due to the subject's denial of negation of primal loss." And whereas Ann Fisher-Wirth uses Kristeva's work on abjection to discuss gender issues in McCarthy's fiction, Guillemin's Kristevan analysis ultimately links abjection to McCarthy's "allegorization of a melancholy sentiment."

Linda Townley Woodson's "Leaving the Dark Night of the Lie: A Kristevan Reading of Cormac McCarthy's Border Fiction" examines the "semiotic foundation" of McCarthy's border fiction. "In the trilogy," she contends, McCarthy's exploration of language "asserts the idea that truths can never be known in conscious reasoning through language, [and] that humans use language as a way of becoming and of holding against the other." *Blood Meridian*'s Judge Holden uses this truth about language to consume the characters and the natural environment through which they move; but in the Border Trilogy, Woodson notes, McCarthy's protagonists also come to appreciate and employ an "oral discourse"—what I referred to earlier as "storytelling"—that "affirms a sacredness of life beyond all conscious knowing": "In coming to know one's heart through the witnessing of others, through holding their memory into the future, through listening to the rhythms of the heart in their oral discourse, their narratives, one can come to a process of living where one recognizes the importance of all things in that universe whose order we can never know, the sanctity of blood, the sanctity of all." John Grady Cole, for example, soon learns that his heroic actions, rooted in the sociolinguistic codes of the "Old West," have lost their currency within the Mexican landscape south of the border—a landscape that challenges the "assumption that he can move into Mexico and take control of whatever he desires." Here he becomes a "victim of the language of those communities." But by the close of *All the Pretty Horses* and, Woodson argues, throughout *The Crossing*, McCarthy's protagonists learn the "sanctity of hearing the narrative of others, narratives of their individual and created histories . . . [through] a reverent acknowledgment of the existence of the other." McCarthy's dedication to storytelling—to "oral discourse"—attempts, then, to "demystify language itself and to call for a different kind of [discourse] outside of sociocultural identities."

In "'Hallucinated Recollections': Narrative as Spatialized Perception of History in *The Orchard Keeper*," Matthew R. Horton further explores McCarthy's storytelling techniques. *The Orchard Keeper*, McCarthy's first novel, "foregrounds distortion as an integral part of conveying historical perception." However, "McCarthy's style of storytelling, his narrative technique, goes beyond the idea of distortion . . . [and] deliberately warps conventional appearance, reveals multiple dimensions of perception, and jumbles the sequence of his narrative to simulate how man reconceives the past with memory." Indeed, Horton's analysis of McCarthy's fiction, like Linda Townley Woodson's, reveals an author deeply concerned with reconceiving and restructuring the experience of narrative and story. McCarthy's storytelling techniques, Horton argues, help to form "a new [narrative] structure that overturns the more conventional notions of historical perception." Within this new structure, the reader is pulled along by an "impenetrable tension" between coherence and disorder. Horton's detailed reading of *The Orchard Keeper* reveals an intricate narrative structure that continually blurs past and present in order to "convey how nearly impossible it is to separate them." At the close of the novel, John Wesley begins to appreciate how his life has been "contained by his memory of the past," and yet his newfound appreciation of the storytelling process enables him to "overcome the obstacles to making sense of history by reordering its sequence . . . [and breaking] through the barriers against moving ahead." Horton's reading of *The Orchard Keeper* reminds me again of the closing words of *Cities of the Plain*. After all, McCarthy urges John Wesley, now fully aware of how word and flesh penetrate and pattern each other, *"Turn the page."*

Robert L. Jarrett further explores the intricacies of McCarthy's storytelling techniques in "McCarthy's Sense of an Ending: Serialized Narrative and Revision in *Cities of the Plain*." In his discussion of the final installment of the Border Trilogy, Jarrett argues that McCarthy, "obsessed with rearticulating and wrapping up the narrative threads of the earlier novels in the trilogy, . . . scrutinizes the act, the possibility, and the significance of postmodern narration." For Jarrett, McCarthy's postmodernism entails "a shift away from direct experience of the world"—a shift that causes his characters to "'fall' into a series of self-conscious . . . dialogic renarration[s] of their experiences to a fictionalized witness." Jarrett terms this narrative technique "postmodern transcendentalism," a powerful authorial strategy that reaches its "supreme instance" at the close of the trilogy with the "gnomic dream-parable" told to Billy by a Mexican hitchhiker. Within this parable McCarthy envisions an author "who acts as both witness to and narrator of his own dream tale and whose dream world, through writing, intersects the dream world of the reader-witness."

Jarrett's "postmodern transcendentalism" involves a fusion of witness and narrator, reader and author reminiscent of *The Crossing*'s storyteller God, who sits "weaving the world" (149). It is my hope that the essays that follow will encourage and help you to single out your own thread of order from the tapestry of Cormac McCarthy's fiction, to post your own witnesses, to tell your own stories.

Notes

1. *Whales and Men* is an unpublished screenplay that is part of Southwestern Writers Collection in the Albert B. Alkek Library at Southwest Texas State University. I am indebted to Edwin Arnold for bringing this screenplay to my attention, and to the Albert B. Alkek Library for its help with this project. I discuss *Whales and Men* at length in my essay "Of Wolves and Men: The Dynamics of Cormac McCarthy's Environmental Imagination."

Works Cited

Kristeva, Julia. *Powers of Horror: An Essay on Abjection.* Trans. Leon Roudiez. New York: Columbia University Press, 1982.

Lilley, James D. "Of Wolves and Men: The Dynamics of Cormac McCarthy's Environmental Imagination." *Southern Quarterly* 38.2 (2000): 111–22.

Limón, José. *American Encounters: Greater Mexico, the United States, and the Erotics of Culture.* Boston: Beacon Press, 1998.

McCarthy, Cormac. *All the Pretty Horses.* New York: Alfred A. Knopf, 1992.
———. *Blood Meridian.* New York: Random House, 1985.
———. *Child of God.* New York: Random House, 1973.
———. *Cities of the Plain.* New York: Alfred A. Knopf, 1998.
———. *The Crossing.* New York: Alfred A. Knopf, 1994.
———. *The Stonemason.* Hopewell, N.J.: Ecco Press, 1994.
———. *Whales and Men.* Unpublished screenplay. Southwestern Writers Collection, Albert B. Alkek Library, Southwest Texas State University.

History and the Ugly Facts of *Blood Meridian*

Dana Phillips

> *These horsemen would dismount in camp at nightfall*
> *and lie looking at the stars, or else squat about the fire*
> *conversing with crude sombreness . . . speaking of*
> *humans when they referred to men.*
>
> **Owen Wister, "The Evolution of the Cow-Puncher"**

> *But what sort of literature remains possible if we relin-*
> *quish the myth of human apartness? It must be a liter-*
> *ature that abandons, or at least questions, what would*
> *seem to be literature's most basic foci: character,*
> *persona, narrative consciousness. What literature could*
> *survive under these conditions?*
>
> **Lawrence Buell, *The Environmental Imagination***

THE 1992 National Book Award for fiction given to *All the Pretty Horses* brought Cormac McCarthy his first widespread recognition as a writer of importance. Throughout most of his career, which began in the mid-1960s, McCarthy had worked and published in obscurity. Promotional campaigns meant little to him; he refused the interviews, personal appearances, and academic sinecures that might have made his name more widely known sooner. And for many years his readership was limited to a small group of admirers, mostly from the South. *All the Pretty Horses* helped change all that, but it is not McCarthy's most noteworthy book. That honor belongs to *Blood Meridian, or, The Evening Redness in the West* (1985), which, like *All the Pretty Horses,* might be called a "Western." Both novels trace the adventures of teenaged boys who run away to Mexico, but *Blood Meridian* is only very loosely centered on the character identified to the reader simply as "the kid." Its opening pages offer a summary of the kid's early life in the Tennessee hills, his flight to Texas in 1848, and his recruitment by a troop of filibusters, most of whom are slaughtered by a force of Comanches as their expedition makes its way into Mexico. The kid then joins up with Captain John Joel Glanton's band of scalphunters, who have a contract to provide the Mexicans with the hair of Apache raiders preying on isolated borderland villages and towns. Glanton and his men begin their own bloody campaign of depredations, which lasts for a year or two and several hundred pages. The kid is one of the few survivors of this campaign. The last chapters of the novel offer a compressed account of the final twenty-eight years of his life of wandering and of his eventual death in an outhouse at the hands of his old comrade-in-arms, the seven-foot-tall, three-hundred-pound, hairless albino Judge Holden, a man of incredible savagery and great intellectual facility. All these events are described in prose remarkable for its syntactic complexity, its recondite vocabulary, its recording of minute detail, and its violent intensity, as well as for an uncanny, almost scriptural stateliness.

Blood Meridian is a very complicated book—although complication is not a quality often associated with the label "Western." Early reviewers attempting to map this novel's outlandish aesthetic and moral territories resorted to striking but desperate oppositions. To them, the novel seemed a blend of Hieronymus Bosch and Sam Peckinpah; of Salvador Dali, Shakespeare, and the Bible; of Faulkner and Fellini; of Gustave Doré, Louis L'Amour, Dante, and Goya; of cowboys and noth-ingness; of Texas and Vietnam.[1] These oppositions, because they were produced by readers still under the novel's spell, evoke rather than inter-pret it. To do the latter has proven extremely difficult. McCarthy's work seems designed to elude interpretation, especially interpretation that would translate it into some supposedly more essential language.

The few readers who have given *Blood Meridian* deliberate and prolonged consideration have generally fallen into two camps, which (simply to make their differences clear) can be distinguished geograph-ically. "Southern" readers have tended to see McCarthy as the heir of William Faulkner and Flannery O'Connor. Given the Appalachian settings and country-folk characters of *The Orchard Keeper* (1965), *Outer Dark* (1968), *Child of God* (1973), and *Suttree* (1979), and given McCarthy's Faulkner-like verbal range and the O'Connor-like grimness of his humor, seeing him as a southern writer in the great tradition is not unreasonable. It is nevertheless a mistake, particularly with regard to *Blood Meridian,* and not just because the sources and setting of this novel are more western than southern. Those who read McCarthy as a "southern" writer tend to want to find in each of his novels something redemptive or regenerative, something affirming mysteries similar to those that O'Connor's fiction is supposed to affirm (mysteries of a Christian or Gnostic variety). McCarthy's fiction resembles O'Connor's in its violence, but he entirely lacks O'Connor's penchant for theology and the jury-rigged, symbolic plot resolutions that make theology seem plausible. In McCarthy's work, violence tends to be just that; it is not a sign or symbol of something else. There is, moreover, an astonishing amount of it: the body count for *Blood Meridian* alone runs into the hundreds. The "southern" camp there-fore wants to defend McCarthy from the heinous charge of nihilism, to make him seem more like O'Connor than he really is.[2]

"Western" readers see in the trajectory of McCarthy's career a move toward wider relevance and a broader worldview. For these readers, *Blood Meridian* marks McCarthy's progress toward address-ing not just the Wild West but also Western culture as a whole, especially its philosophical heritage. According to the "western" camp, McCarthy's antecedents are not only great American writers like Faulkner and O'Connor or Melville and Hemingway, but figures from world literature as well—specifically Dostoyevsky (the judge adopts a sidekick known as "the idiot") and Conrad (especially *Heart of Darkness*), less specifically Nietzsche and Heidegger.[3] McCarthy's "nihilism" is not, therefore, something he must counter by crafting a symbolic redemption of the fallen world or narrating the moral regeneration of his characters. On the contrary, it is just what one would expect from a writer who has fed on such corrosive, demystifying influences.

But the provenance of *Blood Meridian* is still difficult to specify; fittingly for a work set in a borderland, it seems curiously suspended, not just between regions and geographies, but also within literary history. It is a difficult text to place within a literary period. Obviously, given its publication date (1985), it was written after the heyday of high modernism—in fact, at a time when the failure of modernism had been thoroughly assimilated as a working philosophical assumption of contemporary literature. Yet it avoids the apocalyptic tone and the jaded manner of much postmodern fiction (the novels of Thomas Pynchon or Don DeLillo, for example).[4]

McCarthy's allegiance to either the modernist or postmodernist paradigm, or to the "southern" or the "western" camp, is doubtful. He has always been unforthcoming about his intentions but has admitted this: "The ugly fact is that books are made out of books. The novel depends for its life on the novels that have been written."[5] Although this statement may not seem particularly revealing, it does offer clues to understanding McCarthy's novel. What books, then, has *Blood Meridian* been "made out of"? McCarthy acknowledges that the novel is partially constructed out of his research in Mexican and American records detailing the bloody exploits of Captain Glanton and his band of scalphunters (including the historical figure Judge Holden) in the years following the Mexican-American War.[6] Knowing that Glanton and other members of his band are not pure fictions may excite some readers. I doubt, however, that this knowledge offers any real hermeneutic advantage. What distinguishes *Blood Meridian* from the many other works of fiction that also retell the true history of the American West—to be specific, from another contemporary novel in which Glanton and his men also appear, George MacDonald Fraser's *Flashman and the Redskins*? Fraser's novel is so very "historical" that he provides detailed notes describing the sources on which his fiction is allegedly based.[7] *Flashman and the Redskins* is an elaborate pastiche of historical "research," adventure, and sexual farce; in it, Glanton and his band appear broadly comic. *Blood Meridian* also makes detailed use of Glanton's history, but it is not an elaborate jape, nor is it a tour de force. And it is not a pastiche of its sources; it does not, in the postmodern manner, hollow out a space in other texts in order to comment ironically on the cultural fabric they form. It does not much resemble other contemporary novels constructed from similar historical sources. Thomas Berger's *Little Big Man*, to cite a second example, is overtly moral in tone and somewhat sentimentally favors the "savage" side of its protagonist Jack Crabb's character. (Crabb has been raised as a white man and as a Cheyenne, and he claims to be the sole white survivor of the battle of the Little Big Horn.) A third work of historical fiction set in the American West, the definitively postmodern *Silver Light* by film critic David Thomson, borrows characters from classic Western films like *Red River* and *The Man Who Shot Liberty Valance*, treats them as historical figures, and interweaves their lives with those of fictional residents of the present-day Southwest, some of whom are said to be the blood descendants of Matthew Garth, Liberty Valance, and other "historical" figures of popular culture.[8] McCarthy does not have Thomson's archness, and the story of Captain Glanton and his men is not well enough known to qualify as an insider's joke for Western history buffs. McCarthy can neither "allude" to it, as a modernist might, nor can he incorporate it into the fabric of a fictional pastiche in order to riff on it in the postmodern manner.

An awareness of John Joel Glanton's history is therefore of little help in sorting out McCarthy's "philosophy of composition."[9] This concept is developed by Lukács in his 1936 essay "Narrate or Describe?" and although his theories are overly prescriptive, they enable us to characterize McCarthy's book as a historical novel—to place *Blood Meridian* in terms of period and genre and to begin to "historicize" it properly.

However, historicizing it will not mean coming to see *Blood Meridian* as cozily embedded in a particular context that determines its themes, its content, and its style; the novel strongly resists such pigeonholing. If, as McCarthy has said, the novel is "made out of" both his own historical research and "the novels that have been written," its relationship to its context cannot be a simple one. We must consider the complex relationship between its apparent "philosophy of composition" and its implied philosophy of history. "Compositional principles of a poetic work," Lukács writes, "are a manifestation of an author's view of life" (140). The remainder of this essay will explore *Blood Meridian*'s point of view. I will try to show, however, that this is not necessarily the same thing as the "author's view of life," and to describe, finally, how *Blood Meridian* is related to McCarthy's other work, especially the more recent novels of his Border Trilogy.

NARRATION VERSUS DESCRIPTION

Lukács argues that novelists should narrate and not merely describe events. Narration, from his Marxist-humanist perspective, involves the articulation of the ways in which individual characters relate to the events they witness and to the social, cultural, and political contexts in which those events occur. Description involves unflagging attention to objective details and little more. Lukács deplores description as a "philosophy of composition" because it seems to entail the abandonment of a sense of human values and of an active human relationship to the world: "Representation declines into genre. . . . One state of mind at any moment and of itself without relation to man's activity is as important or as irrelevant as another. And this equivalence is even more blatant when it comes to objects" (130). The decline of "representation" into "genre" results, according to Lukács, in the rise of debased forms of popular literature in which narrative complexity and insight have withered away. Lukács has in mind subliterary forms like the detective story; we might, in the present context, think of the Western.[10] The descriptive novel (that is, the "naturalist" novel) attempts no statement of an ideology, and Lukács insists that "without ideology there is no composition" (142). "Ideology" for the early Lukács means historical awareness. Without historical awareness, description fixates on the merely material; this fixation "transforms the novel into a kaleidoscopic chaos" (133).[11]

To some, "kaleidoscopic chaos" might seem an accurate characterization of *Blood Meridian*. McCarthy's novel does not attempt to engage history, to explore the psyches of the characters and explain the meaning of the events it describes in the explicit, consciously critical way that Lukács requires. What does this say about McCarthy's "philosophy of composition"? To answer this question, it helps to be aware of *Blood Meridian*'s use of *Moby-Dick*. As a number of readers have noted, *Blood Meridian* bears some resemblance to Melville's novel. *Moby-Dick* seems to have provided McCarthy with some of his novel's language; for example, his hint about "the awful darkness inside the world" echoes Melville's "the blackness of darkness."[12] Philosophically, however, McCarthy is much more assured than Melville that there is a "darkness inside the world"—and less disturbed by it. For McCarthy, it is just darkness. The desert floor is literally a "hollow ground" across which Glanton and his band ride, where they can hear "the dull boom of rock falling somewhere far below them in the awful darkness inside the world," in the literal darkness of a deeply buried cave or fault in the earth (111). In *Blood Meridian* darkness is not a "theme," a dire metaphysical possibility mad characters can urge upon saner men, but a reiterated fact.

As a place of literal darkness, the Mexican desert is a proving ground, as McCarthy puts it early in the novel, "to try whether the stuff of creation may be shaped to man's will" (5). This also sounds Melvillean, but McCarthy does not go on to portray the tragic downfall of characters guilty of cosmic presumption. Whereas Melville was anxious to record his horror of darkness by having his characters react to it, *Blood Meridian* treats darkness, violence, sudden death, and all other calamities as natural occurrences—like the weather, which can also be vicious in McCarthy's border landscapes. Accordingly, the novel soon makes it clear that creation cannot be shaped to man's will, at least not for very long. Man's will does not seem a very relevant or potent force in this novel, nor does there seem to be some other will shaping his fate:

> Far out on the desert to the north dustspouts rose wobbling and
> augered the earth and some said they'd heard of pilgrims borne
> aloft like dervishes in those mindless coils to be dropped broken
> and bleeding upon the desert again and there perhaps to watch
> the thing that had destroyed them lurch onward like some
> drunken djinn and resolve itself once more into the elements
> from which it sprang. Out of that whirlwind no voice spoke and
> the pilgrim lying in his broken bones may cry out and in his
> anguish he may rage, but rage at what? And if the dried and
> blackened shell of him is found among the sands by travelers to
> come yet who can discover the engine of his ruin? (111)

Nature here is no longer symbolic of some greater fatality that engineers the novel's events, but it is nonetheless deadly.

Because his "philosophy of composition" is not the same as
Melville's, McCarthy's novel realizes some of the unfulfilled potential
of *Moby-Dick*. Melville had begun to suspect that violence and death
(as opposed, say, to liberty and justice) defined American history. That
is why the bloody business of whaling, and not something more
benign such as the spread of railroads or the annexation of new territories (which were, of course, only relatively benign), stands as his
metaphor for American capitalist and imperial aspirations. For
McCarthy, what Melville only suspected has been confirmed, as one of
the epigraphs to *Blood Meridian* suggests: "Clark, who led last year's
expedition to the Afar region of northern Ethiopia, and UC Berkeley
colleague Tim D. White, also said that a re-examination of a 300,000-
year-old fossil skull found in the same region earlier shows evidence of
having been scalped."[13] Violence and death, it would seem, are the
more or less objective truths of all human experience.

The novel's implied insistence on the failure in the mid-nineteenth
century (and in the mid-1980s, too) of the human desire for utopia, as
we might read it, calls into question the very concept of "history," tied
as it is to notions of progress, of the social evolution of human consciousness. "Save for their guns and buckles and a few pieces of metal
in the harness of the animals," nothing about Glanton's men, McCarthy
writes, suggests "even the discovery of the wheel" (232). Given its

apparent rejection of history as a meaningful category, we must conclude that *Blood Meridian* is not "historical" according to the criteria developed by Lukács, although it does incorporate the husk of a historical romance, not just the husk of *Moby-Dick* but that of the Western as well—perhaps of all the Westerns "that have been written."

Other aspects of the historical novel also go by the board in *Blood Meridian*. Character may be the most important of these. Lukács argues that the dramatic representation of character is necessary if an author wishes to explore the ideological complexities of a given era: "An artist achieves significance and typicality in his characterization only when he successfully exposes the multifarious interrelationships between the character traits of his heroes and the objective general problems of the age and when he shows his characters directly grappling with the most abstract issues of the time as their own personal and vital problems" ("Intellectual Physiognomy" 154). In this connection, we might recall how Lukács, in *The Historical Novel*, praises Sir Walter Scott's heroes and (more pertinent here) Cooper's Leatherstocking—that first of all Western heroes—for their awareness of historical conflict and its determining effect on their lives: "Cooper's greatest artistic achievement is his singular development of Scott's middle-of-the-road hero" (64).

The characters in McCarthy's novel resemble not those of *Waverly* or *The Deerslayer* but those of *Moby-Dick*. The likeness of "the kid" to Ishmael, of Captain Glanton and the judge to Ahab, and of Glanton's band to the *Pequod*'s motley crew is fairly obvious. But *Blood Meridian*'s echoes of Melville's text also help make clear their differences. The rhetorical excess of *Moby-Dick*'s attempts to represent character may have suggested to McCarthy the possibility of rewriting character as something else—character not as self but as language, as a suggestive artifact or trace of the human, like the Anasazi potsherds Judge Holden collects. Character in *Blood Meridian* is something written, something "made out of" the sherds of characters McCarthy discovers in the middens of history, literary and otherwise. "The kid," for example, is a remarkably reduced version of Ishmael. Ishmael's fondness for the "furious trope" is partly responsible for the constant swing in *Moby-Dick* from idiom to idiom and, indeed, from genre to genre, as Ishmael interrupts his narrative with parodic, grotesque byplay (Father Mapple's sermon, Queequeg's Ramadan), thumbnail sketches of maritime law, moralistic natural history essays, rhetorical flights of fancy, dumb puns and dirty jokes, imitation Shakespearean tragedy, and other writerly indulgences. With the possible exception of the judge's speeches, there is nothing comparable to Ishmael's furious troping (see Melville 161) in McCarthy's book. Indeed, the kid spits as often as he speaks. It would not really be accurate, therefore, to call him the main "character" in *Blood Meridian*, inasmuch as McCarthy seems to have largely dispensed with the concept of character in fashioning his material. "All history" may be present in the kid's face (3), but this does not make him a "world-historical individual" with the sort of "dramatic character" Lukács admires (*Historical Novel* 104). It is the kid's "taste for mindless violence" that marks his face and makes it historically significant (3); "history" is not a form of awareness in McCarthy's novel but merely the arena in which brutal, "mindless" events unfold.

Judge Holden appears to be an exception to the rule defining character in *Blood Meridian*: he is loquacious, even multilingual, and an intellectual with a great store of both practical and arcane information. His voice seems to be in implicit dialogue with the impersonal, highly detailed, and verbally ingenious narration. But it is a mistake (one that many readers find easy to make because the judge is such a remarkable creation) to regard his speeches as representative of his character. Because they are first and foremost literary performances, the sum of his speeches does not equal a whole person. They are delivered as highly ironic and playful lectures; the judge never misses an "opportunity to ventilate himself" (240). For example, during a confrontation in the desert after most of Glanton's band has been massacred, the judge tries to persuade two other survivors (the kid and the ex-priest Tobin) to join him: "They lay under the boardlike hide of a dead ox and listened to the judge calling to them. He called out points of jurisprudence, he cited cases. He expounded upon the laws pertaining to property rights in beasts mansuete and he quoted from cases of attainder insofar as he reckoned them germane to the corruption of blood in the prior and felonious owners of the horses now dead among the bones. Then he spoke of other things" (293). The judge's speeches are more than lawyerly in their expansiveness: they are also nihilistic. But his is a thoroughly rhetorical, somewhat ersatz nihilism, and the judge offers it up with relish, suggesting that what Melville found so alarming (that behind the facade of the brute, material world there might be something indifferent or malevolent—or nothing at all) McCarthy can retail as if it were just another and quite familiar chapter in the annals of thought (which, after all, it is). The judge's "nihilism," very much on display in the following speech, is an intellectual artifact from a time long past, and thus no cause for alarm:

> God meant to interfere in the degeneracy of mankind would he not have done so by now? Wolves cull themselves, man. What other creature could? And is the race of man not more predacious yet? The way of the world is to bloom and to flower and die but in the affairs of men there is no waning and the noon of his expression signals the onset of night. His spirit is exhausted at the peak of his achievement. His meridian is at once his darkening and the evening of his day. He loves games? Let him play for stakes. (146)

Although many of his speeches, like this one, are nihilistic compounds of Nietzschean (and Spenglerian) rhetoric, the judge is not a nihilist (nor a Spenglerian). That his "character" has no real-world analogue and is not intended to suggest one is made apparent several times.[14] Consider, for example, the quandary of the young boy who offers Judge Holden his choice of two puppies for sale: "The boy looked at one and then the other of the animals. As if he'd pick one to suit the judge's character, such dogs existing somewhere perhaps" (192). Or consider the judge as he appears in a fevered dream the kid has while recovering from an arrow wound: "A great shambling mutant, silent and serene. Whatever his antecedents he was something wholly other than their sum, nor was there system by which to divide him back into his origins for he would not go" (309). There was, McCarthy writes, "no trace of any ultimate atavistic egg by which to commence his reckoning" (310). No calculus, moral or otherwise, will explain the judge.

Having dispensed with "character" as a hermeneutic concept, one cannot then latch onto the judge's speeches as authorial pronouncements. Holden is not a ventriloquist's dummy perched on the novelist's knee, and we should not strain our eyes to see whether McCarthy's lips move when the judge speaks. He is not sounding the novel's "themes."[15] By dispensing with character as a concept, McCarthy is able to deploy the language he uses heuristically as a tool for exploring the liminal concerns the novel takes up, such as whether human beings have any privileged position in relation to the rest of the world. Thus traditional concepts of the narrator as a "person" or "voice," a sort of meta-character with an interest in certain "themes" that help to structure a text, also do not apply to *Blood Meridian.*

The novel's narration is omniscient, but there seems to be no knower providing us with the knowledge it imparts. And this knowledge does not really develop; it merely accrues. The most often repeated sentence in *Blood Meridian* is "They rode on." So the plot moves, but it does not thicken. Because all the novel's complexities are fully present from the first page, it can scarcely be said to have been "composed" at all in the Lukácsian sense. The novel does not seek to resolve "conflicts" that trouble its characters, much less its narrator or author. It is not really a narrative, then, but a description—and some would say it is not really a novel either.

OPTICAL DEMOCRACY

As a book that describes rather than narrates its events, *Blood Meridian* constructs a remarkably consistent, philosophically rigorous, and somewhat uncanny point of view (a misleading metaphor, really, as I try to show later). From this point of view, persons are not privileged as subjects, just as Lukács says must be the case when novelistic representation is abandoned.[16] *Blood Meridian* has been called "a critique of our culture's anthropocentrism" (Bell 124). In it, the human does not stand out among the other beings and objects that make up the world. The question of human spiritual animation—of the human being's status as a subject, as a special kind of object set apart in the landscape of ordinary objects, when it arises at all (the book's critique of anthropocentrism is almost entirely implicit) is a rhetorical one, perhaps designed to tweak our readerly nostalgia for novels (Westerns most especially) in which men were men and the landscape was something else:

> In the neuter austerity of that terrain all phenomena were bequeathed a strange equality and no one thing nor spider nor stone nor blade of grass could put forth claim to precedence. The very clarity of these articles belied their familiarity, for the eye predicates the whole on some feature or part and here was nothing more luminous than another and nothing more enshadowed and in the optical democracy of such landscapes all preference is made whimsical and a man and a rock become endowed with unguessed kinships. (247)

In its insistence on "optical democracy," on the equality of being between human and nonhuman objects, this passage, like many others in *Blood Meridian*, realizes a possibility with which Westerns (films and novels) have long flirted. Jane Tompkins has argued that "the genius of the Western" is that "it seems to make the land speak for itself" (71). But in the Western, if the land speaks "for itself," it also speaks to the hero, who figures as the focal point in any landscape he enters. Tompkins makes this clear in her description of the role of landscape in Louis L'Amour's novels: "The hero's passage across the landscape has ultimately a domesticating effect. Though it begins in anxious movement and passes through terror and pain, it continually ends in repose. A welcoming grove of aspens, a spring, and a patch of grass provide shelter and sustenance. A campfire and the setting sun give visual pleasure and comfort, while trickling water and a horse cropping grass make soothing noises. If nature's wildness and hardness test his strength and will and intelligence, they also give him solace and refreshment. . . . Perhaps more than anything, nature gives the hero a sense of himself" (81).

But L'Amour's landscapes are perfunctory: his descriptions name only a few representative features of the land (mesa, butte, skyline) and its flora and fauna (greasewood, aspens, quail, Gila monsters). In his many novels, the West is a generic place where a windburned saddle tramp rides Old Paint through a paint-by-numbers landscape, grunting with satisfaction at its familiarity.

Blood Meridian, a novel in which none of the protagonists has anything remotely like "a sense of himself," is a Western without a hero (and thus, some would say, not really a Western at all). In it the land speaks for itself—perhaps it would be more accurate to say it "acts for itself"—in a much more thoroughgoing and less mediated fashion than traditional Western formulas permit. Compared to McCarthy's, L'Amour's landscapes seem hopelessly naive. Potent landscapes inform all of McCarthy's work, from The Orchard Keeper, his first novel, to Suttree and Blood Meridian, helping to shape the best-selling and supposedly more humane All the Pretty Horses. In all these texts, McCarthy describes terrain of which we are ordinarily only fleetingly aware, a landscape that looms in the background of the opening frames of many movie Westerns and through which many a literary cowboy has ridden. But as McCarthy shows, this landscape is capable of more than looming.

This landscape is, then, both familiar and unfamiliar. Having seen it only piecemeal before, in Blood Meridian we are shown both its largest and smallest features, "even to the uttermost granulation of reality" (247). It is as if the real American West were being imagined for the first time; imagined, that is, as terribly and finally real:

They rode in a narrow enfilade along a trail strewn with the dry round turds of goats and they rode with their faces averted from the rock wall and the bake-oven air which it rebated, the slant black shapes of the mounted men stenciled across the stone with a definition austere and implacable like shapes capable of violating their covenant with the flesh that authored them and continuing autonomous across the naked rock without reference to sun or man or god. (139)

If any one of the things described in this passage seems more potent, more animate, than another, it is not Glanton's men but the shadows they cast. The suggested independence of light and dark reinforces the lack of precedence, of referential order, in the natural world and helps make apparent the "unguessed kinships" between objects as diverse as goat turds, the sun, men, and gods. This kinship, however, neither ennobles the turds nor debases the gods but merely makes them equal in that both are putatively factual.

The same "optical democracy" (247) characterizes a scene in which the scalphunters take refuge in a stable on a cold night:

> One by one they began to divest themselves of their outer clothes, the hide slickers and raw wool serapes and vests, and one by one they propagated about themselves a great crackling of sparks and each man was seen to wear a shroud of palest fire. Their arms aloft pulling at their clothes were luminous and each obscure soul was enveloped in audible shapes of light as if it had always been so. The mare at the far end of the stable snorted and shied at this luminosity in beings so endarkened and the little horse turned and hid his face in the web of his dam's flank. (222)

Here "obscure souls" are "enveloped in audible shapes of light," but there is no contradiction because the phenomenon of static electricity is a natural one. McCarthy always treats familiar assumptions about character or "soul" as hypotheses ("as if it had always been so") and makes them seem dubious at best. In this scene, the horses seem more animate, perhaps even more conscious than Glanton's men. Of course, horses are more sensitive than men to some things, especially to things in the natural world, and they often get the last word in McCarthy's fiction (this passage concludes a chapter).

These apparent paradoxes are not the only ones in McCarthy's book. Less obviously, he also confounds the categories of narration and description, the purity of which Lukács himself describes as illusory: "What is important . . . are philosophies of composition, not any illusory 'pure' phenomenon of narration or description" ("Narrate or Describe?" 116). Lukács's categories of narration and description rewrite the vulgar Marxist distinction between material base and ideological superstructure in literary terms. His own favorite novelists (Scott, Balzac, and Tolstoy, among others) figure in his essay as heroes of consciousness because of their ability to articulate an ideology in their novels. Ironically for a materialist, Lukács has least admiration for those novelists (Zola especially, but also Flaubert) in whose works the material world is given attention more or less for its own sake: "A 'poetry of things' independent of people and of people's lives does not exist in literature" ("Narrate or Describe?" 136). But McCarthy's philosophy of composition ignores the distinction Lukács makes between description and narration. Description "debases characters to the level of inanimate objects" only if one assumes that characters occupy a higher level than objects in the first place (133); otherwise they cannot be seen as "debased." Thus Vereen Bell's treatment of McCarthy's style does not recognize how radically unanthropocentric it is: "the human beings constitute one protagonist and the natural world another. Narrative and description collaborate with each other in conventional ways, but what is ultimately important is that, even ontologically, they compete" (133). My argument is that this competition has been decided in favor of description and the natural world even before *Blood Meridian* begins. For McCarthy, description and the natural world as categories contain both narrative and human beings. Human beings and the natural world do not figure as antagonists—*Blood Meridian* does not have that kind of dramatic structure. They are instead parts of the same continuum and are consistently described by McCarthy as such. If a grizzly bear eats one of Glanton's Delaware scouts or a wild bull gores one of their horses, it is business as usual as far as the scalphunters are concerned. They ride on.

Blood Meridian does not grant Lukács's humanist premise about novelistic representation. There is no supernatural elevation of consciousness, no "poetry of people," so to speak, in it. Moreover, this lack arises as an issue only occasionally in the speeches of Glanton's men, whose attempts at interpreting the events they witness are soon enough revealed as limited, provisional, and quite naive, as the judge likes to point out: "Your heart's desire is to be told some mystery. The mystery is that there is no mystery" (252). *Blood Meridian*'s universe is a natural one, even when its landscapes are simultaneously earthly and unearthly. At such moments the universe is described as a continuum, a more or less even distribution of existence throughout a radically unbounded space: "The stars burned with a lidless fixity and they drew nearer in the night until toward dawn he was stumbling among the whinstones of the uttermost ridge to heaven, a barren range of rock so enfolded in that gaudy house that stars lay awash at his feet and migratory spalls of burning matter crossed constantly about him on their chartless reckonings" (213). The limits of perspective are left behind in a passage like this one: it is cosmic without being metaphysical, as if the sentence had been written by a transparent eyeball that has learned how not to be Emersonian. It suggests, to paraphrase Melville, an "ungodly, godlike" view of life. In this sense, it is true that McCarthy's "descriptive method lacks humanity," as Lukács would say ("Narrate or Describe?" 140).

It is precisely its lack of human implication that some find *Blood Meridian*'s most disturbing feature. In the raw orchestration of the book's events, the world of nature and the world of men are parts of the same world, and both are equally violent and indifferent to the other. In one scene a man dies when a pitcher of aguardiente is poured over his head and ignited by a cigar: "A man ran outside mute save for the whoosh of the flames and the flames were pale blue and then invisible in the sunlight and he fought them in the street like a man beset with bees or madness and then he fell over in the road and burned up. By the time they got to him with a bucket of water he had blackened and shriveled in the mud like an enormous spider" (268). Human failure to be other than brutal is not treated here as a departure from the ordinary course of events. It is just another event.

This is true as well of the failure of the natural world to take into account human feelings. In another important scene, in which the kid and his companion Sproule lie wounded (Sproule's arm is gangrenous and maggot-ridden) and asleep on the desert sands, a huge bat attacks Sproule: "They slept like dogs in the sand and had been sleeping so when something black flapped up out of the night ground and perched on Sproule's chest. Fine fingerbones stayed the leather wings with which it steadied as it walked upon him. A wrinkled pug face, small and vicious, bare lips crimped in a horrible smile and teeth pale blue in the starlight. It leaned to him. It crafted in his neck two narrow grooves and folding its wings over him it began to drink his blood" (65–66).

We have learned before this gruesome scene, in one of the book's choicest exchanges of dialogue, why the unfortunate Sproule has come out west:

> He was coughing again. He held his chest with his good hand and sat as if he'd get his breath.
> What have you got, a cold?
> I got consumption.
> Consumption?
> He nodded. I come out here for my health.
> The kid looked at him. He shook his head and rose and walked off across the plaza towards the church. There were buzzards squatting among the old carved wooden corbels and he picked up a stone and squailed it at them but they never moved. (58)

Salvation history, which understands the natural world and man's travails in it as symbols of the spirit, has long since been played out, as the ruined, eroded, and vulture-draped mission churches in *Blood Meridian* suggest. Only natural history, which regards neither nature nor man as symbolic, is left. It seems newly potent as a result.

Nevertheless, McCarthy is not writing what Lukács dismisses as a "poetry of things." Vereen Bell points out that the world in McCarthy's novel is "mysterious enough without involving ideas" (3), but I doubt that he intends this remark to imply that McCarthy's work contains the sort of mystery that Flannery O'Connor deliberately injected into hers. In his chapter on *Blood Meridian*, Bell suggests that McCarthy's style "seems to move us toward an epiphany, though only the kind that a seasoned gnostic might construe" (132). I take this as a warning to seasoned gnostics everywhere. Neither the history of the American West nor natural history is put forward in *Blood Meridian* as the last vestige of the mysterious or lyrical. Natural history makes the provisional quality of all human interpretations of events—poetic ones perhaps most especially—painfully apparent. This is why Judge Holden, for all his willful solipsism and despite his casual attitude toward murder, is described as a good dancer and boon companion: "He bows to the fiddlers and sashays backwards and throws back his head and laughs deep in his throat and he is a great favorite, the judge" (335). Nothing in nature prevents his being both a murderer and the life of the party.

The speech of McCarthy's protagonists (perhaps his own as well) is no longer, then, an index of characterological or personal traits, the instrument with which to divine some hidden and occult order in the world, but simply a historical and literary artifact. For that reason, it is available to the writer without regard for psychological or moral or political propriety of the sort that worried Lukács. Once psychology, morality, and politics come to be seen as mere languages, propriety becomes a highly relative question, even an uninteresting one. At any rate, *Blood Meridian* certainly cannot be read as suggesting some moral insight on the order of "scalphunting is wrong." Nor does it try to adumbrate a more sophisticated, more political version of that insight, something on the order of "scalphunting is imperialism by other means."

McCarthy's language has a strange equanimity of tone, strange because of the virtuosity with which it details what seems unspeakable and what once it has been spoken requires no further comment:

Now driving in a wild frieze of headlong horses with eyes walled and teeth cropped and naked riders with clusters of arrows clenched in their jaws and their shields winking in the dust and up the far side of the ruined ranks in a piping of boneflutes and dropping down off the sides of their mounts with one heel hung in the withers strap and their short bows flexing beneath the out-stretched necks of the ponies until they had circled the company and cut their ranks in two and then rising up again like funhouse figures, some with nightmare faces painted on their breasts, riding down the unhorsed Saxons and spearing and clubbing them and leaping from their mounts with knives and running about on the ground with a peculiar bandylegged trot like crea-tures driven to alien forms of locomotion and stripping the clothes from the dead and seizing them up by the hair and pass-ing their blades about the skulls of the living and the dead alike and snatching aloft the bloody wigs and hacking and chopping at the naked bodies, ripping off limbs, heads, gutting the strange white torsos and holding up great handfuls of viscera, genitals, some of the savages so slathered up with gore they might have rolled in it like dogs and some who fell upon the dying and sodomized them with loud cries to their fellows. . . . Dust stanched the wet and naked heads of the scalped who with the fringe of hair below their wounds and tonsured to the bone now lay like maimed and naked monks in the bloodslaked dust and everywhere the dying groaned and gibbered and horses lay screaming. (53–54)

No explanation of this event is necessary. Moreover, McCarthy's use of vivid similes (such as the dead "lay like maimed and naked monks in the bloodslaked dust") does not give the event a symbolic dimension. On the contrary, the similes seem designed to increase the intensity and accuracy of focus on the objects being described rather than to suggest that they have double natures or bear hidden meanings.[17] Consider also his description of a survivor sitting amid the ruins of an ambushed camp of Tigua Indians: "All about her the dead lay with their peeled skulls like polyps bluely wet or luminescent melons cooling on some mesa of the moon. . . . In the circuit of few suns all trace of the destruction of these people would be erased. The desert wind would salt their ruins and there would be nothing, nor ghost nor scribe, to tell to any pilgrim in his passing how it was that people had lived in this place and in this place died" (174). Whatever the language *Blood Meridian* offers us (monks, polyps, or melons), it is meant not to evoke a symbolic netherworld but to describe to the "pilgrim in his passing" the salt ruins of humanity.[18]

NOT FORMS, BUT FORCES

It is perhaps for this reason that McCarthy approaches the ugly fact of violence in such a detached, almost forensic manner, as he does, for example, when he reconstructs a shootout in a cantina in the Mexican village of Nacori: "There were twenty-eight Mexicans inside the tavern and eight more in the street including the five the expriest had shot" (180). A different, less clinical approach would seem anthropomorphic or all too human. But *Blood Meridian* is not so much inhuman as non-human. It is thoroughly dispassionate. The book's odd power derives from its treating everything and everybody with absolute equanimity; its voice seems profoundly alien, but not alienated. With imperturbable calm, it speaks the words of the nineteenth- and twentieth-century narratives and the masterworks it rewrites (Melville, but Dostoyevsky, Conrad, Hemingway, and Faulkner, too), as well as the words of natural history and material history. (McCarthy describes equine accoutrement, antique tools, and hardware, most especially guns, in remarkable detail.) It speaks "Mexican." It draws on the occult and other esoteric matters. It conflates the Old Testament with the Western. It does all this as if these many texts, discourses, foreign tongues, disciplines, scriptures, and literatures all formed a single language. Which they do, at least in this book.[19]

The concatenation of these discourses suggests a "purview," something Charles Newman argues postmodern fiction cannot offer: "We live in a time when no purview is possible."[20] But the purview of *Blood Meridian* is not a source of comfort, nor is it empowering, as Newman imagines such a perspective of totality must be. Its only rule is the relativity of force. All forms (presumably, even its own) are merely provisional, heuristic devices. McCarthy's purview is visionary, but not in the usual sense of that term.[21] It is literally visionary and what it sees is an "optical democracy" in which "all preference is made whimsical" (247).

McCarthy's purview is also complicated in relation to its time, which Newman cites as the chief factor delimiting the possibility of purview. On its surface *Blood Meridian* does not seem to be very much of its time, at least not in any limiting sense. One might even say that it is "premodern," in that it seems to have adopted the purview of the epic. Lukács describes the epic world as follows: "There is not yet any interiority, for there is not yet any exterior, any 'otherness' for the soul. The soul goes out to seek adventure; it lives through adventures, but it does not know the real torment of seeking and the real danger of finding; such a soul never stakes itself; it does not yet know that it can lose itself, it never thinks of having to look for itself. Such an age is the age of epic" (*Theory of the Novel* 30). Some of this passage might also serve as a description of the kid's adventures in *Blood Meridian*. But if it were merely a question of McCarthy's having simulated the epic worldview "by purely formal means," as Lukács puts it, "after the transcendental conditions for its existence have already been condemned by the historico-philosophical dialectic," then *Blood Meridian* might indeed be dismissed as a tour de force (*Theory of the Novel* 101). But I would argue that the epic and natural history—that is, the descriptive or "earth" sciences such as geology, meteorology, astronomy, archaeology, evolutionary biology, and paleontology—are similar ways of viewing the world. Both the epic and natural history are concerned (albeit in importantly different ways) "with reality *as it is*" and with the "concept of life," which Lukács says "has no need of any . . . transcendence captured and held immobile as an object" (*Theory of the Novel* 47). It is *Blood Meridian*'s adherence in its descriptions of events to the protocols and paradigms of natural history that gives it epic resonance. The present world as McCarthy describes it is an ancient world not of myth but of rock and stone and those life forms that can endure the daily cataclysms of heat and cold and hunger, that can weather the everyday round of random, chaotic violence. Only the "great temporal limitation imposed by geology upon human importance," an awareness of "deep time," can give this world spatial and intellectual order (Gould 1–2).[22] For that reason, the American West in McCarthy's fiction is not the New World but a very old world, the reality of which is bedrock. We might place him in time with some confidence, then, as a writer not of the "modern" or "postmodern" eras but of the Holocene, with a strong historical interest in the late Pleistocene and even earlier epochs.

What the virtual absence of Lukácsian narration in his book seems to say about McCarthy's moral or political worldview is bound to be disturbing to readers who (somewhat datedly) expect novels to offer an imaginary solution to individual or social ills. Lukács writes that "the novel form is, like no other, an expression of . . . transcendental homelessness" (*Theory of the Novel* 41). Mikhail Bakhtin makes a strikingly similar claim: "The novel begins by presuming a verbal and semantic decentering of the ideological world, a certain linguistic homelessness of literary consciousness" (367). *Blood Meridian,* in contrast to most novels and most popular Westerns, accepts homelessness as its inevitable condition. It does not express an aspiration for domesticity and repose—for a home on the range.

The favored discourses of the novel—religion, ethics, psychology, and politics—suffer the fate of most other humanist discourses when the anthropocentric point of view is abandoned. So does nihilism. Philosophically, nihilism was a response to religion, ethics, psychology, and politics: Nietzsche, in *The Genealogy of Morals,* exposed the limitations of the language by means of which religious, ethical, psychological, and political discourses attempt simultaneously to capture human essences and to obscure their own institutional interests in power, and he thus revealed each of these discourses as radically relative. *Blood Meridian* hints at a descriptive discourse that might capture within its net religion, ethics, psychology, politics, and nihilism, too, a discourse that limns the outlines of the arena in which humans—priests, jurists, therapists, kings, and philosophers—contend without any vested interest in the outcome. McCarthy's distance from his subjects is in this respect remarkable: "Above all else they appeared wholly at venture, primal, provisional, devoid of order. Like beings provoked out of the absolute rock and set nameless and at no remove from their own loomings to wander ravenous and doomed and mute as gorgons shambling the brutal wastes of Gondwanaland in a time before nomenclature was and each was all" (172). Such passages do not assert the meaninglessness or utter fragmentation of existence or experience as given. Rather, they suggest meaning on a scale of time and space that we can only dimly perceive, marked by the scraping of rock upon rock (in the case of the ancient megacontinent Gondwanaland, very old and very large rocks). The meaning of these scrapings is not connected to human value. *Blood Meridian* does not wholly reject the notion of value, but the values it describes are not ones for which we have ready terms. For McCarthy, the history of the West is natural history. This is a history of forces and the processes by which these forces evolve into the forms to which we give names are not our own. Thus the present is also "a time before nomenclature" (172).

"In History There Are No Control Groups"

Blood Meridian ends with an epilogue that to some readers seems problematic—more so, that is, than the book's preceding 335 pages. It appears to be a parable of sorts, in which a solitary man with a pair of posthole diggers progresses across the West Texas plains *"striking the fire out of the rock which God has put there"* as he makes holes for a new fence line:

> On the plain behind him are the wanderers in search of bones and those who do not search and they move haltingly in the light like mechanisms whose movements are monitored with escapement and pallet so that they appear restrained by a prudence or reflectiveness which has no inner reality and they cross in their progress one by one that track of holes that runs to the rim of the visible ground and which seems less the pursuit of some continuance than the verification of a principle, a validation of sequence and causality as if each round and perfect hole owed its existence to the one before it there on that prairie upon which are the bones and the gatherers of bones and those who do not gather. (337)

It seems to me that this passage does not offer anything new. Rather, it confirms what the preceding chapters have consistently shown: the action here also has "no inner reality." It is "the verification of a principle" of which the actors themselves may not be at all aware, given their clocklike movements and given that the principle itself is only hypothetical, only a matter of "as if." What is vouchsafed here, however, is a vision of the more contemporary world that informs McCarthy's next novel, *All the Pretty Horses:* a world in which the western plains have been rationalized—settled, fenced, and punctured not by posthole diggers but by oil wells, which also strike fire out of the rock in accord with the dictates of an ideology of progress. Thus the epilogue to *Blood Meridian* begins to return us (but *only* begins) to the familiar terrain of religion, ethics, psychology, and politics. *All the Pretty Horses,* the first volume of the Border Trilogy, is set in a recognizably novelistic world. It does have a main character, John Grady Cole (another teenaged boy), and it addresses the history of the American West (in particular, of the Texas-Mexico border country) in a way that might have satisfied even Lukács. It is also a much more genial text than *Blood Meridian*. But McCarthy has warned that its gentle character may be just "a snare and a delusion" (Woodward 40). *Blood Meridian* fulfills a logic at work in all of McCarthy's work, and the violence described on every page of that book is by no means absent in *All the Pretty Horses*. John Grady Cole is beaten, stabbed, and shot; he beats, stabs, and shoots at others. And in a scene reminiscent of Judge Holden's extemporizing, the Dueña Alfonsa, who witnessed first-hand the Mexican revolution, lectures him on the meaning of history:

> When I was in school I studied biology. I learned that in making their experiments scientists will take some group—bacteria, mice, people—and subject that group to certain conditions. They compare the results with a second group which has not been disturbed. This second group is called the control group. It is the control group which enables the scientist to gauge the effect of his experiment. To judge the significance of what has occurred. In history there are no control groups. There is no one to tell us what might have been. We weep over the might have been, but there is no might have been. There never was. (239)

Thus, despite its greater emphasis on the dramatic representation of its characters, *All the Pretty Horses* gravitates toward the worldview of *Blood Meridian*. Both novels resist the comforts of the "might have been," and both insist that, as the Dueña Alfonsa puts it, the true is not "what is righteous but merely what is so" (240). So much for history. With regard to the future, McCarthy promises in the last line of *All the Pretty Horses* a journey into "the darkening land, the world to come" (302). This journey will also be a return.[23]

Notes

1. See Alan Cheuse, *USA Today,* 8 Mar. 1985: D3; Bill Baines, *Western American Literature* 21 (spring 1986): 59–60; Caryn James, "Is Everybody Dead Around Here?" *New York Times Book Review,* 28 Apr. 1985: 31; Tom Nolan, *Los Angeles Times Book Review,* 9 June 1985: 2; Geoffrey O'Brien, "Cowboys and Nothingness," *Village Voice Literary Supplement,* 15 July 1986: 48.

2. See, for example, Terence Moran, "The Wired West," *New Republic,* 6 May 1985: 37–38; Walter Sullivan, "About Any Kind of Meanness You Can Name," *Sewanee Review* 93 (fall 1985): 649–56; Edwin T. Arnold, "Naming, Knowing and Nothingness: McCarthy's Moral Parables," *Southern Quarterly* 30 (summer 1992): 31–50; and Leo Daugherty, "Gravers False and True: *Blood Meridian* as Gnostic Tragedy," *Southern Quarterly* 30 (summer 1992): 122–33. Fred Hobson does not discuss McCarthy at any length, but his book *The Southern Writer in the Postmodern World* (Athens: University of Georgia Press, 1991) attempts to explore some of the historical limitations of the idea of "the southern writer" in a way that avoids some of the pitfalls of regionalism. Hobson's interest in postmodernism (although insufficiently theorized) and his sense that McCarthy's fiction "is often set . . . in a world of pure concreteness and is often, by intent, devoid of any informing point of view at all" (81) anticipate some of my concerns in the present essay.

3. See chapter 5, "The Metaphysics of Violence," of Vereen M. Bell's *The Achievement of Cormac McCarthy* (Baton Rouge: Louisiana State University Press, 1988), 116–35. See also Steven Shaviro's essay on McCarthy (see the following note) and the review by John Lewis Longley, Jr., "The Nuclear Winter of Cormac McCarthy," *The Virginia Quarterly Review* 62 (autumn 1986): 746–50.

4. McCarthy may be writing in the aftermath of literary modernism, but that does not make *Blood Meridian* postmodernist, as Steven Shaviro has suggested. Shaviro reads *Blood Meridian* as an allegory of poststructuralist, postmodern theory (specifically, of Deleuze and Guattari's *AntiOedipus* and *A Thousand Plateaus*); he describes McCarthy as a "nomadic wanderer, lucid cartographer of an inescapable delirium." And Shaviro contends that "*Blood Meridian* rejects organicist metaphors of growth and decay, in favor of an open topography (what Deleuze and Guattari call 'smooth space') in which the endless, unobstructed extension of the desert allows for the sudden, violent and fortuitous irruption of the most heterogeneous forces" and that its language manages to be "continually outside itself, in intimate contact with the world in a powerfully nonrepresentational way." But this reading converts *Blood Meridian* into the sort of anti-oedipal overthrow of all normative discourses in favor of the unbounded play of the erotic that Deleuze and Guattari admire; Shaviro's is thus yet another redemptive, regenerative reading, albeit in a new idiom. See Shaviro, "'The Very Life of the Darkness': A Reading of *Blood Meridian*," *Southern Quarterly* 30 (summer 1992): 111, 113, 117.

5. See Richard B. Woodward, "Cormac McCarthy's Venomous Fiction," *The New York Times Magazine* (19 Apr. 1992): 31.

6. For example, the 1868 frontier memoir of John C. Cremony, *Life Among the*

Apaches, describes the death of Gallantin (as Cremony spells it) at the Yuma crossing of the Colorado River in western Arizona. It—or for that matter just about any other account of western travels published in the nineteenth century—may have provided McCarthy with a model for the ironically understated chapter headings that index his narrative for the reader in a manner that only increases the plot's obscurity (for example, the phrases "Tree of dead babies" and "Attacked by a vampire" preview events in chapter five; other chapter headings are in Spanish, Latin, or German). For comparison, see John C. Cremony, *Life Among the Apaches* (Lincoln: University of Nebraska Press, 1983).

For a review of historical materials McCarthy may have consulted, see John Emil Sepich's essays "The Dance of History in Cormac McCarthy's *Blood Meridian,*" *Southern Literary Journal* 24 (fall 1991): 16–31; "'What kind of indians was them?': Some Historical Sources in Cormac McCarthy's *Blood Meridian,*" *Southern Quarterly* 30 (summer 1992): 93–110; and "A 'Bloody Dark Pastryman': Cormac McCarthy's Recipe for Gunpowder and Historical Fiction in *Blood Meridian,*" *Mississippi Quarterly: The Journal of Southern Culture* 46 (fall 1993): 547–63. Unfortunately, Sepich's work on the novel tries to see it as a web of "allusions" to McCarthy's historical sources.

7. George MacDonald Fraser, *Flashman and the Redskins* (New York: Alfred A. Knopf, 1982), 457–79.

8. Thomas Berger, *Little Big Man* (1964; reprint, New York: Delta/Seymour Lawrence, 1989); David Thomson, *Silver Light* (New York: Alfred A. Knopf, 1990).

9. Georg Lukács, "Narrate or Describe?" reprinted in *Writer and Critic and Other Essays,* ed. and trans. Arthur D. Kahn (New York: Universal Library, 1971), 116.

10. Lukács refers to narrative representation as "epic," by which he means that it elaborates a coherent worldview of the sort associated with older literary forms. However, because Lukács also distinguishes novelistic narrative from that of the epic—precisely because the novel has to elaborate its worldview (something that comes ready-made in the true epic)—and because I want to avail myself of his distinction later in this essay, I have avoided the use of "epic" here.

For classic accounts of the Western as a genre, see John G. Cawelti, *Adventure, Mystery, and Romance: Formula Stories as Art and Popular Culture* (Chicago: University of Chicago Press, 1976), 192–259, or his *The Six-Gun Mystique* (Bowling Green, Ohio: Bowling Green University Popular Press, 1971); and Will Wright, *Six-Guns and Society: A Structural Study of the Western* (Berkeley: University of California Press, 1975).

11. In another essay from 1936, "The Intellectual Physiognomy in Characterization," Lukács writes, "Characterization that does not encompass ideology cannot be complete. Ideology is the highest form of consciousness" (*Writer and Critic* 151).

12. The phrase "the blackness of darkness" is first encountered in *Moby-Dick* in a comic scene in a black church, into which Ishmael has mistakenly wandered: "A hundred black faces turned round in their rows to peer; and beyond, a black Angel of Doom was beating a book in a pulpit. It was a negro church; and the preacher's text was about the blackness of darkness, and the weeping and

wailing and teeth-gnashing there" (Herman Melville, *Moby-Dick*, ed. Harrison Hayford and Hershel Parker [New York: W. W. Norton, 1967], 18). That the phrase first appears in the novel in this bit of minstrelsy suggests that we probably ought not take Melville's cosmic preoccupations at face value, either.

13. This epigraph comes from a news item in the *Yuma Daily Sun*, 13 June 1982.

14. As a verbal construct, the judge grows out of a much more daring philosophical wager on McCarthy's part than any Melville was prepared (or able) to make. Given Judge Holden's bulk, his hairless white skin, and "pleated brow not unlike a dolphin's" (93), it seems appropriate to view him as a refiguration not of Ahab, as some readers have done, but of the great white whale himself.

15. Vereen Bell has written that "in *Blood Meridian* . . . the thematic discourse is like a dark parody of such idioms" (4). Bell has a point, but *Blood Meridian* is far from being a parody, however "like" one it may sometimes seem. Reading it as such would make its text more comfortable, safer, than it is; the novel challenges our notions of history and literary history more strongly than "parody" permits.

16. Or when it is *exhausted,* as we might want to say if we read McCarthy with Bakhtin in mind. A Bakhtinian reading of McCarthy's novel might regard the prevalence of description over narration as the result of the thorough interweaving of all the discourses, literary and otherwise, that the novel is "made out of." Thus, to appropriate Bakhtin's terminology, *Blood Meridian* is no longer a novel precisely because it is so very novelized, so intensely focused outwardly on the world, with little or no interest in the self or some other similarly transcendent object, such as its own aesthetic form. See M. M. Bakhtin, "Discourse in the Novel," in *The Dialogic Imagination: Four Essays,* trans. Caryl Emerson and Michael Holquist (Austin: University of Texas Press, 1981), 259–422.

17. Perhaps the best of the few essays on McCarthy published to date is Andrew Bartlett's "From Voyeurism to Archaeology: Cormac McCarthy's *Child of God,*" *Southern Literary Journal* 24 (fall 1991): 3–15. Bartlett refuses to sentimentalize the human figures in McCarthy's novel and does not treat them as if they were, after all, rounded characters, focusing instead on "the rhetorics of visibility, ways of *seeing* . . . McCarthy's superb regulation of narrative distance and perspective" (4). Thus McCarthy is able to avoid "complacent perspectives based on a society of armchair storytellers or a system of principled theological uniformity"—two of the standard ploys of southern fiction that Bartlett says "tend to exclude or to overlook the evidence outside their necessarily circumscribed fields of vision" (15).

18. Bartlett argues, apropos of the corpses the necrophilic Lester Ballard collects in McCarthy's *Child of God* and the remnants of Appalachian culture also detailed in that novel, that "those remains, the visualized objects, are precisely remains: they do not speak only of themselves but speak for something other than the empirically self-evident—something ancient, vanished, obscure, enigmatic" (9). I would emphasize that the important thing to notice is that the "remains" in McCarthy's fiction are persistently obscure and enigmatic, especially in *Blood Meridian*. Reading harder or more intently cannot get around this obscurity. I would note that McCarthy's rhetorical questions in the passage describing the slaughtered Tigua camp *are* questions, not statements. The difference is crucial.

19. It is worth noting here that McCarthy told Richard Woodward that he thought the novel could "encompass all the various disciplines and interests of humanity" (Woodward 30). Here, however, I deliberately use the less specific, less valorized term *book* to refer to *Blood Meridian* because it seems to me that McCarthy—by virtue of having achieved, in his use of other languages and discourses, such a remarkable degree of integration—has taken the "novel" beyond the moment of heteroglossia Bakhtin identifies as its essence. An awareness of the oppositions on which the novel depended for its life—the social oppositions suggested by the different speech patterns of various characters, for example, or even the more fundamental opposition between fictional and factual discourses—does not give the reader much purchase on *Blood Meridian*.

20. Charles Newman, *The Post-Modern Aura: The Act of Fiction in an Age of Inflation* (Evanston: Northwestern University Press, 1985), 16. Compare Fredric Jameson's more recent comment on the postmodern: "It is safest to grasp the concept of the postmodern as an attempt to think the present historically in an age that has forgotten how to think historically in the first place" (*Postmodernism, or the Cultural Logic of Late Capitalism* [Durham, N.C.: Duke University Press, 1991], ix). Jameson is speaking here not of postmodern fiction but of theory (both postmodern theory and theories of the postmodern), and what is striking is how both Jameson and Newman identify postmodernism with what Jameson calls "an inverted millenarianism" (1).

21. We might even, following Hayden White, call McCarthy's vision "sublime," in that it is informed by a sense of the terrible powers of the natural world. In his description of the "disciplinization" of history, White argues that a rejection of the "sublime" in favor of the "beautiful" is the founding gesture of the modern historical method based on narrativity: "It was this demotion of the sublime in favor of the beautiful that constituted the heritage from German idealism to both radical and conservative thought about the kind of utopian existence mankind could justifiably envisage as the ideal aim or goal of any putatively progressive historical process" (*The Content of the Form: Narrative Discourse and Historical Representation* [Baltimore: Johns Hopkins University Press, 1987], 70). McCarthy's bracketing of human narrative, which he represents as only one of a variety of natural processes, is what gives *Blood Meridian* its strong dystopian flavor, but it seems perverse to us only because we are so enamored of the "beautiful" for the reasons and as a result of the "demotion of the sublime" White describes.

22. The phrase "deep time" is originally John McPhee's; see *Basin and Range* (New York: Farrar, Straus & Giroux, 1980).

23. *The Crossing* (New York: Alfred A. Knopf, 1994), the second installment of McCarthy's Border Trilogy, describes the adventures of Billy Parham, a New Mexico sixteen-year-old who attempts to return a pregnant she-wolf to the Mexican mountain range from which she has strayed north. In the course of three journeys across the borderland, Billy Parham loses not only the wolf he is attempting to save, but also his parents, his brother, their home, most of his horses, and his sense of the passage of time, especially historical time. (He is unaware, for example, of the outbreak of World War II.) *The Crossing* is even more intensely focused on the lives of animals than *All the Pretty Horses* and nearly as bleak as *Blood Meridian*.

Works Cited

Bakhtin, M. M. "Discourse in the Novel." *The Dialogic Imagination: Four Essays.* Trans. Caryl Emerson and Michael Holquist. Austin: University of Texas Press, 1981. 259–422.

Bell, Vereen M. *The Achievement of Cormac McCarthy.* Baton Rouge: Louisiana State University Press, 1988.

Gould, Stephen Jay. *Time's Arrow, Time's Cycle: Myth and Metaphor in the Discovery of Geologic Time.* Cambridge, Mass.: Harvard University Press, 1987.

Lukács, Georg. *The Historical Novel.* Trans. Hannah and Stanley Mitchell. Lincoln: University of Nebraska Press, 1983.

———. "The Intellectual Physiognomy in Characterization." *Writer and Critic and Other Essays.* Ed. and trans. Arthur D. Kahn. New York: Universal Library, 1971.

———. "Narrate or Describe?" *Writer and Critic and Other Essays.* Ed. and trans. Arthur D. Kahn. New York: Universal Library, 1971.

———. *The Theory of the Novel: A Historico-Philosophical Essay on the Forms of Epic Literature.* Trans. Anna Bostock. Cambridge, Mass.: MIT Press, 1971.

McCarthy, Cormac. *Blood Meridian, or, The Evening Redness in the West.* 1985. New York: Vintage Books, 1992.

Melville, Herman. *Moby-Dick.* Ed. Harrison Hayford and Hershel Parker. New York: W. W. Norton, 1967.

Tompkins, Jane. *West of Everything: The Inner Life of Westerns.* New York: Oxford University Press, 1992.

Woodward, Richard B. "Cormac McCarthy's Venomous Fiction." *The New York Times Magazine,* 19 Apr. 1992: 28–31, 36, 40.

The Lay of the Land in Cormac McCarthy's Appalachia

K. Wesley Berry

A S I read Cormac McCarthy's Appalachian fiction—*The Orchard Keeper, Outer Dark,* and *Child of God*—my gaze draws back from the picturesque vista of the broader Appalachians, back from the sublimity of the panorama, to focus on the harsh realities of the close-up: eastern Tennessee and western North Carolina as mountainous wastelands.[1] My vision is drawn to what other critics of McCarthy's Appalachian fiction have given but slight attention to: the ecological undertones of landscape representation.[2] McCarthy's descriptions of the mountain terrain have more in common with Walker Evans's black-and-white close-ups of poor Alabama sharecroppers in *Let Us Now Praise Famous Men* than with the long view of the land framed by Ansel Adams's landscape photography. As in Evans's photographs, where the quaint ruggedness of the rural people does not obscure their poverty, McCarthy's Appalachia is revealed as a place both beautiful and ruined, a land of scant patches of virgin woodlands juxtaposed with the scars of more than two centuries of pioneering. McCarthy is attentive to a variety of ecological measurements: geologic records, the vegetative and animal life that shaped these records (for instance, the hundreds of millions of years of sea life piled on the land when it was covered with water, and whose corpses decayed into the wealth of mineral matter underlying the present-day mountains[3]), and riparian history.[4] By focusing on details of the land—the surface features and landforms, the vegetation covering it, and the human structures built upon it—we better understand McCarthy's subtle critique of the forces that have laid waste and continue to lay waste to the mountain wilderness and the inhabitants who dwell there.

THE ORCHARD KEEPER: INHUMANISM AND THE YEOMAN ELEGY

A historical awareness of natural resource usage in Appalachia encourages appreciation of the ecological critique of McCarthy's fiction. In *The Southern Appalachian Forests*, foresters H. B. Ayres and W. W. Ashe report the findings of field surveys they undertook in the mountains in 1900 and 1901. About the northwestern slope of the Unaka Mountains, which lie on the eastern edge of Tennessee, the foresters reported: "92 percent is wooded. . . . In the coves . . . the soil is fertile. . . . As a rule the earth is fairly well covered and thus protected from erosion. . . . In this region streams heading in unbroken forest are notably clear and show little fluctuation, while those from cleared lands are muddy and inconstant. While present erosion is limited, there is evidence that it would be very great if large areas of the earth were uncovered" (quoted in Camuto 251).

In one species-rich watershed in the southern Appalachians in 1900, from New River Gap in Virginia to the Hiwassee River in western North Carolina and northern Georgia, at least 137 tree species could be found; add to that 174 species of shrubs, "as well as uncounted varieties of herbs, forbs, grasses, plants, lichens, mosses, ferns, and fungi" (Camuto 251). Wilma Dykeman further praises the richness of botanical life in Appalachia in *The French Broad*. The mountains of eastern Tennessee and western North Carolina support woods "richer in variety of trees than the whole of Europe, for this is the area where Northern and Southern vegetation meet and mingle" (11). She explains that twenty-five thousand years ago a great icecap formed over Labrador and crept across North America, "until at last all the northern United States was buried under ice, and trees and plants once native to Canada made their last stand on the heights of the Southern Appalachians" (11). On these mountains exist "some of the largest stands of virgin spruce and balsam fir in the Eastern United States. Here are the great hardwood forests of America" (11). These forests, Dykeman writes, "were and are the most valuable natural heritage of the French Broad country. Not alone for quantity of board feet, nor for wide variety of species, but for the life they supported and their relation to the vast water resource of the region" (11). These diverse forests have, of course, been the sites of vigorous cutting. Deforestation in the region goes back to the late eighteenth century, when large numbers of homesteading pioneers migrated into eastern Tennessee. Settlers hacked away at the wilderness to construct homes and plant crops. The waste of timber stands was large; many cut trees went unused (Dykeman 51–52). Heavy logging occurred in the region throughout the nineteenth century (Smith et al. 294). Deforestation has been extensive. Of the great forests that once covered most of the state, "less than one-tenth of the primeval stand" still stood in 1939 (Federal Writers' Project 19). A study conducted by the Works Progress Administration discusses the condition of the land in that year: "Fire and wasteful lumbering have taken their toll of the timber regions. Protective grasses have been uprooted from the slopes by overgrazing and by the plow. Erosion has resulted from these careless methods, and today (1939) fourteen million acres in the State need reclamation" (Federal Writers' Project 20).

The land within the political borders of eastern Tennessee has yielded a wealth of natural resources, including some of the world's richest coal seams. Coal was first mined in the state in 1814 in western Roane County (Federal Writers' Project 67). In 1939, the second largest marble quarry in the United States lay near Knoxville (Federal Writers' Project 68). In 1939, too, Tennessee's extensive phosphate rock deposits placed the state second to Florida in production of phosphate for commercial fertilizer. Additionally, the Tennessee Valley Authority took advantage of eastern Tennessee's extensive river system and in 1933 began damming the main rivers and tributaries, building nine dams by 1948. (In *The Orchard Keeper*, that same year, John Wesley Rattner heads for the western road, fleeing an encroaching modernity.) The cheap power generated by hydroelectric plants attracted other industries, notably the nuclear facility at Oak Ridge, built in 1943 to produce enriched uranium for the making of the atomic bomb. Furthermore, ALCOA (Aluminum Company of America), using hydroelectric power from the Little Tennessee River, had constructed fifteen power plants in eastern Tennessee and western North Carolina by 1945, the first of them begun in 1914 in North Maryville, in Blount County, Tennessee.

These real-life economic and ecological conditions are reflected in McCarthy's fiction. McCarthy's "critique" is not altogether specific; nowhere in the fiction are mentioned the Tennessee Valley Authority, coal companies, pulpwood plants, or other prominent industries that take advantage of Appalachia's subterranean and surface resources. Nevertheless, the impact of these industries is an unspoken force behind the agricultural decline in McCarthy's Appalachia. For instance, *The Orchard Keeper*, set in the 1930s and 1940s, presents a landscape beset by erosion and abandoned farmland. By piecing together the few dates and spans of time offered in the text, one can ascertain the narrative present to be around 1940. Kenneth Rattner left Red Branch in 1933. He returned after a year's absence, at which time Marion Sylder killed him. Add Rattner's absence of one year plus the six years Arthur Ownby has guarded Rattner's corpse (52) for the historic time when Ownby enters the narrative. We first see Ownby scavenging for peaches in the orchard, which "went to ruin twenty years before when the fruit had come so thick and no one to pick it that at night the overborne branches cracking sounded in the valley like distant storms raging" (51). The absence of peach pickers twenty years before (circa 1920) points to the impact World War I had on agriculture. Historian Durwood Dunn notes the decrease in farming in Cades Cove, Tennessee (a town in Blount County, southeast of McCarthy's fictional Red Branch) following the war: "The 1920's witnessed a sudden regression as agricultural prices—high before and during the war—suddenly dropped, leaving many cove farmers in desperate financial straits. National prohibition in 1919 suddenly highlighted the advantages of the cove's geographic isolation for distilling illicit whiskey. Distilling had always occupied a small fraction of the community before, but by 1920 many mainstream, respectable citizens turned to moonshining in desperation as farm prices continued to fall" (77).

True to the historical conditions, *The Orchard Keeper* reveals this agricultural decline through such details as the wrecked orchard and farms of Red Branch. Ownby, a farmer in his younger days,[5] no longer keeps swine for his own consumption. Traditional rural hog killings were community affairs, and the absence of neighboring farmers in Red Branch is linked to the "black hog-kettle which [Ownby] didn't use any more" (56). The fictional abandoned farms evoke the historic mass migrations of the yeomanry into towns to claim factory jobs.

In an early review of *The Orchard Keeper*, Walter Sullivan places the novel "in the middle of the Agrarian influence" (721). In a more recent analysis of the novel, Robert L. Jarrett refutes this association with the Nashville Agrarians and claims that Sullivan "misreads as 'agrarian' the text's representation of the relation between man and nature and errs in associating the distinctive features of the tradition of the Southern renaissance with McCarthy" (8). Jarrett proposes instead that McCarthy's first novel "critiques the Agrarians' and Faulkner's assumption of an essential or meaningful continuity between Southern past and present" (11). *The Orchard Keeper* is about disconnection, and hence a break from the Agrarian tradition, Jarrett suggests (12–13). If one limits the term "agrarian" to the Nashville scholars and plantation farming, then McCarthy's texts are indeed a divorce from the tradition. The impoverished yeoman landholders of *The Orchard Keeper*, with their few barren acres, do not fit into the context of "Faulkner's Southern patriarchy," with its sharecropping system rooted in "the chattel slavery of the plantation" (Jarrett 21–22). The novel is, however, "agrarian" within the context of Wendell Berry's agricultural praxis. Berry, a farmer who lives in the foothills skirting Appalachia near the confluence of two rivers—the Kentucky and the Ohio—has written a dozen books of nonfiction, most of which emphasize the ecological importance of small-scale sustainable farming. A few of the most explicitly "agrarian" texts include *A Continuous Harmony* (1972), *The Unsettling of America* (1977), and *The Gift of Good Land* (1981), all bearing subtitles that are variations on the phrase "Culture and Agriculture." Berry calls himself an "agrarian" because he is an advocate of agricultural practices that sustain the ecological integrity of a place. He is a supporter of sustainable forestry and of the ability of a people to live "independently"—that is, not dependent on out-of-region and foreign imports of fossil fuels, food, textiles, and so forth.

The Orchard Keeper is an elegy to yeoman farmers and their descendants. The novel is "agrarian" in its awareness of land abuse in modern Appalachia, abuse that accelerated with the shift of property ownership from the small-scale yeoman to "absentee" (out-of-county or -state) landholders and corporations. One notices the decline of independent agricultural communities in Marion Sylder's story. At the age of sixteen, around 1929, Sylder leaves the community with little more than "a pair of thirty-dollar boots mail-ordered out of Minnesota. . . . Whatever trade he followed in his exile he wore no overalls, wielded no hammer" (12). Sylder's purchase of boots through the mail either testifies to the lack of boot sellers in Red Branch or sets him up as a representative of the new cash economy. Because Sylder probably could have purchased a pair of boots in Knoxville, one assumes he is exercising personal choice in buying mail-order boots from far away, rather than supporting his local economy. Sylder returns to Red Branch "bearing no olive branch but hard coin and greenbacks and ushering in an era of prosperity" (29). A moonshine runner, Sylder acquires quick money with minimal labor. Additional references concerning the shift in Red Branch away from subsistence farming and into a cash economy are to the Tiptons, residents who embody the "new catalog store prosperity" in their china lamps and linoleum floor and "warm morning heater" (105). Other signs appear in Knoxville, where farmers converge to higgle their produce and where butchers sell meat "white-spotted and trichinella-ridden" (82). Replacing subsistence farmers who cultivated corn, wheat, potatoes, beans, and who raised a few hens for eggs, a cow for milk, or a hog for meat are poor farm boys "with no more farm than some wizened tomato plants and a brace of ravenous hogs" (16). Sylder's job at the fertilizer plant near Knoxville, where he worked sometime around 1930 before running whiskey, is another sign that large single-crop agriculture, dependent on factory-made fertilizers and pesticides, is expanding. "Progressive" or "scientific" agriculture had by 1910 "swept Cades Cove as it engulfed the rest of the United States" (Dunn 77). Agribusiness technology made possible the harvesting of larger quantities of agricultural produce with fewer hands, which drove down agricultural prices. Land taxes, however, remained steady; indeed, independent landowners were taxed at higher rates than corporate and absentee owners.[6] This economic discrepancy hurt small farmers and spurred their exodus into towns.

Industrial farming, coupled with mining and other heavy industry, shows its presence in *The Orchard Keeper* in the form of a scarred landscape. Near the ruined orchard stands a spray pit once used for mixing insecticide. The orchard has not been actively "kept" in twenty years, yet weeds still do not grow under the apple trees, attesting to the potency and longevity of the chemicals. Additionally, whenever rain pours in McCarthy's Appalachia, the rivers run red with clay from the eroded land. Ownby walks to where a mysterious government tank—an intruder in his Eden—sits "like a great silver ikon, fat and bald and sinister" atop a knoll. A wooded area has been cleared to make room for the tank. It is "a barren spot, bright in the moonwash, mercurial and luminescent as a sea, the pits from which the trees had been wrenched dark on the naked bulb of the mountain as moon craters" (93). Surrounding this wasteland is a wire fence within which "the great dome stood complacent, huge . . . clean and coldly gleaming and capable of infinite contempt" (93). This once healthy forest has been injured, as evidenced by the mud-choked water, bloodred after a rain. During a storm, Ownby casts himself into a land awash in red: "The road had gone from dust shocked up in dark waterballs to geysers of erupting mud" (171). The land around Ownby's misused farm is "bleeding," the rain "cutting gullies on the hills till they ran red and livid as open wounds" (173). "Rafts of leaves descended the flowage of Henderson Valley Road, clear water wrinkling over the black asphalt. The mud-choked gullies ran thick with water of a violent red, roiling heavily, pounding in the gutters with great belching sounds" (174). A flooded creek churns "a chocolate-dark foam," a "thick brown liquid"—the color of topsoil. All this erosion is a reminder that "forests and water are as inseparable as the heart and its blood. If there is a water problem, there is a forest problem first" (Dykeman 11).

Erosion of land is a natural process. For millions of years before heavy industry, water transformed landscapes; the Grand Canyon, carved by the Colorado River, and Mammoth Cave, formed by water trickling and streaming through limestone, are two examples. Nevertheless, the hand of man lies on McCarthy's bloodred streams, gullied roads, and hillsides with gaping "wounds" where trees once stood. Human industry speeds up the momentum, propels the erosion. The land washed away during the big flood in *The Orchard Keeper* recalls earlier scenes of human violence: Ownby dynamiting the earth in preparation for new roads, the pesticide pit insulting the land like an enduring ulcer, and the young boys dynamiting birds, foreshadowing yet another generation that will, in the manner of Thomas Sutpen in *Absalom, Absalom!,* rip violently from the earth whatever is needed for the building of empire.

Around 1949, Ownby grows nostalgic for the agrarian lifestyle, for a time that has passed. Standing on a high bald knoll on Red Mountain, he gazes at the Great Smokies far in the distance. "If I was a younger man," he says, "I would move to them mountains. I would find me a clearwater branch and build me a log house with a fireplace. And my bees would make black mountain honey. And I wouldn't care for no man." He adds, "Then I wouldn't be unneighborly neither" (55). Ownby expresses here agrarian sentiments—a desire for personal self-sufficiency and neighborliness. It is a vision of the agrarian "hero" of pastoral literature, described by Leo Marx in *The Machine in the Garden:* "Instead of striving for wealth, status, and power, he [the farmer] may be said to live a good life in a rural retreat; he rests content with a few simple possessions, enjoys freedom from envying others, feels little or no anxiety about his property, and, above all, he does what he like to do" (98). John M. Grammer notes, however, that the pastoral dream is obsolete, while adding that *The Orchard Keeper* offers the most positive image of pastoral order in McCarthy's oeuvre, "a kind of touchstone" against which we can examine McCarthy's "later and bleaker examinations of the pastoral impulse" (30). McCarthy's ambivalent presentation of the disappearing farmer-pioneer is demonstrated by a comparison of *The Orchard Keeper* with *Child of God*. In the final lines of *The Orchard Keeper,* the narrator notes the passing of these people: "They are gone now. Fled, banished in death or exile, lost, undone. . . . No avatar, no scion, no vestige of that people remains. On the lips of the strange race that now dwells there their names are myth, legend, dust" (246). This vanquished "race" includes failed subsistence farmers and descendants of farmers, hunters, and moonshiners—those whose ancestors were once independent of "outside" sources of sustenance and entertainment but who are now locked into the broader world of commerce connected with the outroads of Appalachia. McCarthy's characterization of these people is objective, yet one senses nostalgia, a small tribute, some authorly admiration in their stubbornness to remain aloof from the outside world. McCarthy does not romanticize the yeoman farmer, whose scions commit acts of idiotic violence. In *Child of God,* for instance, a community narrator explains that Lester Ballard once broke a cow's neck by pulling her with a rope attached to a tractor (35). Another young yokel sets fire under his oxen team to get it to move (36). The violent pioneer impulse lingers in these twentieth-century farmers. They are complex characters, at once admirable, pitiable, and base.

McCarthy's prose implies a vision of ecological holocaust, as if the collapse of the earth as we know it lurks in the near future—a devastation spurred by our fossil-fuel-driven, hurry-up economy of fire. Violent acts run throughout the novels, dealt by humans, animals, and weather. Destruction to life is overbearing. The declining fauna of McCarthy's Appalachia provides the most obvious evidence of ecological disease. Even readers unimpressed by dirt-choked, bloodred waters and the agrarian critique will recognize McCarthy's ethics of the wild. In *The Orchard Keeper,* Ownby recalls how he has not smelled muskrat for forty years (56). A reason is not given, but one suspects that muskrats, like mink, have been trapped out (143). Ownby laments the decline of the raccoon, overhunted, one supposes, or pushed out of Red Branch with the clearing of forests for cropland and for such structures as the enigmatic government tank. The threat to Red Branch wildlife goes all the way back to the 1870s, when

Ownby worked on road crews in the area. Logging roads cut off wildlife migration paths, and perhaps whatever wildlife has not been overhunted and trapped in John Wesley Rattner's and Ownby's roaming area has moved south to the Smoky Mountain wilderness, the less-developed watershed that from Red Branch looms "like a distant promise" (10).

The most memorable symbol of ecological catastrophe in *The Orchard Keeper* may be the hungry solitary panther. Like the venerable bear of Faulkner's novella, the panther is the last of its kind. After a flood, the cat treads the eroding landscape searching for food. She appears "bedraggled and diminutive, a haunted look about her" (174). She is "very thin and forlorn," because her food sources have been diminished by trappers, hunters, and loggers. The lack of vegetative and animal life in Red Branch can be seen through the panther's search for food. The land the cat inhabits in the environs of Ownby's abandoned farm appears dead: "she came down the patch obscure with parched weeds shedding thin blooms of sifting dust where she brushed them" (216). Because forests have been hewn, there is not much natural cover to protect the soil and few spots where the earth holds moisture on a hot, dry day. The panther crosses into a "dry gully, the cracked and curling clay like a paving of potsherds" (217). A "potsherd" is a fragment of broken pottery, particularly one with archaeological worth, such as the Mimbres pottery unearthed in New Mexico, etched with picture-stories from ancient Indian mythology.[7] We can similarly "read" the cracked clay and deadly drought of Red Branch and comprehend the connection between bone-dry land and absent forests. The panther traverses the baked clay earth and then approaches one lone walnut tree standing in a field, the sole survivor "against axe and plowshare" (217). All is passing: the single walnut tree is sure to fall, along with the last panther, the mink and muskrat, and the old independent pioneers like Ownby.

McCarthy never allows readers long spaces of comfort. Agents of violence quickly penetrate sublime natural settings. In this sense, McCarthy's fiction participates in what Leo Marx calls "complex" pastoral literature. In his account, the "naive" pastoral, such as Emerson's *Nature,* tends to romanticize the whole land as a "garden," an ideal in which peaceful wilderness provides a haven of rest for the weary. The "complex" pastoral, on the other hand, recognizes the penetration of human industry into the sylvan countryside, as when railroads encroach on the quiet of Walden Pond or into Faulkner's Big Woods or into McCarthy's Hurricane Wilderness. In one paragraph of *The Orchard Keeper*, we walk in a picturesque forest, where sunlight flashes among sky-reaching tree trunks in which squirrels frolic; in the next paragraph, the "machine" breaks the calm in the form of a fire trail built by the Civilian Conservation Corps (200). Ownby, who makes his newest home in the wilderness, finds a rattlesnake belly-up on the fire trail. He prods the snake and discovers that someone has cut away the rattles— a human hand again intruding on a sliver of old-growth wilderness. Another complex action—one imparting both hope and heavy loss— occurs near the end of the novel, when John Wesley returns a dead hawk and the bounty he had collected on it to the Knox County courthouse and announces, "I cain't take no dollar. I made a mistake, he wadn't for sale" (233). The gesture is futile, yet it suggests that John Wesley has cultivated an ontological appreciation for wild nature, a change from his earlier utilitarian preoccupation with trapping fur-bearing animals for their hides. John Wesley is a type of American Adam, cast out of Eden and fallen. His returning the dead hawk is an admission of complicity, a form of repentance. He knows there will be no reclamation of wildness in Appalachia—no more abundant mink and muskrat and freedom from bureaucracy—and at the novel's close he accordingly heads westward in search of a new Eden.

The destruction of life is overbearing, yet elements of hope exist in the fiction that readers may miss—a hope centered not on humanity but on the rebounding health of the damaged nonhuman world. Consider how McCarthy presents examples not only of abused nature but also of land not destroyed by human invention. When he first introduces his fictional eastern Tennessee in *The Orchard Keeper*, for example, he sets up the dominating conflict of most environmental writing: the contrast between human-scarred land and healthy wilderness. It is summertime in Red Mountain. The scorching sun has baked the land cleared for roads and crops: "The red dust of the orchard road is like powder from a brick kiln. You can't hold a scoop of it in your hand. Hot winds come up the slope from the valley like a rancid breath, redolent of milkweed, hoglots, rotting vegetation. The red clay banks along the road are crested with withered honeysuckle, peavines dried and sheathed in dust. By late July the corn patches stand parched and sere, stalks askew in defeat. All greens pale and dry. Clay cracks and splits in endless microcataclysm and the limestone lies about the eroded land" (10–11). In the next paragraph, McCarthy presents a healthy forest by which we can gauge the damage done to the adjacent land: "In the relative cool of the timber stands, possum grapes and muscadine flourish with a cynical fecundity, and the floor of the forest—littered with old mossbacked logs, peopled with toadstools strange and solemn among the ferns and creepers . . . has about it a primordial quality, some steamy carboniferous swamp where ancient saurians lurk in feigned sleep" (11).

These borders—the margins where the misused land meets the healthy—lend a sense of hopefulness to the story of wasted nature. Agricultural margins, where land damaged by farming and industry abuts land that has been spared of heavy use, can reveal how much our history in a place has failed, but they also show us what we must aspire to, as Wendell Berry says. The land spared of use "is an indispensable example, a little border of health along the edge of bewilderment and defeat" (*Unsettling of America* 185).

The characters in McCarthy's Appalachia generally walk through wastelands, but they occasionally traverse a marginal landscape where a scarred, abandoned farm or eroded hillside abuts a healthy forest. To escape the law and seek peace, the old "orchard keeper" Ownby moves into the "Harrykin" (Hurricane) Wilderness, a forest showing signs of health: a moss carpet over dark earth where wildflowers grow; fallen timber allowed to decompose and fortify the forest floor; rattlesnakes lurking near each log (a detail by which we infer that the food chain is stable, as the soil supports the plants, grub worms, and insects that nourish birds and rodents on which snakes feed). The woods here are diverse and deep, with "spiring trunks," "regiments of Indian Pipe," "green puffballs." Mountain pheasants dwell here. The plush forest floor yields to the weight of Ownby's brogans: "steps soft now in the rank humus earth, or where carapaced with lichens the texture of old green velvet, or wet and spongy earth tenoned with roots, the lecherous ganglia of things growing" (201). Utilitarians may appraise areas like the Hurricane Wilderness as cluttered "worthless" lands, or as "development potential," or as a "gold mine" of natural resources. An ecologist, on the other hand, knows these marginal areas are busting with life.

The ominous tone generated by the ruination of species and places is to an extent mitigated when the collapse of human structures is viewed in light of the American literary-philosophical tradition of "inhumanism"—a weltanschauung that "contains a vital critique of the prevailing humanism (i.e., chauvinistic anthropocentrism) which has contributed greatly to the [environmental] crisis" (Morris 1). "Inhumanism," as poet Robinson Jeffers defines the term, is "a shifting of emphasis and significance from man to not-man; [it is] the rejection of human solipsism and recognition of the transhuman magnificence" (xxi).[8] Literary scholar Christopher Manes further expresses an inhumanist point of view: "The most that can be said is that during the last 350 million years natural selection has shown an inordinate fondness for beetles—and before that trilobites. This observation directly contradicts the *scala naturae* and its use in humanist discourse. From the perspective of biological adaptation, elephants are no 'higher' than earwigs; salamanders are no less 'advanced' than sparrows; cabbages have as much evolutionary status as kings. Darwin invited our culture to face the fact that in the observation of nature there exists not one scrap of evidence that humans are superior to or even more interesting than, say, lichen" (22).

"Inhumanism" indicates a humble conception of the status of *Homo sapiens* in the world—a perspective similar to the "optical democracy" of landscape representation in McCarthy's *Blood Meridian*. Dana Phillips explains that this "Western" novel presents an "equality of being between human and nonhuman objects" (444); the interplay of the land's "largest and smallest features," and even the shadows cast by objects, manifests "optical democracy": "The suggested independence of light and dark reinforces the lack of precedence, or referential order, in the natural world and helps make apparent the 'unguessed kinships' between objects as diverse as goat turds, the sun, men, and gods. This kinship, however, neither ennobles the turds nor debases the gods but merely makes them equal in that both are putatively factual" (445).

Both "inhumanism" and "optical democracy" question whether humans have a privileged position in the world. A primary difference between the two orientations to landscape is that inhumanism shifts "significance" to the nonhuman, while optical democracy presents ontological equality. *Blood Meridian*, Phillips says, "is not so much inhuman as nonhuman. It is thoroughly dispassionate" (450).[9]

To understand the inhumanist perspective is to understand in part how one can read affirmatively the pervasive decay of human structures in McCarthy's fiction. In his ecospiritual autobiography *The Long-Legged House*, Wendell Berry explains how the deterioration of a cabin on the Kentucky River—a place he has visited since childhood, called affectionately "The Camp"—impresses his ecological awareness: "The Camp was rapidly aging and wearing out. . . . Its floors were warped and tilted. The roof leaked where a fallen elm branch had punched through the tin. Some of the boards of the walls had begun to rot where the wet weeds leaned against them. . . . Decay revealed its kinship with the earth, and it seemed more than ever to belong to the riverbank. The more the illusion of permanence fell away from it, the easier it fit into the flux of things, as though it entered the fellowship of birds' nests and of burrows" (152–53). And again, "It is a truthful house, not indulging the illusion of the permanence of human things" (158).

Berry views the decay of The Camp as a healthy natural process rather than as an affront to human grandeur. The decay in McCarthy's Appalachia can be read similarly. In *The Orchard Keeper*, John Wesley returns to Red Branch from his travels to find the old house where he and his mother lived rotting and returning to earth: "he could see the roof of the house deep-green with moss, or gaping black where patches had caved through" (244). In *Outer Dark*, Rinthy passes a "slattern shack" "grown with a rich velour of moss and lichen and brooded in a palpable miasma of rot" (108–9). Wooden shacks fall back into the earth, and the body likewise returns to clay: "The dead sheathed in the earth's crust . . . at peace with eclipse, asteroid, the dusty novae, their bones brindled with mold and the celled marrow going to frail stone, turning, their fingers laced with roots, at one with Tut and Agamemnon, with the seed and the unborn" (*The Orchard Keeper* 245). And a tombstone, three years planted, is already weathered and glazed with lichen—a species forming an essential part of the food chain. The lichen, like the archaeological references so prominent in McCarthy's fiction, bring to mind the building up of millions of years of life on this earth. The human body is recycled, the tombstones are recycled, nature bounces back—the revolution of life and death moves on, regardless of human striving.

THE STRATA OF LANDSCAPE IN *CHILD OF GOD*

Critics have noted the difficulty of attaching specific moral and philosophical significance to McCarthy's texts. Robert L. Jarrett, for instance, writes, "While McCarthy's landscapes hold significance, their meanings are indeterminate" (138). John M. Grammer calls the novels "notoriously inscrutable" and notes how McCarthy's immaculate prose—his "rendering of the physical world in all its dense, vivid specificity"—has the power "to upend whatever conceptual grids are imposed on it" (28). With the "philosophical attitude" of inhumanism in mind, I will examine the landscape of *Child of God*—the human structures, the plant communities, and the geologic features—for its embedded economic and ecological "meaning." Furthermore, I want to consider how knowledge of the topography of eastern Tennessee can assist one in mapping Lester Ballard's mountain rambles.

In *Child of God,* as in *The Orchard Keeper,* human structures on the land hint at the decline of subsistence agriculture. These include the abandoned quarry Ballard traverses in his rambles. The quarry, probably limestone, is cluttered with industrial artifacts: the "ruins of an old truck lay rusting in the honeysuckle" (38); "old stoves and water heaters," "bicycle parts and corroded buckets" are scattered around. White dust blows "off the barren yard by the quarry shed" (39). Like the abandoned spray pit in *The Orchard Keeper,* the quarry suggests large-scale industrial development gone bad, perhaps made insolvent during the Depression. This ruined industry reminds readers of the businesses that shut down or moved out of the region after exhausting their resource bases, and also of the short-lived prosperity farmers experienced when pulled or tempted from their self-sufficient lifestyles to work in quarries, mines, and fertilizer plants. The cornpicker Ballard observes "snarling through the fields" (40) is another of McCarthy's subtle nods toward the corporate influences abetting the decay of human and nonhuman Appalachian communities.

Referring to the exposition of *Child of God,* when the county government evicts Lester Ballard from the property owned by his father, Grammer writes: "The scene in which the yeoman farmer loses his property is the one which pastoral republics dread—the moment when death enters their world" (37).[10] The loss of land is indeed an old story. In 1981, the Appalachian Land Ownership Task Force published *Land Ownership Patterns and Their Impacts on Appalachian Communities: A Survey of 80 Counties.* Among the committee's concerns was the decline of the small farm in the southern regions of Appalachia, which in 1930 "had the heaviest concentration of self-sufficient farms in the country" (125). The committee documented the decline, placing heavy emphasis on the role absentee timber and coal interests played in the transition of Appalachian population from a modest but independent yeomanry to an impoverished people unable to save from destruction the land from which they draw their sustenance. Beginning in the 1870s, agents from timber corporations came to Appalachia in search of lumber. These agents conducted title searches, and many farmers lost the land that supported them; Appalachian subsistence farmers usually titled only the small portions of land they cultivated, and thus many lost to the timber companies the untitled land on which they hunted and fished.

The timber industry's careless logging of the region's virgin forests resulted in severe siltation and flooding problems, making farming even more difficult for the mountain dwellers. Further displacing the mountaineer from his subsistent lifestyle, the coal industry entered the country before the turn of the century and purchased for a pittance the "mineral rights" to the farmers' lands. The result of this exploitation, in Harry Caudill's words, was that the Appalachian farmer came to be "little more than a trespasser upon the soil beneath his feet." "Many subsistence farmers deserted their ancestral farms to take jobs in the coal camps, but the majority stayed behind to follow the same pattern of agricultural life" (*Land Ownership* 127–28). Dean Pierce describes what happened to those who stuck with farming: "Those who remained on the land attempted to provide more food or whiskey to meet their own increased needs and the demands of the coal camps. The additional foodstuffs raised to sell to these camps led to the eventual and everlasting destruction of the soil. It was these increasing outside pressures that came to overstress the agricultural system and finally to destroy the fertility of all the soil. Moreover, the coal camps, through an unjust control of tax assessment, passed the tax burden back to the landowners, falling heavily upon the subsistence farmer, who could ill afford to pay for the area's desperately needed services" (8).

The farmer, dependent on the coal industry's cash economy and "trespasser" on his own stressed land, was unprepared when the Depression brought on a collapse of the cash economy and required households to support themselves with subsistence agriculture. Much of the land was already exhausted from overuse.[11] Growing enough to eat was difficult, and the burden of property taxes was for many overwhelming. Many farmers consequently sold their land to absolve their tax debts (*Land Ownership* 128).

McCarthy depicts a similar situation in *Child of God*. In the opening pages, the county government is auctioning Lester Ballard's farm for his failure to pay taxes on it (7). The auction occurs on a "mute pastoral morning" (4); this is no idyllic scene, however, but "death" encroaching on the "pastoral republic" in the form of eviction. Several details highlight the pastoral nightmare that is carried throughout the novel: the auctioneer's voice like "a ghost chorus among the *ruins*" (5, emphasis added), the rope Lester's father hanged himself with still dangling from the loft (4), the fact that Lester is a scion of "Saxon and Celtic bloods" (4), races that long ago deforested the Scottish Highlands—the same pioneering people whose descendants settled in Appalachia and "with all the vigor and recklessness of necessity which had been behind their forward push to this very place ... attacked the forests of primeval pine and poplar, walnut and oak, chestnut and maple. With ax and fire they laid the giants low"

(Dykeman 51). Additional details of the broken pastoral include the abandoned farm Lester moves to, the outhouse overgrown with moss, the barn behind it that lies in a clearing bestrewn with "clumps of jimson and nightshade," and the two-room house overgrown with "a solid wall of weeds high as the house eaves" (13–14). Lester Ballard has not inherited agricultural wisdom. We sense that he has not cultivated vegetables for years—perhaps ever—as evidenced by his adroitness with the rifle he carries like an appendage and by the lumpy stool he excretes, indicating a lack of fiber in his diet (13). One cannot know for sure the occupation of Lester's father, who hanged himself in his barn when Lester was about nine or ten (21). The corpse dangling in the barn may suggest the senior Ballard's failure as a farmer, or it may suggest the lack of a good sturdy tree from which to hang a noose. We know that the timber on the land being auctioned in the opening scene was cut about fifteen to twenty years ago (5), and that Lester's father hanged himself about seventeen or eighteen years ago. Perhaps Ballard senior sold the timber off his property as a last desperate means of support and killed himself after exhausting that money.

Ballard's mountain neighbors and their livelihoods further indicate the absence of agriculture in the region. Fred Kirby, for instance, is a whiskey maker who apparently consumes too much of his product, inasmuch as he forgets where he stashes it (11–12). Ruebel, the "dumpkeeper," lives in a shack surrounded by junked cars and car parts and assorted industrial trash (26). The youth of the region exhibit an aimlessness brought on, one supposes, by lack of work. They have an excess of energy that they expel in copulation, these "old lanky country boys with long cocks and big feet" who visit the dumpkeeper's idle female spawn (27). "They were coming and going all hours in all manner of degenerate cars, a dissolute carousel of rotting sedans and niggerized convertibles" (27). These country youth recall the farm boys in *The Orchard Keeper* who tended "no more farm than some wizened tomato plants and a brace of ravenous hogs" (16), who dawdle about Knoxville with too much time on their hands. Indeed, the novel offers only a couple of details to support the existence of agriculture in Sevier County. First, cattle owned by a man named Waldrop muddy a creek when Ballard is about to shoot a bass

(34). Second, Ballard forages field corn (40). What little agriculture exists in the Sevier County that Ballard widely roams does not seem to line the stomachs of the region's human inhabitants. Food is conspicuously absent from *Child of God,* reminiscent of Erskine Caldwell's Depression-era *Tobacco Road* and its characters fighting over turnips. The few references to foodstuffs are nutritionally inadequate: whiskey, "dopes" (soft drinks), a stew with squirrel and turnips, a potato skewered on a coat hanger and roasted over a coal oil lantern, cornbread—each individual food a meal in itself, seldom eaten in combination for a "balanced" meal. The only "balanced" meals Ballard eats are during his nine days in jail, where he has "whitebeans with fatback and boiled greens and baloney sandwiches on lightbread" (53), or when he swipes dollars from a dead man and purchases at the store cans of beans, vienna sausages, bread, "baloney," a quart of sweetmilk, cheese and crackers, and a box of cakes (99). Perhaps Ballard's nutritional carelessness arises from a lack of vegetable cultivation in the worn-out mountain lands of Sevier County, where the only produce raised is feed corn for livestock.

In "Reading the Landscape," geographer John Fraser Hart says we should be able to "read" the way vegetation "tells the tale of how people have used and abused the land." For example, Hart explains that when they are abandoned, no longer farmed, woodlands cleared for cultivation fail to replenish their natural fecundity. In place of the ancient hardwoods grow "broomsedge, blackberry bushes, persimmon sprouts, cedar saplings, old field pines, and other plants [that] send a clear signal that the land is no longer used for agriculture." "The observer of landscape," Hart writes, "should be able to recognize the plants that invade and colonize unused agricultural land" (30). Readers of Cormac McCarthy's novels should likewise be aware of the vegetative "signals" of abused and abandoned land. In the opening scene of *Child of God,* the Ballard farm and the surrounding countryside are seen as having been ill used, as evidenced by the "swales of broomstraw" (3) and other scrub growth in the area: "clumps of jimson and nightshade" (poisonous plants), "bullbriers and blackberries" (14). The absence of vegetation is important to understanding the lay of the land. The auctioneer selling the Ballard homestead emphasizes the utilitarian value of a young timber stand not far removed from its last cutting: "It's been cut over fifteen twenty year ago and so maybe it ain't big timber yet, but looky here. . . . They is real future in this property. . . . Friends, they is no limit to the possibilities on a piece of property like this" (5). The absence of large old timber stands is an early hint of the destructive human consumption carried throughout *Child of God.*

Knowledge of Appalachian forestry also assists the spatial function of narrative mapping—a way for a reader to become better "placed" in the mountains, to realize some structure in Lester Ballard's wanderings. Ballard's primary habitation is Sevier County, Tennessee. References to "Sevier" are explicit and numerous, as when Ballard spends time in the Sevier County jail (52). When Ballard walks the mountain terrain, however, we cannot rely on place names, but the botanical references allow a better orientation. Lester always makes his homes at high elevations; this we know by paying attention to what vegetation exists at various altitudes. From his mountain cabin, Lester descends a slope covered in heavy snow. "When he reached the flats at the foot of the mountain he found himself in scrub cedar and pines" (75). Writing about plant communities in eastern Tennessee, H. R. DeSelm points out that "Virginia (scrub) pine occur everywhere in the [Great] Valley and on the [Cumberland] Plateau, and at lower elevations in the Mountains" (381–82). These regions encompass a broad area, and thus the textual reference to "scrub pine" hardly "pinpoints" Lester's location. The Great Valley is an area thirty to sixty miles wide, flanked by the Smoky Mountains; it begins in northeastern Tennessee and slants southwest into Georgia and Alabama. Its ridges "rise 300 to 800 feet above the valley floor" (Federal Writers' Project 8). It is a region "of fat soils and prosperous farms . . . drained by the Tennessee River and its tributaries" (8). Ballard's stomping grounds probably lie toward the southern edge of the valley in the higher elevations, perhaps in the Smokies, because upper Sevier County is in the lower-lying Great Valley. Southwestern Sevier County is most likely Lester's primary inhabitation. From a road near his cabin, Ballard must walk three hours to get to Sevierville (96). Accounting for a standard fifteen-minute mile, his cabin figures to be about ten to fifteen miles from town. Furthermore, Lester must live near Blount County, which borders Sevier County to the west. Ballard once crosses an unnamed mountain into Blount County, descends into a village to hawk some wristwatches, and returns to his cave in Sevier County in a single day. This unnamed mountain is possibly Chilhowee Mountain, which borders Blount County and Sevier County (DeSelm, "Geography" 219). Chilhowee is a ridge in the Unaka Mountains, part of which lie within the boundaries of the Great Smoky Mountains National Park. The highest peaks and ridges of the Unakas are about 2,800–4,800 feet (219).

The purpose of this topographical niggling is to demonstrate that *Child of God* is moderately mappable, even without the help of place names. In this sense, the novel is unlike *Outer Dark,* where the features of landscape are to a lesser extent defined. One feels totally awash in *Outer Dark,* as if wandering a land that could be any place at any time. The mountains Ballard travels are more vividly drawn. From his cave home high in the mountains during the "dreadful cold" of winter, Ballard thinks that before winter is over "he would look like one of the bitter spruces that grew slant downwind out of the shale and lichens on the hogback" (136). The reference to "hogback" (a sharply crested ridge with steep, sloping sides) and "spruce" identifies Ballard as a high-mountain dweller. In the Appalachians, boreal forests cover ridges exceeding 4,500 feet. "At about 4500 feet, the ridges' dominant hemlock is replaced by red spruce and yellow birch. Between about 5000 and 6000 feet, spruce and Fraser fir dominate the forest" (DeSelm, "Plant Communities" 382). High-elevation spruce are weather-stunted trees; McCarthy mentions this fact in *Suttree,* when Cornelius Suttree takes a solitary sojourn into the Smokies south of Gatlinburg, not far from Ballard's haunts: "Suttree went up the narrow valley and deeper into the mountains. Over old dry riverbeds of watershapen stones that lay in the floor of the wood. . . . At these high altitudes the trees were stunted spruce and dark and twisted. . . . The spruce trees stood black and bereaved of dimension in the shadow of the high cloven draws" (285).

Ballard, like the spruce, is shaped by this harsh environment. He is pummeled by rain, snow, wind, and fire, and thus his likening himself to the "bitter spruces" clinging precariously to the steep slopes of the hogback is appropriate. Ballard also tries to establish roots, but he is "uprooted" time and again: first by the legal system, then by fire and water.

When Ballard crosses the mountain into Blount County, he enters an ancient landscape: "Old woods and deep. At one time in the world there were woods that no one owned and these were like them" (127). This stand of virgin timber comes as a surprise, when one has been accustomed to the lower-elevation settlements full of abandoned farms and quarries, weed-choked clearings, "levees of junk and garbage," and logging roads cutting through second- and third-growth forests. An additional detail of the high-elevation primeval forest demands attention: "He passed a windfelled tulip poplar on the mountainside that held aloft in the grip of its roots two stones the size of fieldwagons, great tablets on which was writ only *a tale of vanished seas with ancient shells in cameo and fishes etched in lime*" (128, emphasis added). The rocks in the Great Valley of eastern Tennessee—the sandstones, shales, limestones, and dolomites—were formed from marine sediment (Federal Writers' Project 11), as McCarthy's nod to the "vanished seas" acknowledges. For the purpose of historical mapping, the geologic record embedded in the enormous boulders accentuates the first three periods of the Paleozoic era—Cambrian, Ordovician, and Silurian—together called the "Age of Invertebrates," "when the only life was shell-forming sea animals and buglike crustaceans," and the Devonian, or "Age of Fishes" (Federal Writers' Project 11). The Age of Invertebrates spans a time from 600 million to 395 million years ago, give or take a few million years. The Devonian period occurred from 400 million to 350 million years ago.

By calling attention to geologic time, McCarthy's fiction again manifests the spirit of inhumanism. When held up against millions of years of prehuman existence, the life span of *Homo sapiens* seems relatively inconsequential. Archaeological records place the earliest chipped stone tools of the Paleolithic at 750,000 years ago. The Neolithic period, marked by the development of agriculture and polished stone tools, began around 10,000 B.C. This reckoning of geologic time, coupled with the other archaeological artifacts

McCarthy tosses to readers—the bones of bison, elk, and jaguar ensconced deep within a cave—carries an aura of imminent doom. These great mammals no longer roam the forests of Appalachia, and neither does the hairy mammoth that once ranged Tennessee. Of this beast, only a tusk remains. The young hunters in *The Orchard Keeper* speak of it: "They used to be cave-men hereabouts," says Warn. "Prestoric animals too. They's a tush over on the other side of the mountain stickin out of some rock what's long as your leg" (140). In his *Natural and Aboriginal History of Tennessee,* John Haywood mentions several teeth, tusks, and skeletal remains of the mammoth discovered in Tennessee: teeth and a jawbone in eastern Tennessee, in Sullivan County; tusks between two to three feet in length in the central Tennessee counties of Maury and Sumner; a tusk eight feet six inches in length in the vicinity of Reynoldsburg, a town that during Haywood's tenure in the state (1807–26) lay somewhere on the south side of the Tennessee River (58–60). As the prehistoric beasts that once rove the land have been obliterated, so too have the grand old timber stands. All this death imagery joins with the muddy creeks of McCarthy's Appalachia—bloodred water carrying the fecundity of the mountains, the piled-up death of ages, tons of organic matter washed downstream with each heavy rain, leaving bone-dry, eroded hillsides— to project an eerie prophecy of the next great extinction.

Notes

1. McCarthy's fourth novel, *Suttree,* is marginally "Appalachian," set primarily in the foothills of the mountains around Knoxville, Tennessee. Additionally, in *Outer Dark,* the features of landscape do not function primarily as ecological critique or as a frame for mapping, but serve to mythologize the narrative—to create a sense of the unreal, a world where time and space are blurred. The reader is easily disoriented in *Outer Dark* because its landscape topography is less defined than in *The Orchard Keeper* and *Child of God.* The unspecific nature of the landscape enhances the allegorical quality of the novel. Because the purpose of this essay is to investigate the ecology of particular places, *Outer Dark,* with its "bafflingly incongruous aspects of landscape" (Bell 33), will not be discussed in depth.

2. Literary critics focusing on landscape representation in Cormac McCarthy's novels have emphasized its symbolic significance and aesthetic value. Natalie Grant, for instance, examines how "the natural world" in McCarthy's novels "often provides what T. S. Eliot has called an 'objective correlative' for defining the most mysterious aspects of his characters' personalities. . . . [which are] revealed in their relationship to a natural world that objectifies their psychological boundaries, or lack of them" (61). In Grant's reading of "nature," the nonhuman world is meaningful chiefly for the insight it offers into *human* character. In another analysis, Robert L. Jarrett offers an artful reading of McCarthy's prose landscapes within the context of "American luminism." Luminist paintings such as Frederic Church's *Mount Ktaadn* situate a human viewer "on a highland vista whose horizontal extension draws the spectator's gaze 'into' the landscape and outward to the farther heights of a distant panorama" (136). Jarrett illustrates how prose landscapes in McCarthy's fiction function similarly. In the exposition of *The Orchard Keeper,* for example, McCarthy's narrator, in the luminist style, "first orients us geographically, pointing us east of Knoxville to Red Mountain" and then invites us "to participate in the fiction by extending our vision from our foreground vantage point at Red Mountain southward to the Appalachian summit" (Jarrett 136). The prose subsequently draws our gaze back from the distant watershed to the "red dust of the orchard road" under our feet. These representations of the landscape, Jarrett says, "continually remind readers of the natural world within our sight, if only we expand our vision. . . . McCarthy's fiction might be termed an environmental fiction, constantly reinserting human society and human reality within a largely ignored yet alien natural environment" (137).

3. On the geological and archaeological history of Tennessee, see Haywood (49–60) and Federal Writers' Project (11–26).

4. For information about East Tennessee's topography and natural/economic history, I have benefited from several sources, including *The Natural and Aboriginal History of Tennessee,* by John Haywood; *An Encyclopedia of East Tennessee,* edited by Jim Stokely and Jeff D. Johnson; and *Tennessee: A Guide to the State,* by the Federal Writers' Project for Tennessee.

5. Robert L. Jarrett calls Ownby "a failure at farming" who "through his archaic lifestyle of living off the land rather than by working in a trade or farming . . . resembles more Wordsworth's leech gatherer . . . than the patriarchal warriors

and slave owners memorialized by Faulkner and the Agrarians" (12–13).

6. See Appalachian Land Ownership Task Force, *Addendum to Land Ownership Patterns,* for an extensive survey of the percentage of land owned in specific Appalachian counties by citizens, by corporations, and by absentees. The study compares percentages of acreage owned with taxes paid and concludes that the citizens who own small pieces of land pay an unjust proportion of property taxes compared to large landholding corporations and absentees.

7. For a collection of stories based on the "reading" of Mimbres pottery, see Pat Carr's *Sonachi: A Collection of Myth-Tales.*

8. From the collection *The Double Axe,* Jeffers's poem "Their Beauty Has More Meaning" exemplifies the "philosophical attitude" (vii) of inhumanism:

> Yesterday morning enormous the moon hung
> low on the ocean,
> Round and yellow-rose in the glow of dawn;
> The night-herons flapping home wore dawn on their wings.
>
> I know that tomorrow or next year or in twenty years
> I shall not see these things—and it does not matter, it
> does not hurt;
> They will be here. And when the whole human race
> Has been like me rubbed out, they will still be here: storms,
> moon and ocean,
> Dawn and the birds. And I say this: their beauty has more
> meaning
> Than the whole human race and the race of birds. (1–4, 9–17)

9. Vereen Bell expresses a perspective comparable to "optical democracy" when he calls *The Orchard Keeper* "a meditation upon the irrelevance of the human in the impersonal scheme of things" (10). Bell's attention to details of the landscape emphasizes "the awareness of nature's elemental power to reclaim its paltry human proteges without motive or warning" (19).

10. In his investigation of the "pastoral impulse" in McCarthy's fiction, John Grammer discovers a vein of "anti-pastoral," "the South's second-oldest intellectual tradition," increasingly existent in the novels (29). Grammer dwells primarily on the human face of McCarthy's fiction, gearing his analysis toward the protagonists; he looks at how characters and human communities in McCarthy's South deal with the mathematical progression of modernism.

11. The farming crisis, escalating after the Civil War and World War I, is investigated in other southern fiction: Ellen Glasgow's *Barren Ground,* Erskine Caldwell's Depression-era *Tobacco Road,* and James Still's *River of Earth,* set in Appalachian coal camps. A few lines from *Barren Ground* are representative of the explicit agricultural concerns of these novels. The soils of Virginia farmland have been "impoverished by the war and the tenant system which followed the war" (4); "abandoned acres were rapidly growing up in sumach, sassafras, and life everlasting" (6); the "land poor" Oakleys "owned a thousand acres of scrub pine, scrub oak, and broomsedge, where a single cultivated corner was like a solitary island in some chaotic sea" (6).

Works Cited

Appalachian Land Ownership Task Force. *Addendum to Land Ownership Patterns and Their Impacts on Appalachian Communities: A Survey of 80 Counties*. Washington, D.C.: Appalachian Regional Commission, 1981.

——. *Land Ownership Patterns and Their Impacts on Appalachian Communities: A Survey of 80 Counties: A Regional Overview*. Washington, D.C.: Appalachian Regional Commission, 1981.

Bell, Vereen M. *The Achievement of Cormac McCarthy*. Baton Rouge: Louisiana State University Press, 1988.

Berry, Wendell. *The Long-Legged House*. New York: Harcourt, 1969.

——. *The Unsettling of America: Culture and Agriculture*. San Francisco: Sierra Club Books, 1977.

Camuto, Christopher. *Another Country: Journeying Toward the Cherokee Mountains*. New York: Henry Holt, 1997.

Carr, Pat. *Sonachi: A Collection of Myth-Tales*. El Paso, Tex.: Cinco Puntos Press, 1988.

DeSelm, H. R. "Geography." *An Encyclopedia of East Tennessee*. Ed. Jim Stokely and Jeff D. Johnson. Oak Ridge, Tenn.: Children's Museum of Oak Ridge, 1981. 219–20.

——. "Plant Communities." *An Encyclopedia of East Tennessee*. Ed. Jim Stokely and Jeff D. Johnson. Oak Ridge, Tenn.: Children's Museum of Oak Ridge, 1981. 377–83.

Dunn, Durwood. "Cades Cove." *An Encyclopedia of East Tennessee*. Eds. Jim Stokely and Jeff D. Johnson. Oak Ridge, Tenn.: Children's Museum of Oak Ridge, 1981. 75–78.

Dykeman, Wilma. *The French Broad*. New York: Rinehart, 1955.

Federal Writers' Project of the Works Projects Administration for the State of Tennessee. *Tennessee: A Guide to the State*. New York: Viking Press, 1939.

Glasgow, Ellen. *Barren Ground*. 1925. New York: Hill and Wang, 1957.

Grammer, John M. "A Thing Against Which Time Will Not Prevail: Pastoral and History in Cormac McCarthy's South." *Southern Quarterly* 30.4 (1992): 19–30.

Grant, Natalie. "The Landscape of the Soul: Man and the Natural World in *The Orchard Keeper*." *Sacred Violence: A Reader's Companion to Cormac McCarthy*. Ed. Wade Hall and Rick Wallach. El Paso, Tex.: Texas Western Press, 1995. 61–68.

Hart, John Fraser. "Reading the Landscape." *Landscape in America*. Ed. George F. Thompson. Austin: University of Texas Press. 23–42.

Haywood, John. *The Natural and Aboriginal History of Tennessee: Up to the First*

Settlements Therein by the White People in the Year 1768. 1823. Jackson,
Tenn.: McCowat-Mercer Press, 1959.

Hudson, Patricia L. "Oak Ridge." *An Encyclopedia of East Tennessee.* Ed. Jim
Stokely and Jeff D. Johnson. Oak Ridge, Tenn.: Children's Museum of Oak
Ridge, 1981. 357–61.

Jarrett, Robert L. *Cormac McCarthy.* New York: Twayne, 1997.

Jeffers, Robinson. *The Double Axe and Other Poems.* New York: Random House,
1948.

Manes, Christopher. "Nature and Silence." *Environmental Ethics* 14 (winter 1992):
339–50. Reprint in *The Ecocriticism Reader: Landmarks in Literary
Ecology.* Ed. Cheryll Glotfelty and Harold Fromm. Athens: University of
Georgia Press, 1996. 15–29.

Marx, Leo. *The Machine in the Garden: Technology and the Pastoral Ideal in
America.* New York: Oxford University Press, 1964.

McCarthy, Cormac. *Child of God.* 1973. New York: Vintage Books, 1993.

———. *The Orchard Keeper.* 1965. New York: Vintage Books, 1993.

———. *Outer Dark.* 1968. New York: Vintage Books, 1993.

———. *Suttree.* 1979. New York: Vintage Books, 1992.

Morris, David Copland. "Inhumanism, Environmental Crisis, and the Canon of
American Literature." *ISLE: Interdisciplinary Studies in Literature and
Environment* 4.2 (1997): 1–16.

Parker, Russell D. "Aluminum Company of America (ALCOA)." *An Encyclopedia of
East Tennessee.* Ed. Jim Stokely and Jeff D. Johnson. Oak Ridge, Tenn.:
Children's Museum of Oak Ridge, 1981. 8–9.

Phillips, Dana. "History and the Ugly Facts of Cormac McCarthy's *Blood Meridian.*"
American Literature 68.2 (1996): 433–60.

Pierce, Dean. "The Low-Income Farmer: A Reassessment." *Social Work in Appalachia*
3 (1971): 7–10.

Smith, Elizabeth S., et al. "Log Rafts." *An Encyclopedia of East Tennessee.* Ed. Jim
Stokely and Jeff D. Johnson. Oak Ridge, Tenn.: Children's Museum of Oak
Ridge, 1981. 294–96.

Sullivan, Walter. "Worlds Past and Future: A Christian and Several from the South."
Review of *The Orchard Keeper. Sewanee Review* 73 (autumn 1965):
719–26.

Wiersema, Harry. "TVA Dams." *An Encyclopedia of East Tennessee.* Ed. Jim Stokely
and Jeff D. Johnson. Oak Ridge, Tenn.: Children's Museum of Oak Ridge,
1981. 465–69.

The Sacred Hunter and the Eucharist of the Wilderness

Mythic Reconstructions in *Blood Meridian*

Sara Spurgeon

O NE of the many complex relationships Cormac McCarthy explores in *Blood Meridian, or, The Evening Redness in the West* is between humans, especially Anglo Americans, and the natural world. He does so in part through the manipulation of several archetypal myths closely identified with the European experience in the New World, and most specifically with the border regions of the American Southwest.

McCarthy moves *Blood Meridian* through the dark and disordered spaces of what Lauren Berlant calls the "national symbolic." Unlike the familiar icons of mythic frontier tales, however, McCarthy's characters seek no closure, nor do they render order out of the chaos of history and myth. The novel functions on the level of mythmaking and national fantasy as an American origin story, a reimaging upon the palimpsest of the western frontier of the birth of one of our most pervasive national fantasies—the winning of the West and the building of the American character through frontier experiences.

Both of these related themes demand a wilderness to be conquered, either literally via ax and plow or metaphorically by defeating the

Indians rhetorically tied to the wild landscape. Annette Kolodny has defined the American obsession with land, especially land-as-woman, as an American pastoral, drawing some images from the European version, yet unique from it. The literary hero within this landscape, she says, is "the lone male in the wilderness" (147) struggling to define a relationship with the female landscape in its troubling metaphorical appearance as both fruitful mother and untouched virgin, one image offering nurturing fertility, the other demanding penetration and conquest.

Blood Meridian chronicles the origin of the "lone male in the wilderness," the modern American Adam—though not the benignly patriarchal John Wayne version. McCarthy's project here is not simply to retell the familiar myths or dress up the icons of cowboys and Indians in modern, politically correct costumes à la *Dances With Wolves;* rather, he is using the trope of the historic frontier and the landscape of the Southwest within the genre of the Western to interrogate the consequences of our acceptance of the archetypal Western hero myths. *Blood Meridian* rewrites and reorders those myths in such a way as to bridge the discontinuity that Patricia Limerick identifies as being perceived by the public to exist between the mythic past of the American West and its modern realities.[1] This gap, marked by a feeling of discontinuity and limned by the continued popular obsession with traditional Western and frontier icons that have thus far failed to cover it, is filled in *Blood Meridian* with a newly structured version of national fantasy, though not one that imposes any kind of hoped-for order or control.

Instead, McCarthy presents a countermemory, a sort of antimyth of the West, illuminating especially the roots of the modern relationship between humans and the natural world. In many ways, McCarthy has produced a counterhistory that contradicts the meaning generated from most official histories of the period. It is within the accuracy of historical detail in *Blood Meridian* that McCarthy finds his mythic history, lurking within the liminal spaces of the familiar rhetoric of Manifest Destiny, the taming of the wilderness, John Wayne's famous swagger, and other pillars of the national symbolic.

The central myth enshrining that relationship and manipulated in *Blood Meridian,* mainly by the judge, is that of the sacred hunter. In

Regeneration Through Violence, Richard Slotkin claims that this ancient form of the archetypal hero quest, twisted and hybridized through the meeting of numerous European and Native American versions, forms the basis of the modern American myth of the frontier, and thus much of the groundwork for our commonly perceived national identity.

Kolodny argues that the American pastoral was structured around the yeoman farmer responding to the female landscape, and discusses this figure as he appears in Jefferson, Crèvecoeur, Freneau, and others. However, as Henry Nash Smith noted, the image of the yeoman farmer was simply not romantic enough to sustain popular interest for long. What emerged instead was an American version of a far older figure, the "lone male in the wilderness"—the hunter. In essence, the myth of the sacred hunter is one of regeneration through violence enacted upon the body of the earth. The hunter must leave the community, track his game (usually a representation of the spirit of the wilderness or an avatar of a nature deity), and slay it. In many versions, the prey allows itself to be hunted and killed, willingly sacrificing its life to sustain the life of the hunter, who must in turn give honor and thanks to the prey and to whichever nature spirit it represents. Following the hunt, he or his community either literally or symbolically consumes the prey in a eucharist of the wilderness, thus renewing the hunter and providing life for those he serves. The eucharist, Slotkin argues, is itself a sublimation of the myth of the sacred marriage, which enacts a sexual union between the hunter and the body of nature. The game the hunter tracks in many versions is revealed at the end of the chase to be some female representative of the wilderness whom the hunter marries instead of slaying, in a parallel renewal of self and community through sexual union with nature.[2]

Slotkin writes that, especially in the modern Anglo-American version, "The hunter myth provided a fictive justification for the process by which the wilderness was to be expropriated and exploited" (554). It did so by seeing that process in terms of heroic male adventure commodified by visual and symbolic proofs of the hunter's heroic stature and, therefore, his rightful and proper triumph over his prey. Slotkin cites the famous image of Davy Crockett standing proudly next to his stack of 150 bearskins, the legend of Paul Bunyan clearing miles of virgin forest with a single stroke of his ax, and the often-photographed mountains of buffalo skulls littering the Great Plains as embodiments of this myth. In *Blood Meridian* these images are echoed in the scalphunters' collections of scalps, ears, teeth, and other trophies, and they are described in detail on the plain of the bonepickers. What is echoed and amplified as well is the subtle shift evident in the modern Anglo version of the myth, from the imaging of the prey as symbol of divine nature sacrificed so that man may live to simply that which deserves to fall before him.

The gigantic figure of Judge Holden, who is both a fictional version of a historical personage and an amalgamation of numerous archetypes from the mythic West, acts throughout the book as the author of the new version of the hunter myth. McCarthy consistently presents the judge as a priest, a mediator between man and nature, shepherding, or more accurately manipulating, the scalphunters' souls even as Glanton guides their physical bodies. The image of the judge as priest is consistent with the dominant mood and tone of *Blood Meridian* as origin myth. Bernard Schopen calls the entire novel "profoundly religious" and claims that it takes place "in a physical and thematic landscape charged with religious nuance, allusion, and language" (191). That is not to say, however, that *Blood Meridian* is a Christian book or particularly interested in presenting any kind of Christian worldview. At its deepest structural and rhetorical levels, *Blood Meridian* uses mythic and religious imagery both Christian and non-Christian.

The first time we see the judge, for example, is at the revival meeting tent where he concocts elaborate lies about the camp preacher, which results in a riot among the congregation and a posse that sets out to hang the innocent man. Significantly, the primary charge the judge levels against Reverend Green foreshadows the betrayal and perversion he will commit as the novel progresses. The reverend, the judge claims, is wanted on "a variety of charges the most recent of which involved a girl of eleven years—I said eleven—who had come to him in trust and whom he was surprised in the act of violating while actually clothed in the livery of his God" (7). This violation of a child and the profaning of a sacred office by a figure entrusted with upholding and protecting it will be enacted repeatedly throughout the novel, with the judge playing the leading role. The judge deliberately cultivates a feel for myth, ritual, and religion and directs it toward his own ends. His goal is to harness the unconscious response to mythic heroes, invoke it with the rituals of the sacred hunter and the eucharist of the wilderness, and reorder, or perhaps disorder, it on a deep and essential level. His aim is no less than the birthing of a new myth.

Throughout *Blood Meridian* the judge both exalts the natural world and strives to contain and destroy it, to usurp its power for his own ends. He is priest here not only of men's souls but also of their minds, and he often appears as the spokesman of what is presented as a sort of new religion—science. As the novel progresses, the figure of the judge becomes increasingly godlike, while that of nature is debased. The judge manipulates the power and mystery of the natural world and its association with the sacred through his scientific knowledge, which gives him the ability to penetrate that mystery and therefore disrupt the assumptions of the other characters about the place of humans within the world. While the scalphunters are camped at an abandoned mine, the judge collects ore samples:

> in whose organic lobations he purported to read news of the earth's origins. . . . A few would quote him scripture to confound his ordering up of eons out of the ancient chaos and other apostate supposings. The Judge smiled.
> Books lie, he said.
> God dont lie.
> No, said the judge. He does not. And these are his words.
> He held up a chunk of rock.
> He speaks in stones and trees, the bones of things.
> The squatters in their rags nodded among themselves and were soon reckoning him correct . . . and this the judge encouraged until they were right proselytes of the new order whereupon he laughed at them for fools. (116)

The acceptance of traditional dogma regarding the world and the place of humans in the natural order of existence is deconstructed by the judge, built anew through the acceptance and belief of his listeners, then destroyed again. His audience may now doubt their own understanding of nature as well as Christian doctrine, but the one figure whose personal power has only increased in the eyes of his followers is Judge Holden. The judge is laying groundwork, gathering "proselytes," participants in the ritualistic myth he is enacting. That nature plays the part of the sacred does not imply the sort of patriarchal relationship imagined by Christianity in which a merciful, all-powerful God cares for and watches over His children. As many critics have noted, in McCarthy's work nature is often brutal and almost always without mercy for humans, and yet the shadow of the sacred and the profane permeates *Blood Meridian* and is constantly evoked by the judge through humankind's relationship to the natural world.

That this destructive version of the myth demands material evidence of its fulfillment does not lessen its ritualistic power, especially as McCarthy has constructed it in *Blood Meridian*. The judge, having symbolically dethroned the priest of the Christian rituals and myths at the revival tent, will make proselytes of the scalphunters and lead them in a cannibalistic perversion of the old myth made new in this place where "not again in all the world's turning will there be terrains so wild and barbarous to try whether the stuff of creation may be shaped to man's will or whether his own heart is not another kind of clay" (5).

Whether the stuff of creation may be shaped to man's will is one of the central questions of the novel. Dana Phillips claims in "History and the Ugly Facts of Cormac McCarthy's *Blood Meridian*" that what McCarthy is questioning is "whether human beings have any privileged position in relation to the rest of the world" (443). His answer is that according to McCarthy they do not, that humans and nature are simply part of the same continuum, ignoring each other throughout the novel. At first glance it would seem that indeed creation *cannot* be shaped to human will, or, as Phillips says, "at least not for very long. Man's will does not seem a very relevant or potent force in this novel" (439). However, a closer examination suggests that in fact man's will is the most potent of forces as well as the central concern in the terrifying relationship between Holden and the kid. It is man's will that ultimately shapes myth, and, McCarthy seems to be implying, it is our myths that ultimately shape the world. The agent of this shaping is not nature but Judge Holden, who, as the only character who truly understands the immense power of will, acts almost as collective human will made flesh in order to shape the stuff of creation through the shaping of the myth that constructs it.

Phillips would disagree with this interpretation. He argues that there is no inherent meaning in the actions of the characters or of the natural world in *Blood Meridian,* that darkness is just darkness, death just death. McCarthy has even "dispensed with the concept of character" (441) in the traditional sense, Phillips says, in order to erase any hint of possible moral redemption for his band of scalphunters and their victims. I would argue, however, that the lack of traditional character development by McCarthy is more than a response to the "furious troping" (441) of Melville's Ishmael or an avoidance of Flannery O'Connor-style moralizing. McCarthy is interested in myths, not morals. It is true, as Phillips notes, that there are no real surprises in the plot of *Blood Meridian,* that "all the novel's complexities are fully present from the first page. . . . The novel does not seek to resolve 'conflicts' which trouble its characters" (443). This is so, not because there is no meaning or symbolism in the world of *Blood Meridian,* but because, like any mythic story, we already know the outcome. The characters are not explored in the Lukácsian sense because, as actors in a myth, their individualities are less important than the roles they are playing. The face of the hero is infinitely changeable—therefore the kid does not need a proper name, Judge Holden can be endowed with faculties that border on the superhuman, and Tobin can be referred to simply as "expriest" as often as he is called by name. What is meaningful are the actions the characters take and the power of their story to shape the world of those who hear it.

It is true that the Christian God and the moral structures He represents are absent in the natural world of *Blood Meridian,* at least as a cipherable entity to the travelers. The judge alone among the scalphunters claims the power to solve the mysteries of the natural world, and he does so through science and a skewed rationality cloaked in the rhetoric of religion. The myth of science, with the judge as its sacred high priest, is now opposed to the earlier myth of nature served by the sacred hunter. Within the space of the national symbolic and in the tradition of the earliest Puritan writings about the New World, his figuring of wilderness as that which must be conquered by man lest it conquer him is a familiar trope, common to almost every Western written after the mid-nineteenth century.

Kolodny argues this is part of the defining structure of the American pastoral, born in conjunction with the first stirrings of the Industrial Revolution, that "implicit in the metaphor of the land-as-woman was both the regressive pull of maternal containment and the seductive invitation to sexual assertion" (67). Henry Nash Smith notes that by the late 1850s, as the myth of the garden and the land as fruitful mother began to fray, the archetypal frontier hero in the American wilderness had lost Leatherstocking's "power to commune with nature. . . . He no longer looks to God through nature, for nature is no longer benign: its symbols are the wolves and the prairie fire. . . . The landscape within which the Western hero operates has become . . . 'a dreary waste.' . . . He is . . . alone in a hostile, or at best a neutral, universe" (89). And yet the relationship McCarthy explores is considerably more complex than the simple nihilism of "Nature does not care for man."

Dana Phillips refutes Vereen Bell's claim that human beings and nature compete in the novel by arguing that "this competition has been decided in favor of . . . the natural world even before *Blood Meridian* begins" (446). Humans and the natural world are not antagonists, Phillips claims, but are instead "parts of the same continuum" (446). That is indeed the case at the outset of the novel, and the balance of power between the various parts of the continuum appears fairly equal, but it is the fundamental change in this relationship, enacted on the level of the mythic and sacred, that McCarthy is interested in uncovering. That the nature of that relationship exists on a level significantly deeper than mutual indifference or antagonism is clear. Again and again, McCarthy invokes archetypal myths and references to the sacred when portraying humans in the natural world. Travelers of all sorts in the wilderness are commonly referred to as "pilgrims" and "proselytes." As the scalphunters cross a dry lakebed, the narrator claims that the earth itself notes their passing, "As if the very sediment of things contained yet some residue of sentience. As if in the transit of those riders were a thing so profoundly terrible as to register even to the uttermost granulation of reality" (247). The narrator continues with the often-quoted passage regarding the quality of light in the desert, which "bequeathed a strange equality and no one thing nor spider nor stone nor blade of grass could put forth claim to precedence . . . and in the optical democracy of such landscapes all preference is made whimsical and a man and a rock become endowed with unguessed kinships" (247). These passages have often been interpreted as "a critique of our culture's anthropocentrism,"[3] and, as Phillips notes, "the human does not stand out among the other beings and objects that make up the world" (443). However, that relationship of indifferent equanimity is neither stable nor unchanging. It is the laying bare of the cataclysmic evolution taking place in the mythic formations that have created the structure that McCarthy seeks to document through the actions of his characters and their mythic roles.

If we view the relationship between humankind and nature in terms of the sacred hunter myth, a clear set of images begins to appear. This myth implies the necessity of a certain kind of relationship—a bloody and violent one, to be sure, and one that does not necessarily hold any moral overtones in the Christian sense of right or wrong or good or evil, but simply a set of rules governing what is, how reality and the natural world work, and a sense of order and balance in the roles of each. That, of course, is the most basic function of myth, to organize and impose order on humans and their worlds, though in McCarthy's antimyth the revelation of the profound disorder at the heart of our myths seems to be the ultimate goal.

The scalphunters as a group can be read as playing the part of the sacred hunter, dark versions of classic Western heroes from the Deerslayer and Daniel Boone to Buffalo Bill, leaving their communities to enter the wilderness for renewal and regeneration through the act of hunting and killing. Although the scalphunters seek a human prey, it is a prey nonetheless rhetorically tied to the wilderness, and the goal of its killing is ostensibly the protection and renewal of the scalphunters' foster community—the Mexicans of Sonora. And yet the fact that their prey *is* human begins the degeneration of the myth, tilts it off its axis. Of course, the epigraph from the *Yuma Daily Sun* that opens the novel implies that such a perversion is equally as old as the myth itself. This idea is furthered by the name of the judge's gun, *"Et in Arcadia Ego"* (even in Arcadia am I [Death]) implying, as Leo Dougherty notes, that "the point of the gun's name is not that because of its appearance in the landscape, or by synecdoche the judge's appearance, death has been introduced into an idyllic Arcadia: the entire novel makes clear (primarily through the judge, who continuously emphasizes the point in his preachments) that the human world is, and has always been, a world of killing" (126–27). But for all its echoes of universality and timelessness, in *Blood Meridian* McCarthy is interested in the specific ways in which the ancient myths of the sacred hunter and the eucharist of the wilderness have been played out upon the particular landscape and within the particular historical context of the southwestern borderlands.

JUDGE AND EXECUTIONER

The figure of the judge within this space is an almost Conradian expression of white American civilization, or perhaps the brutal force of its will. Like Kurtz, he engages in a savage war that is both sanctioned and denied by various authorities; like Kurtz, he carries his war forward from both sides, existing at once as the ultimate expression of Euro-American manhood (poet/scholar/warrior) and as the primitive savage he seeks to destroy and emulate, donning native clothing and defeating native peoples on their own ground. And more importantly, like Kurtz, the judge is the agent of the revelation of the savagery at the heart of the myths and the civilization that produces them. Through the course of the novel, the judge will turn the old myth on its head, pervert it, and cannibalize it. He leads the scalphunters in acts that violate the relationship contained within the sacred hunter myth while still seeming to follow its internal rules, in the same way the Black Mass was seen as an inversion of a sacred ritual and indeed *depended* on the sacred nature of the original for its own symbolic power.

This degeneration of the myth from within sounds a striking note of prophecy, for it marks a change not only in the outer form of the hero and his universe (to be expected with the passage of time), but also in the most basic narrative structure of the myth. A change on this level, Slotkin claims, "reflect[s] a fundamental alteration of the culture's conception of the relationship of man to the universe, a revolution in world view, cosmology, historical and moral theory, and self-concept. Hence such changes may be seen as marking the point at which a new epoch of cultural history or perhaps even a new culture can be said to begin" (9). The neobiblical rhetoric of the novel and its blood-washed, apocalyptic images support this vision of revolution, of violent death and rebirth, of some enormous and profound change in the fabric of things imagined by McCarthy through the perversion of the sacred hunter and his position in the natural world.

The first description in the novel of Glanton and his gang marks them equally as actors within the myth and as deviants from it, as both hunters and cannibals:

> a pack of viciouslooking humans mounted on unshod indian ponies . . . bearded, barbarous, clad in the skins of animals stitched up with thews and armed with weapons of every description . . . the trappings of their horses fashioned out of human skin and their bridles woven up from human hair and decorated with human teeth and the riders wearing scapulars or necklaces of dried and blackened human ears . . . the horses rawlooking and wild in the eye and their teeth bared like feral dogs . . . the whole like a visitation from some heathen land where they and others like them fed on human flesh. Foremost among them . . . rode the judge. (78)

The natural order of the original myth governing the relationship between humans and nature has been upset so profoundly that even the horses are seen as feral, feeding on flesh instead of grass, and the hunters themselves a visitation of the profane rather than the sacred. Although Glanton is their nominal leader, the judge is "foremost among them." Their sacred nature as hunter heroes is evidenced by the "scapulars" they wear, and yet their pollution is obvious as well. The scapulars are formed of scores of human ears collected as trophies in the same skewed capitalistic spirit as Davy Crockett's bearskins or Paul Bunyan's logs. And this disturbing trope of cannibalization and the perversion of the sacred eucharist is continued throughout the novel, as is that of inversion and violation.

The first instance of the judge's symbolic cannibalization of those whom he is engaged to serve occurs when the scalphunters spend the night with the doomed miners at the ruined mines. As the gang prepares to retire for the night, "Someone had reported the judge naked atop the walls, immense and pale in the revelations of lightning, striding the perimeter up there and declaiming in the old epic mode" (118). The next morning the body of the boy is discovered, lying naked and face down, while the judge is seen "standing in the gently steaming quiet picking his teeth with a thorn as if he had just eaten" (118). The sacred marriage and the sacred eucharist in this scene are at once conflated and perverted, the whole echoing and reimagining the sacred hunter myth as well as the Christian crucifixion and eucharist.[4] The naked body of the innocent child, "whose head hung straight down" (119) when the miners grabbed his arms and lifted him, mimics the image of the body of the innocent and sinless Christ on the cross, drooping head ringed by a crown of thorns. As the judge watches these procedures, he employs a thorn with which to pick his teeth clean of the cannibalized flesh of the child.

The connotations of rape in the explicit nakedness of the judge and the murdered boy mock the fertility rite of the sacred marriage with a union that produces only violence and death in much the same way that the cannibalism implied by the judge picking his teeth "as if he had just eaten" mocks the intention of renewal and life in the ritual of the eucharist. The judge both literally and symbolically consumes that which is forbidden, the child as a living representation of the community the sacred hunter is bound to serve and protect. The boy is neither proper prey for the hunter nor a proper bride, and yet as the myth is inverted and turned in on itself he becomes both. His childlike state—weak, helpless, and lost in the wilderness—at once feminizes him and marks him as prey for the foremost hunter in the gang. In the proper fulfillment of this emerging version of the myth, the judge rapes and cannibalizes him, absorbs his essence, and emerges renewed. Indeed, the entire gang appears rejuvenated, associated here with the symbols of life and rebirth; as the narrator tells us upon discovery of the boy's body, they "mounted up and turned their horses to the gates that now stood open to the east to welcome in the light and to invite their journey" (119).

This sequence of actions, enacting the ritual of the hunt and culminating in a perversion of the sacred marriage and sacred eucharist and the resulting regeneration of the hunters, ends chapter IX. The next major action within the narrative begins in chapter X with the ex-priest Tobin relating to the kid the story of how he first met Judge Holden, a story that again involves the judge as priest leading a group of men in the perversion of the ritual of the sacred marriage. Although the reflection of a past event disrupts the sequence of the action, the flashback establishes the ritualistic heart of the judge's new myth, for Tobin's story shows the gang's initiation into their roles as sacred, or perhaps profane, hunters. It is important, therefore, that McCarthy have this tale originate from one labeled "expriest," fallen from the symbolic orders, both Christian and non-Christian, of the past, and ripe therefore to be baptized into the order (or disorder) to come.

Tobin relates the much talked about scene in which the judge appears, alone in the middle of the desert, acting as savior for Glanton and his riders, who are without gunpowder and in a desperate flight from nearly a hundred Apaches. The judge uses an uncanny knowledge of the natural landscape to lead them on a new course to a distant mountain range that holds both a bat cave full of niter and a sulfur-ringed volcano. Tobin recalls that the judge, before commencing his bloody ritual, tells the men "that our mother the earth . . . was round like an egg and contained all good things within her. Then he turned and led the horse he had been riding across that terrain . . . and us behind him like the disciples of a new faith" (130).

And like all converts, the men are required to unite themselves in a group ritual pledging them to this "new faith," legitimizing the degeneration of the myth they have been enacting all along. The judge combines charcoal, the niter from the bat cave, and sulfur scraped from the mouth of the volcano as Tobin continues, "I didn't know but what we'd be required to bleed into it" (131). The scalphunters do pour forth their own bodies, in the form of urine instead of blood, into the hole in the earth the judge has made for the preparation of his eucharist.

> He worked it up dry with his hands and all the while the savages down there on the plain drawin nigh to us and when I turned back the judge was standin, the great hairless oaf, and he'd took out his pizzle and he was pissin into the mixture, pissin with a great vengeance and one hand aloft and he cried out for us to do likewise. . . . We hauled forth our members and at it we went and the judge on his knees kneadin the mass with his naked arms and the piss was splashin about and he was cryin out to us to piss, man, piss for your very souls for cant you see the redskins yonder, and laughin the while and workin up this great mass in a foul black dough, a devil's batter by the stink of it and him not a bloody dark pastryman himself. (132)

Here again the sacred marriage and the eucharist of the wilderness contained within both the hunter myth and Christianity are conflated and perverted. Rather than the flesh of a deer or the sacred host, the judge kneads "a foul black mass, a devil's batter" made of elements of the natural world turned black and stinking by a symbolic and ritualistic rape, with all the men gang-raping the great vaginal hole in "our mother the earth," spewing piss instead of semen. The ritual reaches its violent climax with Glanton firing his rifle, primed with the foul mixture, straight down the open mouth of the volcano. The flesh of men and the flesh of nature are united here by science to create gunpowder used to slaughter every last Apache, with the judge as a midwife and antipriest, a "bloody dark pastryman."

In the aftermath of the rape, as the final ceremonial step cementing the men to the judge as their spiritual leader within this version of the myth, the judge "called us all about to fill our horns and flasks, and we did, one by one, circlin past him like communicants" (134). And indeed, communicants is precisely what the scalphunters are, participants in a ritual of renewal dependent on acts of violence and the perversion of the very myth (and mother) that gave them birth.

In this scene, with its savage rape of the earth and resultant "butchery" (134) of the Indians, is a brilliant condensation of McCarthy's violent countermemory of the winning of the West, his antimyth of the frontier, deconstructing the forms of national fantasy so often and so fondly used in building the space of the national symbolic and shaping the realities of modern America and the West. From this ritual, ceremonially setting down a blueprint for America's future relationship with the natural world and with the West's native inhabitants, McCarthy prophesies the future. Here we see that indeed "the stuff of creation may be shaped to man's will," (5) and the results of the shaping, of the wholesale acceptance of this version of the sacred hunter as the governing myth of the new nation, are played out through the last half of the novel.

Immediately following this narrative, in revenge or perhaps fulfillment of the perversion of the sacred marriage/eucharist, a bear, a powerful symbol of the natural world for McCarthy, steals a Delaware. Like many chapters, this one begins with a detailed description of the natural world through which the scalphunters ride, this time the aspen and pine forests of a high mountain. The bear rises up unexpectedly beside the trail, and Glanton shoots it. "The ball struck the bear in the chest and the bear leaned with a strange moan and seized the Delaware and lifted him from the horse. . . . The man dangling from the bear's jaws looked down at them cheek and jowl with the brute and one arm about its neck like some crazed defector in a gesture of defiant camaraderie" (137). Acting as an avatar of the natural world, perhaps as nature's own sacred hunter, the bear escapes with his "hostage" (137). The relationship between them is something more than simply an unlucky rider falling prey to a random wild beast or indifferent nature. The Delaware has been consumed by the myth, as the narrator states, "The bear had carried off their kinsman like some fabled storybook beast and the land had swallowed them up beyond all ransom or reprieve" (138).

By this time all the scalphunters have been swallowed up beyond ransom or reprieve by the antimyth they are enacting, their disconnection from the wilderness through which they ride so complete that even their shadows on the stones appear "like shapes capable of violating their covenant with the flesh that authored them and continuing autonomous across the naked rock without reference to sun or man or god" (139). The balance of power, which may be perceived as resting on the side of nature at the start of the novel, has by the final scenes shifted to the side of man. The original covenant has been violated, the sacred myths structuring the relationship of humans to the natural world now perverted to an extent that McCarthy suggests cannot be redeemed, reprieved, or corrected.

The first powerful vision we receive of the results of this reordered myth is on the plain of the bonepickers, fifteen years after the main action of the novel. The kid, now a man, camps on the prairie, where he meets an old hunter who tells him of the slaughter of the buffalo herds in which he had participated, an event Tom Pilkington calls "an ecological calamity so stunning as to be almost inconceivable" (317).

Initially, the old hunter paints pictures that, though bloody and full of gore, reflect the sheer abundance of life that once existed on the now empty and silent plains, "animals by the thousands and tens of thousands and the hides pegged out over actual square miles of ground . . . and the meat rotting on the ground and the air whining with flies and the buzzards and ravens and the night a horror of snarling and feeding with the wolves half crazed and wallowing in the carrion. . . . On this ground alone there was eight million carcasses" (317). In contrast to this, the hunter then recalls the "last hunt" in which he and the other hunters searched the empty plains for six weeks for a sign of buffalo. "Finally found a herd of eight animals and we killed them and come in. They're gone. Ever one of them that God ever made is gone as if they'd never been at all" (317).

Here is the new covenant, this hunter and those like him, proselytes of the new order the judge has helped bring into being in which humankind's relationship to the wilderness is one of butchery on a scale scarcely imaginable. The outcome is not regeneration, for no animals remain alive to carry on the relationship. This new version of the ancient hunter myth represents degeneration signified by the images of the enormous mountains of bones, miles long, stretching across the prairies in which the mythic figure of the sacred hunter has been reduced to that of the bonepickers, ragged children gathering dead evidence of the now vanished herds. It is the culmination of the task the judge has set for himself early on, when Toadvine questions his taxidermy of one of every species of bird they have encountered. The judge replies, "Only nature can enslave man and only when the existence of each last entity is routed out and made to stand naked before him will he be properly suzerain of the earth. . . . The freedom of birds is an insult to me. I'd have them all in zoos" (198).

Human will clothed in the sacred rhetoric of science, far from being insignificant, is the most powerful force in the novel. If only nature can enslave man, only man can enslave nature, even if by doing so he leaves a sky as empty of birds as the plains now are of buffalo. Through his will man can make himself suzerain of the earth, though in so doing he must destroy that which he would rule. Kolodny has identified this as "the pastoral paradox" and argues it has been at the heart of the modern American relationship to the natural world. Within this paradox, she writes, "man might, indeed, win mastery over the landscape, but only at the cost of emotional and psychological separation from it" (28).

The judge foreshadows this situation through the allegory he relates at the Anasazi ruins: "The father dead has euchred the son out of his patrimony" (145). In destroying the sacred power of nature and the myth that tied humankind to it, the father has robbed those sons to come of their right to take part in that myth and of the regeneration and rebirth to be had from it. Instead, ironically, by making himself suzerain, the hunter/father engenders his own demise, and thus has ensured that for the son "the world which he inherits bears him false witness. He is broken before a frozen god and he will never find his way" (145). Like the son in the story, these sons will grow to be "killers of men" (145) rather than sacred hunters, resulting in generations of those "not yet born who shall have cause to curse the Dauphin's soul" (327).

The great patrimony of nature has been reduced to the level of a zoo or circus by the final chapter of the novel. The gigantic figure of the bear, formerly the magnificent and terrible avatar of the wilderness able to pluck a Delaware from the midst of the scalphunters, is now dressed in a tutu and dances on a saloon stage to the music of a little girl's crank organ. As the kid watches, a drunk from the judge's table shoots the bear, but there is nothing sacred or holy in this hunt; the prey is killed without even the feeling of power or ritual and its death is a meaningless spectacle: "The bear had been shot through the midsection. He let out a low moan and he began to dance faster, dancing in silence save for the slap of his great footpads on the planks. . . . The man with the pistol fired again . . . and the bear groaned and began to reel drunkenly. He was holding his chest . . . and he began to totter and to cry like a child and he took a few last steps, dancing, and crashed to the boards" (326).

This scene is the antithesis of the one that occurred in the mountains. The bear, like the last few buffalo and the defeated remnants of the native tribes, is now the hostage. In the place of the Delaware with his arm around the neck of the mighty beast that will carry him off crouches the sobbing child with her arms around the neck of the dead bear that "in its crinoline lay like some monster slain in the commission of unnatural acts" (327). The unnatural acts here are many—nature as captive, forced to dance on a stage, crying like a child, its death as the shedding of blood without meaning or significance. This scene is capped with perhaps the most unnatural act of all—the judge's subsequent murder of the little girl, who, like most of the other children in the novel, is betrayed by the sacred hunter who should be her protector but who takes her as prey.

The destruction and reordering of the original myth is now complete. This point for McCarthy is both a meridian and a nadir, the final mastery of humankind over the wilderness and the prophetic embarkation of his descent. The judge tells the scalphunters, "in the affairs of man there is no waning and the noon of his expression signals the onset of night. His spirit is exhausted at the peak of his achievement. His meridian is at once his darkening and the evening of his day" (147). There is the implication here of something inevitable and preordained, perhaps more than the random tragedy of history. As the quote regarding the three-hundred-thousand-year-old skull from Africa that closes the epigraph suggests, neither scalping nor any other vicious perversion is new or unique. The scalphunters and the Indians, the dancers in the saloon, the lone buffalo hunter on the empty prairie, and the long-dead scalper of the unfortunate Ethiopian whose skull now speaks to modern anthropologists are all tabernacled in the other's books (141), "each pass[ing] back the way the other had come, pursuing as all travelers must inversions without end upon other men's journeys" (121) in an "endless complexity of being and witness" (141).

The suggestion is that the myth has always contained within itself the antimyth, the dark shadow double awaiting a Kurtz or a Holden to strip bare the original and turn it inside out. McCarthy's earth in *Blood Meridian* and many other works is hollow, full of empty caves and echoing caverns, at once womb and tomb, signifying the hollowness at the heart of all myths. There is no center to the sacred hunter myth, any more than there is to its antithesis. And yet the power of myth to move and shape us remains, and through *Blood Meridian*, McCarthy has done more than simply invert the sacred hunter and the eucharist of the wilderness; he has altered their form in several significant ways.

The most basic relationship enshrined in that myth, between man and nature, is ultimately replaced with a new ordering based on the relationship between man and man in the form of sacred war. The death of a bear or deer, the sacrificial shedding of the blood of some symbol of holy nature, once an essential part of the ritual on which the sacred hunter myth rested, is no longer sufficient for regeneration. Regeneration depends on ritual, but, as the judge explains, "A ritual includes the letting of blood. Rituals which fail in this requirement are but mock rituals" (329). The myth of science, therefore, is not enough. It must be enacted through the more ancient ritual of war. Because all generations following this one have been euchred of the patrimony of nature, invalidating the blood of bears or deer as sources of regeneration, the prey must now become humanity itself. The new version of the myth demands human blood, for now no other will suffice, and therefore the holiest of all acts is war.

Again, the suggestion is that of inevitable procession toward this end. "War was always here," the judge says. "Before man was, war waited for him. The ultimate trade awaiting its ultimate practitioner" (248). War, in fact, is God, according to the judge, because, as myth or game enhanced "to its ultimate state" (249), it is the perfect embodiment of human will, the force of will made divine, driven to test itself against the very stuff of creation, "a forcing of the unity of existence" (249), beyond what the judge considers the petty concerns of moral judgments. In engaging in the act of war, in forcing the hand of existence to choose who shall live and who shall die, the sacred hunter becomes one with the prey, and humankind itself assumes the cloak of divine power. Moral law, good and evil, wrong or right are simply trivialities enshrined by one church or another, one religion or another. Questions of right and wrong are subsumed by the force of will made manifest in war, and to prove this notion the judge challenges Tobin, the de facto representative of religion and moral order.

> The judge searched out the circle for disputants. But what says the priest? he said.
>
> Tobin looked up. The priest does not say.
>
> The priest does not say, said the judge. . . . But the priest has said. For the priest has put by the robes of his craft and taken up the tools of that higher calling which all men honor. The priest also would be no godserver but a god himself. . . .
>
> I'll not secondsay you in your notions, said Tobin. Dont ask it.
>
> Ah Priest, said the judge. What could I ask of you that you've not already given? (250–51)

The judge's new myth has long ago swallowed up Tobin and the religion and morality he symbolizes, the impotent state of those institutions marked by Tobin's status as "ex" priest. The churches are empty shells, like the Anasazi village, crumbling ruins of an order dead and vanished, now "wondered at by tribes of savages" doomed to erect new churches, new edifices of stone in their attempts to "alter the structure of the universe" (146). But all such attempts, the judge insinuates, will ultimately fail. "This you see here, these ruins . . . do you not think that this will be again? Aye. And again. With other people, with other sons" (147). The judge has proven that the only thing that can truly alter creation is the brute force of human will, sharpened and focused through the lens of a mythic structure unconcerned with morality and bent to the task of godlike war. The eucharist of the wilderness has now become a eucharist of humanity.

Everyone now is a participant in the dance of war, as either hunter or prey. All in the gang have been baptized into the new myth, have partaken in its ceremonies of cannibalism and rape. Only the kid finally attempts to renounce the dance and to assert a will independent of the judge and his antimyth. By giving up his position as a hunter of humans within this new myth, he makes himself prey. At the ruins, the judge supplied the blueprint for raising hunters, explaining that at a young age children should be put into pits with wild dogs, forced to fight lions and to run naked through the desert. Only those with the most perfect wills would survive such tests (mercy, we are to assume, would produce weakness instead of strength) and, ironically of course, only those with the most potent of wills could administer the trials without succumbing to the urge to help the children. The kid faces several such trials throughout the narrative and fails them. He alone of the gang answers David Brown's call for aid in removing an arrow from his leg (162). By the rules of the antimyth, Brown should have been left on his own, like the child in the pit of wild dogs, to triumph by the force of his will alone or to fail and die in the desert. Tobin warns the kid of the danger of his actions, "Fool, he said. "God will not love ye forever. . . . Dont you know he'd of took you with him? He'd of took you boy. Like a bride to the altar" (162–63).

The "he" here refers to the judge, who has earlier refused to help Brown, and who tests the kid later by calling for help himself in the killing of a horse (219). None of the other members of the gang answers, and Tobin again warns the kid not to respond. In doing so, the kid violates the internal order of the myth, though the prospect of being taken "like a bride to the altar" by the judge is perhaps not such an appealing one. Although the phrase echoes the rhetoric of the sacred marriage common to both Christianity and the sacred hunter myth and perverted by the act of rape in this new order, in this instance we can understand Tobin to intend a positive meaning. Although the relationship between the judge and the kid might be more properly characterized as that between father and son rather than husband and bride, the implication at least is of renewal and rebirth, the promise of regeneration that the kid betrays.

As Tobin and the kid crouch in the desert after the slaughter at the ferry crossing, the kid receives his final chance to seize his place as hunter within the new myth and fails once again when he refuses to shoot the unarmed judge. To do so would only have been right and proper within the relationship of hunter and prey, human will against human will in sacred war, as well as within the relationship of father and son, because, as the judge has said at the Anasazi ruins, it is the death of the father to which the son is entitled. When the kid will neither shoot him nor join him, the judge charges, "There's a flawed place in the fabric of your heart. . . . You alone were mutinous. You alone reserved in your soul some corner of clemency" (299).

The kid ignores the judge's warning, and over the final section of the book, covering the last fifteen years of his life, he attempts to return to the previous order, to reestablish the relationship of the sacred hunter as guardian and protector of his community. He becomes a guide for other travelers passing through the wilderness, protecting them from the forces of nature, from Indians, and from those like his old companions who have become hunters of men. Most significantly, he begins to carry a Bible, a book already made defunct by the judge as a false book and symbol of the empty moral laws thrown down before the force of human wills in war. Like the church it represents, the Bible is a kind of ruin here, silent and without reference in the world shaped by the new myth. It is a mute emblem of a fallen system even for the illiterate kid, "no word of which he could read" (312).

Its futility as a symbol within the world shaped by the new order is reified by the kid's encounter with the penitents he finds butchered in a canyon and his attempts to speak with the old woman:

> The kid rose and looked about at this desolate scene and then he saw alone and upright in a small niche in the rocks an old woman kneeling in a faded rebozo with her eyes cast down.
>
> He made his way among the corpses and stood before her. . . . She did not look up. . . . He spoke to her in a low voice. He told her that he was an American and that he was a long way from the country of his birth and that he had no family and

that he had traveled much and seen many things and had been at war and endured hardships. He told her that he would convey her to a safe place, some party of her countrypeople who would welcome her and that she should join them for he could not leave her in this place or she would surely die.

He knelt on one knee, resting the rifle before him like a staff. Abuelita, he said. No puedes escucharme?

He reached into the alcove and touched her arm. . . . She weighed nothing. She was just a dried shell and she had been dead in that place for years. (315)

The kid attempts here to perform the act of confession, a ritual based on the acknowledgment of a moral order that the speaker has in some way violated, but the kid has himself been a participant, as his confession makes clear, in the destruction of that moral order, which has rendered this ceremony empty and meaningless, the authority of the church now "just a dried shell." The kid has turned his back on the new myth he helped bring into being, but it is too late to revive the old ones. He prostrates himself before a dead body that cannot hear his confession and can therefore offer no absolution or forgiveness, cannot even move to accept his proffered aide, and is as mute as the Bible he carries but cannot read. He even clasps his rifle, not like a weapon of divine war, worthy of the name the judge has bestowed on his gun, the tool of death in the garden, but like a staff, symbol of the doomed priest, administrator of an empty office whom the kid is said to have now come to resemble.

The kid has in fact betrayed the sacred office he once occupied as a hunter of men in this new myth, and it is this betrayal for which the judge castigates him in the prison. "You came forward," he said, "to take part in a work. But you were a witness against yourself. You sat in judgement on your own deeds. You put your own allowances before the judgements of history and you broke with the body of which you were pledged a part" (307). And it is for this betrayal that the judge, described as immense and bearlike (having subsumed the figures of the old myths within himself), finally kills the kid in a horrible embrace, a perverted hug, a perversion of the act of reproduction performed in the midst of human excrement (333), and yet despite all this, an act that is holy and proper within the structure of the new myth, for after the killing the judge emerges renewed and rejuvenated to join the dance in the saloon.

If we accept Slotkin's claim that any fundamental alteration of the narrative structure of the myth signals some profound shift in the culture that produces it, then the sense of momentous change is inescapable. Here is the bloody tie binding the West's mythic past to its troubled present, here in this mythic dance is the violent birth of a national symbolic that has made heroes out of scalphunters and Indian killers and constructed the near extinction of the buffalo and massive deforestation as symbols of triumph and mastery, the proud heritage of the modern American citizen.

This is one possible interpretation of the novel's rather obscure epilogue. The man progressing over the silent plain digging postholes is striking out of the rock with his steel the fire, and symbolically the life, "which God has put there" (337), the first step before stringing barbed wire along that "track of holes that runs to the rim of the visible ground" (337). The barbed wire fence is a potent and deeply paradoxical symbol in the American West. On one hand, it is the triumphant emblem of Anglo America's conquest of the land once referred to as the Great American Desert, of the sheer force of human will necessary to empty it of those animals like the buffalo that do not serve Anglo America's needs and to fill it instead with cattle—nature tamed and controlled by the sharp-edged product of Eastern factories.

It is also, for many Westerners, the sign of some final closure, usually expressed nostalgically as the loss of the wandering horseman's right to travel freely and without restriction across the landscape. That wandering horseman, the lone cowboy with his bedroll and his rifle, is the most commonly recognized modern American expression of the sacred hunter, the lone male in the wilderness, here digging the postholes that mark his own demise and performing the final fencing-in of the natural world.

The plain in the epilogue is empty of life, no buffalo, no bears, wolves or antelope, the patrimony of nature gone, only "bones and the gatherers of bones" (337), following behind the diminished hunter striking out hole after hole. The act of the posthole digger "seems less the pursuit of some continuance than the verification of a principle, a validation of sequence and causality" (337), the consequence, perhaps, of our national acceptance of the judge's perverted antimyth, of the disruption of the continuum identified by Dana Phillips in which some balance or relationship between humankind and nature has been destroyed and replaced with a mythic structure few besides Cormac McCarthy have dared to gaze at unflinchingly.

Notes

1. In *The Legacy of Conquest*, Limerick argues that the association of the Western landscape with "a potent and persistent variety of nationalistic myth" (30), coupled with the government's official declaration of the end of the frontier in 1891, has resulted in a public perception of "a great discontinuity between the frontier past and the Western present" (31). The perception has persisted, she claims, in part because of the romanticization of the frontier experience, and in part because such a discontinuity allows the grim realities of conquest and colonization to be viewed from a safe remove, as associated with the distant past and unrelated to the present day.

2. Slotkin argues, for example, that the common and extremely popular folktale regarding Daniel Boone's first meeting with Rebecca Boone is a version of this myth. The story claims that Boone was hunting deer by torchlight one night when he saw two eyes shining among the trees. He raised his rifle to shoot, but at the last moment stayed his hand. What he had believed to be a deer was actually Rebecca, walking at night through the woods. Although this portion of the story may or may not be true (neither Boone nor Rebecca denied it, though their children, feeling it to be too primitive and pagan, did so vehemently), we do know that Boone married Rebecca soon after their first meeting. Within the bounds of the myth working at the level of popular culture, this act would have been the proper fulfillment of the rules of the sacred marriage that culminated the hunt and that decreed that woman or deer, married or slain, the hunter must love and honor that which he hunts for its sacred nature in order to receive union, and communion, with it. For a further discussion of the Boone myth as the first truly American (i.e., combination of European and Indian) version of the sacred hunter story, see *Regeneration Through Violence* 152–56.

3. Bell, 124.

4. Many scholars have noted the connection of the symbolic cannibalism of the Christian eucharist and the figure of Christ with both Old and New World versions of the sacred hunter myth, in which the hunter himself must die in a symbolic mirroring of the hunter as stag and prey. See Slotkin's *Regeneration Through Violence,* especially chapter 2, "Cannibals and Christians."

Works Cited

Bell, Vereen M. *The Achievement of Cormac McCarthy.* Baton Rouge: Louisiana State University Press, 1988.

Berlant, Lauren. *The Anatomy of National Fantasy: Hawthorne, Utopia, and Everyday Life.* Chicago: University of Chicago Press, 1991.

Clifford, James. *The Predicament of Culture: Twentieth-Century Ethnography, Literature, and Art.* Cambridge, Mass.: Harvard University Press, 1988.

Cooper Alarcón, Daniel. *The Aztec Palimpsest: Mexico in the Modern Imagination.* Tucson: University of Arizona Press, 1997.

Daugherty, William. "Gravers False and True: *Blood Meridian* as Gnostic Tragedy." *Southern Quarterly* 30.4 (1992): 122–33.

Kolodny, Annette. *The Lay of the Land: Metaphor as Experience and History in American Life and Letters.* Chapel Hill: University of North Carolina Press, 1975.

———. *The Land Before Her: Fantasy and Experience of the American Frontiers, 1630–1860.* Chapel Hill: University of North Carolina Press, 1984.

Limerick, Patricia Nelson. *The Legacy of Conquest: The Unbroken Past of the American West.* New York: W. W. Norton, 1987.

McCarthy, Cormac. *Blood Meridian, or, The Evening Redness in the West.* New York: Random House, 1985.

———. *All The Pretty Horses.* New York: Alfred A. Knopf, 1992.

———. *Cities of the Plain.* New York: Alfred A. Knopf, 1998.

Nelson, Robert M. "Place and Vision: The Function of Landscape in Ceremony." *Journal of the Southwest* (fall 1987): 281–316.

Phillips, Dana. "History and the Ugly Facts of Cormac McCarthy's *Blood Meridian.*" *American Literature* 68.2 (1996): 433–60.

Pilkington, Tom. "Fate and Free Will on the American Frontier: Cormac McCarthy's Western Fiction." *Western American Literature* 27.4 (1993): 311–22.

Schopen, Bernard A. "'They Rode On': *Blood Meridian* and the Art of Narrative." *Western American Literature* 30.2 (1995): 179–94.

Shaviro, Steven. "'The Very Life of Darkness': A Reading of *Blood Meridian.*" *Southern Quarterly* 30.4 (1992): 111–21.

Slotkin, Richard. *Regeneration Through Violence: The Mythology of the American Frontier, 1600–1860.* Middletown, Conn.: Wesleyan University Press, 1973.

———. *Gunfighter Nation: The Myth of the Frontier in Twentieth-Century America.* New York: Macmillan, 1992.

Smith, Henry Nash. *Virgin Land: The American West as Symbol and Myth.* Cambridge, Mass.: Harvard University Press, 1950.

Stoeltje, Beverly. "Making the Frontier Myth: Folklore Process in a Modern Nation." *Western Folklore* 46.4 (1987): 235–53.

Tompkins, Jane. *West of Everything: The Inner Life of Westerns.* New York: Oxford University Press, 1992.

Wills, Garry. "American Adam." *New York Review of Books,* 6 Mar. 1997: 30–33.

History, Bloodshed, and the Spectacle of American Identity in *Blood Meridian*

Adam Parkes

A T the beginning of *Blood Meridian, or, The Evening Redness in the West* (1985), Cormac McCarthy introduces an unnamed kid, who remains more or less in sight until the end of the book: "See the child," McCarthy begins (3). For most of the following 335 pages, McCarthy concentrates on the seventeenth and eighteenth years of his protagonist's life; he spends only the first three pages on the kid's first sixteen years. But the opening passage provides a crucial foretaste of the violence and bloodshed that dominate this tale of life in the American West of the mid-nineteenth century. "In him broods already a taste for mindless violence," McCarthy writes. "All history present in that visage, the child the father of the man" (3). Running away at fourteen from his father's home in Tennessee, the kid wastes little time in satisfying that taste. His early adventures take him down the Mississippi River to New Orleans, where he is shot by a Maltese boatswain, once in the back and a second time just below the heart; when he recovers, he heads west, and takes part in the scalphunting expeditions that occurred in the aftermath of the Mexican-American War of 1846–48.[1]

Anticipating the bloody progress of the rest of the book, these opening events illustrate McCarthy's belief, which he expressed in a rare interview in the *New York Times,* that there is "no such thing as life without bloodshed" (36). A careful reading of *Blood Meridian* suggests, however, that in addition to the obvious reference to violence, the term *bloodshed* has a second meaning, unnervingly related to the first: the shedding of biological origins, the severance of blood ties. In running away from home, the kid literalizes what is implied in McCarthy's use of Wordsworth's famous line, "The Child is father of the Man." In McCarthy's hands, this phrase suggests a self divorced from the Romantic notion of an organic, developing consciousness. The child is father of McCarthy's man not because he will become a man but because he plays the role of his own father, as if to suggest that such terms as *child* and *man* do no more than designate roles that are available to the same character; either role, in other words, could be said to father the other. In this sense, the kid's biological father becomes irrelevant.[2] Wordsworth, who redeployed this line from "My Heart Leaps Up" as the epigraph to "Ode: Intimations of Immortality from Recollections of Early Childhood," posited a fundamental relation between selfhood and memory, but from the outset McCarthy's narrator denies this version of the self's relation to time.[3]

The kid's birth, which results in his mother's death, combines the antidevelopmental meaning of "bloodshed" with its more obvious connotations of violence: "The mother dead these fourteen years did incubate in her bosom the creature who would carry her off" (3). The kid's first action upon emerging from his mother's womb is to cast off his nearest relative; even as an infant, he seems more predatory than the "few last wolves" harbored by the woods beyond. As if to emphasize the point, this initial movement is repeated when the kid is shot in New Orleans. Nursed back to health by a tavern keeper's wife (a kind of surrogate mother), he sets out once again to put himself to the test, as if reborn, liberated at last from ties of blood: "Only now is the child finally divested of all that he has been. His origins are become remote as is his destiny and not again in all the world's turning will there be terrains so wild and barbarous to try whether the stuff of creation may be shaped to man's will or whether his own heart is not another kind of clay" (4–5). Exiling himself from family ties, the kid is now free to confront the trials of life in the "wild and barbarous" arena of the American Southwest. As he submits to these trials, the kid recapitulates his earlier brushes with death and rebirth, as we see in his narrow escape during a fight with Toadvine (the novel's first jakes episode) and in his reemergence from the carnage of Captain White's slaughtered militia: "With darkness one soul rose wondrously from among the new slain dead and stole away in the moonlight. The ground where he'd lain was soaked with blood and with urine from the voided bladders of the animals and he went forth stained and stinking like some reeking issue of the incarnate dam of war herself" (55).

McCarthy implies that the kid's identity should be considered not as biologically predetermined nor as revealing itself in various family traits, but as something constituted over time through the performance of a series of actions or as the product of various trials. *Blood Meridian,* that is, defines identity along lines rather different from Wordsworth's but strikingly similar to those taken by some contemporary theorists of gender. This may seem an astonishing claim, given McCarthy's reputation as a "reactionary" (Woodward 36–40), but his textual practice implies a performative theory of selfhood that closely resembles arguments made by Judith Butler in particular. Indeed, it might be possible in another essay to delineate the ways in which other parts of the McCarthy oeuvre—especially the shadows and shadowlands of *Outer Dark* (1968), *Child of God* (1973), and *Suttree* (1979)—anticipate this union of fictional and theoretical feminist concerns. But it is in *Blood Meridian* that McCarthy's performative theory of identity comes to fruition and discovers its most powerful embodiment.

A number of feminist theorists, including Joan Riviere, Laura Mulvey, Mary Ann Doane, Mary Russo, and Luce Irigaray, have explored the subversive potential of defining gender as a performance or masquerade.[4] Irigaray, for instance, has asked whether a theory of the masquerade might allow woman "to recover the place of her exploitation by discourse, without allowing herself to be simply reduced to it" (76). Judith Butler's work strikes me as especially significant because it pushes such arguments to their ultimate conclusion by purging them of essentialism (the idea that gender resides in some biological or "natural" essence). "Gender reality is performative," Butler writes, "which means, quite simply, that it is real only to the extent that it is performed" ("Performative Acts" 278). Citing Simone de Beauvoir's claim that "one is not born, but, rather, becomes a woman," Butler characterizes gender as "in no way a stable identity or locus of agency from which various acts proceed; rather, it is an identity tenuously constituted in time—an identity instituted through a *stylized repetition of acts.*" Butler continues: "Gender is instituted through the stylization of the body and, hence, must be understood as the mundane way in which bodily gestures, movements, and enactments of various kinds constitute the illusion of an abiding gendered self" (270). Butler, following de Beauvoir, argues that identity "is an historical situation rather than a natural fact" (271).

In its presentation not only of the kid but also of its entire cast of characters—a cast that is almost exclusively male—*Blood Meridian* anticipates Butler's arguments by representing selfhood as a spectacle that requires the shedding of blood. In McCarthy's novel, this theatrical identity is apprehended as an entity situated in, and inextricable from, the brutal history of the American West, and it is predicated on the shedding of such "natural" or biological ties as might inhibit what Butler calls selfhood's "performative fluidity" (279). But in restaging the history of the Wild West, McCarthy does not merely reinscribe the self in its original form. As Butler has argued, repetition may entail not only confirmation but also an undermining of the original, even an undermining of the concept of originality itself: "If the ground of gender identity is the stylized repetition of acts through time, and not a seemingly seamless identity, then the possibilities of gender transformation are to be found in the arbitrary relation between such acts, in the possibility of a different sort of repeating, in the breaking or subversive repetition of that style" (271).[5] It is by recasting the male self in the fluid forms of *Blood Meridian* that McCarthy breaks with traditional novelistic presentations of character and, as a result, undermines the notion of an essential American identity. This subversion has interesting implications for the concept of American nationhood, because it raises questions not only about the sexual coordinates of that concept but also about its racial coordinates, especially (as I will suggest later) when they are examined in the context of events that took place in the U.S.-Mexico borderland after the Mexican-American War.

PERFORMING AMERICAN SELFHOOD

The brief initial appearance of the novel's second major figure, Judge Holden, in the second episode of the opening chapter, emphasizes the performativity of American selfhood in McCarthy's fictional world. The scene is reminiscent, of course, of various escapades in Twain's *Adventures of Huckleberry Finn* (1884), particularly those involving the king and the duke.[6] The Reverend Green, we are told, "had been playing to a full house daily as long as the rain had been falling and the rain had been falling for two weeks" (5). Enter the judge, an "enormous" man nearly seven feet tall and "bald as a stone," with small hands and a "serene and strangely childlike face," who denounces the minister as an "imposter" wanted by the law in several states on "a variety of charges," including the rape of an eleven-year-old girl and the act of "congress with a goat" (6–7). Escaping the ensuing mayhem, the kid and various other characters join the judge in a bar, only to hear him confess: "I never laid eyes on the man before today. Never even heard of him" (8). Thus the judge reveals himself to be an imposter. But Holden's confession does not necessarily acquit the Reverend Green of the charge of fraud. No figure is immune to such allegations because in this work the concept of character is represented as inherently theatrical. To be Judge Holden is to play the role of Judge Holden. The difference between the judge and the reverend is not the difference between true man and false; nor is it the difference between a character who plays a role and a character who knows he is playing a role. The difference between them is a matter of theatrical range: the judge simply has more roles at his disposal. Because there are no original selves to which we can refer, every character in *Blood Meridian* is, in a sense, an imposter. The more important point, however, is that McCarthy renders the term *character* null and void by subverting the difference between true and false identities. "The truest poetry is the most feigning," wrote Auden (470), echoing Shakespeare, and Judge Holden prevails over the Reverend Green precisely because his calculated acts of imposture realize more completely the theatrical nature of their lives. More powerfully than any other character in this novel, Holden embodies the "performative fluidity" of identity, a notion that *Blood Meridian* turns into the founding principle of existence.

As his subsequent, more extended appearances confirm, the judge is perfectly equipped for the unstable theatrical conditions that define the limits of human agency in the world of this novel. Holden seems less constrained than empowered by those conditions. Apparently unencumbered by the natural laws of growth and decay evoked by the poetry of Wordsworth, he is both an eternal infant who says "that he will never die" (335) and a miraculous creature who has never been born at all: as the ex-priest Tobin puts it, "You couldnt tell where he'd come from" (125). Holden may even be indulging in a grisly parody of our biological origins, or the ties between humankind and nature, as he trudges across the desert with the imbecile, James Robert Bell, carrying a collection of pubic scalps, which they wear as hats.[7] To be sure, in the course of the novel the judge puts in a consummate variety performance, playing by turns the roles of raconteur, orator, philosopher, naturalist, inventor, conjurer, draftsman, lawyer, and dancer. He combines these roles, moreover, with those of various literary figures, most obviously Melville's Ahab, and even (as one reader avers) Melville's whale.[8] Another critic has heard echoes of Satan when Holden, placing his hands on the ground, declares: "This is my claim. . . . In order for it to be mine nothing must be permitted to occur upon it save by my dispensation" (199).[9] The judge also reminds us of Conrad's Kurtz by adopting the attitude of an "icon" (147) and by inspiring Captain Glanton's gang to raise severed heads on poles (168). As these examples show, Holden's ability to assume so many different guises suggests that if identity is, as Judith Butler contends, "a regulatory fiction" (279), such regulation hardly rules out playful or creative interpretation.

As every reader familiar with *Blood Meridian* will have realized, the account I have been offering is expressed by Judge Holden himself in a series of what Dana Phillips has described as "literary performances . . . delivered as highly ironic and playful lectures" (441). Preparing to perform a coin trick, for example, the judge declares,

"The truth about the world . . . is that anything is possible. Had you not seen it all from birth and thereby bled it of its strangeness it would appear to you for what it is, a hat trick in a medicine show, a fevered dream, a trance bepopulate with chimeras having neither analogue nor precedent, an itinerant carnival, a migratory tentshow whose ultimate destination after many a pitch in many a mudded field is unspeakable and calamitous beyond reckoning" (245). The theatrical and performative metaphors that appear in this speech resurface elsewhere in the novel, most notably in the judge's description of war as "the ultimate game" (249) and in his characterization of dancing as the ideal human activity: "What man would not be a dancer if he could?" (327).

As Holden explains to the kid during their last encounter, at Fort Griffin, Texas, in 1878, to be a dancer is to participate in history. Participation, moreover, does not require self-consciousness; we may be dancers without knowing it, like the dancing bear, which is shot for no apparent reason. As Holden puts it: "This is an orchestration for an event. For a dance in fact. The participants will be apprised of their roles at the proper time. For now it is enough that they have arrived. As the dance is the thing with which we are concerned and contains complete within itself its own arrangement and history and finale there is no necessity that the dancers contain these things within themselves as well."[10] Holden further elucidates the significance of the bear slaying by invoking the necessity of bloodshed: "The overture carries certain marks of decisiveness. It includes the slaying of a large bear. . . . One could well argue that there are not categories of no ceremony but only ceremonies of greater or lesser degree and deferring to this argument we will say that this is a ceremony of a certain magnitude perhaps more commonly called a ritual. A ritual includes the letting of blood. Rituals which fail in this requirement are but mock rituals" (329).

Holden brings this ritual to a similarly decisive finale, the precise nature of which McCarthy allows us only to imagine, when he ambushes the kid in the jakes (a scene that recalls the kid's first encounter with Toadvine): "The judge was seated upon the closet. He was naked and he rose up smiling and gathered him in his arms against his immense and terrible flesh and shot the wooden barlatch home behind him" (333). In an uncanny reversal of his earlier actions, the kid's part in the dance of history culminates in the shedding of his own blood. At the beginning of the tale, the kid sheds both of his natural parents; at the end, he is shed in turn by the surrogate father he might have had, the so-called Judge Holden, who had once asked him: "Dont you know that I'd have loved you like a son?" (306). The novel's final image of the judge dancing, "huge and pale and hairless, like an enormous infant" (335), underlines the irony of this reversal in the kid's fortunes.

In his illuminating essay on *Blood Meridian,* Dana Phillips cautions us against employing the judge's speeches as "sounding the novel's 'themes'" or as "authorial pronouncements": "Holden is not a ventriloquist's dummy perched on the novelist's knee, and we should not strain our eyes to see whether McCarthy's lips move when the judge speaks" (442). My point here, though, is not that the judge acts as a faithful guide to the novel's meaning; my point is that the manner and matter of his oratory are united in their playfulness. In the judge's performance, form and content are one. Holden's playfulness is a serious issue; for all his smirks and knowing smiles, the judge says what he means and means what he says. This is not to imply that the judge possesses the high self-consciousness that is often found in fictional characters, or that he is in the business of presenting authorial "views"; as Steven Shaviro has written, *Blood Meridian* "is not a book that sets a high value upon self-consciousness" (153). The world of *Blood Meridian* is not one of psychological depths, but one of surface and display; the mode of Holden's existence is, above all, performative. Thus, although it is often the case that Holden's speeches reflect his actions (and vice versa), they perform this function without indicating a quasi-authorial capacity for reflecting on those actions.

In any case, it is not only to the judge himself that we should look for support for this reading; Holden's fellow performers in the Fort Griffin dancing scene also highlight the mobile theatricality of identity in McCarthy's fictional world. The dancing episode, moreover, draws special attention to the theatricality of gender identities. In our last glimpse of the dance, a naked judge is implicitly juxtaposed with a gigantic female counterpart, whom we have seen in the previous paragraph: "An enormous whore stood clapping her hands at the bandstand and calling drunkenly for the music. She wore nothing but a pair of men's drawers" (334). Even as the garment worn by the whore obviously suggests cross-dressing, her corpulent bulk mirrors the judge's own expanse of hairless, infantine, sexually undifferentiated flesh, which we observe for the last time in the next paragraph. Thus, while the terms judge and whore mark these figures as male and female respectively within a conventional frame of social reference, their bodies tell a different story.

McCarthy emphasizes this sexual ambiguity further by intimating a peculiar relation between the whores and the bear, which is killed earlier in the scene. Biologically, the bear is male, but in other ways he is associated with the "garishly clad" women. He sports a crinoline skirt, for instance, and his manner of death (he is shot through the mid-section and the chest; blood runs down his groin) connects him with images of victimized femininity. McCarthy underlines the latter point by showing us the young female organ grinder lamenting the bear's demise, "the front of her dress dark with blood" (327). When McCarthy writes, "the great hairy mound of the bear dead in its crinoline lay like some monster slain in the commission of unnatural acts" (327), he associates the slaughtered bear with more familiar images of violated female bodies. This passage also suggests that the biologically male body might perform the role of its supposedly natural opposite by displaying openly the signs of a monstrously corporeal femininity. (The Latin root of the word "monster" designates the theatrical nature of McCarthy's simile: monstrare, to show.) McCarthy subverts the opposition of natural versus unnatural by presenting bodies, human and animal alike, as costumes that are equally well suited to masculine and feminine roles. The body, it seems, does not necessarily allow clear-cut divisions between these two genders; it functions instead as a borderland where sexual boundaries often remain obscure or undefined, where other genders and new "unguessed kinships" (247) might become possible.

Another passage, which occurs in the central, twelfth chapter, suggests that such gender-troubled implications lie at the very heart of *Blood Meridian*. Having recently crossed the U.S.-Mexico border, Glanton's riders encounter a company of slain "argonauts":

Five wagons smoldered on the desert floor and the riders dismounted and moved among the bodies of the dead argonauts in silence, those right pilgrims nameless among the stones with their terrible wounds, the viscera spilled from their sides and the naked torsos bristling with arrowshafts. Some by their beards were men but yet wore strange menstrual wounds between their legs and no man's parts for these had been cut away and hung dark and strange from out their grinning mouths. In their wigs of dried blood they lay gazing up with ape's eyes at brother sun now rising in the east. (152–53)

Occurring in the borderland, and in a chapter in which McCarthy's characters cross the threshold to a new level of slaughter and debauchery, this moment in the novel's bloody argosy displays the butchered human body as another kind of costume, the torso adorned with spilled viscera and arrowshafts, the mouth dressed with severed male genitalia, and the former site of those genitals wearing (in uncanny anticipation of the dancing bear's crinoline skirt) "strange menstrual wounds."

Blood Meridian abounds with other kinds of evidence for a performative theory of the self. As we follow the often-interrupted tale of the kid's adventures, first with Captain White's filibusters, then with Glanton's gang of scalphunters, we encounter various conjurers and entertainers, from the bazaar where the kid finds Captain White's head floating in a jar of mescal (69) to the freak show where the judge discovers the character he adopts as his demented sidekick, James Robert Bell. Glanton's gang itself constitutes an "itinerant carnival" or "migratory tentshow," as McCarthy emphasizes by describing their adventures in theatrical terms: an altercation with a detachment of soldiers on the outskirts of Chihuahua City, for example, is a "charade" (84).

McCarthy insists on the carnivalesque theatricality of Glanton's men by having them assume diverse guises. The first time they appear, they are characterized as a "pack of viciouslooking humans" and as cannibalistic killers (78); on subsequent occasions they come before us as adventurers, scalphunters, pilgrims, and refugees. At one point they are called "the Texans" (88), at another "the Americans" (101). Later, they are "tattered campaigners" (166), "outlanders" (189), a "falstaffian militia" (221). Such terms accumulate in this novel because McCarthy, somewhat like his precursors in the picaresque tradition, tends to direct his reader's attention to the external attributes of fictional character—that is, to its theatrical surface.[11]

In *Blood Meridian* these accumulations suggest not an evolution of consciousness but the "performative fluidity" of identity. Rather than indicate psychological or emotional development, each new term signifies a new role or costume, which redefines a character's place in the world. This is why the only difference between an individual and a group in McCarthy's fictional world is numerical. In the absence of psychological laws governing human behavior, there can be no distinctions between individual psychology and group psychology; a group thus turns out to be nothing more than a random aggregation of individuals. Consequently, the technique used to describe Glanton's gang as a whole works equally well for a single member: just as the gang is variously described as scalphunters, pilgrims, refugees, and so forth, the kid is characterized at different times as a castaway, a deserter, a fugitive, and a wanderer. Character, individual or collective, changes only when style or language changes; there are no other principles of order at work. Indeed, McCarthy's men are able to survive in this fictional world as long as they remain, as he puts it, "wholly at venture, primal, provisional, devoid of order" (172)— devoid, that is, of the order that familiar biological and psychological paradigms confer on our view of human conduct.

The point may be made clearer still by contrasting the spectacle of a performative self with various instances of the biologically overdetermined self. In the course of the narrative we encounter three pairs of brothers, all of whom include at least one demented member: Cloyce and the imbecile James Robert Bell; Elrod, whom the kid kills in a late skirmish, and the insane-looking Randall; and the mad Dutch hermits at the Tumacacori mission. On the evidence of these brothers and their canine counterparts—a litter of freak dogs in Tucson, "one of whom had six legs and another two and a third with four eyes in its head" (239)—the prospects for the self that lives by blood alone do not look encouraging. All blood can do, it seems, is recycle itself with ever-diminishing returns. But in *Blood Meridian,* as I have been arguing, this biological self gives way to a performative self, a self that is (to recall McCarthy's phrase) "at venture, primal, provisional, devoid of order." In the language of Judith Butler, this novel construes masculinity as an "identity tenuously constituted in time, instituted in an exterior space"—or, in this context, a narrative space—"through a stylized repetition of acts" (*Gender Trouble* 140).

FORGING AN AMERICAN NATION

In laying bare the seams of historical and cultural constructions of American masculinity, McCarthy's text implies an important possibility to which Butler alludes: instead of enshrining the self as some sort of stable essence, the stylized acts by which identity is constructed contain "the possibility of a failure to repeat, a deformity, or a parodic repetition that exposes the phantasmatic effect of abiding identity as a politically tenuous construction" (*Gender Trouble* 141). For the representation of identity—which in *Blood Meridian* means a masculine, American identity—as a theatrical role, or series of roles, has significant implications for McCarthy's revision of the history of the Wild West. If identity is theatrical, as *Blood Meridian* suggests, then perhaps the forging of an American nation also depends on performance and improvisation.

In *Blood Meridian* this possibility seems all the more powerful because the native tribes of the Mexican-American borderland inhabit the same unstable ground of performance as Captain White's "ghost army" of Saxons and Glanton's bloodstained argonauts. By locating the action in this borderland, McCarthy exerts considerable pressure on the essentialist assumptions that give rise to neat categories of racial, as well as sexual, difference, and thus highlights the protean theatricality of his characters' identities. Consequently, although both White and Glanton justify the slaughter of native tribes as contributions to the cause of racial purification, the novel generates a more complicated political context that frustrates the ideological premises of this genocidal project.

A remarkable example of the way *Blood Meridian* performs this refusal of racial essentialism occurs in a scene that is particularly memorable for its spectacular bloodshed. In a sharply ironic turn of events, Captain White's filibusters are cut to pieces by a Comanche "legion of horribles" decked out in various costumes of war and conquest. The text itself seems to rise to the occasion by assuming an archly parodic tone reminiscent of the "Oxen of the Sun" episode in Joyce's *Ulysses,* and so produces a "phantasmatic effect," as Butler puts it, that reveals the notion of an "abiding identity" to be a "politically tenuous construction":

There rose a fabled horde of mounted lancers and archers bearing shields bedight with bits of broken mirrorglass that cast a thousand unpieced suns against the eyes of their enemies. A legion of horribles, hundreds in number, half naked or clad in costumes attic or biblical or wardrobed out of a fevered dream with the skins of animals and silk finery and pieces of uniform still tracked with the blood of prior owners, coats of slain dragoons, frogged and braided cavalry jackets, one in a stovepipe hat and one with an umbrella and one in white stockings and a bloodstained weddingveil and some in headgear of cranefeathers or rawhide helmets that bore the horns of a bull or buffalo and one in a pigeontailed coat worn backwards and otherwise naked and one in the armor of a spanish conquistador, the breastplate and pauldrons deeply dented with old blows of mace or sabre done in another country by men whose very bones were dust and many with their braids spliced up with the hair of other beasts until they trailed upon the ground and their horses' ears and tails worked with brightly colored cloth and one whose horse's whole head was painted crimson red and all the horseman's faces gaudy and grotesque with daubings like a company of mounted clowns, death hilarious, all howling in a barbarous tongue and riding down upon them like a horde from hell more horrible yet than the brimstone land of christian reckoning, screeching and yammering and clothed in smoke like those vaporous beings in regions beyond right knowing where the eye wanders and the lip jerks and drools.

Oh my god, said the sergeant. (52–53)

Mimicking first the language of medieval epic romance ("a fabled horde . . . bearing shields bedight with bits of broken mirrorglass"), then modern evangelical rhetoric ("like a horde from hell more horrible yet than the brimstone land of christian reckoning"), and ending in a comic deflation that is sustained in the next paragraph as the kid's horse sinks "beneath him with a long pneumatic sigh" (53), this passage offers a mock-Dantesque vision of hell, in which the Comanches put on a pantomime on the theme of death and slaughter. The irony is clear: if the conqueror's cap fits for now, the gesture may be merely temporary, as this "company of mounted clowns" is about to be swept aside by the inexorable progress of westward expansion. But there is a further implication as well, as we see in a number of parodic evocations of the medieval Crusades, including a description of one man with "an arrow hanging out of his neck," who "was bent slightly as if in prayer" (53), and the sight of the "unhorsed Saxons" lying at the end of the slaughter "like maimed and naked monks in the bloodslaked dust" (54). McCarthy intimates that perhaps no victory or conquest can be more than temporary, and thus implies that the role of conqueror is less the innate property of a particular sacred tribe than a mantle that repeatedly changes hands over time.

Two important incidents involving Glanton's own "legion of horribles" operate along similarly pantomimic lines. On one occasion the gang encounters a band of Chiricahuas dressed up as "stoneage savages daubed with clay paints in obscure charges," wearing "naught but boots and breechclouts and . . . plumed helmets" (228). Later, Glanton and his men meet a party of Yumas, who, if they seem comical in their "fool's regalia" of braided scarlet coats, silk blouses, and "pantaloons of gray cassinette" (254), have the last laugh when they wipe out almost the entire gang, including Glanton himself, in a surprise attack on their camp at the Yuma crossing.[12]

It is not my contention that such moments as the Yuma and Comanche attacks render historically accurate representations of the inhabitants of the American Southwest. What I do wish to argue, however, is that McCarthy's borderland identities, whether Saxon, Comanche, or Yuma, prove to be no less (if no more) flexible and changeable than theatrical roles. As Steven Shaviro has argued, *Blood Meridian* "savagely explode[s] the American dream of manifest destiny, of racial domination and endless imperial expansion" (144), but not merely for the obvious reason that it exposes the extreme violence incurred in the pursuit of that dream; by locating identity on the uncertain terrain of performance, McCarthy's novel subverts the essentialist premises on which the dream is founded. It is by representing the shedding of blood in this second, nonviolent sense that *Blood Meridian* resists both the cause of racial domination and the imperialist versions of American history to which it has been wedded. In *Blood Meridian,* the concept of American nationhood turns out to be no more fixed or stable than the notions of racial and sexual identity on which it depends.

McCarthy subtly develops the notion of a fluid racial borderland in a further direction in chapter VII by introducing two characters, one white, one black, who share the same name:

> In this company there rode two men named Jackson, one black, one white, both forenamed John. Bad blood lay between them and as they rode up under the barren mountains the white man would fall back alongside the other and take his shadow for the shade that was in it and whisper to him. The black would check or start his horse to shake him off. As if the white man were in violation of his person, had stumbled onto some ritual dormant in his dark blood or his dark soul whereby the shape he stood the sun from on that rocky ground bore something of the man himself and in so doing lay imperiled. The white man laughed and crooned things to him that sounded like the words of love. (81)

Playing on essentialist theories of racial difference, McCarthy intimates a kinship between black and white that is itself predicated on play, or, to be precise, on shadow play. Black Jackson's shadow is invested with something of black Jackson's person or character, and thus imitates him (conveying the Elizabethan sense of "shadow," that is, "actor"). For this reason, white Jackson's efforts to ride in the black man's shadow may be regarded as actual (rather than merely displaced) attempts to trample on black Jackson himself. But as the relation between black Jackson and his shadow reflects (or puns on) the relation between his blackness and white Jackson's whiteness, such that the black man plays the white man's shadow, this passage deconstructs manifest differences between man and shadow, or white and black. That is, if black Jackson's shadow "bore something of the man himself," black Jackson bears something of white Jackson, and vice versa: white Jackson is as much the shadow of black Jackson as black Jackson is the shadow of white Jackson. The "bad blood" that lies between them does not necessarily signify racial impurity or incompatibility; this blood may be their common element.

Indeed, it is this blood that unites the two Jacksons in their shadow play—even, paradoxically, in its bloody conclusion at the end of the next chapter. Having been forced by racial slurs and the threat of violence to vacate his place by the fire, the black man suddenly reappears to decapitate his white double: "Two thick ropes of dark blood and two slender rose like snakes from the stump of his neck and arched hissing into the fire" (107). This violent sundering bears witness to the self's insistently doubling motions, for the action of blood itself embodies the pairing of opposites, giving the lie to the essentialist thinking that underlay the dead man's racism. And so, at one level, the apparently obvious irony that the white man's earlier croonings, which "sounded like the words of love," were really expressions of the bad blood between them turns out to be no irony at all: if love is, as Joyce's Leopold Bloom says, the "opposite of hatred" (333), in some sense love is also, by virtue of that opposition, identical with it.

It might possible, of course, to gloss the story of the two Jacksons as a mini-allegory of race relations in America. One might read the image of a headless white Jackson, for instance, as signifying the irrationality of racism, and black Jackson's revenge as a foretaste of things to come in the Civil War. Alternatively, one might construe their feud as symbolic of hostilities that have projected themselves forward into the twentieth century; in this case, black Jackson would be regarded both as a literary echo and as a historical precursor of Richard Wright's decapitator, Bigger Thomas. And yet, as I have been suggesting, McCarthy tends to destabilize the oppositions on which such allegorical readings are predicated. The Civil War itself, moreover, is glossed over in *Blood Meridian*. In chapter XXII the narrative moves rapidly from the hanging of Toadvine and Brown (June 1850) to the kid's wanderings in the spring of his twenty-eighth year (1860), and then, at the beginning of chapter XXIII, to the kid's roamings on the north Texas plains in the winter of 1878: in the world of this fiction, the Civil War is a nonevent.

The actual historical context on which McCarthy draws in *Blood Meridian* serves to emphasize the provisionality and contingency of an American nationhood defined in theatrical terms. Much of the novel, as I have noted, concerns events that occurred in the Mexican-American borderland in the late 1840s—that is, in the aftermath of the Mexican-American War, when the geographical and political borders of the United States were being renegotiated. The point is powerfully brought home by the massacre of Glanton's gang in April 1850 at a place—the Yuma crossing—where the Colorado River defines the present-day borders of Mexico, California, and Arizona, or what were in 1850 the new borders of Mexico, California, and the New Mexico Territory. In the context of *Blood Meridian* this convergence of history with fiction (in which black John Jackson is the first casualty) implies that in some fundamental sense the project of establishing these borders is inseparable from the attempt to define an American self, and that as long as one of these endeavors is incomplete, the other must remain unfinished as well. Furthermore, *Blood Meridian* allows us to infer that perhaps American history is still in the process of manifesting a course subject not to predestination but to subtle shifts and unpredictable changes of direction. Although certain events have turned out *this* way, in other words, it is equally true that they might have turned out differently, and that they might turn out differently yet.

The spectacle of masculine identity in *Blood Meridian*, I have been suggesting, intimates that the borders of American selfhood, like the geographical borders of the nation, are fluid, permeable, and negotiable. By indicating the inevitability of bloodshed, *Blood*

Meridian resists the notion that identity might be reduced to the terms of essentialist discourses of race and gender. McCarthy's novel, like the work of such theorists as Judith Butler, represents identity as the performance of a script; it is grounded not in nature but in style, which proves susceptible to perpetual reformulation and reinterpretation. But in *Blood Meridian* the implications of this form of representation run deeper still. In showing the connections of a performative version of identity with the larger project of creating an American nation, McCarthy's novel suggests that the script of American history remains open to rewriting. For, as Butler too might argue, there is always the possibility of a failure to repeat, and repetition itself might constitute a kind of failure.

Notes

1. For extensive discussion of some of the historical sources McCarthy may have consulted, see John Emil Sepich's essays, especially "'What kind of indians was them?': Some Historical Sources in Cormac McCarthy's *Blood Meridian*."

2. It is important to distinguish between this reading and the idea that the kid's actions constitute some kind of oedipal reflex. As Steven Shaviro has noted, McCarthy displays no "nostalgia for lost—primitive or uterine—origins," for in this novel the "oedipal myth of paradise lost and regained, of patrimonial inheritance and promised land, has been abolished once and for all" (144).

3. The full epigraph reads: "The Child is father of the Man; / And I could wish my days to be / Bound each to each by natural piety" (Wordsworth 4: 279; see also 1: 226).

4. See Riviere's 1929 essay "Womanliness as a Masquerade," as well as Mulvey's "Visual Pleasure and Narrative Desire" (1975), Doane's "Film and the Masquerade" (1982), and Irigaray's *This Sex Which Is Not One* (1977; trans. 1985), especially "The Power of Discourse and the Subordination of the Feminine" (65–85).

5. Butler elaborates this argument at greater length in *Gender Trouble* (see, especially, 134–41) and, more recently, in *Bodies That Matter* (see, especially, 27–55). In the second work Butler refines her previous arguments to counter the claim, made by some feminist critics, that her deconstructive account of identity is politically disabling because it denies both the supposedly irreducible materiality of the body and possibility of human agency. Butler responds to the first objection by observing that the concepts of materiality and discourse, or "signification," are inextricable from each other. Language itself is material, Butler contends, while materiality, in turn, "is bound up with signification from the start" (30). As for the second objection, Butler insists that agency is a "reiterative or rearticulatory practice, immanent to power, and not a relation of external opposition to power. . . . [It] cannot be conflated with voluntarism or individualism . . . and in no way presupposes a choosing subject" (15).

6. There are other echoes of *Huckleberry Finn* in *Blood Meridian*. Near the beginning of the novel, for example, the kid takes a journey down the Mississippi that may cause him to cross paths with Twain's hero: the date of the kid's journey, 1848, suggests that such a coincidence is possible. The kid aligns himself even more closely with Huck when he runs away from home, turning himself, in effect, into an orphan. This connection seems to be emphasized when Judge Holden offers himself retrospectively as a potential foster-father (306). Holden also evokes Twain's pseudo-aristocratic imposters, the king and the duke, as he lumbers across the desert, "like some scurrilous king stripped of his vesture and driven together with his fool into the wilderness to die" (282).

7. "The judge on his head wore a wig of dried river mud from which protruded bits of straw and grass and tied upon the imbecile's head was a rag of fur with the blackened blood side out. The judge . . . was bedraped with meat like some medieval penitent" (282).

8. See Phillips (440, 458 n. 19), who follows Shaviro (144, 148–49) in comparing

Ahab not only with the judge but also with Glanton and in likening Ishmael to the kid. It is Phillips who notes Holden's resemblances to Melville's whale, particularly in such features as his great hairless bulk, the "blinding white" of his enormous domed head, and his "pleated brow," which is "not unlike a dolphin's" (*Blood Meridian* 79, 93, 128, 167).

9. See Sepich, "A 'blood dark pastryman'" (555 n. 25).

10. To add another layer to Judge Holden's assortment of disguises, this speech contains echoes of Emerson's claim in "Nature" that "every man's condition is a solution in hieroglyphic to those inquiries he would put. He acts it as life, before he apprehends it as truth. In like manner, nature is already, in its forms and tendencies, describing its own design" (4).

11. There are apparent affinities here with Bakhtin's notion of the carnivalesque, which gives a similar emphasis to the grotesque. But although McCarthy's "itinerant carnival" suggests resistance to conventional ideas of social order and effectively parodies that order by conferring the titles of "Judge" on Holden and "Captain" on the likes of Glanton and White, *Blood Meridian* refuses to be assimilated into a Bakhtinian theory because, as I argue, it denies real meaning to the notion of a collective identity that subsumes and transforms the individual's behavior. McCarthy, that is, discounts the very concept of the *social* that underwrites Bakhtin's theory of the carnival. Here I should add that my reading of McCarthy's work differs fundamentally from a Bakhtinian interpretation because I am seeking to make visible precisely those gender relations that are suppressed, as Mary Russo has pointed out (219), in Bakhtin.

12. Readers interested in historical accounts of this incident might consult Douglas Martin (138–51) and Samuel Chamberlain (267–97). Sepich discusses the second in "'What kind of indians was them?'"

Works Cited

Arnold, Edwin T., and Luce, Dianne C. *Perspectives on Cormac McCarthy.* Jackson: University of Mississippi Press, 1993.

Auden, W. H. *Collected Poems.* Ed. Edward Mendelson. New York: Random House, 1976.

Butler, Judith. *Bodies That Matter: On the Discursive Limits of "Sex."* New York: Routledge, 1993.

———. *Gender Trouble: Feminism and the Subversion of Identity.* New York: Routledge, 1990.

———. "Performative Acts and Gender Constitution: An Essay in Phenomenology and Feminist Theory." *Performing Feminisms: Feminist Critical Theory and Theatre.* Ed. Sue-Ellen Case. Baltimore: Johns Hopkins University Press, 1990. 270–82.

Chamberlain, Samuel E. *My Confession.* New York: Harper, 1956.

Doane, Mary Ann. "Film and the Masquerade: Theorising the Female Spectator." *Screen* 23.3–4 (1982): 74–87.

Emerson, Ralph Waldo. *The Complete Works of Ralph Waldo Emerson.* Vol. 1. Ed. Edward Waldo Emerson. Boston: Houghton Mifflin, 1903–4.

Irigaray, Luce. *This Sex Which Is Not One.* Trans. Catherine Porter. Ithaca, N.Y.: Cornell University Press, 1985.

Joyce, James. *Ulysses.* 1922. New York: Vintage, 1990.

Martin, Douglas D. *Yuma Crossing.* Albuquerque: University of New Mexico Press, 1954.

McCarthy, Cormac. *Blood Meridian, or, The Evening Redness in the West.* 1985. New York: Vintage Books, 1992.

———. *Child of God.* 1973. New York: Vintage Books, 1993.

———. *Outer Dark.* 1968. New York: Vintage Books, 1993.

———. *Suttree.* 1979. New York: Vintage Books, 1992.

Mulvey, Laura. "Visual Pleasure and Narrative Cinema." *Screen* 16.3 (1975): 6–18.

Phillips, Dana. "History and the Ugly Facts of Cormac McCarthy's *Blood Meridian.*" *American Literature* 68.2 (June 1996): 433–60.

Riviere, Joan. "Womanliness as a Masquerade." *Formations of Fantasy.* Ed. Victor Burgin, James Donald, and Cora Kaplan. London: Methuen, 1986. 35–44.

Russo, Mary. "Female Grotesques: Carnival and Theory." *Feminist Studies/Critical Studies.* Ed. Teresa de Lauretis. Bloomington: Indiana University Press, 1986. 213–29.

Sepich, John Emil. "The Dance of History in Cormac McCarthy's *Blood Meridian.*" *Southern Literary Journal* 24.1 (fall 1991): 16–31.

———. "A 'blood dark pastryman': Cormac McCarthy's Recipe for Gunpowder and Historical Fiction in *Blood Meridian.*" *Mississippi Quarterly* 46.4 (fall 1993): 547–63.

———. "'What kind of indians was them?': Some Historical Sources in Cormac McCarthy's *Blood Meridian.*" *Perspectives on Cormac McCarthy.* Ed. Edwin T. Arnold and Dianne C. Luce. Jackson: University of Mississippi Press, 1993. 121–41.

Shaviro, Steven. "'The Very Life of the Darkness': A Reading of *Blood Meridian.*" *Perspectives on Cormac McCarthy.* Ed. Edwin T. Arnold and Dianne C. Luce. Jackson: University of Mississippi Press, 1993. 143–56.

Twain, Mark. *Adventures of Huckleberry Finn.* 1884. New York: Oxford University Press, 1996.

Woodward, Richard B. "Cormac McCarthy's Venomous Fiction." *New York Times Magazine,* 19 Apr. 1992: 28–31, 36, 40.

Wordsworth, William. *The Poetical Works of William Wordsworth*. Vol. 1. Ed. E. de Selincourt. Oxford: Oxford University Press, 1940.

———. *The Poetical Works of William Wordsworth*. Vol. 4. Ed. E. de Selincourt. Oxford: Oxford University Press, 1947.

Abjection and "the Feminine" in *Outer Dark*

Ann Fisher-Wirth

I N a talk he gave on *Blood Meridian* at the University of Mississippi in spring 1996, James Lilley wondered aloud where woman is in that novel. It occurred to me suddenly that woman is in the mud— both literally, in that the book is full of nameless dying (male and) female bodies whose primary action is to hit the dirt, and metaphorically, in that, in *Blood Meridian*, woman is the mud. That realm of physicality and death against (and toward) which the males relentlessly struggle has long been linked both mythically and psychoanalytically with the feminine. In Hinduism, for instance, the realm is represented by Kali, in Jungian archetypes by the Terrible Mother. In the French feminist psychoanalytic theory developed by Julia Kristeva, derived from Freud and Lacan, "the feminine"—the body of woman, the body of the mother, and those elements in nature such as mud and blood that are associated with woman—is terrifying and alluring to the male subject[1] precisely because it both represents and threatens abjection. It is important to define "the feminine" carefully; for Kristeva it does not signify merely "woman," but also that realm of experience or existence that lies outside what Jacques Lacan calls the symbolic order, and that must be repressed or repudiated if the subject is to retain his illusion of autonomy, of identity. "What we designate as 'feminine,'" Kristeva writes in *Powers of Horror*, "far from being a primeval essence, will be seen as an 'other' without a name, which subjective experience confronts when it does not stop at the appearance of its identity" (58).

In order to construct an identity, Kristeva argues, the child must pass beyond the (imaginary) preoedipal state of nondifferentiation from, or union with, the mother. Acquiring language, entering the symbolic order, he accomplishes the formation of a "more or less beautiful image" in which he beholds or recognizes himself by repelling and rejecting "what, having been the mother, will turn into an abject" (13, 12). The abject then becomes those things—among them blood, pus, sweat, shit, unclean beasts, corpses, or the physicality of women—that stand in for the repudiated mother, and that the self and the community continually and ritualistically reject anew in order to maintain "identity, system, order" (4). However, existing at the border between identity and loss, "the border of [one's] condition as a living being," the abject is not merely cast off but also ambivalently desired, for its sheer existence reveals "the inaugural loss"—the loss of union with the mother—"that laid the foundations of its own being." All abjection, Kristeva writes, "is in fact recognition of the *want* on which any being, meaning, language, or desire is founded" (5). The fact of abjection, therefore, is "the violence of mourning for an 'object' that has always already been lost" (15). This is why, though rejected, the abject also allures, and why, though despised, the abject also possesses the power of the sacred. It testifies to the frailty of identity, indeed "of the symbolic order itself" (69), and conversely to the power of the feminine, the maternal, the "'other' without a name" that lies beyond the borders of the individual/communal "clean and proper body" (72)[2] and that confronts the subject with his own undoing, his own helplessness and death.

Fully developed female characters do not exist in McCarthy's novels, though some have felt that he works in this direction with Alejandra and her grandaunt Alfonsa in *All the Pretty Horses*,[3] or with John Grady Cole's lover, the whore from Chiapas, in *Cities of the Plain*. But paradoxically, McCarthy's female characters become more interesting the less he attempts to develop them, for their power is poetic, gestural. McCarthy is a brilliant symbolist of "the feminine"; unforgettably, he articulates the dread, loathing, desire, and fascination that, Kristeva says, characterize the subject's response to whatever would undo it. What would in another novelist's work be sensationalism, even pornography—the corpse brides, the incest victims, the raped and mute and scalped and maimed—is in McCarthy's fiction apprehended so powerfully at the level of the unconscious that it becomes the stuff of nightmare and beauty. What Kristeva writes of Louis-Ferdinand Céline (in other ways quite a different writer) is true as well of McCarthy: he is a "borderlander" (55) between being and nonbeing, whose "journey to the end of the night" (58) becomes the "privileged signifier" of the power and meaning of horror. "Far from being a minor, marginal activity in our culture," Kristeva continues, literature like his "represents the ultimate coding of our crises, of our most intimate and most serious apocalypses. Hence its nocturnal power. . . . Hence also its being seen as taking the place of the sacred" (208).

THE FORMATION OF ABJECTION

*Before he slept he saw again the birth-stunned face, the swamp trees in a dark bower above the pale and naked flesh and the black blood seeping from the navel. (**Outer Dark** 27)*

In the last three pages of *Outer Dark*, McCarthy tells briefly of Culla Holme's "later years," after the ghastly events that have comprised the rest of the novel. A wanderer, he comes upon a blind man, "ragged and serene" (239), tapping along the road, who does not so much preach as pray, not so much pray as move along his foredoomed path tranquilly. Holme passes by and continues, "shambling, gracelorn, down out of the peaceful mazy fields" (241), through a burn where "for miles there were only the charred shapes of trees in a dead land," until he arrives at a swamp: "And that was all. Before him stretched a spectral waste out of which reared only the naked trees in attitudes of agony and dimly hominoid like figures in a landscape of the damned. . . . He tried his foot in the mire before him and it rose in a vulvate welt claggy and sucking. He stepped back. A stale wind blew from this desolation and the marsh reeds and black ferns among which he stood clashed softly like things chained. He wondered why a road should come to such a place" (242).[4] Later, retreating from this apocalyptic mire, Culla meets the blind man again, traveling down the road that he has come from. These are the novel's last words: "He wondered where the blind man was going and did he know how the road ended. Someone should tell a blind man before setting him out that way" (242). But in the world of *Outer Dark,* all men are blind, and this road toward the "vulvate welt" is the only road there is. The plot of the novel enacts one long flight from, and one long arrival at, the "mire": one long descent into the abject, and—in helpless revolt against this descent—one long series of outrages against the feminine.

The opening chapter of *Outer Dark* offers a stunning account of the formation of abjection. As has often been remarked, McCarthy presents his characters through action, not reflection; it is therefore difficult to bring psychoanalytic theory to bear on a nonpsychological novel. But as the first chapter of *Outer Dark* abundantly reveals, McCarthy's imagery of landscape and bodies is so rich, so saturated with dreamlike excesses of beauty, terror, violence, that, like imagery in a free verse lyric poem, it serves as a projection of its subjects' psyches. One odd—and suggestive—thing about the novel is that Culla, who responds so vehemently to the birth of his and his sister Rinthy's baby, has not seemed to mind committing incest in the first place. One way to interpret this is to figure that lust just drives people to do lots of things, and given the cheerfulness with which, later in the novel, the pig drover whom Culla encounters tells him, "That's my little brother Billy yander. . . . This is his first time along. . . . Says he goin to get him some poontang when we get sold but I told him he'd be long done partialed to shehogs" (216), that is a definite possibility. But Culla's guilt and sense of damnation, expressed in his dream on the novel's first page, are overwhelming. In his dream, he stands before a prophet among a "beggared multitude," a "delegation of human ruin . . . with blind eyes upturned and puckered stumps and leprous sores," and calls out, "Can I be cured?" The prophet looks down "as if surprised to see him there amidst such pariahs," and answers, "Yes, I think perhaps you will be cured" (5). But though Culla, apparently, has felt superior to this multitude of the abject, it turns out that he alone causes the healing sun to blacken and vanish, and voices are raised against him. "He was caught up in the crowd," McCarthy writes, "and the stink of their rags filled his nostrils. They grew seething and more mutinous and he tried to hide among them but they know him even in that pit of hopeless dark and fell upon him with howls of outrage" (5–6). So extreme is Culla's despair that it is as if he has suffered not a change of heart but a change of ontological status between the incestuous coupling and his son's birth. And so, I suggest, he has.

The incestuous brother/sister union that sets the narrative of *Outer Dark* in motion takes place offstage, before the novel begins; it is known only by its fruit, the baby Rinthy delivers in the novel's first pages. This gives it an air of inevitability; like the adultery between Arthur Dimmesdale and Hester Prynne in *The Scarlet Letter,* it precedes and initiates the narrative, but its specific events remain shadowy. It comes therefore to seem an archetypal, originary transgression; its significance seems to extend far beyond the specific, individual act. In one of the novel's most poignant moments, Rinthy says of this union, "I wasn't ashamed" (156). Her response points up, by contrast, the hysterical nature of Culla's. Though, when Rinthy begs for a midwife, Culla says he can't get one because "She'd tell," his response is nonsense at that level; as Rinthy asks, "Who is they to tell?" (10). And in the world of *Outer Dark,* with its cannibals, killers, and buggers, it seems unlikely that an ordinary act of incest would shock a midwife or a community much, anyway. Instead, Culla's reaction becomes more readily explicable if we see the brother/sister incest as a stand-in for the mother/son incest that constitutes, in Freudian theory, the "second taboo," along with the taboo against the murder of the father, that together founded religion and civilization (*Powers of Horror* 57). Culla's dream of the multitude of abjects, with their blind eyes, puckered stumps, and leprous sores, suggests terror of the whole physical world—terror of castration, terror of vulnerability—yet if he is the incurable one, the worst among "pariahs" (*Outer Dark* 5), that must be because he has already wandered farthest into the outer dark. Breaking the taboo against incest, he has entered what Kristeva calls "those uncertain spaces of unstable identity" and tested "the fragility—both threatening and fusional—of the archaic dyad . . . the non-separation of subject/object, on which language has no hold but one woven of fright and repulsion" (58). That is to say, in his union with the sister/mother, he has become the "borderlander," has crossed back over into nondifferentiation, into what Kristeva describes as a *jouissance* that would annihilate the illusion of self, burst "the shattered mirror" (9).

Out of the mother, back to the mother. His arms "stained with gore to the elbows," Culla brings forth his son from his sister's body, "the scrawny body trailing the cord in anneloid writhing down the bloodslimed covers, a beetcolored creature that looked to him like a skinned squirrel" (*Outer Dark* 14). Immediately he tries to abandon, to negate, this sign of his knowledge of the sister/mother, which is the mark of his guilt, to establish himself as among the saved, in a "clean and proper body" (*Powers of Horror* 72). But, of course, it cannot be done. His incest has already exposed the frailty of the symbolic order, yet, repudiating that incest, he plunges himself still further into the "outer dark," beyond the circle of the family ("a sacred thing, a family," says the squire. "A sacred obligation" [47]), beyond what might conceivably be redemptive fatherhood, beyond the *mater dolorosa*[5] of his sister's uncomplaining, devoted maternal. Birth/death images, images of abjection, flood the body in flight. Dried blood from Rinthy's "vulvate welt" sifts "in a fine dust from the lines of his palm" (15), as if blood will be his fortune. He washes, he runs, carrying the child to what he hopes will be its abandonment, its erasure. But fleeing his knowledge of the mother, everywhere he turns he flees farther into the realm of the maternal. First he reaches a river where "swollen waters" come in a "bloodcolored spume from about the wooden stanchions" of a bridge and fan "in the pool below with a constant and vicious hissing" (15). Then he comes to a cottonwood clearing, where he lays the child down in the wilderness to howl "redgummed at the pending night" (16).

But the more he runs, the more his transgression pursues him. He has broken with creation; the repressed, however, returns all around him. The natural world turns phantasmagorical, possessed of a "spectral quietude . . . as if something were about that crickets and nightbirds held in dread" (16)—and something is; its name is Culla. He comes to a "swampy forest, floundering through sucking quagmires and half running," and follows a creek to where trees like a vengeful womb begin to "close him in, malign and baleful shapes that [rear] like enormous androids provoked at the alien insubstantiality of this flesh colliding among them" (16–17). Utterly lost at last, "with his hands outstretched before him against whatever the dark might hold" (17), he stumbles demented into a clearing, only to find that he has run full circle.

It is a brilliant moment, splendidly overwritten, this journey to the end of the night when Culla, reduced to gibbering, receives by lightning flash his revelation concerning "the feminine":

When he crashed into the glade among the cottonwoods he fell headlong and lay there with his cheek to the earth. And as he lay there a far crack of lightning went bluely down the sky and bequeathed him in an embryonic bird's first fissured vision of the world and transpiring instant and outrageous from dark to dark a final view of the grotto and the shapeless white plasm struggling upon the rich and incunabular moss like a lank swamp hare. He would have taken it for some boneless cognate of his heart's dread had the child not cried.

It howled execration upon the dim camarine world of its nativity wail on wail while he lay there gibbering with palsied jawhasps, his hands putting back the night like some witless paraclete beleaguered with all limbo's clamor. (17–18)

A *camarin,* in Spanish, is the place behind an altar where images are dressed and ornaments destined for that purpose are kept. Culla, then, has arrived at the shrine or temple of existence. The "dim camarine world" of the baby's nativity is, of course, not just the forest clearing but the womb; and the manchild, howling not just from need but already from "execration," takes on a double significance: he is not only the inadmissible sign of his father's *jouissance,* but also a double for Culla himself. Even, perhaps, a double for the phallus, this "shape-less white plasm" that struggles in the grotto like a grotesque incarna-tion of a Hindu *lingam* in a *yoni*. And Culla, having broken taboo, finds that chaos has come again. Grim joke, to think of him as champion of the symbolic order: as the "paraclete"—Holy Spirit or Comforter—helpless to ward off "limbo's clamor," which in this instance is mother speech, the Kristevan "semiotic."[6] Culla has met his match, unmanned by generation.

RINTHY AND CULLA

And stepping softly with her air of blooded ruin about the glade in a
frail agony of grace she trailed her rags through dust and ashes, circling
the dead fire, the charred billets and chalk bones, the little calcined
ribcage. (**Outer Dark** 237)

Lena Grove, the eight-months-pregnant mother in Faulkner's *Light in August,* has little enough. She trudges all the way from Alabama to Mississippi, her possessions in a handkerchief, because her lover has fled and she reckons "a family ought to be all together when a chap comes" (18). But Rinthy, her double, is far more desolate. She wanders through *Outer Dark* after the tinker has taken the baby that Culla abandoned, traveling from farms to shacks to woods in search of "this here tinker . . . got somethin belongs to me" (101), in a patient, useless labor of reclaiming. In the violent pyrotechnics of McCarthy's fiction, it is easy to overlook Rinthy, who hurts nobody, kills nobody. And from a certain kind of feminist point of view, in which male authors are judged for their ability to create female characters, which are then judged for their independence and autonomy, Rinthy—and McCarthy—would be abysmal failures. Rinthy makes Lena Grove look like a nuclear physicist; she is nothing but body and patience. And yet she is one of McCarthy's most important characters, for with Rinthy's story *Outer Dark* attempts to enter, and to represent from within, the story of the abjected "feminine." Only in *Outer Dark* does McCarthy create a female-focused narrative, which, in approximately alternating chapters, he juxtaposes with the male-focused narrative of Culla's wanderings and with the male-focused, italicized interchapters that report the murderous progress of the unholy killer trinity, the minister, Harmon, and the unnamed mute. Only in *Outer Dark*, that is to say, does McCarthy attempt to cross this particular border, to write the story of that Other who/which has been abjected, upon whom/which so much terror, loathing, and desire have been projected by the (male) subject.[7] It is as if, "stepping softly," Rinthy charts a path in her "frail agony of grace" *around* the symbolic order, *around* what Kristeva calls "the braided horror and fascination that bespeaks the incompleteness of the speaking being . . . heard as a narcissistic crisis on the outskirts of the feminine" (*Powers of Horror* 209), and critiques the symbolic system simply by remaining herself, outside.

One of the primary differences between Rinthy and Culla is that, to Rinthy, things of the body still possess their literal meanings. She travels around the countryside like the return of the repressed, trying to undo Culla's mad, obsessively symbolic narrative of "fear of the archaic mother" (*Powers of Horror* 7). The baby Culla abandons, for instance, is not, to her, a "shapeless white plasm" or "boneless cognate of [the] heart's dread" (*Outer Dark* 18); he is, like a litany, simply and heartbreakingly "my chap." Her speech is naked, straightforward: "I'm travelin. . . . Well. I mean I'm not goin to just one place in particular. . . . I'm a-huntin somebody. . . . Just somebody. This feller" (111)—and later, agonized, to the tinker: "Let me have him. . . . You could let me have him. . . . I'd care for him. . . . They wouldn't nobody like me" (193). Her most eloquent language, though, lies in the Kristevan "semiotic," the blood and milk of her body. Blood and milk are just facts of parturition—horrifying, perhaps, to Culla, whose "long shadow" overrides her, but pitiable to more compassionate interlocutors like the old crone who gives Rinthy buttermilk, or the doctor, for the blood and milk express—literally—her innermost being, her transformation into she who has been ruptured, outraged, rendered bereft. The blood that "[starts] again, warm on her leg" (32–33), when she digs an empty pit and discovers that Culla lied, saying he buried her "dead" baby; the milk that runs down her body "like dark tears" (30): these comprise her anguished *jouissance,* her fluid, excessive economy. Milk stains her with the sign of her need, her child's need. It is her body's prayer, betraying her when she hears another woman's baby cry: "Already she could feel it begin warm and damp, sitting there holding her swollen breasts, feeling it in runnels down her belly until she pressed the cloth of her dress against it, looking down at the dark stains" (99). It accompanies her speech in the novel's most wrenching moments, as when she tells the old "stooped and hooded anthropoid" (108) of a crone who feeds her buttermilk, "I'll just tell him. I'll tell him I want my chap. . . . I'd of wanted to see it anyways. . . . Even if it had died" (115).[8]

Rinthy powerfully bears out Margaret Homans's conjecture in *Bearing the Word* that the female subject may retain a greater close-ness to the literal than the male, and the reasons for this, in Homans's theory, fit explicitly as well with *Outer Dark*. In renouncing the mother's body, Homans maintains, the son renounces literality; the pro-hibition against incest consigns him to figural substitutions for that body, a return to which would signify, furthermore, the devolution of his identity. Rinthy, not "ashamed" (*Outer Dark* 156) of either incest or her own maternal body, does not fall under that same taboo. Instead, she inhabits the ground Kristeva claims in "Stabat Mater" for quite a different mother, the Virgin Mary, whose "milk and tears are the signs *par excellence* of the *Mater dolorosa*." Both milk and tears, Kristeva continues, "are metaphors of non-language, of a 'semiotic' that does not coincide with linguistic communication. The Mother and her attributes signifying suffering humanity thus become the symbol of a 'return of the repressed' in monotheism. They reestablish the nonver-bal and appear as a signifying modality closer to the so-called primary processes" (592–93). This is the importance of Rinthy's body-sense, her utterly natural yet near-miraculous knowing. She who "don't live nowheres no more," who "just go around huntin my chap" (156), inhabits what Elaine Showalter has called the "wild zone," the realm of experience not articulated by the symbolic order.[9] She herself is "half wild"—both half wild with grief, and half wild as in *sauvage*—as the doctor perceives when she replies, to his incredulous, "You couldn't still have milk after six months": "If he was dead. That's what you said wasn't it? . . . That means he ain't, don't it? That means he ain't dead or I'd of gone dry. Ain't it?" (154–55). And it is the importance, too, of a sentence McCarthy writes—"She didn't know what to make of it"—when Rinthy wanders at last into the clearing where she finds, among other things, her child's "little calcined ribcage" (237).

In *Outer Dark*, two beings are nameless. The first is the mute, one of the killers, who seems "to sleep, crouched at the [minister's] right with his arms dangling between his knees like something waiting to be wakened and fed" (234). Of the mute, the minister tells Culla, "That'n ain't got a name. . . . He wanted me to give him one but I wouldn't do it. He don't need nary. . . . Some things is best not named" (174–75). The second is the child, who "ain't got nary" (236) a name, either. In contrast to the mute, the child is a pathetic little creature marked by fire, who dangles from his killer's hands "like a dressed rabbit, a gross eldritch doll with ricketsprung legs and one eye opening and closing softly like a naked owl" (235). Both in their different ways inhabit the outer dark, reveal the "frailty of the symbolic order" (*Powers of Horror* 69). The mute, a nightmare creature, is a pure sadistic fantasy from the abject "threatening world of animals or animalism . . . imagined as representatives of sex and murder" (*Powers of Horror* 12). The child is the mute's reverse image: pure outcast, pure victim, equally unspeaking, bereft of the Mother yet forever not called forth into the protection of the Father. And everything in the novel has tended toward the moment when these two mysterious beings—the one somehow embodying Culla's desire, the other Rinthy's—come together in the clearing.

Kristeva writes in *Powers of Horror*: "Abjection, when all is said and done, is the other facet of religious, moral, and ideological codes on which rest the sleep of individuals and the breathing spells of societies" (209). McCarthy's presentation of the murder of the child partakes of the "sacred power of horror" (208), and participates in what Kristeva calls "the various means of *purifying* the abject—the various catharses—[that] make up the history of religions, and end up with that catharsis par excellence called art, both on the far and near side of religion" (17). *Take, eat. This is my body.* When the minister slits the child's throat and hands it to the drooling, whimpering mute, who buries his face in its throat to devour it, the random, seemingly gratuitous sickeningness of the baby's death is perhaps psychologically explicable if the killers are seen as corollary to, implicit in, Culla's hard dream of mastery—the ghastly extension of his desire, earlier, to efface the signs of abjection—and the baby is understood as the best, inadmissible evidence of the body's desire and vulnerability. And it may be that those who live in the lighted spaces sleep more easily, the illusion of order upheld, because of the bloody rituals enacted here, in the dark reaches of the imagination.[10] As Kristeva puts it: "In a world in which the Other has collapsed, the aesthetic task—a descent into the foundations of the symbolic construct—amounts to retracing the fragile limits of the speaking being, closest to its dawn, to the bottomless 'primacy' constituted by primal repression. . . . 'Subject' and 'object' push each other away, confront, each other, collapse, and start again—inseparable, contaminated, condemned, at the boundary of what is assimilable, thinkable: abject. Great modern literature unfolds over that terrain" (18).

IN THE CLEARING

You fear blood more and more. Blood and time. (epigraph to *Blood Meridian*)

But Rinthy?

When she wanders upon the scene of carnage, the tinker hangs invisible in a tree, the child has been burned to ashes and bones, and the killer trinity and Culla have gone off to whatever deadly destination. McCarthy describes her as "half wild and haggard in her shapeless sundrained cerements, yet delicate as any fallow doe . . . [entering] the clearing to stand cradled in a grail of jade and windy light, slender and trembling and pale with wandlike hands to speak the boneless shapes attending her" (237). Arrived at death, where her son's "little calcined ribcage" rests among ashes and bones, Rinthy does "not know what to make of it" (237). I take this in its largest meaning, as a comment not on her ignorance but on the preposterousness of the scene, the sense that it profoundly fails to make to her. She waits, pokes around, but no one returns. Finally she sleeps, as "shadows [grow] cold across the wood and night [rings] down upon these lonely figures" (237–38). There we leave her, "little sister" (238), in the clearing, where time continues, natural process continues, birds and wind and seasons clean the relics of the dead, and death mingles with life in terrible beauty.

Rinthy's presence in the clearing, in the novel, calls into question the whole mad enterprise. She, who does not fear blood and time, speaks another language—she is another language—from the language of horror, entirely.

Notes

1. For this essay, I distinguish the son from the daughter, the male from the female subject. The extent to which gender does or does not define the child's relation to the mother, the nature and severity of the oedipal crisis, and the formation of identity has been endlessly debated in psychoanalytic theory, in ways far beyond the concerns of this essay. In *Outer Dark,* however, McCarthy so dramatically distinguishes between the son's and the daughter's responses to "the feminine" that the novel becomes a perfect example for the most extreme understanding of difference. Therefore, when I use the masculine pronouns for "the child" in Kristeva's theories of abjection, I do so advisedly.

2. In French, *propre* means both "one's own" and "clean." The identity one owns—or has the illusion of owning—is the identity whose borders one polices.

3. Gail Moore Morrison offers an excellent discussion of Alejandra and Alfonsa in "*All the Pretty Horses:* John Grady Cole's Expulsion from Paradise." But I cannot help feeling that Alejandra is a dream from the relatively shallow waters of the psyche, and Alfonsa, potentially far deeper, nevertheless remains circumscribed by her function as Guardian at the Gate, barring John Grady Cole's access to Alejandra.

4. In a famous essay, "The Ambiguous Nihilism of Cormac McCarthy," Vereen Bell reads this passage as exemplary of McCarthy's vision. He writes, with respect to Culla's journey down the dead-end road to the swamp, "This is as close to a conventional paradigm as McCarthy usually comes, and it, of course, is a paradigm of a dead-end, paradigmless world (and for its novel also a kind of gothic, self-referential joke)" (32). A powerful and seminal essay, "The Ambiguous Nihilism of Cormac McCarthy" also, however, exemplifies the ways in which gender theory has generally *not* been brought to bear on McCarthy's novels.

5. Terri Witek uses this phrase in her essay on gender in McCarthy's fiction, "Reeds and Hides: Cormac McCarthy's Domestic Spaces": "Rinthy is Cormac McCarthy's premier example of the *mater dolorosa*" (139). For a discussion of McCarthy and gender, see also two essays by Nell Sullivan, "Cormac McCarthy and the Text of Jouissance" and "The Evolution of the Dead Girlfriend in *Outer Dark* and *Child of God.*"

6. In *Desire in Language,* Kristeva formulates her theory of the "semiotic": a mode of expression and communication that characterizes the (imaginary) state of preoedipal union with the mother, made up not of words and sentences but of body language and sounds.

7. This remark, written before the publication of the final novel in the Border Trilogy, *Cities of the Plain,* must be qualified by McCarthy's characterization of John Grady Cole's beloved, whose history—sold at thirteen, tortured, raped, prostituted—and finally whose murder are the quintessence of abjection. And how appropriate, given Mexico's current political situation, that she is from Chiapas.

8. Milk and blood are signs of Rinthy's abjection. Interestingly, however, it is not Rinthy but several of the novel's male characters who are associated with another common marker for abjection: the animal. Coupling with pigs may be

fine with the drovers, but when Rinthy is coupled with pigs she strongly repudiates the connection. She is speaking with the crone:

> Where's your youngern.
> What?
> I said where's your youngern.
> I've not got nary.
> The babe, the babe, the old woman crooned.
> They ain't nary'n.
> Hah, said the old woman. Bagged for the river trade I'd judge. Yon sow there might make ye a travelin mate that's drowned her hoggets save one.
> That's a lie what you said, the girl whispered hoarsely. (112)

9. The "wild zone," Showalter writes in a famous essay, is the "always imaginary" realm outside "the circle of the dominant structure" and thus neither accessible to nor structured by language. For French feminist critics, in Showalter's phrasings, the "wild zone" would be the "invisible" made "visible," the "silent" made to "speak," and would provide "the theoretical base of women's difference" (262–63).

10. In conversation, James Lilley points out the simultaneous fascination with and horror of diseased bodies that characterize, in particular, the town-dwellers of *Outer Dark,* those who represent the symbolic order—a fascination and horror analogous to both Culla's response to "the feminine," and the reader's response to the killers' bloody rituals, indeed to *Outer Dark* altogether. The passage that follows plays cunningly with the way in which desiring control creates the obsession with loss of control, here instanced as plague and cholera. The diseases run together in the imagination, loathed and ghoulishly wallowed in:

> [Culla] dipped up half a handful of corn from his pocket and began to chew it and then he stopped, his face going from vacancy to disgust, and spat the tasteless meal to the ground. As he did so a man rounding the corner leaped back and began to scream at him.
> What? Holme said dumbly. What?
> Cholera? Cholera?
> Hell, it weren't nothin but a mouthful of corn.
> I lost a whole family to it now don't lie to me like I ain't never seen it goddamn it.
>
> You sure you ain't sick?
> Shit, Holme said. I ain't never been sick a day in my life saving the whoopincough one time.
> I'd shoot a man went around with the plague like ary mad dog, the man said.
> Ain't nobody plagued, Holme said.
> I hope they ain't, the man said. I pray to God they ain't. He came on along the edge of the porch inspecting the damp explosion of chewed corn in the dust there and mounted the steps with a wary cast to his eye. . . . You sure you ain't a little off your feed? You look kindly peaked to me. (137–38)

Works Cited

Bell, Vereen. "The Ambiguous Nihilism of Cormac McCarthy." *Southern Literary Journal* 15.2 (1983): 31–41.

Faulkner, William. *Light in August*. 1932. New York: Random House, 1972.

Hawthorne, Nathaniel. *The Scarlet Letter and Selected Tales*. Ed. Thomas E. Connolly. New York: Penguin Books, 1970.

Homans, Margaret. *Bearing the Word: Language and Female Experience in Nineteenth-Century Women's Writing*. Chicago: University of Chicago Press, 1986.

Kristeva, Julia. "From One Identity to Another." *Desire in Language*. Ed. Leon Roudiez. Trans. Thomas Gora, Alice Jardine, and Leon Roudiez. New York: Columbia University Press, 1980. 124–47.

———. *Powers of Horror: An Essay on Abjection*. Trans. Leon Roudiez. New York: Columbia University Press, 1982.

———. "Stabat Mater." Trans. Arthur Goldhammer. *Contemporary Critical Theory*. Ed. Dan Latimer. New York: Harcourt Brace Jovanovich, 1989. 581–603.

Lilley, James D. "Of Whales and Men: The Dynamics of Cormac McCarthy's Environmental Imagination." *Southern Quarterly* 38.2 (2000): 111–22.

McCarthy, Cormac. *Blood Meridian, or, The Evening Redness in the West*. New York: Random House, 1985.

———. *Cities of the Plain*. New York: Alfred A. Knopf, 1998.

———. *Outer Dark*. New York: Random House, 1968.

Morrison, Gail Moore. "*All the Pretty Horses:* John Grady Cole's Expulsion from Paradise." *Perspectives on Cormac McCarthy*. Ed. Edwin T. Arnold and Dianne C. Luce. Jackson: University Press of Mississippi, 1993. 173–93.

Showalter, Elaine. "Feminist Criticism in the Wilderness." *The New Feminist Criticism: Essays on Women, Literature, and Theory*. Ed. Elaine Showalter. New York: Pantheon Books, 1985.

Sullivan, Nell. "Cormac McCarthy and the Text of Jouissance." *Sacred Violence: A Reader's Companion to Cormac McCarthy*. Ed. Wade Hall and Rick Wallach. El Paso: Texas Western Press, 1995. 115–23.

———. "The Evolution of the Dead Girlfriend Motif in *Outer Dark* and *Child of God*." *Myth, Legend, Dust: Critical Responses to Cormac McCarthy*. Ed. Rick Wallach. New York: St. Martin's Press, 2000. 68–77.

Witek, Terri. "Reeds and Hides: Cormac McCarthy's Domestic Spaces." *Southern Review* (1994): 136–42.

All the Pretty Mexicos

Cormac McCarthy's Mexican Representations

Daniel Cooper Alarcón

> *The task of the narrator is not an easy one. He appears to be required to choose his tale from among the many that are possible. But of course that is not the case. The case is rather to make many of the one. Always the teller must be at pains to devise against his listener's claim—perhaps spoken, perhaps not—that he has heard the tale before.*
>
> Cormac McCarthy, The Crossing

THE comments of McCarthy's fallen priest in *The Crossing* (155) provide a useful way of thinking about the relationship of McCarthy's Border Trilogy to one of the literary traditions within which his border novels may be situated. In this essay I sketch the development of this tradition and its conventions in order to consider whether or not McCarthy's Mexican novels contribute to or challenge the kinds of Mexicanness that tradition supports. I limit my discussion to *All the Pretty Horses,* at the same time noting that similar problems of cross-cultural representation are present in *The Crossing* and *Cities of the Plain.*

Since the turn of the nineteenth century, American and English writers have produced a steady stream of literary works set in Mexico, many of which occupy prominent places within the respective oeuvres of their creators. To cite some of the more famous examples, there are W. H. Prescott's *History of the Conquest of Mexico,* D. H. Lawrence's *The Plumed Serpent,* Katherine Anne Porter's *Flowering Judas,* Graham Greene's *The Power and the Glory,* and Malcolm Lowry's *Under the Volcano.* Defending his novel to prospective publisher Jonathan Cape in 1946, Lowry wrote:

> The scene is Mexico, the meeting place, according to some of mankind itself, pyre of Bierce and springboard of Hart Crane, the age-old arena of racial and political conflicts of every nature, and where a colorful native people of genius have a religion that we can roughly describe as one of death, so that it is a good place, at least as good as Lancashire or Yorkshire, to set our drama of a man's struggle between the power of darkness and light. Its geographical remoteness from us, as well as the closeness of its problems to our own, will assist the tragedy each in its own way. We can see it as the world itself, or the Garden of Eden, or both at once. Or we can see it as a kind of timeless symbol of the world on which we can place the Garden of Eden, the Tower of Babel and indeed anything else we please. It is paradisal: it is unquestionably infernal. It is, in fact, Mexico. . . . (*Selected Letters* 67)

It is, in fact, a mythologized Mexico, constructed to suit the author's needs, a culture to be tampered with freely, as Lowry makes clear in his comment, "we can see it as a kind of timeless symbol of the world on which we can place . . . anything else we please." In this passage, Lowry also suggests the phrase "Infernal Paradise," which Ronald Walker has used aptly to characterize the Mexican works of Lowry, Lawrence, and Greene.[1] The term is particularly appropriate for the Mexican myth that these and other works have fostered in that it vividly suggests the tendency to perceive and represent Mexico in Manichean terms. Lowry's comments are also useful in that they serve as a blueprint for other key features of the tradition and the myth it has fostered. For example, Mexico is frequently perceived as the "meeting place" of the Old World and New World, resulting in "racial and political conflicts of every nature." Another tendency is to portray Mexicans as a "colorful" or exotic people fixated with death. And, in suggesting that Mexico becomes an appropriate site on which to stage the drama of an Englishman's struggle between the power of darkness and light, Lowry points to the use of the Mexican landscape as a symbolic backdrop against which a spiritual quest is played out, a backdrop often represented as "timeless," or ahistorical, its inhabitants frozen in time. Finally, in his references to Ambrose Bierce and Hart Crane, Lowry alludes to perhaps the most curious feature of this tradition: it is one in which the authors themselves have assumed mythic proportions, their legends interwoven and mirrored in their Mexican works.

Shortly before disappearing in Mexico in 1913, Bierce wrote to his nephew's wife, Lora: "If you should hear of my being stood up against a Mexican stone wall and shot to rags please know that I think it is a pretty good way to depart this life. It beats old age, disease or falling down the cellar stairs. To be a Gringo in Mexico—ah, that is euthanasia" (O'Connor 299). Again we have the linkage of Mexico with death, but, significantly, Bierce implies that the death Mexico offers is attractive, an end to be desired and welcomed. This view of Mexico as a place where merciful death awaits the Anglo American or European is one that we find regularly in the Infernal Paradise tradition, for example, in *Under the Volcano* (1947) and in Robert Stone's novel *Children of Light* (1986).[2] Lowry's reference to Bierce suggests that he may have had the dying writer in mind as he created his self-destructive ex-consul. In many ways, Bierce's disappearance has come to symbolize Mexico for English readers, fusing the attraction of the country as a place of spiritual or artistic freedom with the threat of physical danger, and fusing the mystique of the writer-adventurer with the mystique of Mexico. The German author B. Traven would later manage a different sort of disappearing act and become an equally mysterious Mexican cipher by constructing false identities so skillfully that even today his biographers cannot identify his birth name with any certainty.[3]

It is important to recognize that such common Mexican tropes are supported and maintained by a complicated discursive network that comprises not only literature but also film, historiography, photography, journalism, tourist propaganda, and literary criticism.[4] (Despite—or perhaps because of—the many discourses contributing to the Infernal Paradise, scholarship examining it has been sporadic and narrow and has even reinscribed some of the myth's most prominent elements.)

It also needs to be borne in mind that although Anglo writers have been the primary contributors to the Infernal Paradise myth over the last two centuries, it is not purely an Anglo construct. Much of the myth is derived from Spanish colonial texts as refashioned and revisioned by the influential nineteenth-century historians Alexander von Humboldt and W. H. Prescott. Mary Louise Pratt notes that Humboldt's "year in Mexico was spent mainly in and near the capital with Mexican scholars and libraries. The *Political Essays* reflect such research, following lines of reportage laid down by [Spanish] colonial bureaucracies" (*Imperial Eyes* 131). Prescott also relied heavily on Spanish colonial histories in writing his massive history of the Conquest. This connection to Spanish colonial discourse emphasizes the durability of the images and categories that were generated by the first century of contact between Europeans and indigenous Americans. As José Rabasa has suggested, these images and categories "constitute a stock of motifs and conceptual filters prefiguring any possible [later] discovery" (*Inventing America* 194). Keeping this in mind, it perhaps becomes a bit easier to understand how the Mexican images circulated by non-Mexicans writing in the nineteenth and twentieth centuries occasionally bear striking resemblances to the Mexican constructs of Cortés and later Spanish writers. It is also important to note the impact of Mexican nationalism on Anglo writers in the decade following the Mexican Revolution (1911–20). Mexican nationalism, in particular its romanticization and celebration of indigenous pre-Columbian cultures, proved to be very seductive to the expatriate Anglo writers in Mexico at the time, as well as quite adaptable to the Infernal Paradise, as the work of Katherine Anne Porter and D. H. Lawrence attests. Moreover, although cultural nationalism initially may have succeeded in reuniting the war-torn country, the Mexicanness it generated and promoted has come to be just as problematic as foreign versions. As Peter Wollen comments,

"Indeed, the great works of the Mexican muralists have themselves become [depoliticized] tourist attractions. Post-war Mexican artists, from the generation of the Ruptura onwards, have felt compelled to question the idea of an unproblematic Mexicanidad, itself now seen as mythic and folkloric in a problematic sense" (47). Growing out of such seemingly incompatible discourses, the conventions of the Infernal Paradise myth have nevertheless become so much a staple of the literary tradition supporting it, that they have—through repetition—become markers of a literary work's authenticity. Enchanting/repellent, beautiful/desolate, civilized/cruel, dreamlike/bloody, paradisal/infernal—these are the standard oppositional terms with which Anglo writers have consistently represented Mexico.

A preliminary assessment of Cormac McCarthy's *All the Pretty Horses* in terms of action, characterization, and structure easily allows that novel to be located within the Infernal Paradise tradition. As in the work of his predecessors, McCarthy's Mexico functions as a symbolic backdrop, juxtaposing the paradise of the hacienda with the hell of the prison at Saltillo. The Mexican characters, although fleshed out more than in most novels of the tradition, are also fairly standard. The *campesinos* are innocent and generous (or, in the case of the nomadic waxmakers who try to buy Blevins, openly sinister); the *hacendado* is cultured, proud, even a little haughty. About Alejandra we learn very little, other than the fact that she is very beautiful, a characteristic McCarthy repeatedly emphasizes. With the captain, McCarthy walks a fine line between character and caricature, coming very close to the stereotypical, sinister Mexican villain. As for Alfonsa, as riveting as her speeches are, one cannot help but feel that she is brought on stage merely to deliver her lines. Thus, a cursory reading of this popular and highly acclaimed novel offers little evidence that would allow us to position it outside of the Infernal Paradise tradition.

A kinder and potentially more interesting reading of *All the Pretty Horses,* which I am also willing to entertain, is one that considers the Manichean Mexican landscape that John Grady Cole moves through to be a projection of the tension between his steadfast romantic ideals and the cruel, capricious world around him. A brief but telling moment early in the novel suggests such an interpretation, when Cole contemplates an oil painting in the home of his recently deceased grandfather:

> There were half a dozen [horses] breaking through a pole corral and their manes were long and blowing and their eyes wild. They'd been copied out of a book. They had the long Andalusian nose and the bones of their faces showed Barb blood. You could see the hindquarters of the foremost few, good hindquarters and heavy enough to make a cutting horse. As if maybe they had Steeldust in their blood. But nothing else matched and no such horse ever was that he had seen and he'd once asked his grandfather what kind of horse they were and his grandfather looked up from his plate at the painting as if he'd never seen it before and he said those are picturebook horses and went on eating. (15–16)

Coming early in the text, this exchange calls the reader's attention to a distinction between "picturebook" or storybook (i.e., romanticized) ideals and "real" life and suggests that John Grady Cole's code of honor and his romantic longings and leanings are rooted in childhood exposure to storybook ideals.[5] As Gail Moore Morrison puts it, "His journey portrays him not solely as a modern day horse-taming cowboy, although his skills in this regard are the stuff of which legends are made, but as an unlikely knight errant, displaced and dispossessed, heroically tested and stubbornly faithful to a chivalric code whose power is severely circumscribed by the inevitable evil in a hostile world" (176). If this were the case, then would it not follow that the tragedy that unfolds in the latter half of the novel is a result of John's romantic tendencies or his stubborn adherence to a "chivalric code"?

If we accept this idea as a plausible explanation for the kinds of Mexicanness produced by McCarthy, we arrive at an interesting question to ponder: is the novel a demonstration of the dangers of steeping oneself too deeply in storybook values and of trying to live one's life in accordance with romantic ideals? The novel, after all, is called *All the Pretty Horses,* a title that suggests a childlike fascination with horses and a love of horses rooted in childhood; a love and fascination that could easily develop into a romanticization of the animals.[6] Such an idea is strengthened by a possible source of the title, an African American lullaby sung in the antebellum South:

> Hushaby, don't you cry.
> Go to sleepy, little baby.
> When you wake, you shall have cake,
> And all the pretty little horses.
> Blacks and bays, dapples and grays,
> Coach and six-a little horses.
> Way down yonder in the meadow,
> There's a poor little lambie;
> The bees and the butterflies pickin' out his eyes,
> The poor little thing cries, "Mammy."
> Hushaby, don't you cry,
> Go to sleepy, little baby.[7]

According to Rosalinda Méndez González, this lullaby "laments a black mother's inability to be with her newborn child through early motherhood and nursing because she had to tend to the baby of her mistress" (11). Such a lament resonates ironically with Cole's strained relationship with his own mother, who seems to have very little interest in mothering him, and the macabre image of the lamb having its eyes picked out by insects seems very McCarthyesque: the violence that frequently erupts and shatters the idealized dreams and innocence of his border heroes. More importantly, though, the allusion strengthens the notion that McCarthy intends to examine the tragic consequences that arise when one tries to carry storybook values over into adulthood. *All the Pretty Horses* is a coming-of-age novel, and John's maturation depends on the recognition of the destructive potential of his illusory ideals and romantic tendencies. This recognition can be isolated in his confession to the county judge in the fourth part of the novel. If we as readers recognize the danger of such thinking, then one could argue that, though still problematic, McCarthy's stereotypical Mexican representations are to a certain extent offset by a degree of self-reflexivity that problematizes them by calling attention to their discursive origins.

As long as the action of the novel remains north of the U.S.-Mexican border, the reader remains firmly grounded historically within the narrative's chronology of 1949–51, primarily through the use of technological markers. However, as the boys cross over into Mexico, they cross not only into a foreign country but also into the past, as well as into a picture-book landscape ("Drinking cactus juice in old Mexico," exults Rawlins shortly after the crossing [51]). Other critics have commented on the importance of the stark contrast between the United States and Mexico in the novel. Drawing on the work of Alan Cheuse, John Wegner suggests that for John Grady Cole, Mexico is attractive because it is a tabula rasa, a blank space on the map that has no past or history.[8] I would go a step farther and argue that for Cole and Rawlins Mexico is the past, albeit an ahistorical one. McCarthy re-creates the preindustrial world that they enter so vividly that it is a shock to the reader when the boys glimpse an automobile in a small town or when reference is made to Rocha's airplane. But what I find particularly fascinating is that the effect produced by these references is contrary to what one would logically expect: rather than call attention to the anachronistic nature of the preindustrial landscape through which the boys move, it is the cars and planes themselves that appear anachronistic, so deeply rooted are we in John Grady Cole's world of pretty horses. The farther into Mexico the Americans ride, the farther back in time they ride as well, culminating with their arrival at the hacienda, encompassing land home to wild, primordial horses that have never seen a man on foot. One could go so far as to say that—like Don Quixote—Cole's values and his entire adventure are anachronistic.

Wegner focuses on Dona Alfonsa's discussion of Francisco Madero and the Mexican Revolution as an attempt by McCarthy to offset Cole's perception of Mexico as a preindustrial oasis and write Mexico back into history, as well as to explain the lawless and impoverished Mexico that McCarthy presents to the reader. In other words, Mexico is impoverished and lawless because of the failure of the revolution to fulfill the idealistic goals of the Madero brothers. This is an intriguing notion, but it also implies that we look at what changes the revolution *did* bring about, as well as those it did not. Alfonsa's history lesson takes place on a massive cattle ranch owned by her family, a very unlikely possibility given the widespread land reappropriation and breakup of the hacienda system during the Cárdenas administration of the 1930s. So, although I agree with Wegner that Alfonsa's speech is an important historical marker in the text, its effect is both to heighten and to justify the fantastical nature of the Mexico that Alfonsa inhabits and that John Grady Cole moves through, rather than to work against such misrepresentation. Why do the boys go south instead of west? Nostalgia. They can't go west because the industrialization that followed on the heels of westward expansion during the nineteenth century has placed too many obstacles in their path and erased the storybook Wild West. (And, as McCarthy demonstrated so masterfully in *Blood Meridian,* there was never anything romantic about westward expansion and colonization.) That romantic, storybook landscape needs to be relocated in Mexico, where McCarthy's literary predecessors have established a formulaic tradition perfectly suited to his narrative designs: the primitive, preindustrial world where the infernal rests immediately beneath the fragile surface of paradise.

A final observation about the novel: in his last conversation with Rawlins, John says that he doesn't know where his country is or "what happens to country" (299). In this comment is the novel's most interesting irony. It is suggestive of the familiar story of the American male who leaves "civilization" behind to seek a different way of life in the "wilderness" but unwittingly becomes an agent of colonization, transforming his wilderness refuge into the very thing he had sought to escape. That John Grady Cole cannot make sense of it is perhaps indicative of his inability, despite all that has happened to him, to see that he and his romantic ideals are very much a part of what happens to country. Ultimately, McCarthy's Mexican novels fit neatly within the Infernal Paradise tradition, doing little to challenge its assumptions and conventions. Like his storyteller, the fallen priest, he has done a wonderful job of appearing to tell a different Mexican story, when in fact he has retold a very familiar one.

Notes

1. With *Infernal Paradise: Mexico and the Modern English Novel,* Ronald Walker was the first critic to delineate the prominence of this trope and discuss its implications. See also my extended discussion of this tradition in my book *The Aztec Palimpsest: Mexico in the Modern Imagination.*

2. *Cities of the Plain* uses these familiar conventions as well. If the Mexico in *All the Pretty Horses* was the traditional infernal paradise, in *Cities of the Plain* Mexico has become simply infernal, with the exception of the beautiful prostitute who lures John Grady Cole back. His death merely reinscribes the notion of Mexico as a violent and dangerous place.

3. Traven expert Karl S. Guthke has speculated that Traven himself may not have been sure who his parents were. For a fascinating discussion of the Traven mystery see Guthke's essay "In Search of B. Traven, Mystery Man," in his book *Trails in No-Man's Land: Essays in Cultural and Literary History* (114–32).

4. Those interested in examining the portrayal of Mexicanness in film should consult Juan R. García, "Hollywood and the West: Mexican Images in American Films, 1894–1983." I would also briefly point out that the Infernal Paradise conventions are a staple of Hollywood films set in Mexico; three well-known examples are Orson Welles's *Touch of Evil,* Sam Peckinpah's *The Wild Bunch,* and Oliver Stone's *Born on the Fourth of July.*

5. In an interesting comment on this same passage, Gail Moore Morrison has suggested that when John Grady Cole is put in charge of breeding Rocha's horses at the hacienda, he has the opportunity to try to bring the picture-book horses to life. Such a reading supports my view here that there is a tension in the novel between idealized visions and a not so ideal reality, as well as Cole's investment in romantic ideals.

6. One could go so far as to suggest that John Grady Cole not only romanticizes the horses but that he romances them as well. His interaction with the horses is always depicted in sensual, even sexual, terminology, and the narrative makes clear that in choosing Alejandra over the horses, Cole chooses the wrong lover. Ultimately, the horses remain faithful to him while Alejandra does not. There is also a suggestion that the horses reflect homoerotic desire: "What he loved in horses was what he loved in men, the blood and the heat of the blood that ran them. All his reverence and all his fondness and all the leanings of his life were for the ardenthearted and they would always be so and never be otherwise" (6).

7. Quoted in Rosalinda Méndez González, "Distinctions in Western Women's Experience: Ethnicity, Class, and Social Change." I thank Stephanie Athey for bringing this passage to my attention.

8. See Wegner, "Whose Story Is It?"

Works Cited

Cooper Alarcón, Daniel. *The Aztec Palimpsest: Mexico in the Modern Imagination.* Tucson: University of Arizona Press, 1997.

García, Juan R. "Hollywood and the West: Mexican Images in American Films, 1894–1983." *Old Southwest/New Southwest: Essays on a Region and Its Literature*. Ed. Judy Nolte Lensink. Tucson: Tucson Public Library, 1987. 74–90.

Greene, Graham. *The Power and the Glory*. 1940. New York: Penguin Books, 1986.

Gunn, Drewey Wayne. *American and British Writers in Mexico, 1556–1973*. Austin: University of Texas Press, 1974.

Guthke, Karl S. *B. Traven: The Life behind the Legends*. Chicago: Lawrence Hill, 1991.

———. *Trails in No-Man's-Land: Essays in Literary and Cultural History*. Columbia, S.C.: Camden, 1993.

Humboldt, Alexander von. *Political Essay on the Kingdom of New Spain*. Trans. John Black. 4 vols. London: Longman, 1811.

Huxley, Aldous. *Beyond the Mexique Bay*. New York: Harper, 1934.

Lawrence, D. H. *The Plumed Serpent*. 1926. New York: Vintage Books, 1959.

Lowry, Malcolm. *Selected Letters of Malcolm Lowry*. Ed. Harvey Breit and Margerie Bonner Lowry. New York: Capricorn, 1969.

———. *Under the Volcano*. 1947. New York: Penguin Books, 1986.

McCarthy, Cormac. *All the Pretty Horses*. New York: Alfred A. Knopf, 1992.

———. *Blood Meridian, or, The Evening Redness in the West*. New York: Random House, 1985.

———. *The Crossing*. New York: Alfred A. Knopf, 1994.

Méndez González, Rosalinda. "Distinctions in Western Women's Experience: Ethnicity, Class, and Social Change." *Feminist Frontiers IV*. Ed. Laurel Richardson. New York: McGraw Hill, 1997. 9–16.

Morrison, Gail Moore. "*All the Pretty Horses:* John Grady Cole's Expulsion from Paradise." *Perspectives on Cormac McCarthy*. Ed. Edwin T. Arnold and Dianne C. Luce. Jackson: University Press of Mississippi, 1993. 173–93.

O'Connor, Richard. *Ambrose Bierce: A Biography*. Boston: Little Brown, 1967.

Porter, Katherine Anne. *The Collected Stories of Katherine Anne Porter*. New York: Harcourt, 1979.

Pratt, Mary Louise. *Imperial Eyes: Travel Writing and Transculturation*. London: Routledge, 1992.

Prescott, W. H. *History of the Conquest of Mexico*. 1843. New York: Random House, 1951.

Rabasa, José. *Inventing America: Spanish Historiography and the Formation of Eurocentrism*. Norman: University of Oklahoma Press, 1993.

Stone, Robert. *Children of Light*. New York: Alfred A. Knopf, 1986.

Walker, Ronald G. *Infernal Paradise: Mexico and the Modern English Novel.* Berkeley: University of California Press, 1978.

Wegner, John. "Whose Story Is It?: History and Fiction in Cormac McCarthy's *All the Pretty Horses.*" *Southern Quarterly* 36.2 (1998): 103–10.

Wollen, Peter. "Tourism, Language, and Art." *New Formations* 12 (1990): 43–59.

"Blood is Blood"

All The Pretty Horses in the Multicultural Literature Class

Timothy P. Caron

CRITICS have examined Cormac McCarthy's novels from several perspectives, yielding particularly rich results in studying the historical antecedents and philosophical underpinnings of his work or contemplating his indebtedness to Faulkner, Melville, O'Connor, the Bible, and a host of other writers and texts. In addition, scholars are broadening the field of McCarthy studies, examining his work in the light of recent theoretical developments. McCarthy even has an entire web site and an online journal devoted to the discussion of his works. All of this is to say that critics have read McCarthy's works through a variety of lenses, but no one has yet considered him in the context of multiculturalism. Indeed, at first glance, Cormac McCarthy might seem like an odd choice as a subject for an essay on teaching an American multicultural literature class. After all, in the popular conception of the term, McCarthy is not even "multicultural." As a white male of Anglo-Irish extraction, he is not "ethnic" (i.e., Asian, Indian, African American, or Latino) in a way that most people would consider as "multicultural." Such narrow conceptions of multiculturalism reveal a type of essentialist thinking that is problematic, to say the least.

For instance, as my own American multicultural literature students often wonder, do only people of color have an ethnicity? In other words, is there such a thing as "white" ethnicity? Although McCarthy's *All the Pretty Horses* is not a self-conscious exploration of its author's ethnicity in the same way that *Beloved,* for example, is an expression and exploration of Toni Morrison's African American ethnicity, McCarthy's novel can be tremendously effective in a multicultural literature classroom. Specifically, the trials and tribulations of McCarthy's Texan hero, John Grady Cole, can serve as a sobering reminder to students of the peculiar peril—and promise—of encountering the cultural Other. In this essay, I explore the role McCarthy's novel played in my recent teaching of a course called "Contemporary Multicultural American Literature." *All the Pretty Horses* provided an excellent opportunity for the class to explore the dangers inherent within a border contact between two cultures and served as a paradigm for both teacher and students in what to do and not to do as we tried to fashion ourselves into what Gloria Anzaldúa calls *atravesados*—border-crossers.

THE CAMPUS, THE CLASS, AND SOUTHERN CALIFORNIA DEMOGRAPHICS

I first included McCarthy on a multicultural literature syllabus while I was teaching American literature at Biola University, a small, private, Christian, liberal-arts university in Los Angeles County whose student population is largely white.[1] Despite being located within what is arguably the most ethnically and culturally diverse metropolitan area in the United States, our campus is both ethnically and ideologically homogenous. This homogeneity results from the type of student that the university recruits—generally, middle- to upper-middle class Anglos from evangelical backgrounds. For instance, because the school does not actively recruit potential students from Catholic backgrounds, the percentage of Latino/a students will always necessarily be underrepresented on a campus situated in the heart of southern California. Likewise, the African American population is underrepresented because the school's faith strictures exclude students from the Holiness and Pentecostal movements.

Having just participated in a five-week NEH Summer Institute on multicultural American literature a few months before teaching this class, I was anxious to employ many of the curricular and pedagogical insights I had garnered over the summer.[2] However, I was seriously concerned if anyone would be interested in such a class at the university. After all, 70 percent of the total undergraduate population is white (Asian Americans constitute 13.75 percent of the student population, Latinos/as 7.37 percent, and African Americans 3.63 percent). The percentage of minority students who are also English majors is probably even lower than these campuswide statistics. In a class of sixteen (and one very white professor recently transplanted from Louisiana), only three minority students were enrolled: a young Afro-Caribbean woman and two Latinos.

After consulting, primarily through the Internet, with colleagues from around the country who teach at a variety of colleges and universities,[3] I began to realize just how distinctive my overwhelmingly Anglo class composition was with respect to the typical multicultural literature classroom experience. As I have mentioned, the class contained sixteen students, certainly not a staggering number, but an impressive one considering that the normal enrollment for upper-level classes in the English department is ten. This was also the first time such a class had ever been taught at the university.

These sixteen students seemed to realize the importance of a multicultural approach to their education. For the majority of the students, the class would not have many of the usual objectives of a standard multicultural curriculum; reading Amy Tan's *The Joy Luck Club,* Sandra Cisneros's *House on Mango Street,* Louise Erdrich's *Love Medicine,* and Toni Morrison's *Beloved* would not necessarily "foster the development of strong minority-cultural identities" (Wills 366) in the thirteen Anglo students. Rather, reading McCarthy in conjunction with these other authors would create a dialogue that would help students better understand as many facets as possible of the multicultural world in which we already live. Nowhere is the importance of learning these lessons more immediate than in southern California. Currently Los Angeles County is 43.5 percent Latino, 35.1 percent white, 9.9 percent black, and 11.4 percent Asian; however, by the year 2040 Los

Angeles is predicted to be 69.1 percent Latino, 13.8 percent white, 6 percent black, and 10.9 percent Asian (Hicks M1). Experts predict that a similar changing demographic will be reflected behind the "Orange Curtain" of Orange County, the county just south of Los Angeles. Orange County is currently 59 percent white, 27 percent Latino, 12 percent Asian, and 2 percent black, but by the year 2020 Orange County will be 41 percent Latino, 40 percent white, 15 percent Asian, and 3 percent black (Grad A1). Although the campus is situated within this increasingly diverse geography, it remains insulated from outside influences. Students speak of the "Biola bubble," and it was my explicit and expressed intent to render the "bubble" a semipermeable barrier, at the very least.

Because this class was overwhelmingly Anglo (myself included), I sought to construct a framework that would orient students in what was for many of them their first exposure to ethnic writing. The course was constructed around the theme of "borders," and one of our first class meetings was dedicated to a discussion of a student presentation on Gloria Anzaldúa's *Borderlands/La Frontera*. Anzaldúa's work forced the students to reconceptualize their ideas of minority writing and multiculturalism. Students were compelled to think of the benefits of occupying a border position. As Anzaldúa so powerfully demonstrates, borders not only separate but also join. True, borders are primarily areas of contestation and violence, but borders are also those special areas where hybrids flourish, where new languages and new cultures are born. After being exposed to Anzaldúa's work, students were forced to rethink popular conceptions of the phrase "multicultural author": those whom students had thought of as whiners seeking special consideration slowly became transformed in most students' minds into proud claimers of an individual heritage. Misperceptions that multiculturalism meant doing away with Hawthorne and Melville in favor of speech codes and propaganda gave way to a willingness to explore the "borders" of the known and the given regarding America's literatures.

While Anzaldúa forced students to recognize the "borders" of American literature, Héctor Calderón's essay "Reinventing the Border" invited them to imaginatively occupy that border, to realize that the hyphen in so many hyphenated-Americans' designations is not a divider but a link. Calderón's personal reminiscences of his child-hood demonstrated the vibrancy and cultural creativity of occupying the literal border of the United States and Mexico, and his essay modeled an investigative attitude for studying the cultural and ethnic "borders" we would explore. His essay echoed and amplified many of Anzaldúa's insights, an important contribution because, to be honest, many of the students flinched in the face of her militant sexual politics. For the students there were no "distractions" in Calderón's essay, as there were in Anzaldúa's. Thankfully, after having read many of the same ideas in what was for them a more palatable format, most of the students then came to understand more fully and appreciate more closely the role that sexuality plays in Anzaldúa's politics. Furthermore, his investigation of one of her key terms provided us with a specific metaphor that challenged the class throughout the semester: his work offered a challenge to each of us to become an atravesado, a border-crosser. Most of us could never embody the term in the way that Anzaldúa does because we were not products of a *mestizo* culture, as she and Calderón are; however, we could, and did, pledge ourselves to becoming atravesados in the sense in which Calderón uses the term. Not only would we become more aware of and sensitive to borders and boundaries, but we would also commit to becoming informed travelers across borders.

MCCARTHY IN THE MULTICULTURAL MIX

As a novice in the teaching of multicultural American literature, I copied four of the class's novels from the previous summer's NEH Summer Institute: Cisneros's *House on Mango Street;* Tan's *The Joy Luck Club;* Erdrich's *Love Medicine;* and Morrison's *Beloved.* A posting I had listed on an online discussion group of American litera-ture teachers had challenged me to examine Anglo writers as also being a part of the American multicultural literary mosaic. Given the makeup of the class, I also wanted a novel whose main character leaves behind his homeland and encounters the cultural and ethnic Other. *All the Pretty Horses* fulfilled all of these needs. McCarthy's novel provided a solid foundation for the course as we began interrogating John Grady Cole's reasons for traveling to Mexico, his romanticized expectations, and how his lack of knowledge of Mexican history and customs causes so much pain for him.

Our reading and close study of the book allowed us, by examining the case of our young, lovesick hero, to wonder how much historical, contextualizing knowledge must we have before we can understand others and their cultures. For instance, his brutal experiences in Mexico teach John Grady that simply loving horses as much as Alejandra's father, Don Rocha, does, will not make him an acceptable suitor; in a similar manner, what abstract (and often naive) ideals must we as students of literature be willing to move beyond to forge real and lasting literary relationships across cultures? How much truth is there in the vaquero's statement that a man is formed by the land in which he is born (226)? If these men speak truly, what can we do realistically to bridge cultural and ethnic literary borders? These are important questions when we remember that Cole tells Lacey Rawlins that he has no "country" after crossing back from Mexico to Texas (299). Given this conclusion, why does John Grady Cole set out so confidently for Mexico with a "blank map" (34)? How much of that map, and ours, has to be filled in with historical and cultural knowledge? Isn't that what the *dueña* is trying to tell Cole as she explains to him why she will never allow Alejandra to marry him by telling him of the Mexican Revolution? Last, what limits and chauvinisms would an "American" novel with so much Spanish in it force us to confront and, we hope, move beyond?

JOHN GRADY COLE, LACEY RAWLINS, AND JIMMY BLEVINS CROSS THE BORDER

When John Grady Cole sets out for Mexico with his best friend, Lacey Rawlins, and the tag-along Jimmy Blevins, John Grady is the only one of them who speaks Spanish fluently. His *abuela* has taught him the language, but she has not taught him of Mexico. At the conclusion of the first chapter, it seems as if Cole's and Rawlins's romanticized notions were accurate. As they are drifting off to sleep in the bunkhouse at La

Purisima, Rawlins asks, "How long do you think you'd like to stay here?" and Cole replies, "About a hundred years" (96). The boys seem to have found a place that transcends culture, for, as Rawlins says in the bunkhouse, the Mexican vaqueros are "some good old boys," just like themselves (96). But the boys are experiencing only a short grace period because the course of events that will send them to the hellish prison at Saltillo has already been set in motion. McCarthy underscores Cole's and Rawlins's ignorance of Mexico in a conversation the boys have shortly after they arrive at the prison: Rawlins says, "I never knowed there was such a place as this," and Cole replies, "I guess there's probably every kind of place you can think of." Rawlins seems to give voice to both boys' unfamiliarity in his final words in the conversation, "I wouldn't of thought of this one" (184).

Given the fact that the boys first undertake their journey with "an oilcompany roadmap that Rawlins had picked up" (34) at a cafe, it is little wonder that they so quickly "lose their way" once they cross the border, set loose as they are from the familiar culture of their native Texas. This map, which shows "roads and rivers and towns on the American side of the map as far south as the Rio Grande and beyond that all was white," perfectly emblematizes their unfamiliarity with Mexico and its geography, culture, and heritage. John Grady Cole does have a map of Mexico, and he traces their route for his friend. Again, it is the more talkative Rawlins who speaks for them both when, looking at the map, he says, "There ain't shit down there" (34). Even a map that shows Mexican towns, roads, and topographical features remains essentially blank to the boys because of their nationalistic attitudes; Mexico remains an empty space onto which they project their ideas of a cowboy's perfect paradise. As Alan Cheuse puts it, John Grady and Rawlins seek "freedom from the old well-marked Texas spaces in the possibilities of an undiscovered country" (141). The problem, of course, is that Mexico is not "an undiscovered country," and the boys' ignorance of this fact will cost them dearly. In a real sense, their imprisonment at Saltillo is a direct result of the boys' simple nativistic pride.

Most of my students were experienced enough as readers to realize the significance of this textual moment in McCarthy's novel. In our discussions of this passage, students went on to ask two questions: thinking like atravesados in training, the class wondered what the implications might be of crossing a border with a blank map. We began to wonder about the romanticized conceptions that John Grady Cole and Lacey Rawlins have of Mexico. How much of their trouble in Mexico is caused by those idealized notions? This led to a second question—do John Grady Cole and Lacey Rawlins view Mexico in exactly the same way? What attitudes might both boys share, and are there any differences in their outlooks?

We decided that despite the boys' similar expectations, there are important differences between them, especially regarding their attitudes toward the Mexicans themselves. For instance, although Rawlins thinks that the vaqueros on Don Rocha's ranch are "good old boys," he still shows some anxiety that he will become tainted after his blood transfusions in the prison hospital. Cole reassures him, "Blood's blood. It don't know where it came from" (210–11). This conversation resonates with one of the great themes of *All the Pretty Horses*, for John Grady is only partially correct. Blood is blood, and it does not know where it comes from. In a literal sense, there is no such thing as "Mexican blood," and Rawlins need not fear that some sort of latent "Mexicanness" will be transmitted to him through his transfusion. However, for Don Rocha, for Dueña Alfonsa, and, ultimately, for Alejandra, there is such a thing as Mexican blood. As Gail Moore Morrison has pointed out in her essay "*All the Pretty Horses*: John Grady Cole's Expulsion from Paradise," there is a richly ironic parallel between Don Rocha's attempts to "produce a superior cutting horse by crossing his quarter horse mares with a thoroughbred stallion" and his refusal to condone a "similar experiment in cross-breeding between his daughter Alejandra and the Texas import" John Grady Cole (178–79). After Alejandra confesses that she and Cole have been lovers, Don Rocha turns the boys over to the military authorities, who eventually send the Americans to the Saltillo prison. Don Rocha shows that he will go to great lengths to prevent the "dilution" of his family's bloodlines.

Given his temperament, his background, and his social position, Don Rocha could hardly be expected to act otherwise; John Grady shows a similarly predictable doggedness in his relentless pursuit of a doomed love affair with Alejandra. Despite his extraordinary horse skills, John Grady has not yet acquired the simple wisdom of the vaqueros, who know that it is "no accident of circumstance that a man be born in a certain country and not some other and they said that the weathers and seasons that form a land form also the inner fortunes of men in their generations and are passed on to their children and are not so easily come by otherwise" (226). Shaped and molded by the American West's "weathers and seasons," by its emphasis on independence and insistence that ability should overcome class distinctions, John Grady Cole expects his suit to be successful. It is the *dueña*, however, who reminds him that he is in "another country" now (136). Even Alejandra realizes that their love will not be able to overcome cultural obstacles, both at the beginning of their relationship when John Grady Cole sees in "her face and in her figure something he'd not seen before and the name of that thing was sorrow," (140) and at the end of their affair when Alejandra says, "I cannot do what you ask. . . . I love you. But I cannot" (254). Tom Pilkington, in his essay "Fate and Free Will on the American Frontier: Cormac McCarthy's Western Fiction," sums up their inability to overcome the "inner fortunes" bequeathed to them by their respective countries: "Alejandra ends the affair because she is the daughter of her family, class, and nationality. . . . She acknowledges the limitations on individual human action, the obduracy of centuries-old conventions and customs" (320). On the other hand, John Grady Cole is a "*norteamericano*. He believes in individualism, free will, volition. He thinks every man . . . is an Adam, free of memory and external constraint, able to shape his illimitable 'self' in any way he chooses. He is shocked when Alejandra refuses to break all ties to go with him" (320). It was at this reading moment that the class began to clearly see how comparable their views and attitudes were to John Grady's. Almost all of them were hopeful of a "happily ever after" ending where John Grady Cole and Alejandra get married and live the rest of their lives in domestic bliss. Few were prepared for the novel's resolution, which seems to suggest that love simply cannot overcome every barrier.

One of the primary means by which McCarthy suggests humanity's inability to make such happy connections across borders lies in the novel's distinction between the innate nobility of horses and the fallen nature of the men who ride them. As Luis, the *mozo*, says, "the horse shares a common soul and its separate life only forms it out of all horses and makes it mortal" (111). It is significant that it is John Grady Cole who asks if the same is true for men, if there is some link that binds one man to another, some common soul, for if there is a common bond among men, then there is some hope for making himself into a legitimate suitor for Alejandra in Don Rocha's eyes. Luis replies that "among men there was no such communion as among horses and the notion that men can be understood at all was probably an illusion" (111). It seems that if men identify with one another at all in *All the Pretty Horses,* they share only a common extinction. The Indians who lurk at the margins of the novel underscore this point. Immediately following his grandfather's funeral, Cole has a spectral vision of the Comanches who once held the land he himself longs to inherit. McCarthy's evocation of the ghostly procession of Comanches, "lost to all history and all remembrance like a grail the sum of their secular and transitory and violent lives" (5), is a dark foreboding of Cole's own eventual outcast condition. As Gail Moore Morrison notes, *All the Pretty Horses* opens and closes with John Grady Cole among the ghostly presence of Indians, suggesting that he will share their fate (177–78): a lonely, nomadic existence on the fringes of society. This connection is made explicit by Cole's father, when he says in his final conversation with his son, "We're like the Comanches was two hundred years ago. We dont know what's goin to show up here come daylight. We dont even know what color they'll be" (25–26). Cole's father has survived a World War II prison camp, only to return to a cowboy world that no longer exists, a fate sadly parallel to his son's. If our analysis of *All the Pretty Horses* had ended here, the cultural work that I imagined the course performing might never have happened; the students might never have believed in the possibility or desirability of crossing borders, both in literature and life.

The novel, then, seems to offer little hope for successfully crossing cultural boundaries. For all of his efforts, and despite his genuine love for Alejandra, *All the Pretty Horses* ends with John Grady Cole's riding off into the sunset, taking cold comfort from his stoic resignation to live by a code of honor in a "world that was rushing away and seemed to care nothing for the old or the young or rich or poor or dark or pale. . . . Nothing for their struggles, nothing for their names. Nothing for the living or the dead" (301). Not only has he lost the love of his life, but John Grady Cole has also lost something that is distinctively "American" after crossing the border and coming back. In his final conversation with Rawlins when they are reunited in Texas, Cole responds to Rawlins's pronouncement that "this is still good country" by saying, "Yeah, I know it is. But it aint my country." When asked where his "country" is now, the world-weary John Grady can only respond, "I dont know where it is. I dont know what happens to country" (299). Without further investigation, the novel seems to offer only one example of domination and displacement after another: the Comanches are pushed aside because of America's "Manifest Destiny," and now John Grady is a historical relic, still riding a horse while his rival for Mary Catherine's affection is driving a truck and Don Rocha flies to his ranch in his personal airplane.

Such a reading runs contrary to the popular conception of a warm, fuzzy multiculturalism, too often fiercely lampooned in cloying imitations of Rodney King's now infamous question, "Can't we all just get along?" *All the Pretty Horses* seems to suggest that, no, we can't all just get along; we are condemned to live in a world of violence, mayhem, and bloodshed. Richard B. Woodward's article "Cormac McCarthy's Venomous Fiction" quotes McCarthy saying as much: "There's no such thing as life without bloodshed. . . . I think the notion that the species can be improved in some way, that everyone could live in harmony, is a really dangerous idea. Those who are afflicted with this notion are the first ones to give up their souls, their freedom. Your desire that it be that way will enslave you and make your life vacuous" (36).

The novels of the Border Trilogy—*All the Pretty Horses, The Crossing,* and *Cities of the Plain*—along with their "prequel," *Blood Meridian,* seem to exemplify this bleak view of borders. All of these novels document the violence that often occurs along borders, for as

Gloria Anzaldúa reminds us, our borders are often contested sites, especially the borders of the Southwest where "death is no stranger" (Anzaldúa 4). Perhaps the conversation between John Grady Cole and Pérez inside the prison expresses something close to McCarthy's sentiments in this interview. Cole steadfastly maintains that "somebody runs the show," that there must be some ordering principle, even in an environment as chaotic as Saltillo, and Pérez responds, "this confinement . . . gives a false impression. As if things are in control" (195).

Cautious Optimism

To be sure, the class, both students and professor, struggled with McCarthy's statements on humanity's inability to make connections across borders. I began to wonder if I had chosen the best text to demonstrate the possibility of becoming an atravesado. But the reading is just the beginning, for the interpretation, the working through of issues and ideas, continues long after closing the covers of one of his novels. Class discussion, even while ostensibly discussing other works, continued to return to *All the Pretty Horses*. Students reinterrogated the text long after we had moved on because John Grady Cole's situation seemed so analogous to their own. As Anglos themselves, many asked how they were to make contact with the cultural Other. As I have mentioned, the campus is primarily white but is situated in the extremely ethnically and culturally diverse greater Los Angeles metropolitan area. Could McCarthy's work, in conjunction with the other authors from the syllabus, help students to move outside of what students themselves call the "Biola bubble?" I think so, because discussing McCarthy's fictionalized border violence sensitized them to conflicts throughout the Los Angeles area while heightening their awareness of tensions on the campus itself within that "bubble."

As we read other literary and theoretical works, the class continued to return to McCarthy's novel, which seemed to run contrary to so much of the class's attitude and intention. Finally, it began to dawn on us that our individual readings of *All the Pretty Horses* were not nearly as disheartening as our classroom discussions of the novel or as dark as the author's comments on his own works. We had overlooked key passages during our in-class analysis of the novel that suggest that there can be moments of connection, even in a world of alienation and loneliness. Long after the class periods set aside for discussing McCarthy's novel, we remembered the powerfully understated scene of John Grady's father giving his son the brand-new saddle; John Grady's heroic refusal to abandon Jimmy Blevins once they cross the border; and, perhaps greatest of all, John Grady's courageous decision to retrieve "all the pretty horses." These incidents, and others, began to suggest to us a reading strategy and an unforeseen connection between John Grady Cole and ourselves. Our young hero—and John Grady was a hero to many in the class—refused to lose heart in the world completely, for despite all of the cruelties that befall him and the "loneliness" that causes him to feel "wholly alien to the world," "he loved it still" (282). We began to realize that there is much to admire in John Grady's steadfast refusal to abandon his ideals. Borrowing from our hero's compromised idealism, many students began to construct their own cautious optimism. Learning from John Grady's mistakes, students began the hard work of making themselves into atravesados—border-crossers, but with their eyes wide open.

Cole's strength of character derives from his love of horses. For him, the horse embodies all that is good and noble within this world. One of the few glimpses McCarthy allows us into John Grady's soul is the dream we read of where he runs with the horses:

> and in the dream he was among the horses running and in the dream he himself could run with the horses . . . and [they] trampled down the flowers in a haze of pollen that hung in the sun like powdered gold and they ran he and the horses out along the high mesas where the ground resounded under their running hooves and they flowed and changed and ran and their manes and tails blew off of them like spume and there was nothing else at all in that high world and they moved all of them in a resonance that was like a music among them and they were none of them afraid horse nor colt nor mare and they ran in

resonance which is the world itself and which cannot be spoken but only praised. (161–62)

Even in a world as coldly cruel as the one that John Grady Cole inhabits, he does find some transcendence, some hope for something pure and uncompromised and beautiful. We should also remember that what John Grady "loved in horses was what he loved in men, the blood and the heat of the blood that ran them . . . and [that] all the leanings of his life were for the ardenthearted and they would always be so and never be otherwise" (6). Many students from the class were eagerly awaiting McCarthy's concluding volume of the Border Trilogy, anxious to see if John Grady's love of horses has made him any more ready to love other people.

"WHITE GUY WITH A TAN"?

I mentioned toward the beginning of this essay that the multicultural class had three "ethnic" students. Perhaps a more accurate accounting would be two: an Afro-Caribbean woman, a Latino, and one young man who, until enrolling in the class, considered himself a "white guy with a tan," a phrase he used to describe himself in one of the semester's early essays in which students were asked to explore their ethnicity. This student originally came to the conclusion that he had no real Latino ethnicity. After all, he was not even really bilingual. Jon's father is of total Mexican extraction while his mother is Anglo. Growing up in San Diego, Jon never considered himself as anything but an Anglo, too. Jon was in exactly the same situation as most of the other students; the Mexico of McCarthy's *All the Pretty Horses,* along with its people, culture, and language, were as foreign to him as to any gringo in the class. In fact, Jon confided in me that coming to this conclusion while reading the novel served as further impetus for him to undertake his own border crossing. Jon decided to travel to Mexico to search for his cultural and ethnic roots.

Following his graduation, Jon set out for Mexico and traveled for two months by himself, going all the way from Mexico City to the Yucatán peninsula and back again. Jon, however, had learned from many of John Grady's mistakes and, as a result, was a much better atravesado. Jon spent the months between his college graduation and his departure learning Spanish and reading about Mexican culture and customs. In fact, his first reason for traveling to Mexico was to enroll in a Spanish language school, hoping to immerse himself in the language. He was quickly discouraged, however, when he realized that the only people he would meet at the language school were other students like himself who were just as unfamiliar with Mexico. Ironically, he found himself having to drop out of language school to learn more about Mexico. Jon's immersion then became complete because he saw a Mexico outside the walls of the language institute, one that does not appear on a tourist's itinerary. He rode the buses, he ate at roadside cafes, and he occasionally slept on beaches.

I have talked with Jon several times since his return from Mexico, and he says he no longer considers himself a "white guy with a tan." What Jon realized was that his roots are firmly planted on both sides of the border. I will always remember his description of the moment of this realization, an insight that came to him as he was sitting one evening in a Mexican cantina. As he observed the amorous advances of a young man toward a young woman, Jon said that this was the moment he most distinctly felt his own "Mexicanness" because the scene caused him to reconstruct imaginatively what his own paternal grandfather and grandmother's first meeting might have been like. The scene helped him visualize his own family's distinct, and not so distant, Mexican heritage. Some might object that Jon's claims to a Mexican ethnic identity are spurious or based on some Americanized version of Mexico. What is not to be overlooked, however, is the fact that a young man who would have once been happy to have his ethnicity boiled away in the American melting pot is now actively reconstructing his heritage.

Like Jon, the rest of the class never forgot McCarthy, and his work served the useful purpose of tempering our initial optimism and reminding us of the hard work of being full-time atravesados. Given McCarthy's reluctance to talk to the press, we cannot really know with absolute certainty his thoughts on topics like multiculturalism. Despite the bleak nature of the views expressed in the *New York Times Magazine* article, I still maintain that *All the Pretty Horses* serves a tremendous pedagogical function in a multicultural literature class: the novel allows us to understand better the skills necessary to become true border-crossers.

ACKNOWLEDGMENTS

I would like to thank John Wegner and Mel Sanchez for sharing their ideas with me during the writing of this essay. John shared his encyclopedic knowledge of McCarthy and his works, while Mel reminded me that no one crosses borders innocently. I could not ask for better or more willing students than Peter Falk, Marla Grupe, Lance Kayser, Chris Lindley, Jim Mayer, Heather Shook, Veronica Shuffield, Sarah Siebert, Corrie Stanley, Ernestienne Woodstock, Jodie Mugavero, Jon Teran, Shari Kinneman, Juan Sanchez, Matt Silva, and Julie Hunsaker. I continue to learn from them and our experiences together.

Notes

1. I have now completed my third year at California State University, Long Beach, and I continue to include McCarthy in my multicultural American literature syllabi. Although the student population is much more diverse at Long Beach State, *All the Pretty Horses* still serves the same highly useful purpose of investigating the ideas and attitudes inherent in crossing cultural borders.

2. This five-week Summer Institute at the University of California, Irvine, "Bridging the Gaps: Critical Theory, American Literature, and American Cultures," was under the direction of John Carlos Rowe and featured guest theorists Lindon Barrett, A. LaVonne Brown Ruoff, Catherine Stimpson, Gerald Graff, and Paul Lauter. The institute brought together Southern California educators from high schools, community colleges, and colleges and universities to build bridges across segmental lines and to investigate new methods of incorporating multicultural texts and current trends in critical theory into our classrooms.

3. Thanks to all of the participants on the T-AMLIT listserv who helped me to construct this first class in contemporary multiethnic literature. Kara Provost and Ed Gallagher were very helpful in suggesting texts and critical articles. Gregory S. Jay was particularly kind and posted his entire course syllabus for his "Fictions of Multiculturalism" course on the listserv.

Works Cited

Anzaldúa, Gloria. *Borderlands/La Frontera*. San Francisco: Aunt Lute Publishing, 1987.

Calderón, Héctor. "Reinventing the Border." *American Mosaic: Multicultural Readings in Context*. 2d ed. Ed. Barbara Roche Rico and Sandra Mano. Boston: Houghton Mifflin, 1995. 512–20.

Cheuse, Alan. "A Note on the Landscape in *All the Pretty Horses*." *Southern Quarterly* 30.4 (1992): 140–42.

Grad, Shelby. "O.C. Latinos to Outnumber Whites by 2020." *Los Angeles Times* (Orange County Edition), 23 July 1997: A1.

Hicks, Joe R. "The Changing Face of America." *Los Angeles Times* (Orange County Edition), 20 July 1997: M1.

McCarthy, Cormac. *All the Pretty Horses*. New York: Alfred A. Knopf, 1992.

Morrison, Gail Moore. "*All the Pretty Horses:* John Grady Cole's Expulsion from Paradise." *Perspectives on Cormac McCarthy*. Ed. Edwin T. Arnold and Dianne C. Luce. Jackson: University Press of Mississippi, 1993.

Pilkington, Tom. "Fate and Free Will on the American Frontier: Cormac McCarthy's Western Fiction." *Western American Literature* 27.4 (1993): 311–22.

Wills, John S. "Who Needs Multicultural Education? White Students, U.S. History, and the Construction of a Usable Past." *Anthropology and Education Quarterly* 27.3 (1996): 365–89.

Woodward, Richard B. "Cormac McCarthy's Venomous Fiction." *New York Times Magazine,* 19 Apr. 1992: 28–31, 36, 40.

The Cave of Oblivion

Platonic Mythology in *Child of God*

Dianne C. Luce

MURDERING necrophile who lives in caves, hoarding the bodies of his victims as material possessions, Lester Ballard mystifies both his neighbors and the reader. Although his progression in misguided deeds follows a logic of escalation, the narrative offers little grist for the psychoanalysis of its murderer such as that provided by, for instance, Faulkner's *Light in August*. Indeed, Robert Coles remarked in his review of *Child of God* that Cormac McCarthy "seems not to wish our twentieth-century psychological sensibility to influence his work" (87). And Vereen Bell writes, "McCarthy offers nothing in the foreground that would explain him [Lester Ballard], has the good sense not to want to" (61). One may wonder, too, at the contrast between the extremity of Lester's acts and the restraint with which McCarthy presents them; the imagery of murder and necrophilia is handled with exquisite delicacy compared to the imagery of death and gore assaulting the reader's imagination in *Blood Meridian*. Moreover, the novel's title and the narrator's challenge to the reader to identify with Lester (a "child of God much like yourself perhaps" [4]) cannot be dismissed as merely ironic or cynical.

Child of God is undeniably rich in concrete and historical details
that are amenable to empirical verification and that are drawn from
McCarthy's reading or experience. The caves underlying Sevier County,
Tennessee, which form a locus for much of the significant action of the
novel, are verifiable in all their mineral and organic details. Thomas
Barr's 1961 geological survey *Caves of Tennessee* describes nearly every
feature of the cave formations and the animal life in Lester's underground world, and, conversely, McCarthy weaves into his novel each
creature Barr has documented inhabiting the caves of east Tennessee.[1]
K. Wesley Berry has shown that "Ballard's stomping grounds" in southwestern Sevier County can be mapped through the novel's vegetation
and topographical imagery, "even without the help of place names"
(73). Furthermore, as in the spring of Lester's twenty-seventh year
(126), Sevierville flooded regularly until the Little Pigeon River was
widened and rechanneled in 1967 in a TVA flood-protection program.
Floods of fourteen to eighteen feet were recorded in 1875, 1896, 1920,
1928, 1957 (the most likely date for the main action of *Child of God*),[2]
twice in the spring of 1963 (when McCarthy himself was living in
Sevierville), and finally in 1965 (Fox A5). Mr. Wade's reminiscences
about the nineteenth-century White Caps and Bluebills (165–68) can
be traced to historical sources such as Thomas H. Davis's *The Sevier
County White-Caps* (1899) and later revisions of it by Cas Walker: *The
White Caps of Sevier County* (1937, 1974).[3] Lester's murders may be
based partly on the *Chattanooga Daily Times* reports of the murders
of a teenaged couple parked near Lookout Mountain, of which a young
carpenter named James Blevins was accused and tried in the 1960s; on
the treatments of serial killer Ed Gein in journalism and in Robert
Bloch's *Psycho* (1959); and to Alfred Hitchcock's film of the same name
(1960).[4] And many of the details of Lester's motives and behavior relating to necrophilia are drawn from the studies of necrophiles in R. E. L.
Masters and Eduard Lea's curious 1963 compendium *Sex Crimes in
History*, a survey of sexual deviancy that draws on literary and historical accounts as well as psychological profiles, mostly European, but
that includes few modern clinical case studies.[5]

According to Masters and Lea, the necrophile who murders to
obtain corpses is rare and seldom manifests the psychology of the more

common necrophile. They distinguish between the "true necrophile" and the necro-sadist, who might murder and then sexually assault his victim: "The sex act he [the necro-sadist] performs is usually only an extension of his violation of his victim. The necrophile, on the other hand, is often quite incapable of making an effective sexual approach, and especially a sadistic one, to a living person" (116). In *Child of God*, McCarthy departs from the most typical profile, inventing in Lester that rare case of the true necrophile who also murders. The opportunism of Lester's first necrophilic experience identifies him as a genuine necrophile, and his later turning to murder is prompted by his despair of making human contact, his distrust of others, and his pent-up rage. Except perhaps in his attempted murder of Greer, Lester kills as a means to an end, and he is not motivated by the desire to mutilate and destroy, as is the necro-sadist. Granted, Lester's passionate behavior with his first body may have been partially suggested by a detail from the classic case of Sergeant Bertrand, a necro-sadist who described his first sexual experience with an exhumed body: "all the joy procured by possession of a living woman was as nothing in comparison with the pleasure I felt. I showered kisses upon all parts of her body, pressed her to my heart with a madman's frenzy. I overwhelmed her with the most passionate caresses" (Masters and Lea 121–22). However, Lester's scenes of passion are more reverent; and far from mutilating his bodies, as Bertrand always did, he tries against all odds and time to preserve them. He manifests some of the behaviors of the true necrophile Giuseppe Alessandro, who was witnessed passionately kissing a corpse "dressed in an elaborate silken gown with a strand of pearls about its neck" and who, it was discovered, had "disinterred her body and with superhuman strength transported her coffin over the mountains" (Masters and Lea 222).[6]

The experiences that lead to Lester's necrophilia also resemble those of the true necrophiles reported by Masters and Lea, many of whom had lost parents to death when they were young, and for whom the corpse represented the lost mother. The case of Victor Ardisson, particularly, may inform the dynamics of Lester's relationship with the dumpkeeper's daughters and the scantily dressed woman he finds asleep on the road:

> He proposed marriage to the girls of the place, but was
> ridiculed by them. It is not proved that he ever thereupon tried
> to rape a girl.
>
> As a substitute, he would follow the girls when they went to
> urinate, and masturbate at the same time. (124)

Lester's voyeurism, his confusion in the face of death and his painful
confrontations with women—all factors contributing to his
necrophilia—are as grounded in realism as are the caves in which he
dwells. But much of the novel's power comes from McCarthy's con-
joining these realistic elements to exploit their mythic or allegorical
import.[7] As in many of his novels, McCarthy's strategy in *Child of God*
is to employ mythic images and patterns to transcend the material body
of the referential world, inviting allegorical readings and guiding the
reader to ponder metaphysical issues. In *Child of God*, metaphysical
concerns cluster more consistently around analogues to Platonic myth
than around the Christian mythology consonant with either Lester's
background or McCarthy's Roman Catholic heritage.

The influence of Plato on McCarthy's thought was documented
biographically by Garry Wallace in 1992. With his companion Betty
Carey, Wallace traveled to El Paso in 1989 to meet with Carey's friend
Cormac McCarthy about a book she hoped to write. There they also
met book dealer and professor of philosophy Irving Brown, who
apparently spoke with McCarthy regularly and who told Wallace that
"in his opinion McCarthy had over-read Plato" (Wallace 135). Whether
or not McCarthy is guilty of over-reading, he clearly engages Platonic
philosophy in many of his works from *Outer Dark* (1968) on,
beginning with Culla Holme's dream of being told by a prophet that
he might be among the souls who will be "cured" (5). In Plato's *Gorgias*
myth, the myth of the day of judgment, only those souls who after death
are judged capable of cure are subject to purification in "the prison-
house of just retribution, which men call Tartarus" and subsequent
incarnation as men (Stewart 134). The incurable are incarnated as
lower life forms. After *The Orchard Keeper*, McCarthy's novels, in
which his seeking or drifting protagonists are depicted in terms of
quests or antiquests, explore, with varying degrees of realistic

grounding, his great underlying concern with the soul's struggling toward or at least as often blundering away from the healing spiritual insight of which it is capable (although he rarely directly invokes the theological concept of spirit).[8] With some crucial differences, this is also the burden of Plato's myths relating to the soul's progress (or lack thereof) back toward the Truth or the Light to which it was exposed at its creation: a progress involving sequential incarnations of the soul, intervening purifications in the cave of Tartarus, the soul's choice of the circumstances of its next life in accord with the wisdom achieved in Tartarus, its subjection to forgetfulness through imbibing the waters of Lethe, and then its incarnation in "the cave of this world"—"a cave of forgetfulness" or oblivion.

In his 1904 translation and commentary *The Myths of Plato,* revised and reissued in 1960, just a few years before McCarthy was to break forth in fiction, J. A. Stewart shows that while the individual myths embedded in Plato's dialogues are shaped to advance specific arguments, together they form a rather cohesive whole illustrating Plato's cosmology, ontology, and epistemology. Furthermore, Plato's myths profoundly inform Dante's cosmology and his emphasis on the soul's progress in the Divine Comedy, which some reviewers and scholars have seen as analogous to McCarthy's work.[9] Stewart writes that the "theological doctrine of Purgatory, to which Dante gives such noble imaginative expression, is alien to the Hebrew spirit, and came to the Church mainly from the Platonic doctrine of purification" (145). McCarthy understands this resonance between Plato and Dante and employs it throughout his fiction, and that phenomenon, together with his uses of various Platonic and Neoplatonic myths discussed by Stewart, suggests that Stewart's study may be one source of McCarthy's extensive knowledge of Plato.[10]

McCarthy's philosophy is no clone of Plato's, but he shares Plato's emphasis on the importance of the search for value and meaning, and in several works (most notably *Child of God, Outer Dark,* and *Blood Meridian,* but also to some degree in *Suttree* and the Border Trilogy) he evokes the Platonic/Dantean notion of earthly life as a purgatorial experience. Rarely, however, does McCarthy directly invoke the notion of an afterlife or a cycle of reincarnation. (Indeed, when John

Grady Cole dreams of the murdered Jimmy Blevins, Blevins tells him that being dead is "like nothing at all" [*All the Pretty Horses* 225].) McCarthy's novels remain grounded in the life humans experience in this world. He honors the naturalistic world and the world of human culture for good or ill far more than Plato, who, at least for the sake of his philosophical argument, tends to dismiss the material world as illusion at worst or to value selected elements of it as symbols of the Ideal world at best. Nevertheless, in *Child of God* particularly, McCarthy employs elements of Platonic myth to define the metaphysical dimensions of Lester Ballard's trials and crimes, exploring this aspect of his experience more fully than the psychological dimension. In the reading that follows, my intention is not to equate McCarthy's philosophy with Plato's, but to accept McCarthy's implicit invitation to contemplate Lester Ballard through Plato's myths.

FAILURE OF VISION AND THE LOVE OF MATERIAL BODIES

As Lester Ballard's scuttling in darkness through caves would suggest, McCarthy's analogies to Plato's myths largely cluster around problems of vision, and the cave parable is most obviously invoked. When Lester is confined in the hospital, his physical position echoes that of Plato's cave dwellers: "A room scarce wider than the bed. There was a small window behind him but he could not see out without craning his neck and it pained him to do so" (175). Moreover, throughout much of the novel, Lester both dwells and is imprisoned in literal caves. The text employs images of fire casting a "shadowshow" against cave walls or comparable backdrops (159, 183). It associates Lester's cave with Tartarus through allusions to Hades (141) or to stygian mist (158) and in Lester's impression that its stream "ran down through the cavern to empty it may be in unknown seas at the center of the earth" (170). But even before Lester's descent into the caves, the voyeurism and carnality that characterize his approaches to women and lead to necrophilia evoke the Platonic idea that if vision is rightly an avenue to Truth and apperception of Ideals, evil results from blindness and materialism.

In the "Discourse of Diotima" from the *Symposium*, Plato tells the myth of Eros, describing progressive initiation into the love of beauty. This process culminates when the lover's object is no longer transient material bodies but the ideal of eternal Beauty. The true lover—or philosopher—is a seeker or a lover of wisdom rather than one who already possesses it, and his search begins with the love of one, then two, then all beautiful bodies, growing to the love of beautiful customs, then doctrines, and finally eternal Beauty or True Virtue (Stewart 370–77). The narrator Diotima says that because Love is the desire to possess Good always, Love aims at immortality. But Lester's is a perverted version of aiming at immortality in love. Bell writes that Lester's necrophilia derives from his "unprotected exposure to raw time and his conditioned belief that what is living—his mother, his father, and his home—is what is lost"(64). Similarly, in his treatment of *Child of God* as a pastoral, John M. Grammer notes that Lester's collecting corpses constitutes a "mad protest against history itself, against the passing of time." But it is difficult to agree with Grammer's implication that Lester actually achieves among his corpses what he may well aim at: "a timeless order, immunity to change" (40). Lester's bodies are the very image of mortality. No less than the living are they subject to flood and fire; and though Lester pursues the illusion of immortality, he cannot evade time's decay. The blatant failure in necrophilic love of Lester Ballard, this novel's everyman, to transcend the material body constitutes an extreme and obvious emblem of his failure of vision and wisdom, and this suggests that McCarthy employs the figure of the necrophile almost playfully as a grotesque parody of Plato's Diotima myth in this novel in which no one in Lester's materialistic culture achieves the ideal progress she describes.

Yet McCarthy's indictment of this grasping and materialistic culture is quite serious. Lester is emblematic of the society from which he arises. His collection of corpses has its parallels in the dumpkeeper's "levees of junk and garbage" presided over by the upturned remains of two dead cars "like wrecked sentinels" (26), and in the nearby rubble tip of the quarry where he searches for castoff goods (38–39). Though far from middle-class America, the novel's Sevier County is a valley of ashes whose inhabitants hoard material remains or dead and deadening material, and Lester's sifting the ashes of his burned cabin for the remains of his first beloved reflects a similar materialism in his culture.[11] The ruthless opportunism of Lester's neighbors, who legally cheat him of material goods in the auction of his farm or in the barter of watches (129–32), is implicated in the formation of Lester's necrophilia. Lester responds to this society in which the weak are dispossessed by learning to take possession of others forcibly. Moreover, Lester's feat at the shooting gallery parodies the worker's endeavor in a capitalist society: he converts his time and skill into prizes or rewards until he becomes burdened down by these goods, the giant stuffed bears and tiger with which he peoples his cabin (67). Lester's shooting his human victims is an extension of the same: he expends his talents and efforts in amassing material goods— much like ourselves perhaps.[12] The quarry and the dump with their dead machinery are merely less covert versions of Lester's boneyard. The flood scene in which the hardware storekeeper salvages his goods (161–63) immediately follows and parallels that of Lester's carrying his "chattel" or "possessions" to higher ground (154–58). It is apt that when Lester meditates his assault on Greer, he spies on his bespectacled alter ego as he sits (in the most recognizably middle-class image of the novel) in Lester's repossessed farmhouse, engaged in the purchasing of living goods, seeds, from a catalog (109). As Philip L. Simpson says of the serial killer Quentin in Joyce Carol Oates's *Zombie,* Lester's "'asocial' point of view is constructed in part from specific ideological positions. One of these positions is the privileged status of patriarchal science and consumer culture in the United States, which . . . fails to realize or acknowledge its manipulation or destruction of others" (170). From this perspective, Lester's necrophilia functions as a metaphor not only for the materialism Plato rejects, but also specifically for American consumer culture.

Necrophilia shocks because of the practitioner's failure to see that his beloved is mere material. Indeed, the necrophile loves the corpse precisely because she is an illusion. Masters and Lea point out that although the necrophile is usually acutely uncomfortable in encounters with a living being whose will may oppose his own, his necrophilia depends on the humanlike quality of the corpse and its "aura of consciousness" (112). That is, most necrophiles do not love or find arousing death itself or all dead creatures, but only the human dead. This is because it is human connection, human "warmth," that they desire: "it is at bottom the body as a person, not the body as mere felicitously arranged and compounded substance, or even as decaying matter, which he [the necrophile] requires for his gratification. . . . He insists upon a subject that has become an object, but in some sense remains a subject also" (112–13). Lester's first "lover," with whom we see him most actively engaged, is the unresisting receptacle of all his thwarted love and desire. He "poured into that waxen ear everything he'd ever thought of saying to a woman. Who could say she did not hear him?" (88–89). Later he dresses her in lingerie, poses her seductively before the fire so that he can go outside his cabin to gaze at her through the window to become aroused (the most pathetic of many scenes of Lester's window-gazing), and tells her without contradiction, "You been wantin it" (103). When the temperature falls and she becomes a "frozen bitch" (102), or when his enjoyment of a later victim is delayed until he finds her "cold and wooden with death" and he howls "curses until he [is] choking" (152), the extremity of his rage derives only in part from his free-floating anger at the will of all who have previously abandoned or rejected him (beginning with his mother's abandoning the family when he was small, leading to his father's abandoning and orphaning him through suicide); it is prompted at least as much by his frustration at the intrusion of cold reality on his comforting illusion.

As a pursuit of illusions, Lester's very literal progress from the love of one *body* to many subverts and perverts the progress Diotima outlines and constitutes a descent into materialism rather than transcendence. His blindness is progressive. His initial approach to the woman abandoned by the roadside (one of many doubles of Lester himself) is not devoid of empathy or recognition of her humanity: "Ain't you cold?" he asks her (42).[13] It does not occur to him to shoot her, even though he carries his rifle. (But his tearing away her gown as a trophy foreshadows the more extreme behavior to come.) Even after his enraging wrongful arrest for assaulting this woman, he is attracted to a young girl who watches fireworks with wonder and who, for the narrator, presents a vision of timeless loveliness. But here as later the narrative voice encompasses a vision that Lester does not fully achieve; something in his gaze frightens the girl, breaks the spell of her innocent wonderment, and provokes her narcissistic self-consciousness: "she saw the man with the bears watching her and she edged closer to the girl by her side and brushed her hair with two fingers quickly" (65). In accepting the illusion offered by necrophilia, Lester commits himself to progressive blindness, becoming the antithesis of Plato's philosopher-as-seeker. By the middle of the novel, he squats over the ashes of his burned cabin, looking with "eyes dark and huge and vacant" for remains of his first victim (107). Lester's necrophilia, manifesting a self-willed blindness to the decay and materiality of the corpse, both echoes and mocks or complicates the Platonic idea that love (philosophy) aims at immortality and perhaps implies that in aiming at transcendence Plato's system takes inadequate account of the stubborn materiality of the world and its occupants who face first of all the problem of how to live in it.

Just as Lester's response to the beauty of women becomes perverted as he becomes a collector of decaying bodies, his response to the beauty of the natural world is numbed in all but a few scenes, and he fails to access what is for Plato the potentially redemptive power of the sensible world's beauty to evoke recollection of Eternal Beauty and hence of Justice, Knowledge, and Temperance—a concept Plato explores not only in the "Discourse of Diotima" but also in the *Phaedrus* myth. As a squatter in the ramshackle cabin of a kindly neighbor, Lester's circumstances roughly parallel Thoreau's at Walden Pond. But Lester fails to take Thoreauvian sustenance from the natural world.[14] Even when in the narrator's eyes the world is a radiant vision, Lester is often oblivious. In winter, approaching the nadir of his moral/spiritual descent, Lester begins to stalk Greer, who has bought the Ballard homestead. Walking to his old place, Lester sees this landscape: "It was almost noon and the sun was very bright on the snow and the snow shone with a myriad crystal incandescence. The shrouded road wound off before him almost lost among the trees and a stream ran beside the road, dark under bowers of ice, small glass-fanged caverns beneath tree roots where the water sucked unseen. In the frozen roadside weeds were coiled white ribbons of frost, you'd never figure how they came to be. Ballard ate one as he went" (128). McCarthy performs one of his marvels here, placing us simultaneously within Lester's perspective and outside of it (as indeed the novel as a whole accomplishes). The images of winter light and snow and ice are dazzling, but Lester's perception is captured in the metaphors of the lost road, the threatening glass-fanged caverns, and the sucking, invisible water. Though in one sense Lester sees the ribbons of frost, the wonder belongs to the narrator alone. To Lester, the ice ribbons are to be consumed materially, and his eating one parallels his sexual consumption of the material bodies of his "lovers."[15] Similarly, Lester fails to understand the behavior of a pair of hawks he sees coupled in air—they mate on the wing, and some species are thought to mate for life—because he "did not know how hawks mated but he knew that all things fought" (169). Earlier he has paused to watch as hounds harry a boar and it fights back viciously: "Ballard watched this ballet tilt and swirl and churn mud up through the snow and watched the lovely blood welter there in its holograph of battle, spray burst from a ruptured lung, the dark heart's blood, pinwheel and pirouette, until shots rang and all was done" (69). Lester recognizes beauty only in sexually objectified women or in violence.[16]

VOYEURISM, NARCISSISM, AND THE OPPORTUNITY FOR SELF-RECOGNITION

Almost as prevalent as images of Lester's voyeurism, particularly his watching his victims through the windows of cars or houses, are instances of his seeing his own reflection in water, windows, or other people. The primary import of these images of Lester as Narcissus derives neither from the popular interpretation of the Narcissus myth as a warning against self-love, nor especially from the psychological interpretation of the myth as a warning against dependence on others for one's self-image—although this phenomenon is at work in McCarthy's muted delineation of Ballard's psychology. (Abandoned by both parents, he has not had the loving parental gaze mirroring back his own face, thus to establish a strong sense of his own worth and being; later he lives up to and exceeds the negative expectations of the people around him, which are given voice most explicitly by the aptly named Sheriff Fate Turner, whose prediction that "murder is next on the list" of his mean acts Lester soon fulfills [56].) Rather, the Narcissus references in *Child of God* suggest the Platonic idea of the role of vision in achieving wisdom, particularly as presented in Plotinus's allegorical, Neoplatonic interpretation of the Narcissus myth, which Stewart cites:

> Seeing . . . those beauties which appear in bodies, he must not run after them, but knowing them to be images and vestiges and shadows, he must flee to that of which they are the images. And if any one should pursue them, wishing to take them as real, they would be like a fair image borne on water, and when he desires to seize it . . . , plunging to the bottom of the stream, he disappears. In the same way, he who grasps beautiful bodies and will not let them go, is submerged not only in body but in soul, within the dark depth hateful to his own mind, where, remaining blind in Hades, he dwells among shadows, there as here. (Stewart 231–32)

Lester's voyeurism and necrophilia are thus repetitions of Narcissus's fateful error—a mistaken application of vision and erotic attraction resulting in his drowning in materialism. The self-destructiveness of Lester's path, implied in the Narcissus references, is given overt expression when he attempts to ford the flooded creek with his possessions: "Anyone watching him could have seen he would not turn back if the creek swallowed him under" (155).[17]

Plotinus explicitly relates the Narcissus myth to Plato's myths of the soul's drinking forgetfulness from Lethe before incarnation. Stewart summarizes: "Souls . . . descending, at their appointed times, come to the water which is the Mirror of Dionysus [which Plotinus identifies with Lethe], and enamoured of their own images reflected therein—that is, of their mortal bodies—plunge into the water. This water is the water of oblivion, and they that drink of it go down into the cave of this world" (232). All souls drink of the waters of oblivion, but the wisest drink the least. Plotinus's interpretation thus relates the

Narcissus myth to Plato's explanation of the individual's prenatal choosing of the circumstances of his life in accordance with the wisdom he has achieved. In light of these myths, the life of the cave and oblivious materialism is the apparently hapless and fated Lester's chosen world—an environment reflecting the character-defining choice he made before birth and symbolizing his lack of spiritual insight, as the cramped and mean-spirited lives of his self-righteous neighbors symbolize theirs.

Stewart cites also Ficino's Neoplatonic interpretation of Narcissus as "a thoughtless and untried man, [who] does not see his own face. He turns his regard by no means to his proper substance and worth, but pursues his reflection in water and tries to embrace it. That is to say, he admires beauty in a perishable body, like moving water, which is the shadow of his own rational soul" (233). And indeed, Lester's Narcissus-like moments are all near misses, lost opportunities to see his own face truly—as when his voyeurism is turned back on him and he is mirrored and confronted by the image of the dead girl he sees through the car window ("Out of the disarray of clothes and the contorted limbs another's eyes watched sightlessly from a bland white face" [86]), or by the retarded boy who watches him set his house afire ("the last thing he saw through the smoke was the idiot child. It sat watching him, berryeyed filthy and frightless among the painted flames" [120]).

The clearest reference to the myth of Narcissus in *Child of God,* occurring just before Lester's vision of the ice fangs and sucking water, implies that he approaches vision or understanding yet shies away from it. Lester comes to a mountain spring: "Kneeling in the snow . . . Ballard leaned his face to the green water and drank and studied his dishing visage in the pool. He halfway put his hand to the water as if he would touch the face that watched there but then he rose and wiped his mouth and went on" (127). The scene ambiguously suggests both his near-recognition of his "proper substance and worth" and his pursuit of shadows or illusions. Similarly, late in the novel, in another of the scenes of reversed voyeurism that always offer the potential for recognition, Ballard sees a boy watching him from the window of a church bus: "He was trying to fix in his mind where he'd seen the boy when it came to him that the boy looked like himself. This gave him the fidgets and though he tried to shake the image of the face in the glass it would not go" (191). This is as close to epiphany as Ballard comes, yet he tries to refuse it.[18] Nonetheless, such scenes play off of the Platonic idea that the opportunity for insight always lies before a man because, even though he has imbibed the waters of forgetfulness at his birth, knowledge of Truth inheres from his creation.

A less philosophically loaded image that contributes to the Narcissus pattern occurs when Lester visits the dumpkeeper's house in hopes of seeing his favorite of the man's daughters, perhaps intending her for his second object of necrophilia: "Behind the house stood the remains of several cars and from the rear glass of one of them a turkey watched him" (110). In its mirroring of the novel's other images of reversed voyeurism, and especially in its foreshadowing of the little boy who seems to watch Lester from the window of the church bus, this image is parodic, yet it hints of an opportunity for Lester to catch a glimpse of his material, animal impulses, and it reinforces the psychological pattern of self-consciousness that characterizes Lester— his obsession not only with watching but also with being watched. Such self-consciousness punctuates his furtive encounter with the first dead couple: in Lester's perception, the dead man winks at him ("he lay staring up with one eye open and one half shut") and watches what he does to the dead girl, and even the girl's breasts appear to be "peeking" at him "from her open blouse" (88).[19]

The function of such images is modified again in the case of the man with the shotgun who squats in the truck bed watching Lester through the rear window of the truck while his companions are preparing to lynch the small necrophile (181). The scene echoes those of Lester himself peering at his potential victims through car windows, and, significantly, here the Narcissus figure is not Lester but the man, a representative of the community, who fails to see his own face in that of Ballard.[20] In terms of the Platonic myths, the man fails to recognize that his own and all men's positions in the world are similar to Lester's: condemned to imperfect wisdom by the conditions of his existence and offered sequential chances for correction through seeking insight. The community consistently tries to explain Lester's evil acts in such a way as to prove his constitutional difference from them, that he is *other*. The consensus is that Lester was "never . . . right" (21): "You can trace em back to Adam if you want and goddamn if he didn't outstrip em all" (81). They neither recognize Lester's potential for a different kind of life, nor acknowledge their essential kinship with him. Furthermore, McCarthy's juxtaposition of the dissection of Lester's body with the exhuming and bagging of his corpses as "Property of the State of Tennessee" (196) at the novel's end suggests a parallel between Lester's descent into the materialism of necrophilia, a kind of inquiry into the human body (he inspects "her body carefully, as if he would see how she were made" [91–92]), and that of the socially approved legal, forensic, medical, and undertaker's professions. (Significantly, Masters and Lea document several necrophiles whose fantasies of the dead led them to become undertakers or to study anatomy; see, for example, 127–29.)

McCarthy's deft manipulation of narrative stance in *Child of God* positions the reader to recognize Lester as a being much like himself or herself—making the novel itself a Narcissus reflection for the reader. Although McCarthy's novel is not entirely typical of the American serial-killer fiction and films that became prominent in the post-*Psycho* decades, Philip Simpson's observation that such works can fruitfully be read as cultural criticism holds true for *Child of God* as well. The serial killer is "never as Other as might be supposed at first glance" Simpson writes. Such fiction "compels thoughtful observers to acknowledge their own murderous impulses" and invites us to recognize that "serial killers literalize spiritual and nationalistic ideals that most of their fellow Americans share" (24). Some American traits we might recognize in Lester include his armed individualism, his perverted consumerism, his clumsy improvisation, and his resilience as the underdog. Or, as Vereen Bell observes, "McCarthy has conceived pathetic Lester as a berserk version of fundamental aspects of ourselves—our fear of time, our programmed infatuation with death, our loneliness, our threatening appetites, our narcissistic isolation from the world and the reality of other people" (55).

CELESTIAL INTIMATIONS AND THE ORACLES
OF DREAMS

In the intervals between his egregious offenses, Ballard's narrative is punctuated with opportunities for insight—glimmerings and intimations. His sightings of stars invoke the creation myth in Plato's *Timaeus,* which tells that in making souls, God divided a mixture of the elements of fire, air, water, and earth into as many souls as there are stars, "and to each star he assigned a Soul, and caused each Soul to go up into her star as into a chariot, and showed unto her the nature of the All, and declared the laws thereof which are fixed and shall not be moved" (Stewart 261).[21] In Plato, this is the original source of the soul's wisdom, forgotten at birth. But God also created vision "to the end that, having observed the Circuits of Intelligence in the Heaven, we might use them for the revolutions of Thought in ourselves, which are kin, albeit perturbed, unto those unperturbed celestial courses; and having throughly [*sic*] learnt and become partakers in the truth of the reasonings which are according to nature, might, by means of our imitation of the Circuits of God which are without error altogether, compose into order the circuits in ourselves which have erred" (Stewart 266). Thus Plato stresses that the order humans perceive in the movement of heavenly bodies should both remind them of their inherent understanding of the Truth and inspire them to imitate that order in their lives. But when Lester looks at the stars, he sees them as voyeurs like himself, watching him with "lidless" fixity, "remote" (133) and alien even when they prompt questioning, as when he witnesses the awakening of bats in a "false spring" and sees them "ascend . . . like souls rising from hades" and depart through a hole in the roof of his cave: "When they were gone he watched the hordes of cold stars sprawled across the smokehole and wondered what stuff they were made of, or himself" (141).[22]

Lester cannot perceive a creative order in the world, inferring only the principle that "all things fought" (169), a principle that both McCarthy and Plato acknowledge, but that both would view as a half-truth or worse. Like many of McCarthy's protagonists who lack the maturity, patience, openness, or imagination to perceive a cosmic order in the world, Lester wishes to arrogate to himself the prerogative of the creator: "Coming up the mountain through the blue winter twilight among great boulders and the ruins of giant trees prone in the forest he wondered at such upheaval. Disorder in the woods, trees down, new paths needed. Given charge Ballard would have made things more orderly in the woods and in men's souls" (136). Lester's longing for order derives from the immortal part of his soul; his inability to see an acceptable order (for Plato the transcendental order; for McCarthy the order that results from the synthesis of the life of the body in a real world and the life of the inner spirit: from perception of one's place within "the world itself"[23]) marks the ascendance of the mortal or appetitive part of his soul—the part that, Plato says in *Timaeus,* "hath in itself passions terrible, of necessity inherent—first, Pleasure, evil's best bait, then Pains that banish good things, also Confidence and Fear, two heedless counsellors, and Wrath hard to entreat, and Hope easily led astray. These did they [the lesser gods to whom God delegated the responsibility to mould and guide the mortal part of man] mix with Sense that lacketh Reason, and Love that dareth all, and so builded the mortal kind of Soul" (Stewart 268).

This passage virtually catalogues the passions wracking Lester and only occasionally calmed by his immortal soul. After his day and night of desperate removal from his flooded cave to one on higher ground, during which he nearly drowns, loses many of his possessions, and soils all of them, Lester emerges exhausted from his new cave to survey a "dead and fabled waste. . . . He had not stopped cursing. Whatever voice spoke him was no demon but some old shed self that came yet from time to time in the name of sanity, a hand to gentle him back from the rim of his disastrous wrath" (158). Regarded in light of Plato, this old shed self, kin to the "old foreboding" that has earlier stayed Lester's hand from senselessly killing a bluebird (25), may be the immortal soul, or the consciencelike daemon assigned to guide the soul through life. Similarly, the passage reflects the story in *Timaeus* that the gods positioned the liver close to the appetitive soul, which resides in the breast, so that, mirrorlike, it could reflect the intelligence of the immortal part into the Appetitive soul and "might fill [it] at one time, with fear, [. . .] at another time might make it mild and gentle, and give unto it a space of calm at night, wherein it should receive the Oracles of Dreams, meet for that which is without Reason and Understanding" (Stewart 269). These calming oracles of dreams, to which the immortal soul makes the appetitive soul receptive, are what later lead to Lester's transient recognition of the beauty of the world even as he reconfirms the fatality of his course in his dream of riding a mule through sunlit woods: "Each leaf that brushed his face deepened his sadness and dread. Each leaf he passed he'd never pass again. They rode over his face like veils, already some yellow, their veins like slender bones where the sun shone through them. He had resolved himself to ride on for he could not turn back and the world that day was as lovely as any day that ever was and he was riding to his death" (170–71).

However, for Lester this dream offers yet another ungrasped opportunity for insight.[24] In the next scene, dressed in skirt and scalp and presenting an image utterly at odds with Plato's notion of the man guided by his immortal part,[25] Lester attempts to murder Greer and to enforce his own temporal idea of order and justice.

THE HEEDLESS BLACKSMITH AND THE ORIGIN OF EVIL

Plato's myths concerning the limited wisdom manifested in humankind's earthly incarnations often coincide with his etiological myths of the soul's creation and its nature, and thus they explain the human potential for both good and evil. In Tartarus, all souls may ultimately be cured of their forgetfulness and foolishness through their punishment and their witnessing of the warnings of other foolish souls—other children of god much like themselves (*Gorgias* myth, Stewart 136). When the soul finally achieves this wisdom, it ascends to the Plain of Truth or the star of its origin, no longer subject to correction and reincarnation. In Plato's mythology, human failings are sometimes explained by the partial or intermittent agency of God, who created the immortal part of the soul and exposed it to truth, but who left the body and the mortal soul to the design of the young gods, as in the *Timaeus* myth (Stewart 262), or who created the world and then withdrew for a period, during which time humans forgot their maker and governed themselves less well, surviving only because of such gifts of the gods as seeds and herbs, fire, and the mechanical arts of Hephaestos, as in the *Politicus* myth (Stewart 189).

Defending the *Politicus* myth's naive treatment of the problem of evil, Stewart describes the comparable myth of the Birth of Iron in the Finnish epic, the *Kalewala*. In accordance with Finnish belief that to overcome a difficulty one recites its origins, the Birth of Iron myth is an elaboration of a charm-formula that must be told by the magician-hero if he is to cure a wound. As an etiological myth, the Birth of Iron tells of the origin of evil in iron, as does McCarthy's own blacksmith's creation story, introduced in *Child of God* when Lester takes an ax to be sharpened. Though the events of the two stories are not identical, they have interesting affinities where they touch on the problem of evil in iron, or in men.

The Birth of Iron myth partly explains the origin of evil as a lapse on the part of the blacksmith. He intends to create iron for good purposes only, and the myth tells of his care at each stage in the process. At one point, Iron, who fears Fire, begs the Smith to withdraw him; but he answers, "If I take thee now out of the Fire, thou mightest grow up to be evil, and all too dangerous; thou mightest murder thy nearest-of-kin" (202), and he leaves Iron in the Fire until he swears never to do harm. (*Child of God* inverts this myth when Lester angrily throws his frozen-up rifle into the fire: "But fetched it out again . . . before it had suffered more than a scorched forestock" (159)—saving it to do further harm.) Because Iron needs to be hardened, the Smith next prepares a bath, asking the bee to add its honey. But the evil Wasp overhears the Smith and substitutes her venom for the "noble" honey, a ruse undetected by the Smith: "without heed he cast the metal therein, when he had drawn it out of the Fire. . . . Then came it to pass that Iron was made hurtful" (203). Significantly, however, the old man who hears this tale, narrated by the wounded hero, concludes that Iron alone—not his well-intentioned though momentarily heedless creator—is responsible for the evil he does: that no one coerces him to do evil (Stewart 199–204).

In McCarthy's similar myth of the creation of iron, the blacksmith describes the principles of his craft as he dresses the ax, using language that establishes the analogy between the blacksmith and the creator of man. Like the events of the Birth of Iron myth, the lecture of McCarthy's blacksmith suggests that evil may be introduced by the creator's heedlessness: "Never leave steel in the fire for longer than it takes to heat. Some people will poke around at somethin else and leave the tool they're heatin to perdition but the proper thing is to fetch her out the minute she shows the color of grace. . . . It's like a lot of things, said the smith. Do the least part of it wrong and ye'd just as well to do it all wrong" (72–74). While this set piece seems to suggest that the creator bears responsibility for the evil in man, its analogous relationship to the Birth of Iron story, and its context within a larger fiction that invokes analogues to Platonic myth, temper that view considerably. In Plato, human suffering is finally and most consistently attributed to the lack of wisdom with which the soul approaches Lethe, succumbing to thirst on its release from Tartarus, drinking too deeply of forgetfulness, and thus choosing the circumstances of its earthly life foolishly (in the most extreme cases missing the opportunity to choose in such a way as to avoid doing unredeemable evil), and subsequently conducting its life without wisdom. In the "Myth of Er" in the *Republic*, Plato emphasizes that no one is constrained to choose an evil life: "Even for him whose turn cometh last, if he hath chosen with understanding, there is prepared a Life, which, if only a man bear himself manfully, is tolerable, not wretched" (Stewart 153). Thus, according to Plato, the fate that Lester bemoans, feeling himself "so grievous a case against the gods" (189), results from the soul's own first choice and remains his responsibility. Stewart's comments on the "Myth of Er" resonate with all of McCarthy's work from *Outer Dark* on:

> The Soul, choosing the circumstances, or Life, chooses, or makes itself responsible for, its own character, as afterwards modified, and necessarily modified, by the circumstances, or Life. . . . To be free is to be a continuously existing, self-affirming, environment-choosing personality, manifesting itself in actions which proceed, according to necessary law, from itself as placed once for all in the environment which it has chosen . . . the environment which is the counterpart of its own character. . . . The

momentary prenatal act of choice . . . is the pattern of like acts which have to be performed in a man's natural life. Great decisions have to be made in life, which, once made, are irrevocable, and dominate the man's whole career and conduct afterwards. (176–78)[26]

Lester curses his fate and considers himself grievous evidence against the creator; the novel implicates his community of similarly blinded men and women and delineates the purgatorial world of Sevier County (and America) as one in which humans participate in mutual torture and persecution (much as in McCarthy's previous purgatorial nightmare, *Outer Dark,* and his later *Blood Meridian*). No one in Sevier County achieves the status of Plato's seeker/philosopher.

Through its evocation of both Hades and Plato's cave parable, with its implications of the limits of human vision and of humanity's bondage to materiality, Lester's descent into the caves implies that his life as experienced is an outward manifestation of his inner spirit and thus reconfigures questions of fate and responsibility. Lester himself dimly recognizes the cave as a metaphor for his whole existence when he imagines that after his death in the cave, mice will nest in the "lobed caverns where his brains had been" (189)—although, typically, he conceives this in terms of his fleshly brains rather than his spirit. Regarded through the lens of Platonic myth, Lester's retreat to the caves of Sevier County stands as the most metaphysically explicit element in the pattern of like acts that define his life and make him the community's scourge and scapegoat. Lester's early life prefigures his cave life, and indeed the earthly cave of oblivion is Lester's environment throughout; his imprisonment in the cave after he eludes his persecutors is a parable of his whole life (as well as those of his neighbors), and his release from the underground cavern is a "rebirth" into the cave of this world. After long searching for a way out of the cavern, Lester sees a shaft of sunlight: "It occurred to him only now that he might have passed other apertures to the upper world in the nighttime and not known it" (188). But Lester remains unenlightened, and though "He'd cause to wish and he did wish for some brute midwife to spald him from his rocky keep" (189), his rebirth is no resurrection but merely a Platonic transmigration from Tartarus to earth, or from one purgatory to another. When he gives himself up to the hospital, that revered human institution for the study and cure of the material body, Lester's eyes remain "caved and smoking" (192).

ACKNOWLEDGMENTS

Some of the reading for this article was done at Australian National University in Canberra, New South Wales. I am grateful to ANU's English Department for hosting me as a visiting fellow in the winter and spring of 1996. This article was presented in an earlier version at the Southern Writers/Southern Writing Conference at the University of Mississippi in July 1996.

Notes

1. Lester's caves appear to be composites of the various caves Barr describes, and although I am convinced that McCarthy read *Caves of Tennessee* for his work on *Child of God* and *Suttree*, it also seems possible that McCarthy had done some spelunking in east Tennessee and that his imagining of Lester's caves was drawn from his own observation. McCarthy and his first wife Lee were living in Sevierville in 1963 when a Knoxville newspaper article listed them among the out-of-town guests at the marriage of McCarthy's sister Maryellen ("Miss McCarthy" 6).

    Through his father, chief attorney for the Tennessee Valley Authority, McCarthy may also have known Berlen Moneymaker, the TVA's chief geologist, and/or his unpublished thesis on east Tennessee caves, which Barr consulted in the writing of *Caves of Tennessee*. I have not seen Moneymaker's thesis. Another study is Larry E. Matthews's *Descriptions of Tennessee Caves* (Nashville: State of Tennessee, Division of Geology, 1971).

2. Because time markers other than seasonal imagery are rare in *Child of God*, the flood reference helps us tentatively to date the action of the novel. Mr. Wade, the old man who tells the deputy about White Caps, says he was born in the flood year of 1885—not a flood year Fox lists, which suggests that McCarthy relied on his own experience and contemporaneous news reports more than on historical accounts of nineteenth-century floods on the Little Pigeon (166). Lester dies in April 1965 (193–94), and, although the text is not explicit on this point, it seems he has spent significant time in the state mental hospital before his death. The flood that forces him to move his possessions from one cave to another on higher ground occurs in late winter (154); the actual flood of 1957 came on February 1, earlier than the more typical spring floods in March and April (Fox A5). If we conceive the action of the novel to take place in the flood year of 1957, that would make old Mr. Wade seventy-two, and it would mean that Lester is incarcerated for seven years before his death; it would place Lester's birth in 1930 and make his twenty-seven-year life in Sevier County flood-free until the year of his arrest, which might help explain his naive wonder at the disorder of the winter world. Further, this would place in the Depression years both his mother's abandonment of the family and his father's selling off of the timber. Berry writes, "We know that the timber on the land being auctioned in the opening scene was cut about fifteen to twenty years ago (5), and that Lester's father hanged himself about seventeen or eighteen years ago. Perhaps Ballard senior sold the timber off his property as a last desperate means of support" (71).

3. Another edition of the White Cap book was prepared by Marion Mangrum in the 1960s. For a journalistic account of the White Caps, which gives some indication of the complex revision and republication history of Davis's book, see Mike Gibson, "Blue vs. White," *Metro Pulse* [Knoxville], 29 June 2000. Online at <http://metropulse.com/dir_zine/dir_2000/1026/t_cover.html> (1 Aug. 2000). Gibson also refers to a University of Tennessee master's thesis on the White Caps by Joe Cummings (1988). I am grateful to John Cant for directing me to this online article.

4. McCarthy's interviewer Richard Woodward writes that Lester Ballard "is based on newspaper reports of such a figure in Sevier County" (31), and there are some indications that McCarthy hinted that a case that inspired the novel occurred in Sevier County. However, in a letter of August 16, 2000, Sevier County historian Beulah Linn wrote me, "I am 88 years old and I do not recall this murder case. . . . The surname Ballard is a very old and respected Sevier County family." The novel dates Lester's death and the exhuming of his victims' remains in April 1965, but no articles appear in the Knoxville *News-Sentinel* in either April or May of that year that could be sources for *Child of God*. However, in a search of the *News-Sentinel* I found reports of the James Blevins case and was able to supplement these with related articles from the *Chattanooga Daily Times*. My unpublished paper on McCarthy's use of the Blevins case and that of Wisconsin serial killer Ed Gein, "Voyeur, Necrophile, Psycho: The Homicides behind the Scenes of *Child of God*," was delivered at the Cormac McCarthy Society International Colloquy in El Paso, Texas, October 16, 1998.

5. The book closes with a ponderous fictional tale by Masters, "The Writer and the Black Beauty," which seems to me to have had almost no direct influence on *Child of God*; however, "The Writer and the Black Beauty" may well have served McCarthy as a negative model of literary treatment of the necrophile, as it manages to be both prurient and pedantic—as is, indeed, its narrator, the Writer.

6. When the floods come, Lester works all night to haul "his possessions" to higher ground (158). Earlier, carrying one victim to his cave, Lester has performed a feat similar to Alessandro's—one that he must have performed many times—yet the imagery stresses that he is overburdened both physically and metaphysically by the gross material body he has sought to possess: "Scuttling down the mountain with the thing on his back he looked like a man beset by some ghast succubus, the dead girl riding him with legs bowed akimbo like a monstrous frog" (153).

7. However, I also endorse Andrew Bartlett's assertion that "the aesthetic power of *Child of God* results from McCarthy's superb regulation of narrative distance and perspective" (4).

8. For treatments of spirituality throughout McCarthy's novels, see Edwin T. Arnold's "Naming, Knowing and Nothingness: McCarthy's Moral Parables" and his "'Go to sleep': Dreams and Visions in the Border Trilogy." For treatments of spiritual themes in *The Crossing*, see Arnold's "McCarthy and the Sacred: A Reading of *The Crossing*" in this volume, and my "The Road and the Matrix: The World as Tale in *The Crossing*." I have also explored such issues in *Blood Meridian* in "Ambiguities, Dilemmas, and Double-Binds in Cormac McCarthy's *Blood Meridian*," *Southwestern American Literature* 26.1 (fall 2000): 21–46. For McCarthy's use of Roman Catholic theology, see Jason Ambrosiano, "Blood in the Tracks: Catholic Postmodernism in *The Crossing*," *Southwestern American Literature* 25.1 (fall 1999): 83–91.

9. Most critics have simply noted the influence in a generalized way. For a few specific parallels, see Arnold, "Naming, Knowing and Nothingness" (Arnold and Luce 45–69). In an unpublished paper, "The Border Trilogy: McCarthy's Marriage of *Figura*," Jennifer Fraser has gone much further in discussing McCarthy's specific uses of Dante.

10. I have explored McCarthy's use of *The Republic* in "The Confluence of Plato's *Republic* and Mexican History in *All the Pretty Horses,*" *Proceedings of the 2nd Annual International Conference on the Emerging Literature of the Southwest Culture* (El Paso: University of Texas at El Paso, 1996), 177–85.

11. One is reminded of the gitano's admonishment to Billy Parham as he strives to recover Boyd's body from Mexico in *The Crossing*: "*La cáscara no es la cosa*" (The husk is not the thing [411]).

12. Christine Chollier observes that Lester as outsider is excluded from the monetary exchange system and that he does not aim to accumulate money. As a boy, he worked just long enough to earn the money for his rifle (seven hundred fenceposts' worth), and then he quit (Chollier 172). When Lester finds the asphyxiated couple, he steals their money only as an afterthought (*Child of God* 89). Whenever he comes into a few dollars this way, he immediately exchanges them for food or for alluring clothing to enhance his sexual illusions. But Lester's rifle and ammunition themselves become means of exchange when he shoots targets for stuffed bears and when he hunts human victims. He does aim to accumulate material goods. The abstraction of money means less to him because money cannot buy the inert material he most wants. For Lester, a well-placed bullet has more currency.

13. However, Lester's compassion is more easily prompted when he thinks this woman is dead, or at least sleeping. Nell Sullivan rightly observes, "As long as the woman is sleeping and de-animated, she receives the approbative term *lady,* but waking, she becomes 'a goddamned whore'" (74; *Child of God* 52). Lester may see his faithless mother in her, and she too seems to confuse him with someone else when she says, "I knowed you'd do me thisaway" (42). While Lester fumbles awkwardly around desirable women, once this "lady" assaults him with a rock he exhibits no fear of verbally or physically confronting her. Her behaviors certainly reinforce the lesson that dead women are quieter, safer, less likely to put the law on him.

14. Similarly, Robert Jarrett writes, "Unlike Thoreau at Walden Pond, Ballard's isolation in nature neither regenerates nor restores a lost innocence; it corrupts this contemporary inversion of the American Adam" (41).

15. More than he will admit, Lester is akin to the man in a nearby cell who has been convicted of opening people's skulls and "eat[ing] the brains inside with a spoon" (193).

16. Bell notes that he is "oblivious" to beauty because "he is not an observer. He is innocent of, and uninterested in, the nature of the materials of the world and of how processes and procedures produce specific results" (64). The one exception, of course, is Lester's interest in the material of and fashion in which his girlfriends' bodies are made.

17. Several other images reinforce the notion of Lester's self-destructiveness. Just as he is overburdened by his possessions, including the corpse of a girl who rides him like a succubus (see note 6), Lester bears his "rifle on his neck like a yoke" (25–26) or carries it on his lonely night vigils "hanging in his hand as if it were a thing he could not get shut of" (41).

18. Bartlett finds in this scene an "enigmatic conversion" that causes Lester to

return to the hospital, a choice which, whether "resignation or repentance . . . is a kind of suicide" (15). I find the scene even more ambiguous as to its effects on Lester and question whether it causes either a conversion or his return to the hospital, where he is already headed.

19. He does not close the man's eyes, but he does the girl's—perhaps both to further the illusion that she is not dead but sleeping and also to avoid her gaze (87–88).

20. Bartlett was the first to emphasize the importance of the voyeurism trope in the novel, but his observation that "the recurrent image of the voyeur in *Child of God* is that of a hunter who focuses on a presence or a scene of actual or potential death" (4) is only sometimes accurate, as I hope my discussion of variations on the image shows. Indeed, many scenes of voyeurism foreground not the hunter's acute eye but the oblivious perspective of Ballard's neighbors—Bartlett's second degree "of proximity to Ballard"(4)—and also Ballard's own obliviousness, especially to himself. The mirroring images always suggest doubling of Ballard by others, but seldom do any of the characters recognize this doubling.

21. At birth, the souls fall to earth from the stars or shoot from the river Lethe like meteors, according to the "Myth of Er" in the *Republic* (Stewart 155), a myth that resonates with the kid's birth on the night of the 1833 meteor shower in *Blood Meridian* (3).

22. Dante's depiction of Hades as a cavern in the earth (like Tartarus) is one of the elements of his cosmography drawn from Plato.

23. Relevant here is a 1989 letter from McCarthy paraphrased by Garry Wallace. Challenging Wallace's scientific skepticism, McCarthy wrote that "the mystical experience is a direct apprehension of reality, unmediated by symbol, and he ended with the thought that our inability to see spiritual truth is the greater mystery" (138). For commentary on the importance of "the world itself" in McCarthy's works, see my "The Road and the Matrix" and J. Douglas Canfield's "Crossing from the Wasteland into the Exotic in McCarthy's Border Trilogy," in *A Cormac McCarthy Companion: The Border Trilogy*, ed. Edwin T. Arnold and Dianne C. Luce (Jackson: University Press of Mississippi, 2001), 256–69.

24. Edwin T. Arnold demonstrates that in many of McCarthy's works, dreams both function as the characters' extrarational visions and offer the reader moments of insight into their souls, taking the place of psychological probing. Arnold concludes that McCarthy's use of dreams is more Jungian than Freudian. He reminds us, "This unanticipated glimpse into Lester's distraught soul comes immediately after he sits high above the world 'that he'd once inhabited' (169) and weeps as he watches the 'diminutive progress of all things in the valley, the gray fields coming up black and corded under the plow, the slow green occlusion that the trees were spreading' (170). There is an awful need for love and belonging even in a creature such as Lester, his dream affirms, and in this manner McCarthy opens Lester's heart to us in all its twisted yearning" ("Dreams" 42).

25. In my unpublished paper, "Voyeur, Necrophile, Psycho: The Homicides behind the Scenes of *Child of God*," I have argued that Lester's dress and fright wig are traces of serial killer Ed Gein and of his fictional descendant Norman Bates of *Psycho*.

26. One is reminded of Culla Holme's choice of evasion in *Outer Dark,* which becomes the pattern that keeps him circling in darkness. Consider also Lacey Rawlins's counsel to John Grady Cole in *All the Pretty Horses:* "Ever dumb thing I ever done in my life there was a decision I made before that got me into it. It was never the dumb thing. It was always some choice I'd made before it" (79). In the Border Trilogy, the repetition-compulsions that lead to so much of the sorrow in Billy Parham's long life, and even more so in John Grady Cole's brief life, can also be viewed from this Platonic perspective.

Works Cited

Arnold, Edwin T. "'Go to sleep': Dreams and Visions in the Border Trilogy." *A Cormac McCarthy Companion: The Border Trilogy.* Ed. Edwin T. Arnold and Dianne C. Luce. Jackson: University Press of Mississippi, 2001. 37–72.

———. "Naming, Knowing and Nothingness: McCarthy's Moral Parables." *Perspectives on Cormac McCarthy.* Rev. ed. Ed. Edwin T. Arnold and Dianne C. Luce. Jackson: University Press of Mississippi, 1999. 45–69.

———, and Dianne C. Luce, eds. *Perspectives on Cormac McCarthy.* Rev. ed. Jackson: University Press of Mississippi, 1999.

Barr, Thomas C., Jr. *Caves of Tennessee.* Nashville: Tennessee Department of Conservation and Commerce, Division of Geology, 1961.

Bartlett, Andrew. "From Voyeurism to Archaeology: Cormac McCarthy's *Child of God.*" *Southern Literary Journal* 24.1 (fall 1991): 3–15.

Bell, Vereen M. *The Achievement of Cormac McCarthy.* Baton Rouge: Louisiana State University Press, 1988.

Berry, K. Wesley. "The Lay of the Land in Cormac McCarthy's *The Orchard Keeper* and *Child of God.*" *Southern Quarterly* 38.4 (summer 2000): 61–77.

Chollier, Christine. "'I aint come back rich, that's for sure,' or The Questioning of Market Economies in Cormac McCarthy's Novels." *Myth, Legend, Dust: Critical Responses to Cormac McCarthy.* Ed. Rick Wallach. Manchester: Manchester University Press, 2000. 171–82.

Coles, Robert. "The Stranger." *New Yorker,* 26 Aug. 1974: 87–90.

Fox, John. "March 26, 1965: Sevierville's Last Great Flood." *Mountain Press* [Sevier County], 26 Mar. 1984: A5.

Grammer, John M. "A Thing against Which Time Will Not Prevail: Pastoral and History in Cormac McCarthy's South." *Perspectives on Cormac McCarthy.* Rev. ed. Ed. Edwin T. Arnold and Dianne C. Luce. Jackson: University Press of Mississippi, 1999. 29–44.

Jarrett, Robert L. *Cormac McCarthy.* New York: Twayne, 1997.

Luce, Dianne C. "The Road and the Matrix: The World as Tale in *The Crossing.*" *Perspectives on Cormac McCarthy.* Rev. ed. Ed. Edwin T. Arnold and Dianne C. Luce. Jackson: University Press of Mississippi, 1999. 195–219.

Masters, R. E. L., and Eduard Lea. *Sex Crimes in History: Evolving Concepts of Sadism, Lust-murder, and Necrophilia—from Ancient to Modern Times.* New York: Julian Press, 1963.

McCarthy, Cormac. *All the Pretty Horses.* 1992. New York: Vintage Books, 1993.

———. *Blood Meridian, or, The Evening Redness in the West.* 1985. New York: Vintage Books, 1992.

———. *Child of God.* 1973. New York: Vintage Books, 1993.

———. *The Crossing.* 1994. New York: Vintage Books, 1995.

———. *Outer Dark.* 1968. New York: Vintage Books, 1993.

"Miss McCarthy Marries Mr. James A. Jaques [Jacques] III." *Knoxville Journal,* 10 June 1963: 6.

Simpson, Philip L. *Psycho Paths: Tracking the Serial Killer through Contemporary American Film and Fiction.* Carbondale: Southern Illinois University Press, 2000.

Stewart, J. A. *The Myths of Plato.* Ed. G. R. Levy. London: Centaur Press, 1960.

Sullivan, Nell. "The Evolution of the Dead Girlfriend Motif in *Outer Dark* and *Child of God.*" *Myth, Legend, Dust: Critical Responses to Cormac McCarthy.* Ed. Rick Wallach. Manchester: Manchester University Press, 2000. 68–77.

Wallace, Garry. "Meeting McCarthy." *Southern Quarterly* 30.4 (summer 1992): 134–39.

Woodward, Richard B. "Cormac McCarthy's Venomous Fiction." *New York Times Magazine,* 19 Apr. 1992: 28–31, 36, 40.

From *Beowulf* to *Blood Meridian*

Cormac McCarthy's Demystification of the Martial Code

Rick Wallach

IN his essay "Blood Music," Peter Josyph notes the generic (if not genetic) relationship between *Blood Meridian* and *Beowulf*. There is much substance to this observation, and not only because the novel, like the poem, which Josyph calls one of its "grandfathers" (179), depicts an escalating process of violence. The two texts are really most alike in their detailed depiction of martial codes, by which I mean structured social systems that justify and promulgate conflict, represent violence as craft, and conventionalize destructive activity in a craftsmanly way.

Despite the outlandish violence of Cormac McCarthy's epic anti-western, this sanguine narrative cannot be considered nihilistic, even though some critics argue that its pervasive mayhem represents not much more than amoral naturalism. As Vereen M. Bell puts it, "the whole experience of McCarthy's work . . . is that nothing can be taken to stand as the truth. Anything that *stands* in this sense by definition cannot be true" (135). For Steven Shaviro, the gist of *Blood Meridian* "is only war, there is only the dance. Exile is not deprivation or loss, but our primordial and positive condition" (145). Novelist and surgeon

Richard Selzer, for whom the application of benign violence is a matter of craft, remarks that McCarthy's violence "is there for its own sake" (Josyph 176). Yet, despite the claim by *Blood Meridian*'s narrator that the child in whom "broods a taste for mindless violence" is father to the man (3), the novel evolves beyond the Old English epic, because it exposes the psychological and cultural mechanisms behind the martial code instead of merely chronicling the code's effects. In reality, *Blood Meridian* possesses a precise moral compass whose poles are the narrative voice and the voice of the monstrous Judge Holden, who, as Harold Bloom has observed, "has no ideology except blood, violence, war for its own sake. And that is what makes him so astonishing a figure, so frightening and foreboding" (Josyph and Bloom 11). However, Holden's voice is not the narrator's, and much of the narrative's aleatory value results from an implicit dialogue with its Anglo-Saxon antecedent.

The anonymous narrator of *Beowulf* foreshadows the carnage of its hero's battles by recounting the violent origins of Scyld Scefing's dynasty. The poem then deploys a series of conflicts initiated by Beowulf's friendly contest with Breca, intensified in the hero's verbal duel with Unferth, which finally breaks into physical violence with Grendel. In a struggle more furious yet, Beowulf battles Grendel's mother, and his climactic fight with the dragon is the most vicious of all. Stitched among these battles, soldierly braggadocio reprises yet other battles like subterranean percolations between eruptions. Even the denouement averts resolution, as Wiglaf predicts the disintegration of the entire world of the poem into another cataclysm of war. Beyond the litter of shattered bodies and kingdoms, only the martial code itself prevails.

Critics have traditionally accused Beowulf of hubris for choosing to battle the dragon for mere riches when the welfare of his kingdom is at stake. Such criticism begs the issue. The welfare of Beowulf's kingdom is irrelevant. Under the terms of the code he serves, he may not refuse to give battle and still continue to legitimize his sovereignty. The code of martial honor consumes imperatives of nationhood, blood relations, and friendship. Because everything is ultimately sanctified by and sacrificed to that code, the conflicts related by the poem belong to the order of sacrificial rituals. As Girard (1977) observes: "As the sacrificial conflict increases in intensity, so too does the violence. It is no longer the intrinsic value of the object that inspires the struggle; rather, it is the violence itself that bestows value on the objects, which are only pretexts for a conflict. From this point on it is violence that calls the tune. Violence is the divine force that everyone tries to use for his own purposes and that ends up using everyone for its own" (144).

Blood Meridian exposes this contagion of systematized violence by invoking *Beowulf* in its representation of another culture whose vitality derived from obedience to the martial code, the mid-nineteenth century American "Wild West." In some cases the invocation is explicit, as when Captain White's fallen filibusters are described as "unhorsed Saxons" (54), dispatched by Comanche spears and clubs rather than guns. The novel's philosopher of the code, Judge Holden, asserts the primacy of violence over form when he insists, "If war is not holy, man is nothing but antic clay" (307). But how does an ethos of violence perpetuate itself if its practitioners are so routinely consumed by their own conduct? According to Girard (1977), the code *appears* to reconstitute through a doubling effect that he ascribes to mimetic desire. The code assumes that a rival will always be available. The eternal regression behind this concept—that every object has already been and always will be desired by a rival—is itself doubled by the persistent regression into violence. By alternating between object-desire and revenge, all conflict assures that each successful rival will become a model of aggression for a subsequent challenger. Dianne Luce appreciates how Holden himself hides this doubling effect in plain sight of the gang when he spins his parable of the traveler and the harnessmaker. The judge obfuscates his own revelation by ascribing to mere "jealousy" the mimetic effect of the code: "By confessing that he has murdered the Christ-like traveler, the harnessmaker defines humanity and manhood to his son and may harness his son to that image, creating the same behavior in him" (28).

Girard believes that because mimetic desire depends upon opposition, it often appears as its own opposite. Thus, in both *Beowulf* and *Blood Meridian,* as in any jingoistic appeal to patriotic fervor, the solipsism of mimetic desire disappears behind a masquerade of ennobled emptying of the self into a commonhood. In operation, however, this charade is less an abnegation of desire than the abnegation of individual will. So disguised, the code may be especially seductive, and otherwise astute scholars of the poem have been taken in. The bonds of loyalty forged by the "bloody-minded ferocity behind the *comitatus* oath," the declaration of absolute fealty to one's king or captain, nevertheless strikes Howell Chickering as "a noble bond between men and not very far from what we now call brotherly love" (260). Dazzled by the illusion of self-sacrifice, which is no more than the desire to imitate and possess the authority of another, Chickering does not pause to reconsider the logical inconsistency between love and the bloodthirstiness he correctly deduces behind the oath. Neither does the anonymous *Beowulf* poet, for whom, like the Scylding *scop* or bard who is his own double within the text, the celebration of martial glory is the sole objective of his art.

However, "for the judge and his slow-witted pupils," as Bell notes, "the authority of [the judge's] presence compels all such incompatible distinctions to seem as one. The fact that his rhetorical authority obscures real contradictions for both himself and his listeners is a sign that he has contrived a belief system for which unwavering conviction is itself the objective" (125). The "noble bond" forged by such conviction finds the same self-subverting expression in the Glanton gang, comitatus of *Blood Meridian*, but its contradictions are vividly bared by the narrative: "They rode like men invested with a purpose whose origins were antecedent to them, like blood legatees of an order both imperative and remote. For although each man among them was discrete unto himself, conjoined they made a thing that had not been before and in that communal soul were wastes hardly reckonable more than those whited regions on old maps where monsters do live and where there is nothing other of the known world save conjectural winds" (152).

This is a geography of latent violence whose "conjectural winds" are the capriciousness of desire seeking objects to appropriate, from the heads and arms of dismembered monsters to the scalps of murdered Indians. The "whited regions" evoke ancient maritime charts with their spatially abbreviated terra incognita, spouting whales, coiling serpents, and krakens.

The same images pervade the contest between Beowulf and Breca upon "the sea roads, / the ocean of wind" (514–15). They not only dominate Beowulf's first battle with the monsters of the whited spaces, but they also expose the sacrificial aspect of Beowulf's dedication to the code, whose claim on his loyalty supercedes all personal relationships. His argument with Unferth entails an unblinking dismissal of his friend Breca in order to reaffirm his own triumph under the terms of the code. Beowulf's derision conflates his friend with his antagonist: "I never have heard / such struggle, sword-terror, told about you. / Never in the din and play of battle / did Breca or you show such courage" (581–85).

Thus Beowulf stops distinguishing friends from adversaries as soon as he realizes that they desire the same glory he does. He lashes out verbally, accusing Unferth of code violations, in this case patricide (587). Once he has attacked Unferth, he seemingly cannot contain himself and all but vomits hostility; in short order he accuses Hrothgar's entire comitatus, and by extension his host as well, of the most grievous code violation of all, cowardice: "But [Grendel] has discovered he need not dread / too great a feud, fierce rush of swords, / not from your people" (595–96). "Doubles are the final result and truth of mimetic desire," writes René Girard (1978), "a truth seeking acknowledgment but repressed by the principal characters because of their mutual antagonism" (41). Girard's observation accounts for Beowulf's insult to Hrothgar and his men in such gross violation of the laws of hospitality. At the same time, it explains why his outburst is nevertheless subsumed by the sham amiability of Heorot. The narrator merely glosses over the antagonism and xenophobia churning beneath his narrative.

Beowulf intrudes into the Scyldings' utter abjection in the wake of their humiliation by Grendel. As Julia Kristeva notes, "There looms, within abjection, one of those violent, dark revolts of being, directed against a threat that seems to emanate from an exorbitant outside or inside, ejected beyond the scope of the possible, the tolerable, the thinkable. It lies there, quite close, but it cannot be assimilated. It beseeches, worries, and fascinates desire . . . a vortex of summons and repulsion places the one haunted beside himself" (1). Inasmuch as abjection is pathologically averted desire, the Scyldings seem to confuse a disruptive element that is part of the original whole, Unferth, with Beowulf, an intruder from outside. This points to the illusion of mimetic doubling: even though Beowulf has arrived as an ally and savior, Unferth's derision and Beowulf's acrimonious response (499–594) remind us that custom and ceremony may be bent to channel violence, but violence is never permitted to disappear completely beneath superficial etiquettes.

Grendel, in fact, is a *product* of an uneasy interregnum between battles. He first intrudes into the celebration that follows the raising of Heorot, interrupting Hrothgar's consolidation of rule and its fatuous quietude. In social systems founded on violence, conflict always erupts anew. Like some psychic form of spontaneous combustion, violence first presents itself as an otherness to the illusion of peace: "Then the great monster in the outer darkness / suffered fierce pain, for each new day / he heard happy laughter loud in the hall" (86–88). Grendel is no less than the spirit of ineffectually elided violence, and represents that "massive and sudden emergence of uncanniness" Kristeva asserts to have been "familiar . . . in an opaque and forgotten life" but that "now harries [one] as radically separate, loathsome" (2). Moreover, it is precisely the scop's song of the world's creation, of delivering order out of chaos, that in direct narrative sequence triggers the monster's attacks (90–101). The ogre is uncanny because he is at once monstrous to the peace and utterly familiar by the terms of the martial code. Superficially unrecognizable as the Scyldings' ideal wish fulfillment, he nevertheless objectifies their obsession with violence and their discomfort with mere orderliness.

It is no accident that *Blood Meridian* is also set during a martial interregnum, in 1849, at the conclusion of the Mexican-American War and the United States' transcontinental territorial consolidation. Like Grendel invading Heorot, Judge Holden invades Reverend Green's tent (5) to disrupt his sermon and incite a riot, the tent collapsing amid another invocation of monstrous sea creatures, "like a huge and wounded medusa" (7). Similarly, Captain White's filibusters, like the restless warriors of Heorot, cannot abide the peace. Their dimly comprehended itch for combat, interpreted, as always, as patriotic fervor, sets the catastrophic narrative of the kid's encounter with the Glanton gang in motion.

Blood Meridian also exposes the conflict of doubles. Its narrative encodes complementarity in the physiognomies of the kid and Judge Holden, whose "animosities were formed and waiting before ever we two met" (307). The judge, himself a "massive and sudden emergence of uncanniness," is as bizarre a departure from physical norms as Grendel, "close on to seven feet in height," with a "serene and strangely childlike" face, and hands that are "small and delicate" (6). By contrast, the kid "is not big but he has big wrists, big hands" (4) and a scarred face whose eyes are "oddly innocent." In what may well be an allusion to Grendel in his mere and the nautical expertise of Beowulf, the kid "lives in a room above a courtyard behind a tavern and comes down at night like some fairybook beast to fight with the sailors" (4).

On closer examination, Beowulf also proves to be Grendel's rival double. The code effectively inhabits its subject as well as its object, in this case glory; the poem is amply seeded with Beowulf's claims to glory. Heorot is a monument "which the sons of men should hear of forever" (70), and this fame, as his risky derision of Hrothgar's comitatus implies, is precisely what Beowulf covets. Thus Beowulf and Grendel, in their mutual desire to possess Heorot, collide over the same object. But the object of desire always remains unattainable, because it is so defined by the other's desire that victory, which necessitates the liquidation of the other, evaporates the value of the object. Osborn cites Grendel's inability, after twelve years of all but unchallenged hegemony over Hrothgar's hall, "to approach the hall's numinous center" (116); Beowulf also fails to possess the barrow-treasure in the wake of his pyrrhic victory over the dragon. Similarly, the kid seems to lose everything he struggles toward; he cannot approach a burning mesquite clearly meant to parody the biblical burning bush (215), and shortly thereafter discovers that Glanton's retreating scalphunters have burned their valuable scalp collection (216); his last act before he dies is a visit to the whore, which is aborted by his impotence (332). Glanton's fleecing of Mangas Coloradas with a dummy whiskey barrel (241–42) constitutes a reductio ad absurdum of the theme of futile desire.

Once the code-hero triumphs over his rival, not only does his object lose its allure but, as Girard notes, "the [rival's] prestige vanishes. [The victor] must then turn to an even greater violence and seek out an obstacle that proves to be totally insurmountable" (148). Hence Beowulf tests his fealty to the code in progressively more violent struggles with progressively more *elemental* beings. Beowulf's battles suggest deflected sexuality because they enable him to connect physically with organic entities like Grendel, his mother, and even the dragon. Grendel is barely manlike; his mother, her femininity desecrated by her monstrousness, is even less so. The epiphallic judge's homoerotic death-embrace of the kid, whom he "gathered . . . in his arms against his immense and terrible flesh and shot the wooden barlatch home behind him" (333), redacts the she-beast's death embrasure by Beowulf within the deformed vulva of her mere. We would not be mistaken in inferring an inversion of phallic swordplay in this narration, especially considering that the kid had, apparently without success, availed himself of a whore scant moments before his fatal trip to the outhouse (332–33), even as Beowulf's sword had melted in the blood of Grendel's mother like a detumescent phallus.

The dragon is the most phallic and elemental rival of all. Beowulf swears that "I would carry no sword or weapons / against the serpent if I knew how else / to grapple proudly, wrestle the monster / as I did with Grendel" (2518–21). In its penile limblessness the creature, like the sexually perverse, bald, suggestively penile judge, is a manifestation of "immense and terrible flesh." In yet another expression of their mimetic rivalry, both the kid and the judge attempt to gratify themselves with figures of diminished sexuality as the children Holden rapes and murders, and the kid's "dwarf of a whore" (332). Like Beowulf, the kid, whose sexuality has been mitigated so completely by its deflection into violence, cannot survive direct contact with such unmitigated configurations of erotic desire as the judge or the dragon.

Juxtaposing similar or identical narrative elements reveals variations in emphasis as well as different levels of awareness on the part of the narrators, but this technique, in which McCarthy engages so powerfully, also tells us much about gendered role-playing in the etiology of violence. Claude Lévi-Strauss has observed that the meanings accorded to the narrative "gross constituents" of myth, or mythemes, depend as much on their relation as on their situational content (209–13). Following Lévi-Strauss, then, I want to pose a more paradoxical correlation, also rooted in the mythic representation of violence, and featuring the same elements of thwarted order, disrupted kingship and irrational deviations from an ideally ordered social norm. The Scyld's conflict with Grendel features all the mythemes of Euripides's *Bacchae,* with protagonists and antagonists exchanging roles. Grendel is in this sense Pentheus revisited. Dismembered by those whose rituals he intrudes on, Grendel dies in his mother's presence. Pentheus's mother's recovery from her intoxication symbolizes restoration of order, whereas Grendel's mother initiates another round of conflict. When the she-beast appears to wreak havoc, Hrothgar admits that he already *knew* of the existence of Grendel's mother (1345–56). The lateness of Hrothgar's revelation well serves dramatic recitation, but it also accentuates, by reinvoking the antifeminine bias of the poem, the effect of doubling or mirroring that Girard, Lévi-Strauss, and others find so central to myths and codes of violence. Her lair, wet, dank, hidden between hills, edged with "roots that sag and clutch" (1361–76), invokes both the Bacchae's grove and the male's terror of the feminine genitals. For all the exaggeratedly vulvic imagery of her fen, though, Grendel's mother reproduces mysteriously; there is no mention of a sire (1355–56). The ogre's apparently parthenogenetic descent from his hideous dam incarnates the warrior code's rejection of domesticity, and his cannibalism objectifies the self-consuming aspect of the code itself. James Earl observes that Grendel's mother "wreaks legally justifiable revenge for her son's death. That Beowulf was also justified in killing Grendel for revenge is not the point in Germanic law, and when Grendel's mother kills Æschere, Beowulf is justified in pursuing revenge once again. A legal system that encourages such a chain reaction contains a terrible contradiction: though vengeance is intended to inhibit violence, once it breaks out it is almost impossible to contain until it has run its awful course" (75). As Girard points out, this reconfiguration of gendered roles flags the sacrificial crisis: "The tendency to attribute to women what is probably a masculine trait of violence can be related to a major thematic motif of *The Bacchae:* the loss of sexual differentiation. As we have remarked, one of the effects of the sacrificial crisis is a certain feminization of the men, accompanied by a masculinization of the women. . . . The abolishment of sexual differences—for that matter, of all differences—is a reciprocal phenomenon, and the mythological redistribution has been carried out, as always, at the expense of reciprocity" (141).

Beowulf responds to Hrothgar's disclosure of the female monster's existence by undertaking the resolution of such gender confusion. When he wins his explicitly sexualized body-to-body battle with Grendel's mother, he effects a restabilization of gender roles, reenfranchising masculine sexuality, and restores social order while vindicating the masculine war code. Power, not generation, characterizes such sexual metaphors. In this ferocious spirit, the gang in *Blood Meridian,* out of ammunition and trapped by Indians, watches as the judge prepares an emergency ration of gunpowder out of bat shit and their collective urine. As the ex-priest Tobin describes the episode, "we hauled forth our members and at it we went and the judge on his knees kneadin the mass with his naked arms and the piss was splashin about" (132). The men fill their powder horns with the mixture "one by one circlin past him like communicants" (134) and slaughter their pursuers. Bill Spencer reminds us that "the prominent display of male genitals in this Eucharistic parody seems to reinforce another symbolic implication of the judge's complex character, for the judge himself appears to be a phallic symbol. . . . The phallus is of course an ambiguous symbol because of its positive associations with potency and creation and its negative association with male aggression" (103).

The same mythemes are assembled in their most negative formulations elsewhere in *Blood Meridian.* We find degradation of the feminine in the ritualistic slaughter of a crinoline-clad dancing bear during the saloon brawl the judge instigates. A patron demiurge of northland warriors like the wolves revered by Tobin and the gang members, the bear's masculinity is desecrated by its ballerina costume, and its murder is a "ritual [that] includes the letting of blood," as the judge explains, adding, "rituals which fail in this requirement are but mock rituals" (329). The bear's death symbolizes the exhaustion of an entire epoch of the code, but it also heralds a new one as surely as does the eradication of the buffalo, that symbol of the Native American masculine hunt ethos. Fort Griffin's bison-bone trade implies that the code has been reinscribed in a new, commercial, guise of jingoistic capitalism. The nature of this system has been hinted at already, in the commodification of human body parts, especially scalps. In effect, the socioeconomic system that has taken root along the newly "civilized" frontier provides "legal sanction, public opinion, and racism," which "have obscured the scalphunters' perception of the Indians' humanity" (Luce 37). This is a socioeconomic system that, like the martial code of which it is an extension if not an end product, consumes the land, consumes the life upon it—as is plainly demonstrated by Fort Griffin's hills of bison bones—and consumes its votaries as well. According to Christine Chollier, in *Blood Meridian* "general massacre replaces trade. However, the judge argues that war is 'the ultimate trade awaiting its ultimate practitioner' [248]. So violence, which first appeared as complete annihilation of trade, is reestablished as the ultimate form of trade" (174–75). David Holloway argues *Blood Meridian*'s linkage of capitalism with violence even more explicitly, perceiving that "as writing which is made in the closing decades of the twentieth century" the novel "seems to raise broad questions about the difficulty in thinking and articulating an oppositional voice under late capitalism" (195).

Blood Meridian concludes in a locale that mirrors the fens of *Beowulf*. The "mudded dogyard behind the premises" (334) is situated among windrows of buffalo bones behind a saloon that, like Hrothgar's hall, is a scene of feasting, incipient sexuality, and explosive violence. In a reaffirmation of the primacy of the code, the little girl whose father owned the bear disappears after accompanying the carcass out the door of the saloon. She has become another victim, we suspect, of the malevolent judge (333). Meanwhile, whatever is left of the kid, as two cowboys behold inside the dogyard outhouse, is too horrible to describe; asked what he has seen there, the first refuses to speak and merely walks back to the bar (334). He has witnessed the aftermath of another sacrifice to the code and responded to it with the silence befitting a mystery.

Inside the saloon an "enormous drunken whore"—sexuality once again rendered nongenerative and subject to masculine utility—wears "nothing but a pair of men's drawers" as a counterpoint to the bear's crinoline, and rollicks androgynously through the hall, "clapping her hands at the bandstand and calling drunkenly for music" (334). Sure enough, the judge is once again restless. Like the deaths of the bear and of Beowulf himself, the "lunar dome" (335) of Holden's skull connotes the passing of the initial age of American frontier exploration, with its special brand of genocidal violence. His dance underscores the ultimate frangibility of any lineage based on a patriarchal model of violence; indeed, his murder of the kid extinguishes the last surviving member of the gang. Yet how easily the judge recruits another nameless disciple to explode into violence and slaughter the bear.

The conclusion of *Blood Meridian* exposes the mechanism by which the code perpetuates itself. In textual terms, the code becomes a parody of the life force. It lives through sequences of disposable individual bodies and disposable extended social bodies. Social order in a patriarchy demands the differentiation of male and female sexuality, yet sexuality is disposable as well, inasmuch as the code reconstitutes itself solely through conflict. As in *Blood Meridian,* "There is no place for women in the masculine economy of *Beowulf;* they have no space to occupy, to claim, to speak from" (Overing 222). Androcentric institutions and lineages prove ultimately transient, swept away by the violence on which they were founded in the first place. Yet that very fragility of patriarchal structures is a virtual necessity for the code's perpetuation. As our juxtaposition of the mythemes of *Beowulf* and *The Bacchae* suggest, the feminine is the code's rival double. Thus the code substitutes violence for the feminine object of masculine desire, enabling it to deform and parody natural law. Holden may well be suggesting as much when he asserts that Reverend Green had been caught "having congress with a goat" (7) and thereby incites a thug in the audience to open fire.

Operating as if it were an organically generative process, the code canalizes mimetic desire solely to assure that another rival will always be available, perfectly capable of constructing the delusional grandeur of a new and equally doomed Heorot around itself. As Clare Lees notes of the warriors in *Beowulf,* "their desires are channeled into a social ethos that ritualizes desire as heroic choice, thus ensuring the preservation of that ethos. The institution of the warrior caste encodes the desires of its members, and warriors choose death as a means of its reproduction" (143). Hence, when the judge retrieves the idiot from the river following the solicitude of Sarah Borginnis and reenacts a twisted scenario of birth with him (258–59), and when he insists that the kid's demonstration of even minimal compassion has "poisoned . . . in all its enterprise" the gang's mission (307), he enacts once more the rout of the feminine by the ethos of the code. Holden understands that compassion dissolves the difference between self and other, which alone makes rivalry and violence possible. The kid's double-negative rebuke of the judge—"You ain't nothin" (331)—betokens his suspicion of the illusion and an attempt to withdraw from the ethos of the code. Mere instinct, inadequately focused by rhetoric, cannot counterweigh the code's mystifying appeal. Its absolute violence is not susceptible to half-formed insights.

Compared to the bombastic, self-deluded orations of code heroes like Beowulf and Hrothgar, Judge Holden's proclamations indicate a sophisticated grasp of his role as antagonist and the subterfuges necessary to advance his purposes. His facile comparisons of war to dance, to religion, and to desire itself recall Elaine Scarry's observation that war "requires both the reciprocal infliction of massive injury and the eventual disowning of the injury so that its attributes can be transferred elsewhere, as they cannot if they are permitted to cling to the original site of the wound, the human body" (64). Critics who have accused McCarthy of amorality ought to bear in mind Scarry's and Kristeva's disclosure of the necessity of expelling the sites of pain. However, as Andrew McKenna insists: "If [violence] is the 'subject' of all literature and criticism—indeed, of all possible cultural discourse—it is because violence, as Girard argues, is the true subject, the active and passive agent, the agendum and dilendum, of all cultural institutions, of institutional formation and dissolution. Whereas for Derrida literature consists in deferring this total dissolution, for Girard it has superior merit, in its greatest moments, of referring directly to it" (111). Just so; in *Blood Meridian*'s graphic depiction of the evisceration of Captain White's troop (54), the decapitation of the white Jackson (107), the murder of Owens the hosteller (236), and numerous descriptions of scalpings and other assorted mayhem, the narrator holds the damage before the reader and keeps it there. The rudimentary insight of the illiterate man—formerly the kid—though inadequate in itself, incrementally contributes to a progressive, millennium-long process of such literary references to the code.

Thus, far from identifying itself with the judge's amorality, the narrative voice of *Blood Meridian* consistently subverts his philosophy. As the incarnation of the property of the code that obscures pain, Holden is an archon of language and inscription. This master of many tongues effaces the physical subjects of his journal as he records them so that the site of injury is indeed erased from memory. Less concerned with "writing the body" than with the necessity of *over*writing it, his access and accession to violence is so acute that in his persona violence turns in upon itself in an extended parody, a mimesis of consciousness. As I have argued elsewhere (1995), he well understands that conflict of doubles underlies the violence obtaining not only between himself and the kid but also between all men:

> Everbody dont have to have a reason to be someplace.
> That's so, said the judge. They do not have to have a reason. But order is not set aside because of their indifference.
> [The kid] regarded the judge warily.
> Let me put it this way, said the judge. If it is so that they themselves have no reason and yet are indeed here must they not be here by reason of some other? And if this is so can you guess who that other might be?
> No. Can you?
> I know him well. (331)

The progress of the narrative, from the kid's "taste for mindless violence" to his resistance to the judge's discourse, cannot reasonably be interpreted as an amoral representation of violence for its own sake. *Blood Meridian,* facing its precursor across an eon, well and truly applies the darkened mirrors of language to the task of demystifying mimetic violence.

Works Cited

Bell, Vereen M. *The Achievement of Cormac McCarthy.* Baton Rouge: Louisiana State University Press, 1988.

Beowulf. Ed. and trans. Howell D. Chickering, Jr. New York: Doubleday, 1977.

Chollier, Christine. "I ain't come back rich, that's for sure,' or, The Questioning of Market Economies in Cormac McCarthy's Novels." *Myth, Legend, Dust: Critical Responses to Cormac McCarthy.* Ed. Rick Wallach. Manchester: Manchester University Press, 2000. 171–76.

Earl, James W. *Thinking about Beowulf.* Stanford: Stanford University Press, 1994.

Girard, René. *To Double Business Bound.* Baltimore: Johns Hopkins University Press, 1978.

———. *Violence and the Sacred.* Trans. Patrick Gregory. Baltimore: Johns Hopkins University Press, 1977.

Holloway, David. "'A false book is no book at all': The Ideology of Representation in *Blood Meridian* and the Border Trilogy." *Myth, Legend, Dust: Critical Responses to Cormac McCarthy.* Ed. Rick Wallach. Manchester: Manchester University Press, 2000. 185–200.

Josyph, Peter. "Blood Music: Reading *Blood Meridian*." *Sacred Violence: A Reader's Companion to Cormac McCarthy.* Ed. Wade Hall and Rick Wallach. El Paso: Texas Western Press, 1995. 169–88.

———, and Harold Bloom. "Tragic Ecstasy: A Conversation with Harold Bloom about Cormac McCarthy's *Blood Meridian*." *Southwestern American Literature* 26.1 (fall 2000): 7–20.

Kristeva, Julia. *Powers of Horror: An Essay on Abjection.* Trans. Leon S. Roudiez. New York: Columbia University Press, 1982.

Lees, Clare A. "Men and Beowulf." *Medieval Masculinities: Regarding Men in the Middle Ages.* Ed. Clare A. Lees. Minneapolis: University of Minnesota Press, 1991. 129–48.

Lévi-Strauss, Claude. *Structural Anthropology.* Trans. Claire Jacobson and Brooke Grundfest Schoepf. New York: Basic Books, 1963.

Luce, Dianne. "Ambiguities, Dilemmas and Double Binds in Cormac McCarthy's *Blood Meridian*." *Southwestern American Literature* 26.1 (fall 2000): 21–46.

McCarthy, Cormac. *Blood Meridian, or, The Evening Redness in the West.* New York: Random House, 1985.

McKenna, Andrew. *Violence and Difference.* Urbana: University of Illinois Press, 1992.

Osborn, Marijane. "The Great Feud: Scriptural History and Strife in *Beowulf*." *Beowulf: Basic Readings.* Ed. Peter S. Baker. New York: Garland, 1995. 111–25.

Overing, Gillian. "The Women of *Beowulf*: A Context for Interpretation." *Beowulf: Basic Readings*. Ed. Peter S. Baker. New York: Garland, 1995. 219–60.

Scarry, Elaine. *The Body in Pain*. New York: Oxford University Press, 1985.

Shaviro, Steven. "The Very Life of the Darkness: A Reading of *Blood Meridian*." *Perspectives on Cormac McCarthy*. Ed. Edwin T. Arnold and Dianne C. Luce. Jackson: University Press of Mississippi, 1993. 143–56.

Spencer, William. "Evil Incarnate in *Blood Meridian*: Cormac McCarthy's Seductive Judge." *Publications of the Mississippi Philological Association* (1995): 100–105.

Wallach, Rick. "Judge Holden: *Blood Meridian*'s Evil Archon." *Sacred Violence: A Reader's Companion to Cormac McCarthy*. Ed. Wade Hall and Rick Wallach. El Paso: Texas Western Press, 1995. 125–36.

McCarthy and the Sacred

A Reading of *The Crossing*

Edwin T. Arnold

F OR readers of his play *The Stonemason* and his novel *The Crossing*, both published in 1994, that Cormac McCarthy is a writer of the sacred should be beyond dispute. The two works bring to the forefront spiritual issues that have been an essential, though often disguised, part of his fiction from his first book onward. Expressed largely in Christian terminology—sin, guilt, grace, and redemption—in the so-called southern novels (*The Orchard Keeper* through *Suttree*), these concerns have taken on a broader, more metaphysical quality in the later works, those set in the American Southwest and Mexico (*Blood Meridian* and beyond). Indeed, with the greater emphasis on the natural world in these books (though certainly present in the southern works, landscape and animals play an increasingly larger role in the western novels) and the self-conscious use of interpolated "oral" parables within the narratives (which cause us to reconsider the essential role of narrative itself), one might posit that in moving west McCarthy developed a worldview more in keeping with Native American cosmology than with traditional Eurocentric Christian perspectives. There is still, however, a definite Christian sensibility underlying his narrative, one related, I think, to the esoteric philosophical and religious views of mystical thinkers like Jacob Boehme. We might rightly, in fact, identify McCarthy as a mystical writer himself, a spiritual author who venerates life in all its forms, who believes in a source of being and order deeper than that manifested in outward show and pretense of human individuality, and who acknowledges the inevitability of death not as absurdity or tragedy but as meaningful transition from one plane of existence to another.

The Crossing illustrates these ideas more explicitly and with greater insistence than any of McCarthy's previous works, including *Blood Meridian* and *The Stonemason,* his other most overtly philosophical/theological narratives.[1] In ecological terms, it asks that we reconsider our position and role in the natural world. In religious terms, it asks that we recognize how limited our perception of the spiritual realm remains. The title alone encourages a kind of religious exegesis. In plural form, it would identify the three excursions or quests the protagonist, Billy Parham, makes across the U.S.-Mexico border; that McCarthy groups these journeys into one inclusive movement in his title suggests, then, a concern greater than geographical or cultural passage. Given the amount of suffering, both physical and emotional, that Billy experiences, the title also carries with it a sense of punishment and abasement, leading, perhaps, to refined understanding or even redemption, as is common in tales of visionary journeys. As James Keegan writes, "Billy is certainly a picaro and an Everyman, a human sufferer in a landscape so apparently meaningless that it paradoxically and consistently evokes the most basic existential and theological questions, continually returning us to consider meaning at its primary level" (1). And yet the reading experience itself resists any reductive attempt to impose order. It demands of us another state of understanding altogether, something beyond the rational or symbolic or psychological.

The novel requires—of Billy and the reader—a willingness to contemplate at no remove the mystical and the sacred. For an author who details so often and so explicitly the violence and despair and apparent randomness of life, the possibilities of grace, love, and charity in the world might seem remote, and yet these qualities appear repeatedly in his work. "You think God looks out for people?" Lacey Rawlins asks John Grady Cole in *All the Pretty Horses,* and when John Grady answers affirmatively, Rawlins agrees: "Way the world is . . . you dont know what's goin to happen. I'd say He's just about got to. I dont believe we'd make it a day otherwise" (92). In one sense this is a simplistic answer, made before both boys experience the awful consequences of their journey, but in another it seems to be a core belief in McCarthy's work, and nowhere more so than in *The Crossing.*

The world as depicted by McCarthy, composed of the temporal, day-to-day series of individual acts and multiplying consequences, works on its own level, makes no choices based on such philosophically derived concepts as "justice" or "intention" or "merit." "The events of the world can have no separate life from the world," the hermit priest tells Billy Parham in the first of the interpolated tales. "And yet the world itself can have no temporal view of things. It can have no cause to favor certain enterprises over others. The passing of armies and the passing of sands in the desert are one. There is no favoring, you see. How could there be? At whose behest?" (148). But in McCarthy's fiction this fact does not thereby negate the larger, comprehensive essence of a sentient, animistic universe, or of a spiritual "awareness" that lies at the heart of that universe.

Such a reading opposes that of Dana Phillips and others who feel that in McCarthy there is no deeper meaning to things than the things themselves, that history or identity or even consciousness are really not "meaningful categor[ies]" (Phillips 440) in McCarthy's lexicon. "But what sort of literature remains possible if we relinquish the myth of human apartness?" Phillips quotes Lawrence Buell as asking in *The Environmental Imagination.* "It must be a literature that abandons, or at least questions, what would seem to be literature's most basic foci: character, persona, narrative consciousness. What literature could survive under these conditions?" (433). McCarthy does indeed ask that we "relinquish" this "myth," that we alter our anthropomorphic view of existence, that we acknowledge and engage our oneness with the natural, atomic, and finally cosmic world. And in this sense, he does require us to speak what Christopher Manes calls "a language of ecological humility," one that is "free from the directionalities of humanism, a language that incorporates a decentered, postmodern, post-humanist perspective" (17). But McCarthy, I think, does more than that. He is unquestionably among our finest nature writers, possessed of brilliance in describing the naturalistic details of the physical world, and his ecological awareness is at the heart of much of his work.[2] Yet, at the same time, he posits the existence of a deeper, truer life, an "invisible" world suggested by, and sometimes disguised by, the physical. Indeed, the insubstantiality, the "fragility" of the perceived physical world is explored at length in *The Crossing*.[3] "You cannot touch the world," Don Arnulfo, the native wolf trapper, tells Billy near the beginning of the novel. "You cannot hold it in your hand for it is made of breath only" (46). "Stones themselves are made of air," the priest says. "What they have power to crush never lived" (158). The blind man cautions that "because what can be touched falls into dust there can be no mistaking these things for the real. At best they are only tracings of where the real has been. Perhaps they are not even that. Perhaps they are no more than obstacles to be negotiated in the ultimate sightlessness of the world" (294). "The world has no name," the *gerente* Quijada tells Billy. "The names of the cerros and the sierras and the deserts exist only on maps. We name them that we do not lose our way. Yet it was because the way was lost to us already that we have made those names. The world cannot be lost. We are the ones" (387). And, finally, the gypsy who heals Billy's horse tells the young man that the essential world "cannot be quit for it is eternal in whatever form as are all things within it" (413).

The image that unites these two readings of the world, the natural and the spiritual, is that of the matrix.[4] A matrix can be conceived in two ways: as both the primal substance, the "mother," out of which other essences or forces develop and, in more modern terms, as a network of interconnected or intersecting forces. In both cases the emphasis is placed on the basic unity and interdependence of all elements, no matter how individual or separate each apparent "entity" might seem when privileged or placed in arbitrary isolation. Such a belief is at the heart of contemporary ecological concepts of nature and the human's place in it. The First Law of Ecology, according to Barry Commoner, is that "everything is connected to everything else." "All of nature has utility, all is important," is how ecologist Neil Evernden states it. "There are no discrete entities" (93). And this is one of the "truths" that Billy Parham must learn. "So everything is necessary," the priest tells him. "Every least thing. This is the hard lesson. Nothing can be dispensed with. Nothing despised. Because the seams are hid from us, you see. The joinery. The way in which the world is made. We have no way to know what could be taken away. What omitted. We have no way to tell what might stand and what might fall" (143).[5]

The first emblem of this network of necessity is the wolf Billy Parham traps and then attempts to set free in the beginning section of the novel. Like Faulkner's bear, Old Ben, the wolf signifies a (super)natural thread of the world that threatens a domesticated people and therefore must be controlled or destroyed. At the same time, its inherent freedom and sovereignty speak to some disregarded but essential desire within these people to experience such knowledge and existence. After Billy has caught the wolf, he sits by the campfire watching the fettered animal. We are told:

> When the flames came up her eyes burned out there like gate-lamps to another world. A world burning on the shore of an unknowable void. A world construed out of blood and blood's alcahest and blood in its core and in its integument because it was that nothing save blood had power to resonate against that void which threatened hourly to devour it. . . . When those eyes and the nation to which they stood witness were gone at last with their dignity back into their origins there would perhaps be other fires and other witnesses and other worlds otherwise beheld. But they would not be this one. (73–74)[6]

The wolf, in its natural world, "reads" its environment by engaging it in an intimacy unknown to or forgotten by man. For example, as she approaches the traps Billy and his father have hidden, "She circled the set for the better part of an hour sorting and indexing the varied scents and ordering their sequences in an effort to reconstruct the events that had taken place here" (26). This is admittedly a physical existence she is ordering, "indexing," but it also suggests a deeper knowledge. Don

Arnulfo tells Billy that "the wolf is a being of great order and that it knows what men do not: that there is no order in the world save that which death has put there" (45). The wolf bait, alchemistically prepared by the old magus Echols (who, like Merlin, has disappeared, vanished from the modern world Billy inhabits), is intended to lure the animal to its death and extinction by manipulating the natural order. The potions are black magic, perversions of the pattern of the natural world. "In the jars dark liquids. Dried viscera. Liver, gall, kidneys. The inward parts of the beast who dreams of man and has so dreamt in running dreams a hundred thousand years and more. Dreams of that malignant lesser god come pale and naked and alien to slaughter all his clan and kin and rout them from their house. A god insatiable whom no ceding could appease nor any measure of blood" (17).[7] The potion chosen, a "Number Seven Matrix" (44) prepared from meat and fluid of the slaughtered animals, serves as sensory simulacrum of some otherwise concealed and indefinable knowing now lost to the human.[8]

In the course of his journey with the wolf, Billy Parham grows more aware of this other world. He has always had a sense of kinship with this aspect of nature, as indicated by his early dreams and visionary experiences.[9] But he has retained his separation. In his determination to "save" the wolf, he has also attempted to make himself master of the animal, has tried to determine what is right and good for her.[10] His good intentions have resulted in the wolf's greater suffering and finally in its death, killed by Billy's own bullet. Afterward the boy carries the wolf's body to the mountains as he had promised. Don Arnulfo has told him, "El lobo es una cosa incognoscible. . . . Lo que se tiene en la trampa no es mas que dientes y forro. El lobo propio no se puede conocer. Lobo o lo que sabe el lobo. Tan como preguntar lo que saben las piedras. Los arboles. El mundo" (45) (The wolf is an unknowable thing. That which one has in the trap is no more than teeth and fur. One cannot know the true wolf. Wolf or what the wolf knows. It's like asking what the stones know. The trees. The world).[11] But Billy tries to know. He samples her blood, "which tasted no different than his own" (125).[12] As he waits until dawn to bury the body, he "sat by her and put his hand upon her bloodied forehead and closed his own eyes that he could see her running in the mountains, running in the starlight where the grass was wet and the sun's coming as yet had not undone the rich matrix of creatures passed in the night before her . . . all nations of the possible world ordained by God of which she was one among and not separate from" (127). This vision of the "rich matrix of creatures," so different from the artificial matrix of human device, is one of McCarthy's loveliest passages (echoing as it does Robinson Jeffers's magical poem "Hurt Hawks"). Indeed, the narrator's voice speaks directly to us here, as if to validate Billy's experience, not to question or amend the moment:

> He took up her stiff head out of the leaves and held it or he reached to hold what cannot be held, what already ran among the mountains at once terrible and of a great beauty, like flowers that feed on flesh. What blood and bone are made of but can themselves not make on any altar nor by any wound of war. What we may well believe has power to cut and shape and hollow out the dark form of the world surely if wind can, if rain can. But which cannot be held never be held and is no flower but is swift and a huntress and the wind itself is in terror of it and the world cannot lose it. (127)

This passage elevates the idea of the matrix from the physical to the spiritual world and anticipates the more theological concerns that follow.

In such descriptions McCarthy suggests a biocentric view of nature. Billy enters into an afterworld of animals and, in doing so, momentarily transcends his human perception. Neil Evernden asks in his essay "Beyond Ecology," "Where do you draw the line between one creature and another? Where does one organism stop and another begin? Is there even a boundary between you and the non-living world? . . . How, in short, can you make any sense out of the concept of man as a discrete entity?" (95). The same questions are inherent in *The Crossing*. "This flesh is but a memento, yet it tells the true," the priest instructs Billy. "Ultimately every man's path is every other's. There are no separate journeys for there are no separate men to make them. All men are one and there is no other tale to tell" (156–57). But this "literal interrelatedness" of man and man, and of man and environment (Evernden 102) does not thereby reduce the mystery of life and being. When Billy shortly afterward wakes "at some unknown hour and started up to see a figure watching him from the doorway but it was only the clay olla hanging there . . . and not some other kind of figure of some other kind of clay" (160), this description is not meant to say that there is no more to people than the clay of their flesh. McCarthy does not deny that bodies, like all physical things, are temporal and frail and will return to earth, often in manners violent and gross to our sensibilities. But when, for example, in *Blood Meridian* he describes the scalphunters "crackling" with sparks as they undress and then notes that "each man was seen to wear a shroud of palest fire. Their arms aloft pulling at their clothes were luminous and each obscure soul was enveloped in audible shapes of light as if it had always been so" (222), he is not, as Dana Phillips holds, simply reducing this moment to the natural phenomenon of static electricity (435). He instead implies a spiritual essence and connection, a temper or affinity that resides in "each obscure soul" and links one with another in a common bond of being.

And here is found a second concept of the matrix, that of the primal condition or source, the "divine protoforce laden with all the qualities and potentialities in the world" (Weeks 198). One of the epigraphs to *Blood Meridian* is taken from Jacob Boehme, the seventeenth-century religious mystic and philosopher.[13] Among Boehme's conceptions was that of the *Mysterium Magnum,* the title of one of his major treatises (1623). Boehme believed that all life came from this one source: "Everything in the depths above the earth, upon the earth, and within the earth interacts reciprocally like a single thing . . . having various forces and effects, but only one matrix *(Mutter),* from which every thing originates and flows. And all creatures are made out of these qualities, and originate and live therein, as within their matrix. Thus, too, earth and stones take their origin therefrom, as does everything that grows out of the earth. All of this lives and flows from the force of these qualities" (quoted in Weeks 65).

Because all forms of nature, animate and inanimate, human and nonhuman, come from this source, and because this source is from God, then all forms hold an aspect of God, a divinity, within. Thus,

"All human beings are fundamentally only one man," Boehme writes (149). This divine essence could be found in the most evil of people, the most savage of beasts. Evil itself was not the opposite of good; rather, it was "the type of the good that has been stunted and perverted in its growth" (Weeks 181). Although evil disrupts the order and unity of the world, it is also necessary to the world. As Boehme put it, "This world is rooted in evil and good, and there can be neither one of them without the other. But the great misfortune in it is that evil is preponderating therein over good, and the wrath stronger than love, and this is due to the sin of the devil and of man, who excited nature by their perverted desires, so that the world is now powerfully qualified in wrath, acting like a poison within the body" (173).

Boehme saw humankind existing in three states simultaneously: the external world composed of the natural elements; the world of darkness "wherein is born the fire as the eternal torment"; and the world of light, "wherein resides happiness and the Spirit of God" (267). "The external world has been outbreathed from the holy and from the dark world," Boehme wrote in *Mysterium Magnum*. "It is, therefore, evil and good, and in love and wrath; but, compared with the spiritual world, it is only like a smoke or a fog" (172). As David Weeks explains, using Boehme's *Six Theosophic Points* as his source, "The three worlds are not located and separated from one another by boundaries. They are the three moments in a process of self-revelation of the divine will. . . . The external principle of nature is caught up in a perpetual war and strife. . . . The life of nature and the warfare which rages in the human domain are one. Even the forms of nature accuse each other of evil and engage in mutual destruction. The dark-world is like the tyranny of this world; the more evil and vicious a creature, the greater its power" (179). Thus, there is, in Boehme's view, no "justice" inherent in this "external" world, no eventual righting of wrongs or even a "natural" balance of good and evil. This is a world of woe, where the righteous suffer and the corrupt, the "godless" (although God does reside in the "abyss" of even the most depraved soul) are free to explore and expand their evil as they wish. Indeed, the most perverted may attain enormous power in the terrestrial world, and against them those who seek the good may have little defense or strength.

Boehme held that in the terrestrial state, man isolates himself from the rest of creation, caught up in his (illusive) individual consciousness and will, a state of essential exile, separated from the whole; whereas in the celestial state he will return to his place in the matrix, resign his individual personality, his "selfish will," to the greater "nothingness" of spiritual existence. In *Forty Questions on the Soul*, Boehme described the Deity's mystical essence as the "Ungrund" (the "unground"), implying both nothingness and all, that which in being everything is equally an incomprehensible "No thing" (Weeks 147). The evil of the world, even death itself, provide, in a sense, a foundation against which this "nothingness" can be set and are thus necessary components of terrestrial existence that lead to salvation through self-recognition and the "acknowledgment of the tragic ground of life." As Weeks puts it, "Because the three worlds are inextricably bound together, there is no redemption without terror and tragedy. Not only is grim death a root of life, there would be no joy if not for woe" (179). This moment, this "shock" of knowledge and recognition (the *Schrack:* the sudden awareness and terror inspired in the one who suddenly comprehends both his corruption and divinity), is thus a transforming event, and beyond it all perception must be forever changed.

The three major interpolated narratives in *The Crossing*—those of the priest, the blind man, and the gypsy—told to Billy on his three journeys into Mexico, reflect Boehme's philosophy and serve as warnings to the boy against his own spiritual peril. In the first of these encounters, Billy meets the hermit priest living in the ruins of Huisiachepic, the deserted town where the priest has come "seeking evidence for the hand of God in the world" (142). The story he tells Billy concerns a "heretic," a "certain man" (142) who is also all men. Billy meets the priest after his failed attempt to return the wolf to the mountains of Mexico but before he returns home to discover the terrible events that have occurred during his absence. Nor does he yet know of his partial responsibility for the murder of his parents through his unintentional complicity with the strange Indian lurking near their home and his heedless abandonment of the family, taking with him his father's rifle, in order to save the wolf. But Billy is by this time aware that he has separated himself from family and community, for he has now spent weeks wandering alone in the mountains, confronting his own wildness, his own capacity for alienation.

The essence of the priest's tale is that man cannot reason with God, cannot require balance or justice or even understanding.[14] "It seemed that what he wished, this man, was to strike some colindancia with his Maker. Assess boundaries and metes. See that lines were drawn and respected. Who could think such a reckoning possible?" the priest asks. "The boundaries of the world are those of God's devising. With God there can be no reckoning. With what would one bargain?" (151). To "reckon" in this way would separate God from man, externalize the divine. What the heretic comes to realize is that God is all-encompassing. "Here was a God to study," the priest says, describing the heretic's dream. "A God with a fathomless capacity to bend all to an inscrutable purpose. Not chaos itself lay outside of that matrix. And somewhere in that tapestry that was the world in its making and in its unmaking was a thread that was he and he woke weeping" (149). The heretic also learns (as many others will tell Billy) that God cannot be "eluded nor yet set aside nor circumscribed about and it was true that He did indeed contain all else within Him even to the reasoning of the heretic else He were no God at all" (156). As the priest tells the boy (repeating image and language previously used by the narrator in describing the death and burial of the wolf [127]):

> His voice is not to be mistaken. When men hear it they fall to their knees and their souls are riven and they cry out to Him and there is no fear in them but only that wildness of heart that springs from such longing and they cry out to stay his presence for they know at once that while godless men may live well enough in their exile those to whom He has spoken can contemplate no life without Him but only darkness and despair. (152)

The "exile," according to the priest, results from man's attempts to remove himself from the matrix by declaring his independence from, his superiority over the rest of the natural world, and furthermore by assigning to himself an individual uniqueness within the race of humans that separates him from the common fellowship. "To God every man is a heretic," the priest concludes. "The heretic's first act is to name his brother. So that he may step free of him. Every word we speak is a vanity. Every breath taken that does not bless is an affront. . . . In the end we shall all of us be only what we have made of God. For nothing is real save his grace" (158).

At the end of his lengthy parable, the priest tells the boy, "Go home" (159). Others have told and will tell him the same thing. Indeed, "Go home" and "Vaya con Dios" become the repeated instructions and benedictions in this book, and in each case Billy looks back at the one he is leaving as if to fix that person in a certain time and place. In ecological understanding, things are defined in large part by their environment: they *belong* to a place and to be elsewhere is to be "out of context" (Evernden 100). In a religious sense, the divinity within the flesh and matter of the terrestrial world yearns for the spiritual world of light, for ultimate unity with God. Billy represents both kinds of displacement, geographical and spiritual. "I aint sick . . . and I aint lost," Billy insistently tells the priest (139), but clearly he is both.

When Billy meets the blind man, the boy is making his second journey into Mexico, this time with his brother Boyd, their ostensible purpose to retrieve their murdered father's stolen horses. Why do so, he is asked more than once. What purpose will thus be served? The horse trader Gillian puts the question directly to him, again indicating the interconnectedness of all things:

> What remedy can there be? What remedy can there be for what is not? You see? And where is the remedy that has no unforeseen consequence? . . . You do not know what things you set in motion, he said. No man can know. No prophet foresee. The consequences of an act are often quite different from what one would guess. You must be sure that the intention in your heart is large enough to contain all wrong turnings, all disappointments. Do you see? Not everything has such a value. (202)

Gillian warns against attempting to impose one's will on the world itself. In returning the wolf to Mexico, Billy, for all his good intentions, placed his youthful, romantic desires above the needs of his family, and the results were disastrous. Now he repeats the same mistake by demanding a personal justice, an accounting, having failed to heed the meaning of the priest's story. Billy is more serious now—he has been tempered by tragedy—but he has not yet learned that the world works according to its own devices and not those of the individual. And once more he encounters disaster, his brother shot and the horses again lost.

It is in this state that he meets the blind man and hears the second tale. The blind man cautions, through his experience, against despair and estrangement. When he loses his eyes to the grotesque German captain Wirtz, the blind man loses the physical world as well. And yet the absence of the physical world and the subsequent plunge into the dark one (where he gives in to his grief and attempts suicide) lead him eventually to a deeper understanding, one he attempts to relate to Billy. The blind man echoes Boehme's theology throughout. The physical world is not the real world; indeed, it is both fragile and "perilous": "That which was given him to help him make his way in the world has power also to blind him to the way where his true path lies" (293). This world, moreover, contains little in the way of justice. Evil has the greater power, for the good man "will not know that while the order which the righteous seek is never righteousness itself but is only order, the disorder of evil is in fact the thing itself" (293). The blind man's final "truth" (for he tells Billy he has "no desire to entertain him nor yet even to instruct him," only to "tell what was true" [284]) is, again, the temporal and secondary nature of the physical world: "Lo que debemos entender . . . es que ultimamente todo es polvo. Todo lo que podemos tocar. Todo lo que podemos ver. En éste tenemos la evidencia más profunda de la justicia, de la misericordia. En ésta vemos la bendición más grande de Dios" (293) (What we should understand . . . is that finally everything is dust. All we can touch. All we can see. In this we have evidence more profound than justice, than mercy. In this we see the greatest blessing of God).

Like the horse trader Gillian, the blind man argues against trying to remake the past. Only by losing himself in his blindness does he find the place, the "ground," to discover the true meaning of being. He calls for an acceptance of acts and consequences. The man who attempts to "impose order and lineage upon things which rightly have none" will bring about his own destruction. In seeking justice, he may "indemnify his words with blood" (293), as does Boyd, who is described in the *corridero* after his death as the "youth who sought justice" but followed a "bloodfilled road" (375) in doing so. The blind man reminds Billy that there is no guarantee of justice in this world, only "la bendición más grande de Dios" (293), and it is this grace of God all must await. Until then, the best that one can do is to "begin again" each day (291).[15]

On his third journey, this one undertaken to find and return Boyd's body to his native country, Billy hears the last parable, told by the gypsy who stops to treat Billy's wounded horse. The gypsy attempts to show Billy, through his story of the two airplanes, that the "vanity" of his need to "reclaim" his dead brother is as selfish and misguided as the rich man's attempts to recover the plane in which his son died. As Billy's recent dream (400) has indicated, "Boyd" no longer exists. ("I think the dead have no nationality," Quijada has earlier told Billy. "No. But their kin do," Billy answers [387], revealing his true motivation.) The "legends" of the lost plane (which resembles Hemingway's snow leopard in "The Snows of Kilimanjaro") and of the desperado Boyd, whether "factual" or not, have a living truth for all who hear or tell the tales. But the actual plane and Boyd's desiccated corpse, as physical objects, no longer have any inherent meaning, and for the father or Billy to appropriate them in such a fashion is, to the gypsy's thinking, a selfish act. "He said that as long as the airplane remained in the mountains then its history was of a piece. Suspended in time. Its presence on the mountain was its whole story frozen in a single image for all to contemplate" (405). But to remove the plane, or Boyd's body, is to place the needs of the one above that of the many and to insist on a specificity that does not exist. Thus the significance of the gypsy's father's collection of old photographs, portraits of people now forgotten and unknown (412–13): the pictures possessed meaning only to those who knew the individuals represented, but the number of such people is limited and bound by time, and with their forgetting and passing, the pictures become anonymous representations of humanity in general, not identifiable portraits of individuals in particular. What were originally attempts to confer special status on the one become instead proof of the common matrix of the many.

Thus the gypsy, in his view of the temporal world and the role of the individual within that world, reiterates the "truths" expressed by both the priest and the blind man. He argues that "the great trouble with the world was that that which survived was held in hard evidence as to past events" (410) but that "in any case the past was little more than a dream and its force in the world greatly exaggerated. For the world was made new each day and it was only men's clinging to its vanished husks that could make of that world one husk more" (411). Then he adds, "La cáscara no es la cosa" (411) (The husk isn't the thing). Finally, he salutes Billy as a fellow "man of the road," one who knows that "oblivion cannot be appeased" but also realizes that "the world cannot be quit for it is eternal in whatever form as are all things within it" (413).

"Yo no soy un hombre del camino" (414) (I am not a man of the road), Billy insists, denying his companionship to the gypsy. But if he isn't, he surely is well on his way to becoming one. "Perhaps he was a crazy person. Perhaps a saint," the priest says of the heretic, the "anchorite" residing in the ruined church of Caborca (150, 158), and we might rightly consider Billy in similar fashion. "Have you always been crazy?" the old rancher who first finds Billy with the wolf asks. "I dont know. I never was much put to the test before today," Billy answers truthfully (59). The next rancher he meets says, "You a very peculiar kid. . . . Did you know that?" "No sir. I was always just like everbody else far as I know," Billy responds. "Well you aint," the rancher declares (68). Billy's "difference" grows more pronounced as the "tests" continue. "In that outlandish figure they beheld what they envied most and what they most reviled," the narrator says when Billy returns to New Mexico after his first crossing. "If their hearts went to him it was yet true that for very small cause they might also have killed him" (170). By the end of the book Billy believes that he will never belong to any family, that he will eventually be buried "in some distant place among strangers" (346),[16] the very fate from which he thinks he has rescued his brother. But Boyd, in his violence and death, had become a "man of the people," whereas Billy, in his isolated wanderings, must be, as the gypsy identifies him, a "man of the road."

Billy begins his journey in innocence and love. His heart is "outsized in his chest" (31) when he takes the wolf back to Mexico. He sees himself as ordained by God to fulfill his mission. He explains to those strangers who want to take the wolf "that the wolf had been entrusted into his care but that it was not his wolf and he could not sell it. . . . He said that the wolf was the property of a great hacendado and that it had been put in his care that no harm come to it" (90). Billy's improbable relationship with the wolf is at this point almost mythic, and of the many man-wolf tales we might draw on, the story of St. Francis of Assisi is the most intriguing. Lynn White, Jr. has called St. Francis the "greatest spiritual revolutionary in Western history" because he "proposed what he thought was an alternative Christian view of nature and man's relation to it; he tried to substitute the idea of the equality of all creatures, including man, for the idea of man's limitless rule of creation" (14). St. Francis believed in the existence of the animal soul, befriended a murderous wolf, and later buried it in holy ground, and so, likewise, does Billy.

But Billy at this early point in the novel is still untested. Later, the failures with the wolf and the horses and his own brother make him bitter. When Boyd deserts him, leaving with the unnamed Mexican girl, Billy goes in search, apparently out of jealousy and anger. During this bleak quest he finds in his pocket a "milagro," a "small silver heart" (298) previously offered him by a small child in the hamlet of Mata Ortiz, and he "held it in the palm of his hand and he studied it long and long" (331). Returning to New Mexico, he discovers the world at war and attempts to join the army, but he is rejected three times because of a heart defect. "There aint nothin wrong with my heart," Billy protests to the first doctor, again in denial. "Yes there is," the doctor replies (340). Soon thereafter, Billy stops by the ranch of his old friend Mr. Sanders. "Bless your heart," the elderly man smiles (350). It is this blessing that Billy must learn, for *The Crossing* is surely a story of the heart, of the need for compassion, charity, and fellowship in such an uncertain world. Spiritual virtues, all.

Which brings us to the ambiguous conclusion of this long, complex novel. After burying Boyd's poor corpse, Billy continues his wanderings, coming at last in the rain to an abandoned way station. There he prepares to sleep in the hay, already used for bedding by another animal. That creature, an old, crippled dog, "wet and wretched and so scarred and broken that it might have been patched up out of parts of dogs by demented vivisectionists," attempts to enter the building from the storm. It sniffs the matrix "to pick up the man's scent and then raised its head and nudged the air with its nose and tried to sort him from the shadows with its milky half blind eyes" (423). Billy's reaction is one of disgust, and he chases the dog back out into the rain, where it disappears howling, "a terrible sound. Something not of this earth. As if some awful composite of grief had broke through from the preterite world" (424). During the night Billy wakes suddenly to the "white light of the desert noon" (425), breaking not to the east but to the north, followed shortly by the return of dark and the coming of a cold wind, a wind anticipated in the first pages of the book (5). In that enigmatic setting, that inexplicable moment of improbable illumination, Billy calls for the dog, and when the dog fails to appear he sits despondently in the empty road in the traditional posture of the penitent. As the narrator tells us: "He took off his hat and placed it on the tarmac before him and he bowed his head and held his face in his hands and wept. He sat there for a long time and after a while the east did gray and after a while the right and godmade sun did rise, once again, for all and without distinction" (426).

This conclusion, both devastating and strangely hopeful, summarizes the novel's main ideas and images. The dog "had perhaps once been a hunting dog, perhaps left for dead in the mountains or by some highwayside. Repository of ten thousand indignities and the harbinger of God knew what" (424), the narrator tells us, connecting the animal to Boyd's dog (whose throat the murderous Indian cuts), to the wolf, and to Billy himself. Its three-legged stance communicates again the recurring tripartite imagery in the novel: Billy makes three journeys into Mexico; the wolf is wounded in one leg and walks on three; the ruined church of Caborca stands on three "legs"; Billy weeps three times: once for his parents, once for Boyd, and finally, one might assume, for the dog, and for himself, and for the earth and all that exists on it. It also suggests the Trinity of Father, Son, and Holy Spirit, and Boehme's three worlds (each composed of three in one).

And perhaps one step more. Don Arnulfo tells Billy at the beginning of his search that to discover the essence of the world he will need to find that "place where acts of God and those of man are of a piece," where "God sits and conspires in the destruction of that which he has been at such pains to create" (47). Trinity, New Mexico, is such a place. The Trinity Project resulted in the first atomic explosion, detonated on July 16, 1945, at 5:29:45 A.M. As others have convincingly argued, the light Billy witnesses this night comes from this explosion. The description includes hints of biblical apocalypse—the "broken rainbow or watergall" that stands in a "dim neon bow" suggests that God's covenant with man has now been concluded. The "alien dusk" and "alien dark" (425) that follow lend credence to that possibility. The basic structure of the natural matrix has been violently shattered, undone by man in an act of tremendous hubris, the final cost and consequences unknown. No wonder Billy hides his face in his hands and cries, for how better could humankind's separation and alienation from the natural world be illustrated?[17]

At the same time, this moment might also be seen as an act of spiritual illumination and revelation. As Billy rides to bury the wolf at the end of Book I, he crosses a river as fireworks from the town soar and explode in the night sky behind him: "A last lone rocket rose over the town and revealed them midriver and revealed all the country about them, the shoreland trees strangely enshadowed, the pale rocks. A solitary dog from the town that had caught the scent of the wolf on the wind and followed him out stood frozen on the beach on three legs standing in that false light and then all faded again into the darkness out of which it had been summoned" (125). In this place Billy has his vision of the wolf in the spiritual world. The similarities between this episode and the concluding one are many, the three-legged dog and the "false light" of the rocket being the most obvious. Jacob Boehme's first great work was *The Aurora* (1613), which Boehme himself had intended to call *The Rising of the Glowing Day* or *The Morning Redness* (Cheney 249), a clear inspiration, as others have noted, for McCarthy's title *Blood Meridian, or, The Evening Redness in the West.* Boehme once summarized the book as follows: "I saw and comprehended the Being of all Beings, the Byss and the Abyss; and the generation of the Holy Trinity. I saw the original and primal existence of this world and of all creatures. Within myself I perceived creation entire, in its order and movement; I saw, first, the divine world, of the angels and of paradise, second, the darkened world, the fiery realm, and third, the world around us, visible and tangible, as an issue and expression of the two inner, eternal, hidden worlds" (quoted in Cheney 249).

Perhaps in this moment of sudden, terrible illumination, Billy experiences a similar moment, or *Schrack*. McCarthy had earlier described Billy's staring into a campfire, watching "the last few embers of his fire at their dying and the red crazings in the woodcoals where they broke along their unguessed gridlines. As if in the trying of the wood were elicited hidden geometries and their orders which could only stand fully revealed, such is the way of the world, in darkness and ashes" (130). But this is a greater revelation, followed later by the natural rising of the sun, Boehme's predominant symbol of God and grace.

McCarthy ends the book with a paraphrase of Matthew 5:45, taken from Christ's Sermon on the Mount. The verses that precede it are significant:

> Give to him that asketh thee, and from him that would borrow of thee turn not thou away.
>
> Ye have heard that it hath been said, Thou shalt love thy neighbor, and hate thine enemy.
>
> But I say unto you, Love your enemies, bless them that curse you, do good to them that hate you, and pray for them which despitefully use you, and persecute you.
>
> That ye may be the children of your Father which is in heaven; for he maketh his sun to rise on the evil and on the good, and sendeth rain on the just and the unjust. (Matthew 5:42–45)

This is Christ's description of the common grace of God, offered "without distinction" to all. It recognizes the shared need of all for God's mercy because the external world is a place of evil and hatred and injustice, but it also emphasizes the need for human charity and sacrifice, and ultimately for love, compassion, and forgiveness.

If this is such a moment of spiritual illumination for Billy, we may be hard pressed to explain his subsequent character in the third novel of the trilogy, *Cities of the Plain*. Set some seven years later, this novel gives us a Billy who at first seems a degraded version of the young boy we follow in *The Crossing*. And yet this Billy soon reveals his enduring capacity to love, even to risk once again losing the object of that love. John Grady Cole assumes Boyd's place in his still-damaged heart, and by the end of the book they are one in his memory. At the end of *The Crossing*, Billy sits weeping until he is blessed by the "godmade sun." At the end of *Cities of the Plain*, an old man in a house of strangers, he is blessed by the mother Betty, who offers him final absolution described in a final image of flesh and earth and light:

> She patted his hand. Gnarled, ropescarred, speckled from the sun and the years of it. The ropy veins that bound them to his heart. There was map enough for men to read. There God's plenty of signs and wonders to make a landscape. To make a world. (291)

Notes

1. For other discussions of such issues in these works, see Wade Hall, "The Hero as Philosopher and Survivor: An Afterword on *The Stonemason* and *The Crossing*," *Sacred Violence: A Reader's Companion to Cormac McCarthy*, ed. Wade Hall and Rick Wallach (El Paso: Texas Western Press, 1995), 189–94; R. Dean Reed, "Of Ancients and Moderns: Cosmology and Spirituality in *The Crossing*," *Proceedings of the 3rd Annual International Conference on the Emerging Literature of the Southwest Culture* (El Paso: University of Texas at El Paso, 1997), 401–4; Jason Ambrosiano, "Blood in the Tracks: Catholic Postmodernism in *The Crossing*," *Southwestern American Literature* 25.1 (1999): 83–91; and J. Douglas Canfield, "Crossing from the Wasteland into the Exotic in McCarthy's Border Trilogy," *A Cormac McCarthy Companion: The Border Trilogy*, ed. Edwin T. Arnold and Dianne C. Luce (Jackson: University Press of Mississippi, 2001), 256–69. I also discuss *The Stonemason* at greater length in "Cormac McCarthy's *The Stonemason*: The Unmaking of a Play," *Southern Quarterly* 33.2–3 (1995): 117–29, and in "'Go to sleep': Dreams and Visions in the Border Trilogy," *A Cormac McCarthy Companion: The Border Trilogy*, ed. Edwin T. Arnold and Dianne C. Luce (Jackson: University Press of Mississippi, 2001), 37–72.

2. In addition to his novels, McCarthy has written an unfilmed screenplay, "Whales and Men," that clearly reveals his ecological philosophies. The title resembles Barry Holstun Lopez's book *Of Wolves and Men* (New York: Charles Scribner's Sons, 1978). See James D. Lilley, "Of Whales and Men: The Dynamics of Cormac McCarthy's Environmental Imagination," *Southern Quarterly* 38.2 (2000): 111–22; Dianne C. Luce, "The Vanishing World of Cormac McCarthy's Border Trilogy," *A Cormac McCarthy Companion: The Border Trilogy*, ed. Edwin T. Arnold and Dianne C. Luce (Jackson: University Press of Mississippi, 2001), 161–97; and my "'Go to sleep: Dreams and Visions in the Border Trilogy," for further discussion of this screenplay and its connection to the Border Trilogy.

3. In Leslie Marmon Silko's novel *Ceremony* (1977) this idea is expressed using the same term. The old man Ku'oosh tells Tayo, "But you know, grandson, the world is fragile." Silko continues, "The word he chose to express 'fragile' was filled with the intricacies of a continuing process, and with a strength inherent in spider webs woven across paths through sand hills where early in the morning the sun becomes entangled in each filament of web. It took a long time to explain the fragility and intricacy because no word exists alone, and the reason for choosing each word had to be explained with a story about why it must be said this certain way" (35). The intertextuality between McCarthy's western novels and Silko's work, including *Ceremony* and *Almanac of the Dead* (1991), offers intriguing possibilities for further study. See Ellen L. Arnold, "An Ear For the Story, an Eye For the Pattern: Rereading *Ceremony*," *Modern Fiction Studies* 45.1 (1999): 69–92, for a discussion of these issues in Silko's work. I have also benefited from conversations with James Lilley and his insights on McCarthy and Native American writers.

4. For a somewhat different discussion of the matrix image in the novel, see Dianne C. Luce, "The Road and the Matrix: The World as Tale in *The*

Crossing," *Perspectives on Cormac McCarthy,* rev. ed., ed. Edwin T. Arnold and Dianne C. Luce (Jackson: University Press of Mississippi, 1999), 195–219.

5.   The priest is describing the importance of narrative here, the elements that go into the making of a tale. But, as he says, narrative gives order to life. "For this world also which seems to us a thing of stone and flower and blood is not a thing at all but is a tale. And all in it is a tale and each tale the sum of all lesser tales and yet these also are the selfsame tale and contain as well all else within them" (143). See Luce, "The Road and the Matrix," for further discussion of tale and narrative in *The Crossing.* One might again compare this idea to the Native American concept presented in Silko's *Ceremony,* in which stories create the world, narrative makes reality: "You don't have anything/if you don't have stories" (2). The imagery, however, also relates to that of stonemasonry and recalls this passage from McCarthy's play *The Stonemason:* "According to the gospel of the true mason God has laid the stones in the earth for men to use and he has laid them in their bedding planes to show the mason how his own work must go. A wall is made the same way the world is made. A house, a temple. This gospel must accommodate every inquiry. The structure of the world is such as to favor the prosperity of men. Without this belief nothing is possible. What we are at arms against are those philosophies that claim the fortuitous in mens' [*sic*] inventions. For we invent nothing but what God has put to hand" (10). Or, as God says to Job, "Where were you when I laid the earth's foundations?" (Job 38:4).

6.   This description calls to mind Boyd Parham's earlier dream: "There was this big fire out on the dry lake. . . . These people were burnin. The lake was on fire and they was burnin up" (35). Unlike Billy, in his quest for "justice" Boyd will participate in the violence of the world, symbolized by fire and blood. The scene also recalls the moment Boyd sees himself reflected in the eyes of the murderous Indian he and Billy find near their home: "He stood twinned in those dark wells with hair so pale, so thin and strange, the selfsame child. As if it were some cognate child to him that had been lost who now stood windowed away in another world where the red sun sank eternally. As if it were a maze where these orphans of his heart had miswandered in their journey in life and so arrived at last beyond the wall of that antique gaze from whence there could be no way back forever" (6). Both descriptions foreshadow Boyd's violent death.

7.   For other discussion of McCarthy's treatment of wolf trapping in this novel, see S. K. Robish, "The Trapper Mystic: Werewolves in *The Crossing*," *Southwestern American Literature* 25.1 (1999): 50–54; and Dianne C. Luce, "The Vanishing World of Cormac McCarthy's Border Trilogy."

8.   In the gypsy's tale near the end of the book, the gypsy describes the body of the drowned man brought into view by the flooded river. The corpse suggests an equally mysterious knowledge:

>   He'd come already a long way in his travels by the look of him for his clothes were gone and much of his skin and all but the faintest nap of hair upon his skull all scrubbed away by his passage over the river rocks. In his circling in the froth he moved all loosely and disjointed as if there were no bones to him. Some incubus or mannequin. But when he passed beneath them they could see revealed in him that of

which men were made that had better been kept from them. They could see bones and ligaments and they could see the tables of his smallribs and through the leached and abraded skin the darker shapes of organs within. He circled and gathered speed and then exited in the roaring flume as if he had pressing work downriver. (408–9)

9. For further discussion of these matters, see my essay "'Go to sleep': Dreams and Visions in the Border Trilogy," esp. 57–64.

10. See Nell Sullivan, "Boys Will Be Boys and Girls Will Be Gone: The Circuit of Male Desire in Cormac McCarthy's Border Trilogy," *A Cormac McCarthy Companion: The Border Trilogy*, ed. Edwin T. Arnold and Dianne C. Luce (Jackson: University Press of Mississippi, 2001), 228–55, for a thoughtful discussion of yet other aspects of this relationship. She argues, "Perhaps the characterization of Billy Parham in *The Crossing* most clearly demonstrates the destabilization of gender roles that both complicates and transgresses the generic conventions of the Western in the Border Trilogy. An apparent reference to Billy's three forays into Mexico, the titular 'crossing' is equally a reference to his 'gender crossing,' as he crosses the illusory yet socially-endorsed boundaries between the masculine and the feminine" (233).

11. Translations of the Spanish passage are aided by those provided by Lt. Jim Campbell in "A Translation of Spanish Passages in *The Crossing*," <http://www.cormacmccarthy.com/spanishcrossingtrans.htm>.

12. Earlier, Billy "wondered if the wolf were so unknowable as the old man [Don Arnulfo] said. He wondered at the world it smelled or what it tasted. He wondered had the living blood with which it slaked its throat a different taste to the thick iron tincture of his own. Or to the blood of God" (51–52).

13. Both Leo Daugherty and Steven Shaviro have noted Boehme's possible influence on McCarthy, and I am indebted to their work. See Daugherty, "Gravers False and True: *Blood Meridian* as Gnostic Tragedy," 159–74; and Steven Shaviro, "'The Very Life of the Darkness': A Reading of *Blood Meridian*," 145–58.

14. See Keegan for a detailed comparison of this tale to the Book of Job.

15. The destructiveness of such "justice," of attempting to remake the past, is an idea expressed in McCarthy's first novel, *The Orchard Keeper* (1965). John Wesley Rattner's mother demands that the boy seek his father's killer, but John Wesley never does so. His later mentor, Marion Sylder (who, unknown to them both, is the slayer), warns the boy against revenge.

16. This will, in fact, be Billy's fate to some degree. At the end of *Cities of the Plain*, as an old man, he has come to live with a family that takes him in, accepts him as a member. With no other kin, he seems prepared for death in this household.

17. I have discussed the ending of *The Crossing* in similar terms but with a somewhat different emphasis in "'Go to sleep': Dreams and Visions in the Border Trilogy," 62–64.

Works Cited

Boehme, Jacob. *Personal Christianity: The Doctrines of Jacob Boehme*. Ed. Franz Hartmann. New York: Frederick Ungar, 1958.

Cheney, Sheldon. *Men Who Have Walked with God*. New York: Alfred A. Knopf, 1945.

Daugherty, Leo. "Gravers False and True: *Blood Meridian* as Gnostic Tragedy." *Perspectives on Cormac McCarthy*. Rev. ed. Ed. Edwin T. Arnold and Dianne C. Luce. Jackson: University Press of Mississippi, 1999. 159–74.

Evernden, Neil. "Beyond Ecology: Self, Place, and the Pathetic Fallacy." *North America Review* 263.4 (winter 1978): 16–20.

Keegan, James. "'Save yourself': The Boundaries of Theodicy and the Signs of *The Crossing*." *The Cormac McCarthy Online Journal* (2000). <http://www.cormacmccarthy.com/journal/>.

Lopez, Barry Holstun. *Of Wolves and Men*. New York: Charles Scribner's Sons, 1978.

McCarthy, Cormac. *All the Pretty Horses*. New York: Alfred A. Knopf, 1992.

———. *Blood Meridian, or, The Evening Redness in the West*. New York: Random House, 1985.

———. *Cities of the Plain*. New York: Alfred A. Knopf, 1998.

———. *The Crossing*. New York: Alfred A. Knopf, 1994.

———. *The Stonemason*. Hopewell, N.J.: Ecco Press, 1994.

Manes, Christopher. "Nature and Silence." *Environmental Ethics* 14 (winter 1992): 339–50.

Phillips, Dana. "History and the Ugly Facts of Cormac McCarthy's *Blood Meridian*." *American Literature* 68 (June 1996): 433–60.

Shaviro, Steven. "'The Very Life of the Darkness': A Reading of *Blood Meridian*." *Perspectives on Cormac McCarthy*. Rev. ed. Ed. Edwin T. Arnold and Dianne C. Luce. Jackson: University Press of Mississippi, 1999. 145–58.

Silko, Leslie Marmon. *Ceremony*. New York: Viking Penguin, 1977.

Walsh, David. *The Mysticism of Innerworldly Fulfillment: A Study of Jacob Boehme*. Gainesville: University Press of Florida, 1983.

Weeks, Andrew. *Boehme: An Intellectual Biography of the Seventeenth-Century Philosopher and Mystic*. Albany: State University of New York Press, 1991.

White, Lynn, Jr. "The Historical Roots of Our Ecological Crisis." *Science* 155 (10 Mar. 1967): 1203–7.

"See the Child"

The Melancholy Subtext of *Blood Meridian*

George Guillemin

AMONG the many melancholy moments in the Old Testament, we find the Israelites' mourning of their forced exile by the rivers of Babylon in Psalm 137. Strangely, it ends with an image at odds with the woeful tone of the preceding verses:

> O daughter Babylon, who art to be destroyed; happy shall he be, that rewardeth thee as thou hast served us. Happy shall he be, that taketh and dasheth thy little ones against the stones. (8–9)

The children whose murder the Hebrew expatriates are advocating are to them the offspring of heathen. Homicidal expatriates, too, are the desperadoes of Cormac McCarthy's *Blood Meridian,* taking unwarranted revenge on the "heathen" (as they sometimes label Native Americans) in a manner not unlike what the psalmist may have had in mind:

> and one of the Delawares [in the gang] emerged from the smoke with a naked infant dangling in each hand and squatted at a ring

of midden stones and swung them by the heels each in turn and bashed their heads against the stones so that the brains burst forth through the fontanel in a bloody spew. . . . (156)

The two textual images are comparable because both are excerpted from melancholy contexts, and because in both texts the melancholy sense is conveyed by the complete indifference of the speaking voice to the agony thus reported. What further legitimizes the parallel are the constant references in McCarthy's fiction to biblical iconography and rhetoric, among them many involving the death of children.

Let us introduce a third analogy, this time a critical assessment of the role that scenes like Herod's infanticide play in baroque drama: "Gryphius' early work in Latin, the Herod epics, show most plainly what captured the interest of those people: the seventeenth century sovereign, the paramount of creation, erupting into rage like a volcano and annihilating himself along with the entire court around him. Paintings reveled in the picture of how he, holding two infants in his hands in order to smash them, succumbs to madness" (Benjamin 52).[1]

McCarthy's novel, it seems, draws on a traditional motif that subsumes melancholia, rage, and infanticide. Here I want to inquire into the nature of this motif and to try to determine why images of slain children keep haunting the pages of *Blood Meridian*. In interpreting these images, I will show that nowhere in the novel does the narrative voice devote itself to the question of ethics, not even by pointing out the conspicuous absence of moral positions. In order to define the causality underlying the novel's morally indifferent *narration* of epidemic destruction, I will focus in this reading on the patent melancholia permeating the text of *Blood Meridian* in the form of a discursive meta-narrative. The reason this "melancholy subtext"— which will take some time to define—seems to ignore ethical standards is simply that its motivation and essence draw on a posthumanist ethics. The gist of the argument to follow is that at times McCarthy seems to adopt an almost baroque mode of narration grounded in weltschmerz.[2] By transporting melancholy meaning via allegoresis, the structural device of the "melancholy subtext" constitutes something of a quasi-baroque strain that weaves its way through the text. The terms *melancholia* and *allegory* represent the woof and the warp of this discursive web, "melancholia" connoting here a form of aesthetic conditioning rather than depression in the clinical sense; "allegory" implying a rhetorical mode diametrically opposite to, rather than complementary to, that of the symbol; and "baroque" defining a stylistic category combining the elements of allegory, melancholia, and an egalitarian view of nature rather than an epochally defined aesthetics. In short, allegoresis functions as the structural mode used to convey a baroque discursivity steeped in death and melancholia.

A good way to start is by looking into the textual evidence on victimized children (who figure prominently in the proposed "melancholy subtext"), such as the instance of a Mexican boy who is dropped with a rock off the wall from which he and his friends have been urinating onto sleeping prisoners. The "kid,"—the novel's nameless teenage protagonist—who has pitched the rock at the boy hears "no sound other than the muted thud of its landing on the far side" (71). The child has probably been killed. Later, the scalphunting desperadoes come across the site of a massacre, strewn with "the tiny limbs and toothless paper skulls of infants like the ossature of small apes at their place of murder" (90). Elsewhere, "children tottering and blinking in the pistolfire" (174) find their untimely end during the scalphunters' massacre of the Tiguas. A Mexican boy is found naked and dead among "great numbers of old bones" (118), presumably one of the small victims abused by Judge Holden. At one point, the judge—in a sense the novel's Mephisto figure and second protagonist—adopts an Apache boy orphaned during a raid, "a strange dark child covered with ash" (160), only to kill and scalp him three days later (164). The belligerent boy whom the kid kills in self-defense in the last chapter also recalls the kid's own feistiness at the outset of the novel. Among the most haunting references to infantility is the following moment:

The way narrowed through rocks and by and by they came to a bush that was hung with dead babies. They stopped side by side, reeling in the heat. These small victims, seven, eight of them, had holes punched in their underjaws and were hung so by their throats from the broken stobs of a mesquite to stare eyeless at the naked sky. Bald and pale and bloated, larval to some unreckonable being. (57)[3]

The surreal miniature is neither prepared by the text, nor elaborated, nor ever taken up again, so that it stands in structural isolation, a decontextualized "still death." Crimes committed on and by children abound in *Blood Meridian,* but the representation of the child as a leitmotif extends to countless "unharmed" children in the text as well, including orphans, street urchins, juvenile delinquents, and childlike aspects in adults, corpses, and imbeciles. The child motif marks the novel's overture and its finale—both told in the present tense—as *Blood Meridian* opens with the strange prompting "See the child" (3) and concludes (excepting the epilogue) with the dreamlike scene of the naked judge dancing, "huge and pale and hairless, like an enormous infant" (335). The childlike, or rather fetal, features of the judge are repeatedly alluded to through references to his baldness, hairlessness, paleness, smallness of extremities, and nudity. Although children expire in his hands, the judge, who himself looks like a demonic child revenant, outlives the entire cast of the novel.

Yet while the child motif stands centrally in *Blood Meridian,* in what sense should the still life of the bush hung with infant bodies be read as an allegory rather than a symbol? An interpretation of the image in symbolical terms would have to read it as a sign—complete with signifier, signified, and an objective referent concurrent with subjective meaning—but what would this lurid metaphor signify? A society hostile to children? The cruelty of ethnic cleansing? The dead babies fail to lend themselves to symbolic divination because—decontextualized as they are—they carry no significatory weight outside the textual moment. The image does not accommodate individual adaptations of meaning and is devoid of any signified beyond itself, the image of a mesquite bush with dead babies representing just that: the image of a mesquite bush with dead babies. Dana Phillips argues when writing in the context of a like instance in *Blood Meridian* that "McCarthy's use of vivid similes . . . does not give the event a symbolic dimension. On the contrary, the similes seem designed to increase the intensity and accuracy of focus on the objects being described rather than to suggest that they have double natures or bear hidden meanings" (450).

But Phillips's assessment belies evidence to the effect that images in *Blood Meridian* such as this one—though lacking a "double nature or hidden meaning" of the *symbolic* order—do contain a secondary plane of meaning that may not be essential to the perusal of the text on the plot level but that is nevertheless there. The image at hand seems to separate into elements of a mimetic foregrounded narrative and those of a nonmimetic meta-narrative in the sense that it is intrinsically structured by a hybrid discursivity typical of allegoresis, consisting of a literal surface meaning perfectly coherent in itself, and an anterior level of meaning that is more or less accessible. The clearly autonomous, ambiguous meaning of allegory stands in stark contrast to the subjective accessibility of symbolic meaning. For, unlike the symbol, which unites subject and object in a subjective, contextual meaning that is never quite the same, allegory functions as "a sign that refers to one specific meaning and thus exhausts its suggestive potentialities once it has been deciphered" (de Man 200). Being confined to its temporal placement, the meta-level of allegorical imagery points to the reiterated meaning "of a previous sign with which it can never coincide, since it is of the essence of this previous sign to be pure anteriority" (de Man 209–10). What is more, in this typological reference to something anterior (present only in its signified absence), allegory always signifies the facticity of death as absence absolute. In this sense, allegory transports melancholy meaning by basing its semantics on the sine qua non implication of death; therefore, "Allegories are in the realm of thoughts what ruins are in the realm of things" (Benjamin 146). It is the problem of signifying the unsignifiable—death—that allegory addresses via its modus operandi, "its reference to a meaning it does not itself constitute" (de Man 200).

The terrible vignette of the bush hung with dead infants, then, translates into a pure memento mori motif confronting the beholder above all with an atemporal, if historical, fact that transcends the historical reality of the southwestern borderlands in 1849, reminding us not only that even infants may be subject to murder, let alone death, but also that the world is essentially indifferent to this fact and to such incidents. If we read the image as a symbolic act of violence, we cannot but suspect an excessive degree of cynicism in the narrator. If we commit ourselves to the allegorical mode, however, the image reveals itself as an expression of profound melancholia, something akin to medieval depictions of the *danse macabre,* death dancing. It then transforms into a baroque type of memento mori, or even a *vanitas* motif, grounding its indifferent rhetoric in the vanity of all human efforts vis-à-vis inevitable death. The source for melancholy-allegorical discursivity and the *vanitas* motif itself is biblical: "Vanity of vanities, saith the preacher, vanity of vanities; all is vanity" (Ecclesiastes 1:4). The melancholy rhetoricity of Ecclesiastes clearly reverberates through the very first sentence of *Blood Meridian,* "See the child." Nowhere else does the narrator address his audience as directly as in this line, and only one other time after the first subchapter does he speak of the protagonist as a "child."[4] Now, if the function of the unique first line was to define the character first introduced as the protagonist, it would hardly do to designate him as "child" and then drop the term after two pages, and if it was to draw our attention to that person's childhood, the unctuous rhetoric of the opening line would be out of place. In fact, this singular exhortation would seem justifiable only if it referred to something more than the kid's childhood and to someone other than the child he ceases to be on page 4. As it instructs us from the start to watch for a figure transcending personal boundaries, a child all allegorical and yet very real, the line "See the child," in fact, advises us on the presence of the melancholy subtext.

But let us look at the fantastic "child" who enters the text as soon as the kid outgrows his childhood.[5] Roughly a page after the "child" is "finally divested of all that he has been" (4) and metamorphoses into "the kid" (5), the figure of Judge Holden is introduced as "strangely childlike" (6), and a child he keeps mimicking in many ways.[6] Curiously, the very same sentence comparing the judge to "an enormous infant" because he has "small feet" and is "naked," "pale and hairless," concedes that he is "towering" and "huge" (335). His height is given as "close on to seven feet" (6), his weight is determined on a livestock scale as being "twenty-four stone" (128), or 336 pounds: "an enormous infant" indeed. The paradoxical persona of the judge becomes all the more monstrous as the narrative turns him into something of an Antichrist persona with Nietzschean rhetoric; a confidence man altering his appearance and appearing anywhere, any time; a conjurer adept at tricks and magical feats; a master of ceremonies at many a dance; a walking encyclopedia. He remains "little changed or none in all these years" (325), even immortal: "He says that he will never die" (335). These concluding words and the oxymoronic picture of the "enormous infant" suggest that the judge has apparently come to monopolize the child motif.

SENEX, SATURN, JUDGE

In order to trace the interstices between the "monstrous child" and melancholia, allegory, and death, we need to borrow an analytical model that will legitimize interpretation of the judge and the kid as archetypal figures. Concentrating on the circumstance that despite his childlike aspects, the judge, more than the gang's Faustian leader John Joel Glanton, tyrannizes the company as well as the textual semantics via his sermons, the judge's tyrannical profile may be identified with the help of the Jungian archetypes of "senex" and "puer."[7] This interpretative undertaking is invited by the text's prototypical, larger-than-life psychograph of the judge, which suggests that we subsume his figure under an allegorical typology rather than interpret him symbolically. Establishing the Jungian typology will subsequently afford a smooth transition to the doctrine of Saturn and the four humors, and eventually to Lacanian psychoanalysis.

Roughly speaking, Jung's senex archetype comprises a broad range of positive and negative qualities associable with old age, though the senex connotes senescence less than the maturity, wisdom, and petrified power structures established in the course of a lifetime. Within the archetypal dualism the senex is pitched against the archetype of the puer, who corresponds to youth and attendant attributes such as revolt, transcendence, idealization, and the crossing of boundaries. The puer represents childhood less than "the Divine Child, the figures of Eros . . . the Trickster, and the Messiah" (Hillman 23), and arguably the kid represents the puer counterfigure to the judge's senex features in *Blood Meridian*. Governed by historical sequence and the continuity of time, eternity, past, death, the senex translates into the figure of Kronos or Saturn in Greco-Roman mythology. In fact, the iconography of Jung's senex matches the profile of Saturn as the deity ruling melancholia among the four humors,[8] although neither Jungian psychology nor the doctrine of the four humors defines Saturn as a mythical icon but as a typological back-reference. Henceforth, both terms are used interchangeably, *senex* to emphasize psychological qualities, *Saturn* mythological ones.

Accordingly, it is essential to clarify that the judge is not to be read as someone who is *like* Saturn but *as if* he was in fact Saturn. As in fairy tales (which constitute a strictly allegorical genre), where sinister personae are not only stylized to be as evil as the devil but *are* the devil himself, the judge does not symbolize Saturnian energies in an otherwise realistic character but is an allegorical incarnation of the Saturnian archetype despite all realistic detail. The figure of Saturn handed down from antiquity is a castrating, child-devouring ogre, identified with gluttony and human sacrifice as the ultimate expression of omnipotence. He is the god of childlessness, orphanhood, and the lonely god of the dead, an eater of the newly born and of raw flesh. As if in analogy, the judge is often directly or indirectly implicated in the death of children, orphans, and puppies, and among the judge's smaller victims may also count the kid, a child of sorts, who succumbs to the judge in the jakes of a saloon.[9] Saturn indulges in "cold, cut-off satanic sexuality" (Hillman 33), whereas the judge habitually practices child abuse, involving, for instance, a girl flung over a wall with superhuman strength after her violation (239), "a girl of perhaps twelve years cowering naked in the floor" (275) of his room, and "a Mexican or half-breed boy maybe twelve years old" (116) raped and murdered of a night during which the judge has walked the premises stark naked.

The judge also displays the senex's omnipotent aspirations: "A suzerain rules even where there are other rulers. His authority countermands local judgements" (198). He goes on to specify that the earth he walks "is my claim. . . . In order for it to be mine nothing must be permitted to occur upon it save by my dispensation" (199). Both senex archetype and the judge are obsessed with boundaries, the anality of order, and a Nietzschean will to power. The protofascist claim to sovereignty is complemented by the senex's inclination to destructiveness, to "cruelty, cunning, thievery and murder" (Hillman 18), and the judge is certainly not innocent on any of these counts.[10] Viewing the world from the outside as "lord of the nethermost," Saturn's greedy and despotic rapacity has him govern "coins, minting, and wealth" (Hillman 17), a circumstance shedding light on the kid's strange dream of graver and judge[11]:

> It is this false moneyer with his gravers and burins who seeks favor with the judge and he is at contriving from cold slag brute in the crucible a face that will pass, an image that will render this residual specie current in the markets where men barter. Of this is the judge judge and the night does not end. (310)

Like this coldforger, the kid is under the sway of the judge's dark patronage, and here the opportunity presents itself to look in turn into the archetypal characteristics of the kid. As suggested earlier, the kid in his role as picaresque hero is supposed to fill the shoes of the puer archetype, offering resistance to the judge's senex authority. Yet, as he fails to defy the judge and to usurp the senex position in his stead, it becomes clear that the kid does not constitute much of a traditional hero, even less of a picaro figure, and none but the flipside of the puer. Rather, he comes to function as a reflector for the all-too-prominent figure of the judge until he is almost reduced to a structural fixture: a rudimentary third-person narrator nearly speechless out of an overwhelming sense of indifference. Even as his point of view governs the narrative perspective, his motives and thoughts are never disclosed. Even after acknowledging the judge—an ambiguous substitute father bent on undoing him—as his antagonist late in the story, he dodges his advances with an air of inner paralysis. Belonging therefore in the category of the "negative puer" (Hillman 27)—passive, narcissistic, cynical[12]—the kid leads a disenfranchised picaresque existence marred by gratuitous acts of violence, intoxication, and melancholia.

Melancholia, however, constitutes the principal aspect of Saturn and his saturnine children. Rather than being invested with omnipotence, being born under the sign of Saturn means to be subsumed under Saturn's typology.[13] Although Saturnian characteristics are easily traced in the judge—singling him out as a tyrannical, cruel, intellectual senex figure—the novel contains a whole variety of details linking the judge with the typological melancholia of Saturn—such as animals and symbols associated with Saturn—which we cannot possibly go into here. As will become evident later, the judge, being grounded in both Saturnian *and* saturnine energy, is more deeply implicated in the melancholy subtext than his braggadocio suggests. Not just symbolizing but also personifying Saturn, the judge contains melancholy in the manner of an emblematic figure. He unites in his persona (not as a psychic affect but as an aesthetic effect) the somber mood of land and people around him, among them two facets of the melancholy mind: the vision of reality as a process of incessant decay on one hand and an alternative vision of a pastoral paradise—timeless yet secular—on the other. The ambivalence is captured in the motto engraved into the gunstock of the judge's rifle, reading *"Et In Arcadia Ego"* (125): Even in Arcadia I, death, exist.[14] This particular phrase— a memento mori motif in itself—more or less sums up everything the judge stands for when contextualized with the allegorical, melancholy meta-narrative of *Blood Meridian*.

Nevertheless, while reading the judge as a personification of melancholia, we must remember to read him simultaneously as the historical figure he represents and to restrict our typological interpretation of him to certain quintessentially allegorical aspects, the most prominent among which is the child imagery we initially isolated, and which surfaces not only in descriptions of the judge's infantile features but also in his rhetoric:

> That feeling in the breast that evokes a child's memory of loneliness such as when the others have gone and only the game is left with its solitary participant. A solitary game, without opponent. Where only the rules are at hazard. Dont look away. We are not speaking in mysteries. You of all men are no stranger to that

feeling, the emptiness and the despair. It is that which we take arms against, is it not? (329)

Compare this constellation of child, loneliness, violence—familiar by now—with Hillman's summary of the senex archetype: "[The senex] is there from the beginning as are all archetypal dominants and is found in the small child . . . who is the last to pity and the first to tyrannize, destroys what it has built, and in its weakness lives in oral omnipotence fantasies, defending its borders and testing the limits set by others" (Hillman 21).

Here, in the aspect of the child contained within the senex archetype, we encounter once more the idea of the "monstrous child," and having illustrated the allegorical role of the judge as Saturn, lord over the melancholy humor, we need to define in what way the judge's Saturnian-while-saturnine character and his oxymoronic aspect as an "enormous infant" combine in an overall allegorization of melancholia.

THE MONSTROUS INFANT

Let us return to the words set into Judge Holden's rifle stock: *"Et In Arcadia Ego."* Within the narrative context, the baroque aphorism states that even the idyllic pastoral world is encroached upon by death. *Blood Meridian*'s third epigraph on the scalped skull three hundred thousand years old adapts this aphorism to the novel's context, stating in effect that the earth has been a place of mayhem and murder since time immemorial. Being equally adapted to both context and the notion of ubiquitous death, and being moreover true to his Saturnian character, the judge explicitly favors the fortunes of war—the epitome of violence—as the most sincere vocation of man. Not only is war holy, he claims, but in a secular Orcus of total anarchy, war alone is holy:

This is the nature of war, whose stake is at once the game and the authority and the justification. Seen so, war is the truest form of divination. It is the testing of one's will and the will of another within that larger will which because it binds them is

> therefore forced to select. War is the ultimate game because war
> is at last a forcing of the unity of existence. War is god. (249)

This could easily be passed off as campfire bombast, but the gist of the
judge's argument paraphrases certain effects of the unconscious that
refer us to the workings of the Thanatos. What else might "unity of
existence" imply if not the longed-for restoration to a continuity
whose loss conditions the formation of the subject and unleashes the
dynamics that strive to terminate the ego's discontinuous existence?
The notions of Saturn, war, and melancholia afford little leverage if we
decide to read the desperadoes' rampages as symptomatic of a suici-
dal/homicidal melancholia, but they read almost like a case history
when contextualized with Lacanian psychoanalysis.

Not until he recognized that the human subject may actively seek
to incur pain or to inflict it upon himself, and that, moreover, sadism
constitutes nothing but extroverted masochism, did Freud propagate
the Thanatos in *Beyond the Pleasure Principle*. Aggressivity, as he
understood it, is always also auto-aggressivity, so that violence must
be seen in link with self-destructive impulses. The story of the kid (as
well as that of the gang) evidently bears this hypothesis out, because
the kid never hesitates to endanger his own life when wreaking havoc
on others. His very first appearance in the text is overshadowed by
mention of his "taste for mindless violence" (3), that is, an inclination
for exacting irrational and subliminal aggression. Having run away to
New Orleans at fourteen, he frequents a tavern "at night like some
fairybook beast to fight with the sailors" (4), for no good reason. At
Nacogdoches he fights a gunslinger over the rights to a boardwalk (9),
then helps this same character set fire to a hotel and beat another man
senseless, no questions asked (12–13). At San Antonio de Bexar he
challenges an entire cantina and kills the barman over a drink refused
(24–25). He partakes in Captain White's suicidal campaign into
Mexico mostly for lack of anything else to do. In captivity he almost
jeopardizes his and his fellow prisoners' lives by killing an obnoxious
Mexican child (71). Indifferent to the point of suicide, he fetches water
right before the eyes of the—by then inimical—judge (285), and all too
indifferent, he declines to shoot the judge when twice the opportunity

presents itself (285, 298). Nor does he flee the saloon at Fort Griffin to save himself after the judge has virtually told him to his face that he will be sacrificed. While being indifferent to the lives of others, shooting "as if he'd done it all before in a dream" (109), and leaving his companion Shelby to die in the desert, he is just as indifferent regarding his own soul, as becomes apparent when he fails to understand Tobin's parable of the voice of God (124).

The same self-destructive impetus manifests itself in the chronicles of the Glanton gang as a whole, for they refuse to quit their marauding until massacred by the Yumas in much the same way as they in turn massacred the Apaches.[15] At one point black Jackson verbalizes the gang members' belief "that he that lives by the sword shall perish by the sword" (248), and in the present context this credo seems to suggest not adherence to Mosaic law but a deferred death wish. Moreover, the narration of the gang's westward migration often paints the western sky in apocalyptic overtones, as if to suggest a suicidal quest for death on the blood meridian. Thus, we at one time read that the "sun to the west lay in a holocaust" (105), another time that "to the west lay reefs of bloodred clouds" (21), but the point is most clearly driven home by the following allegorization of a latent death wish:

> Within a week of their quitting the city there would be a price of eight thousand pesos posted for Glanton's head. They rode out on the north road as would parties bound for [the safety of] El Paso but before they were even quite out of sight of the city they had turned their *tragic* mounts to the west and they rode *infatuate* and *half fond* toward the *red demise of that day,* toward the *evening lands* and the distant *pandemonium* of the sun. (185, emphasis added)

Visions of "suicide and terrorism" (Kristeva, *Sun* 186), as expressed in his fiction, marked Fyodor Dostoyevsky's response to psychic suffering, and one could probably diagnose the desperadoes as suicidal terrorists acting out their nonsublimated unconscious want in paranoid violence. It is the work of Julia Kristeva more than that of

Freud or Lacan that ties melancholia, suicidal violence, and allegorical writing together. Kristeva specifies "that *want* and *aggressivity* are chronologically separable but logically coextensive" (*Powers* 39), and that failure to link the two (libido and Thanatos)—by speaking of aggressivity alone—reduces the transference of aggressivity onto an object to a symptom of paranoia. It is important to note, however, that aggressivity aims at violating the "imaginary form of the body that models the ego" (Boothby 39), the Thanatos being not directed at the physical destruction of the subject but concerned with destroying the integrity of the self. Nonetheless, aggressivity manifests itself cognitively in starkly physical images: "Among these *imagos* are some that represent the elective vectors of aggressive intentions, which they provide with an efficacity that might be called magical. These are the images of castration, mutilation, dismemberment, dislocation, evisceration, devouring, bursting open of the body, in short, the *imagos* that I have grouped together under the apparently structural term of *imagos of the fragmented body*" (Lacan 11).

Interestingly, textual instances substantiating every one of the "imagos of the fragmented body" can be found throughout the novel.[16] The impulses working toward the destruction of the self function as incessant reminders that the subject has constituted itself through alienation from itself, that is, by excluding those (of its own) aspects that fail to enter into the formation of the infantile subject and remain unrepresented. These excluded aspects—never-silent tokens of the lost continuity with one's own (and the maternal) self—return one way or another. In the "normal" subject, this return of the repressed occurs in the wake of the subject's entry into the symbolic order of language. They will find the representation initially denied to them in the subject's very ability to negate their absence discursively and to repress their existence through sublimation as "the possibility of naming the pre-nominal, the pre-objectal" (Kristeva, *Powers* 11). Hence, "the child needs a *solid implication* in the symbolic and imaginary code, which, then and only then, becomes stimulation and reinforcement" (Kristeva, *Sun* 36). In this manner, primal loss enters the economy of the unconscious via language and is assimilated by the subject's (libidinal) objects.

Yet in case discursive sublimation fails, the excluded aspects cause the subject to abject not the excluded aspects, which can neither be forgotten nor remembered, but itself. That is, if the subject rejects the mirroring object (usually the mother) on which to base its ego, and if so its identification with the imaginary "other" as well as its implication in the symbolic order fail, then the subject enters into an abject life based not on desire but on exclusion, because it preserves the impossible memory of a primal loss that is preliminary to being itself. Melancholia due to abjection is experienced when the site of "me" is taken up by "an 'Other' who precedes and possesses me, and through such possession causes me to be" (Kristeva, *Powers* 10), and when both this alienating, tyrannical "Other" (the symbolic order of the Dead Father) and the non-negated, immemorial aggression caused by primal loss unite in the dismemberment of the ego: "The abjection of self would be the culminating form of that experience of the subject to which it is revealed that all its objects are based merely on the inaugural *loss* that laid the foundations of its own being. There is nothing like the abjection of self to show that all abjection is in fact recognition of the *want* on which any being, meaning, language, or desire is founded" (Kristeva, *Powers* 5).

Abjection—the return of the "real," in Lacan's terminology—emerges as a "primordial internal conflict in the subject even as it institutes the most basic formation of psychic identity and mobilizes the most primitive forms of intentionality" (Boothby 65). Accordingly, abjection seems to be what determines the kid's subjective identity in *Blood Meridian*, for his birth entails not just the loss of continuity with the maternal body, but also the loss of his mother who dies in childbirth (3). The kid's abortive ego formation and experience of want is complemented by a failed initiation into the symbolic order: "He can neither read nor write" though his father "has been a schoolmaster." The latter "lies in drink" (3) and the kid watches him as the abject figure that he is, internalizing the image of an all but dead father, tyrannical in its immutability and its loathing of the son. Thus the kid could be subsumed under the judge's disquisition on something like the stalling of the oedipal conflict:

> The father dead has euchred the son out of his patrimony. For
> it is the death of the father to which the son is entitled and to
> which he is heir, more so than his goods. He will not hear of the
> small mean ways that tempered the man in life. He will not see
> him struggling in follies of his own devising. No. The world
> which he inherits bears him false witness. He is broken before a
> frozen god and he will never find his way. (145)

Seen so, the kid's father waxes into something of an absconding deity,
withdrawn into inebriation and the world of literature into which he
neglects to initiate his son. Small wonder that the kid is mesmerized by
the judge, a terrible (Saturnian) father figure who smiles at and
watches him even during their first encounter in Nacogdoches (14).
Simultaneously, the kid is unable to negate the loss of the mother (the
imaginary object), because "the father never speaks her name, the
child does not know it" (3). The abjection the kid experiences over an
unrepressed and always inexpressible want merges with the tyranny of
the "frozen god" that his "dead" father represents. And so "in him
broods already a taste for mindless violence" (3), an insuperable
aggressivity he can neither appease nor place. His abjection causes him
to become an exile to himself, asking "'*Where* am I?' instead of '*Who*
am I?,'" a feckless picaro, "a stray . . . [who] is on a journey, during
the night, the end of which keeps receding."[17] He becomes a nomad
traversing a space that "is never *one*, nor *homogenous*, nor *totalizable*,
but essentially . . . catastrophic" (Kristeva, *Powers* 8). The horrifying
tally of the kid's (and his comrades') "mindless violence" cannot
mitigate the primal loss he himself is traumatized by. Endlessly the
abject, melancholy person pursues what ultimately is "not an Object
but the Thing . . . the real that does not lend itself to signification"
(Kristeva, *Sun* 13). It is here that the "monstrous child" enters into the
picture as an emblem of that unrenounceable, abject "Thing," because
both melancholy literature and psychoanalytical theory on melancholy
psychosis use the image of the "monstrous child" to find a discursive
expression for the terrifying return of the real.

The monstrous child exists as a memory of something that never
was, a memory constantly evoked (rather than being repressed) by the

melancholic's "denial of negation" (Kristeva, *Sun* 46) until it induces the type of melancholy psychosis marking the kid as well as certain narrative moments in *Blood Meridian*. As an omnipotent presence, "terrifying, tyrannical, or indestructible" (Blanchot 71), this monstrous child—the emblem of the abjected aspects of self which the destructiveness of the Thanatos seeks to recover—rules the life of the melancholic and the suicide whose violence either against others or the own self is meant to kill the monstrous infant but is bound to fail because "the child always still to be killed is the child already dead and . . . thus, in suicide—in what we call suicide—*nothing at all happens*" (Blanchot 69). In this sense, death itself does not (come to) pass, for even in suicide there remains the narcissistic child within, "always already dead and nonetheless destined to a fragile, attenuated dying" (Blanchot 126).[18] We find as an analogous phenomenon (yet to be interpreted) in *Blood Meridian* the dying of live children and the survival of one "enormous infant," a demonic agent that "will never die." This monstrous child, projected from the kid's inside onto the judge's outer appearance as a child revenant, lives on beyond the death of the kid. In this sense, the kid—or rather, the "child" inside the kid— survives himself in this particular aspect of the judge, and sure enough, the text fails to pronounce the kid's death explicitly. Moreover, we could say that, when the narrative voice recognizes "All history in that visage, the child the father of the man" (3), it refers us from the start to the timeless presence of the monstrous child that haunts the kid.

Because the melancholic has not learned to repress his loss through sublimating language, he is silent. Unsurprisingly, the kid remains mostly silent and talks only in random, monosyllabic utterances hardly enough to sustain a dialogue. It is the narrator who speaks for, but not through, the kid, while the judge (the monstrous child) monopolizes the novel's monologues. As Walter Benjamin writes, the tragic hero (in baroque drama) is silent because he has severed his ties to God and the world; he is empty, without soul, and has himself the character of an allegorical sign signifying the violence of death "because death entrenches most deeply the jagged line of demarcation between physical nature and signification" (145). The baroque vision of history translates into a melodrama of human sorrow, the Passion of mankind, intelligible in its essence only as allegorical stages of decay that in turn find their analogies in an equally allegorized and sorrowful nature. In a brilliant reading of *Blood Meridian* as a nonanthropomorphic rewriting of the American West (a reading that similarly places man and nature on an existential par, if from a thoroughly secular angle), Dana Phillips argues that "natural history makes the provisional quality of all human interpretations of events—poetic ones most especially—painfully apparent" (449). This "painfully apparent," "provisional" quality bespeaks an air of despondency, too, and yet, in order to identify the melancholy strain in the novel, the baroque angle in *Blood Meridian* must be contextualized with the novel's representation of nature and its sense of the pastoral.

THE MELANCHOLY SUBTEXT

The one instance of melancholy discursivity we have studied so far is the image of the mesquite bush hung with dead babies. Another example would be the following:

> They rode on into the mountains and their way took them through high pine forests, wind in the trees, lonely birdcalls. The shoeless mules slaloming through the dry grass and pine needles. In the blue coulees on the north slopes narrow tailings of snow. They rode up switchbacks through a lonely aspen wood where the fallen leaves lay like golden disclets in the damp black trail. The leaves shifted in a million spangles down the pale corridors and Glanton took one and turned it like a tiny fan by its stem and held it and let it fall and its perfection was not lost on him. (136)

The passage continues in the same narrative mode until the silence, darkness, and solitude of the moment are invaded by death when a bear slays one of the Delaware Indians. The passage describes a moment removed from the butchery, the lewd dialogues, and plot progression, a sublime moment within a pastoral sanctuary. In the baroque withdrawal from the secular sordidness of the world, "Not eternity confronts the dismal course of the world's chronicles but the restoration of paradisical timelessness" (Benjamin 73). Analogously, the gunman's contemplation of the aspen leaf amounts to an allegorical moment because the leaf whose "perfection was not lost on him" functions as a reminder of both his own depravity and his mortality, just in the way nature functions in baroque discourse: Nature and man as such may still be perfect in their design, and yet they have always already lost any prelapsarian continuity to the fact that all things must die. By virtue of nature's allegorical adaptation to *human* nature, nature shares man's fall from grace and his melancholia in the face of death: "Because it is mute, fallen nature is grieving. But the inversion of the sentence introduces even more deeply the essence of nature: its grief makes it fall silent" (Benjamin 200). The point is that man and nature are on equal standing in *Blood Meridian,* and that reflection of this equality implies sorrow over the vanity of human efforts. Here we find the very essence of the *vanitas* motif. Following another line of argument, Phillips derives a similar, if less resigned, conclusion from the novel's concept of "optical democracy" (*Blood Meridian* 247): "For McCarthy, description and the natural world as categories contain both narrative and human beings. Human beings and the natural world do not figure as antagonists—*Blood Meridian* does not have that kind of dramatic structure. They are instead parts of the same continuum and are consistently described by McCarthy as such" (Phillips 446).

It is certainly not the plot structure that calls for the allegorical image of Glanton and the leaf, and within the context of our argument its insertion must be motivated alone by the narrator's "melancholy gaze" (in the Lacanian sense). The moment stands as isolated and enigmatic within the surrounding text as does the image of the mesquite bush, or that of the burning tree (215), or many other images like them. What both miniatures—bush there, leaf here—share and what makes them so interesting is, first, the precise descriptive mode that restricts itself to the very materiality of nature; second, the silence of nature due to this materiality-bound representation of it, which fails to infuse the passage with any "supernatural elevation of consciousness" (Phillips 447); and, third, the melancholy dynamics of this textual moment of existential parity, which, as an allegory outside the narrative progress, transports the negative implication of nature's materiality and silence, namely death. In short, the two moments match in terms of allegorical mode and melancholy mood, and both ought to be read as memento mori motifs. Their language balances precariously between callous indifference and a confounding sense of enigma; and yet these images in their material opulence—the novel's "baroque density" (Bell 129)— refuse to signify more than the full measure of death and indifference in nature (and characters). "It is precisely its lack of human implication that some find *Blood Meridian*'s most disturbing feature," writes Phillips. "In the raw orchestration of the book's events, the world of nature and the world of men are parts of the same world, and both are equally violent and indifferent to the other" (447).

The images of babies and leaves represent in one way or another material evidence of consummated death and the universal indifference toward it. Having little intrinsic meaning besides, all other deferred meanings that crowd the respective picture—such as the cruelty of men, the beauty of nature, and the hostility of the desert—are subsumed under what we should call the material historicity of McCarthy's discourse, the allegorical vanishing point of which is death. The intrinsic meaning of "nature," "beauty," "death," and their material representations cannot be signified except allegorically, and this because the semantic overdetermination attendant on these images ultimately gives way to a semantic void.[19] But although nothingness, the negative materiality of death, remains unspeakable, its impossible essence can be pointed to allegorically as an absence (e.g., as the absence of a building whose ruinous remains we behold). Signification without (enunciable) meaning constitutes the very heart of allegory, and it grounds the allegorical function of nature, ruin, and corpse. To signify "without meaning," while the silence conveyed by the allegory's failure to signify amounts to a "meaning without signification," this is what elevates allegorized silence to an allegorical (non-) enunciation of death.

Again, silence and unspeakable meaning also mark the return of the "real," the "Thing," the "enormous infant" in the melancholy unconscious. So we are now in a position to synchronize allegory and melancholia. Let us recall that the failed formation of the melancholy subject takes place in abjection of the self. Let us further recall that the melancholic's denial of negation of the "Thing" that he has lost and that he endlessly pursues implies his alienation from the symbolic order of discourse as well. Kristeva describes the language of the melancholy person as "repetitive and monotonous," and she goes on to say that it may eventually deteriorate "into the blankness of asymbolia or the excess of an unorderable chaos" (*Sun* 33). A case in point, the kid speaks only in one-liners, sits "mute as a tailor's dummy at [the governor's] board" (169), retorts to the judge's rhetoric with a mere "That's crazy" or "You aint nothin" (331), and vents his unverbalized want in mindless violence instead. To him apply Blanchot's words that "*When all is said, what remains to be said is the disaster. Ruin of words, demise writing, faintness faintly murmuring: what remains without remains* (the fragmentary)" (33). If we now take the fact that the melancholic experiences his unspeakable-because-unsublimated want (and his speechlessness as such) in images of the fragmented body that reverberate through his allegorical words or acts of (self-)destruction, we could paraphrase Benjamin to say that the fragmented body, in the realm of the psyche, is what ruins are in the realm of things, and what allegories are in the realm of thoughts. Considering it something of a "hypersign," Kristeva identifies allegory "as lavishness of that which *no longer is*, but which regains for myself a higher meaning because I am able to remake nothingness" (*Sun* 99). Allegory offers its voice to melancholia, it lends expression to inexpressible death, it introduces the imaginary into the world of things, translates sorrow into (sublime or picturesque) landscapes, it analogizes nature with history, it spatializes ideas and time.

In the context of the three allegorical moments quoted, we found that reflection of the equality of man and nature implies sorrow over the vanity of human efforts, and that this constitutes the essence of the *vanitas* motif. We may now realize that allegorization of the melancholy gaze inversely instrumentalizes the equality of man and nature as expressed in the *vanitas* motif to find expression for itself, for a melancholy view of history. This circumstance would explain the rhetorical specificity and contextual isolation of the three quotes as well as of all those representations of nature in *Blood Meridian* that are invested with the silence and negative materiality of death.[20] The possibility of re-presentation that allegory opens up for the melancholy artist, and that allows for the "monstrous child" to transfer from *imaginary* opacity into the *significatory* opacity of the emblem, all this induces a strange euphoria in the melancholy narrator crafting the allegory, and perhaps also in the reader susceptible to its melancholy meaning. Allegory "endows the lost signifier with a signifying pleasure, a resurrectional jubilation even to the stone and corpse, by asserting itself as coexten-sive with the subjective experience of a named melancholia—of melan-choly jouissance" (Kristeva, *Sun* 102). Stephen Shaviro, for one, seems to read *Blood Meridian* along similar lines when suggesting that "bloody death is our monotonously predictable destiny; yet its baroque opulence is attended with a frighteningly complicitous joy" (146). At the same time, he seems to overlook how complexly intertwined—and not at all contradictory—death, melancholia, allegory, tragedy, and relief are, or else he would not confess later that "the scariest thing about *Blood Meridian* is that it is a euphoric and exhilarating book, rather than a tragically alienated one, or a gloomy, depressing one" (156). As terrible and scary as the minutes of the story may be, the sense of euphoria accompanying its perusal may signal not sadistic glee over the bloodshed but a sense of subtle elation the melancholy recluse in his mysterious lucidity experiences when contemplating from afar the world in its vanity and the turning wheel of fortune.

Before I summarize my findings, let us look at what is perhaps the most stereotypical *vanitas* allegory in *Blood Meridian*:

> He wanders west as far as Memphis, a *solitary migrant* upon that flat and *pastoral* landscape. Blacks in the fields, lank and stooped, their fingers spiderlike among the bolls of cotton. A *shadowed agony in the garden.* Against *the sun's declining* figures moving in the slower dusk *across a paper skyline.* A *lone dark husbandman* pursuing mule and harrow down the rainblown bottomland *toward night.* (4, emphasis added)

The text all but announces its melancholy intentionality: a solitary migrant (the child who becomes the kid), agony in the garden, decline, dusk, night, the world a stage with paper skyline, a lone dark husbandman whose harried aspect almost evokes the grim reaper himself. As he offers us an almost pure example of baroque allegoresis, the narrator seems to turn his back on a moribund world corrupted by decay, melancholia, and twilight. Some pages later, San Antonio de Bexar is similarly described alternately as a house of mirth (cf. 39) and a pesthouse (cf. 26 and 30–31).[21] But unlike its baroque precursors, this kind of "subtext" invariably grounds itself in the here and now, allowing not even for the hope of transcendence, and advancing the dogma of a secular deity, nature itself, who, as the judge phrases it, "speaks in stones and trees, the bones of things" (116).

From among textual instances such as these, then, *Blood Meridian* recruits its melancholy subtext, and we ought to summarize our findings: we have identified a meta-narrative in *Blood Meridian* devoted to the allegorization of a melancholy sentiment. Melancholy psychosis, the eruption of "a mindless violence" due to the subject's denial of negation of primal loss, evidently guides the representation of both death and nature throughout the hybrid text, if only within a secondary discursive strain we defined as the novel's "melancholy subtext." The analogy between the imaginary object of melancholia—called the "Thing" by Kristeva—and the motif of the monstrous child are evidently reiterated in the allegorical aspects of the figure of Judge Holden, although neither the authentic figure of the judge nor the desert landscape alone contains the sense of melancholia ascribed to both. Instead, we found the melancholy aspects to be projected onto the textual material by the narrative gaze, which in turn is channeled through the eyes of the protagonist, the kid, and which gaze defines—by literally taking them in—both the kid's and the reader's gaze-*cum*-subjectivity. We may now conclude that the novel combines historical material with the fictional psychograph of an unidentified, amorphous narrator whose melancholy state of mind qualifies the representation of major parts of the text and thus the representation of the novel's historical background as well. Consequently, we may assume that the aesthetic function of *Blood Meridian* as a work of fiction is to stylize certain episodes out of frontier history into something we may call with Phillips an egalitarian "natural history" of humankind and nature. This we moreover identified as being analogous to the melancholy allegoresis of the Baroque. In the latter point, the argument for a melancholy subtext disagrees with Phillips's conclusion that "traditional concepts of the narrator as a 'person' or 'voice,' a sort of metacharacter with an interest in certain 'themes' that help to structure a text, also do not apply to *Blood Meridian*" (443).

"See the child," the novel starts out, and we have seen it, some of it anyway. Yet in light of the narrative mosaic of melancholia thus identified questions arise. Whose melancholia is it? Whose subtext? Whose child is it we are to see? Is it the child of that drunken schoolteacher and the mother who dies in childbed? Is it the judge, that "enormous infant," we are to see, or the "monstrous child" inside the narrator? If we recall Steven Shaviro's phrase of the scary, "complicitous joy" *Blood Meridian* inspires, could it not be a melancholy side in ourselves that we find reflected in the novel's melancholy subtext, and whose enactment in mindless violence and projection into the desert landscape causes our fascination with the novel? Although many readers dislike *Blood Meridian* and refuse to enter into this kind of complicity with it, McCarthy's fiction belongs to what Roland Barthes designated "writerly" (as opposed to "readerly") literature, the meaning of his writings being dependent on what we make of them and their epidemic destructiveness. The approach put forth here—the identification of a melancholy subtext—not only permits us to read *Blood Meridian* as something more than a revisionist Western awash in blood, it also elevates McCarthy to the ranks of other master craftsmen of melancholy discourse, such as Conrad, Dostoyevsky, or Faulkner. All of McCarthy's works are permeated by the same melancholy energy, surrendering to a retrospective vision dominated by memory and storytelling. The work of memory heralds the future in the Benjaminian sense that the stories of the past are told in expectance of future generations implicated in, while alienated from, a past not theirs. Let us speculate in closing that the readers of *Blood Meridian* have been expected, too: expected by the monstrous child of melancholia that is signifying what cannot be signified, pushing itself up front and prompting us from the start: "See the child."

Notes

1. The Benjamin quotes are my translations from the German original, because the English translation now in print is incomplete in places.

2. The term *weltschmerz,* denoting the sorrow over a world gone to ruin, expresses most cogently the apocalyptic state of mind of the Baroque.

3. The imbecile James Robert Bell, who can be grouped with the novel's infants because the text once calls him "this child" (258), is similarly described as having "dark larval eyes" (282). He appears to be party to "some unreckonable being" as well.

4. The one exception being the sentence "This child just sixteen years on earth" (310).

5. Except for the first subchapter, where he is identified as "the child," and part of the very last chapter, where he meets his end as "the man," the protagonist is referred to as "the kid" throughout the bulk of the text.

6. Up to the very moment he dances off the novel's penultimate page like "an enormous infant," his features are described in similes suggesting infancy. As instrumental a role as allegories are going to play in this argument, their prominence in *Blood Meridian* in no way obscures the fact that the text frolics in a welter of tropes that are not allegorical. Nevertheless, the child motif as such, in its insistent, surreal redundancy, comes across as strictly allegorical.

7. The delineation of the senex and puer aspects in the novel will follow James Hillman's argument, which seems almost custom-made for the present purpose. The analogies between the Hillman essay and the characterization of the judge are at times eerily graphic.

8. The following account of Saturnian characteristics is mostly excerpted from *Saturn and Melancholia,* which Hillman, too, identifies as one of his principal sources on the subject.

9. Coming as no surprise, the judge's murder of the kid presents the culmination of a long-standing animosity, something on the order of an oedipal conflict. Years before, the judge has verbalized his regret over the kid's emotional reticence toward him by saying, "Dont you know that I'd have loved you like a son?" (306). From the lips of someone resembling child-eating Saturn, the words sound like the ominous threat that ultimately does fulfill itself in the judge's murderous embrace of the kid at Fort Griffin. Interestingly, the murder site itself may not be coincidental, inasmuch as Saturn is also the god of privies.

10. Saturn also presides over the Saturnalia. Analogously, the judge arranges Roman holidays more than once, fiddling and/or dancing at the governor's reception in Chihuahua City (170), at Jesús María (190), at Ures (201), at Tucson (240), and of course at Griffin (335).

11. Besides minting, the passage contains also the Saturnian elements night, cold, underworld, tyranny, and markets. The judge's eloquence and prolix manipulation of language matches the brainpower associated with the senex: "His *intellectual qualities* include the inspired genius of the brooding melancholic, creativity through contemplation, deliberation in the exact sciences

and mathematics, as well as the highest occult secrets such as angelology, theology, and prophetic furor" (Hillman 18). Hardly wanting for prophetic furor, the judge also displays deep erudition in geography (85), geology (116), jurisprudence (239), astronomy (240), anthropology (84), paleontology (251), chemistry (127–35), history (224), and phrenology (238), among other fields.

12. The negative puer is also characterized by effeminacy, and it so happens that the kid deflects homosexual advances at least three times and succumbs to the last one (hermit, 20; Sonorans, 263; saloon patron, 311; and judge 333). Then there is his childlike face (4) to consider, his homophobia when naked (28), his impotence in the brothel (332), and Tobin's warning that Brown would have taken him (into the grave with him) "like a bride to the altar" (163).

13. Much in the same way Christ, the new Adam, functions less as a *symbolic* representation of Adam within Christian iconography than as a replication of Adam, able to redeem him by redeeming himself.

14. "Arcadia" is an ideal place, a pastoral utopia. For the meaning and history of the aphorism see Erwin Panofsky's essay "Et in Arcadia Ego," reprinted (among other places) in *Pastoral and Romance,* ed. Eleanor T. Lincoln (Englewood Cliffs, N.J.: Prentice Hall, 1969), 25–46.

15. Here, a Girardian argument for a collective relapse into a pattern of mimetic, reciprocal violence could be made. In this context, however, psychological aspects are more at issue than anthropological or social ones.

16. Textual evidence from *Blood Meridian* can be given for each of Lacan's exemplary imagos, such as castration, 153; mutilation, 54; dismemberment, 220; dislocation, 179; devouring, 88; and bursting open of the body, 269.

17. Kristeva's words are almost literally paraphrased in the description of the kid's nightmare of the coldforger, who is "an exile . . . hammering . . . all through the night of his becoming . . . and the night does not end" (310).

18. Compare Suttree's traumatization by his impossible memory of his stillborn twin brother. To understand Blanchot's words as more than a rhetorical stunt, let us rephrase them in light of the foregoing argument: Even as the suicide undoes himself and thus resurrects in death the lost aspects of his self—which were always already dead while never having died—he only consummates the dying of his ego that has been going on all his life, and through his death restores himself to the continuity that preceded his discontinuous existence and that never was (experienced consciously) at all.

19. Here, materiality opens onto what Ronald Schleifer calls "the negative materiality of death," which he defines—quoting Derrida—as "the worst violence, the violence of primitive and prelogical silence, of an unimaginable night which would not even be the opposite of day, an absolute violence which would not even be the opposite of non-violence: nothingness or pure non-sense" (8).

20. When Bell writes about *Blood Meridian*, "The human beings constitute one protagonist and the natural world another" (133), he could not be more right, except that he fails to specify that we are looking at two equal, congenial protagonists, costarring rather than competing. Phillips goes a step farther when saying by way of comment on Bell "that this competition has been decided in favor of description and the natural world even before *Blood Meridian* begins" (446).

21.   The term *pesthouse* is explicitly used earlier, when it is said that the kid "works
      in a diphtheria pesthouse" (5), a place that most likely serves to epitomize the
      nightmarish country he travels through.

Works Cited

Bell, Vereen M. *The Achievement of Cormac McCarthy.* Baton Rouge: Louisiana State
      University Press, 1988.

Benjamin, Walter. *Ursprung des deutschen Trauerspiels.* Frankfurt: Suhrkamp, 1977.

Blanchot, Maurice. *The Writing of the Disaster.* Lincoln: University of Nebraska
      Press, 1986.

Boothby, Richard. *Death and Desire.* New York: Routledge, 1991.

de Man, Paul. "The Rhetoric of Temporality." *Critical Theory since 1965.* Ed. Hazard
      Adams and Leroy Searle. Tallahassee: Florida State University Press, 1986.
      199–222.

Hillman, James. "Senex and Puer: An Aspect of the Historical and Psychological
      Present." *Puer Papers.* Ed. James Hillman et al. Irving, Tex.: Spring
      Publications, 1979. 3–53.

Klibansky, Raymond, Erwin Panofsky, and Fritz Saxl. *Saturn und Melancholie.*
      Frankfurt: Suhrkamp, 1994.

Kristeva, Julia. *Black Sun: Depression and Melancholia.* New York: Columbia
      University Press, 1989.

————. *Powers of Horror: An Essay on Abjection.* New York: Columbia University
      Press, 1982.

Lacan, Jacques. *Écrits: A Selection.* New York: W. W. Norton, 1977.

McCarthy, Cormac. *Blood Meridian, or, The Evening Redness in the West.* 1985.
      New York: Vintage Books, 1992.

Phillips, Dana. "History and the Ugly Facts of Cormac McCarthy's *Blood Meridian.*"
      American Literature 68.2 (June 1996): 433–60.

Schleifer, Ronald. *Rhetoric and Death.* Urbana: University of Illinois Press, 1990.

Shaviro, Steven. "'The Very Life of Darkness': A Reading of *Blood Meridian.*"
      Perspectives on Cormac McCarthy. Rev. ed. Ed. Edwin T. Arnold and
      Dianne C. Luce. Jackson: University Press of Mississippi, 1999. 145–58.

Leaving the Dark Night of the Lie

A Kristevan Reading of Cormac McCarthy's Border Fiction

Linda Townley Woodson

A T the end of Cormac McCarthy's *Blood Meridian,* Judge Holden makes a prediction, "As war becomes dishonored and its nobility called into question those honorable men who recognize the sanctity of blood will become excluded from the dance, which is the warrior's right, and thereby will the dance become a false dance and the dancers false dancers" (331). If *dance* in this passage is understood as a Nietzschean metaphor for life itself, with its inevitable struggles for dominance and power, then the *sanctity* of blood is its existence as the substance that makes possible the identity of the individual. Blood provides the possibility of a holding against the *other,* of which the rest of the substance of the corporeal individual is a part. According to Nietzsche, the will to power, the basic human motive, is an effort to gain control over chaos, a stay against the brevity of human existence, a maintaining of the self against other people: "Therefore, he needs to make peace and strives accordingly to banish from his world at least the most flagrant *bellum omni contra omnes* [war of each against all]. This peace treaty brings in its wake something which appears to be the first step toward acquiring that puzzling truth drive:

to wit, *that* which shall count as 'truth' from now on is established" ("Truth and Lies" 81).

If blood holds us against the other, then spilling the lifeblood of the other in war to establish the ultimate power of the self is the most extreme recognition of the other. Sharing with Nietzsche an understanding of how language works to separate us and to establish dominance, Julia Kristeva describes this act of sanctioned murder as "the potentialities of *victim/executioner*" ("Women's Time" 210), an act in historical time often designated *moral* if it is accomplished in the name of national values, defined by "economic homogeneity, historical tradition and linguistic unity" ("Women's Time" 188).

Thus, in *Blood Meridian* the atrocities and horrors of the act of war are displayed vividly and are justified by the participants in the ruse of cause/consequence, means/end, called Manifest Destiny. This system of logic is made possible by the sociocultural, collective memory of writing or inscription, identified clearly in the character of Judge Holden in *Blood Meridian* (Wallach 124–36), a memory that makes possible words as "things" that create a "formal agenda of an absolute destiny" (85). Because humans can perceive the world only through patterns of thought inherent in the human brain, they can never know the world exactly as it is. Patterns such as cause/consequence may not exist in the outside world but function for the human to make sense of otherwise chaos. Humans call up stored images of experiences in various combinations based on the working of the brain by what we call "memory" and apply these combinations to the storing of new images. Without these patterns, we would be forced to see each new situation as if for the first time. Collectively, only the recording of these patterns in writing prevents their dissolution with the passing of the individual or of his or her immediate group. Only the recording of these patterns historically makes possible acts of aggression among groups as large as those involved historically in Manifest Destiny. Thus, the potential of large groups to act as *executioners* relies on sight, the most intellectual of all the senses; the absence of reliance on the other senses is symbolized in *Blood Meridian* by the wearing of scapulars of ears belonging to the dead by the participants (87, 270).

The coming of World War II, the period on either side of which the first two novels of the Border Trilogy, *All the Pretty Horses* and *The Crossing,* take place, signaled the end of the possibility of a national identity. As Kristeva posits, although World War II was fought as if for national values, it "brought an end to the nation as a reality: it was turned into a mere illusion which, from that point forward, would be preserved only for ideological or strictly political purposes, its social and philosophical coherence having collapsed" ("Women's Time" 188). It brought, too, the creation of atomic weapons drawn graphically in the "white light of the desert noon" (425) at the end of *The Crossing.* Whereas in *Blood Meridian* the judge describes war as the ultimate game because of the value of "that which is put at hazard," which "swallows up game, player, all" (249), the release of radiation through nuclear power upped the stakes to a level never before conceived. This release of radiation had the power to speed up the dying of the natural world.

In that scenario, the false dance (Nietzsche's *will to power* in order to make sense of the chaos and to maintain identity) is enacted in language, the other means humans have to maintain themselves against the other. This alternative means is chosen out of necessity because of the value of what would be hazarded by taking the other's life. Nietzsche describes language use as the will to know devised by the intellect to detain humans for a moment in existence. The old man at the church in Caborca in *The Crossing* describes this drive as "something to contain us or to stay our hand. Otherwise there were no boundaries to our own being and we too must extend our claims until we lose all definition. Until we must be swallowed up at last by the very void to which we wished to stand opposed" (153). At one level in the trilogy, then, McCarthy is exploring language, the false dance that *is* the human activity and the creation through that dance of individual and national identities. At the same time he exposes, through the presented philosophies, the truth about *truth* as humans know it. Although these books rely on semiotic systems, they are honest about how those systems work, or, as Claude Lévi-Strauss describes it, "no key to no mystery" (quoted in Kristeva, "Semiotics" 78). By exhibiting the concepts of Nietzsche's "On Truth and Lies in a

Nonmoral Sense" throughout both *All the Pretty Horses* and *The Crossing* (see my essay "'The Lighted Display Case': A Nietzschean Reading of Cormac McCarthy's Border Fiction"), McCarthy asserts the idea that truths can never be known in conscious reasoning through language, that humans use language as a way of becoming and of holding against the other, that humans are controlled by inner drives (energy) that determine paths toward the common destiny, and that the movement of these drives exists at a level below signifier and signified in the rhythms and rhymes of that surface language. Literature then becomes a way of exhibiting these rhythms, and each individual's narrative and the witnessing to it in the memory of another become a way of existing for a temporary moment in history. This existence is possible despite the fact that in the world outside human existence, the conceptual truths created through language, such as cause, consequence, responsibility, and morals based on those concepts and on intention, have little meaning.

That is not to say, though, that McCarthy creates an amoral literary universe in his border fiction. In coming to know one's heart through the witnessing of others, through holding their memory into the future, through listening to the rhythms of the heart in their oral discourse and their narratives, one can come to a process of living where one recognizes the importance of all things in a universe whose order we can never know, the sanctity of blood, the sanctity of all. The universe affirms a sacredness of life beyond all conscious knowing.

Controlling McCarthy's literary vision in his border world are themes established first in *Blood Meridian*. Early in the novel, the kid encounters a hermit who speaks first of the controlling truth in the novel, a truth that goes far to explain why the judge ultimately kills him: "A man's at odds to know his mind cause his mind is aught he has to know it with. He can know his heart, but he dont want to" (19). Throughout the novel the kid has studied the judge (in Kristevan terms, historical record and the violence caused by that record) but is unable to kill him in the desert; Language/Law/the Father can never be completely destroyed because, as Kristeva reminds us throughout her work, language *is* the human activity, or, as Tobin exclaims, significantly without pause after *God*, "God the man is a dancer . . ." (123).

As the kid begins to understand what the ex-priest already knows about the judge (the foibles of the father, the knowledge of which, according to Freud, allows the son to break free of the burden of the father), "they spoke less and less between them" (303). Later, the kid, placed outside of historical language by his separation from the judge and by his inability to read, tries to convey the horrors he has witnessed in oral language ("he began to speak with a strange urgency of things few men have seen in a lifetime" [305]), but he is not understood and ultimately resorts to silence. He moves among others (312), carrying a Bible "no word of which he can read" (312) and seeming to travel with "no news at all" (312), the result of a motive the judge quickly recognizes: "Was it always your idea . . . that if you did not speak you would not be recognized?" (328). In the kid's dream he has seen the judge joined by a "false moneyer with his gravers and burins who seeks favor with the judge" (310), like Nietzsche's coiner of illusory language: "Truths are illusions which we have forgotten are illusions; they are metaphors that have become worn out and have been drained of sensuous force, coins which have lost their embossing and are now considered as metal and no longer as coins" ("On Truth and Lies" 84). Although the judge suggests that he could have loved the kid like a son (306), he (Language, Law, History, and the Father, in Freudian/Kristevan terms) destroys the kid. The "flawed place in the fabric" (299) of the kid's heart has been his refusal to act fully on the will to power. Earlier, the judge has been candid with the men about the ability of the mind to know, as candid as the hermit is, as candid as semiotic systems must be about themselves, "for existence has its own order and that no man's mind can compass, that mind itself being but a fact among others" (245). And because the kid's dream reveals that he has begun to understand something about the judge, about language and its role in the execution of the will to power, something about human *truth* and its lie, in the end he has the potential to be useless to the judge (306).

Having laid the foundation for exploring the relationship of language to reality in *Blood Meridian*, McCarthy continues the exploration of how language transforms reality, of how reality transforms language, and of the nature of truth in *All the Pretty Horses*.

The rhetorical structure of *All the Pretty Horses* presents an intertextuality in which the words of the principal teachers whom John Grady Cole encounters reveal Nietzschean concepts like those of *Blood Meridian,* while the narrative itself demonstrates the truth about those concepts. Just as *truth* for the men of *Blood Meridian* was the establishment of national identity through the misguided logic of Manifest Destiny as cause and its resultant consequences, no matter the cost to others, throughout *All the Pretty Horses* John Grady Cole encounters evidence that the truth is what a particular society wants or wishes it to be: the truth of Mexico, of the pueblo La Encantada, of the prison, and of the hacienda, where the Dueña Alfonsa, to protect her niece, becomes the ultimate judge. In a setting more real than metaphorical, Cole, like the kid, is manipulated and controlled by language, the judge. In spite of Cole's belief that the "truth is what happened. It aint what come out of somebody's mouth," he is forced to realize the significance of the captain's words, "We can make the truth here" (168). In the prison Pérez informs Cole that in the Mexican system of justice, individuals can be accused of crimes at will, "a matter of choosing" (193). John Grady Cole assumes that he can move into Mexico and take control of whatever he desires (Alejandra and the hacienda), much like a modern reenactment of Manifest Destiny. His desire to create a world like the one that was lost to him in the selling of his grandfather's ranch is overcome, however, by the *say* of Alfonsa, a woman who has spent her life as an exile from the larger language and law of her country.

Alfonsa has been made an exile both because of her gender and because of her reading of her father's books and her education in Europe. Made cynical about human nature by observing the fate of the Madero brothers, she speaks words that bear many of the Nietzschean concepts of the book, in particular, her words to Cole as she explains her decision against him: "If there is a pattern there it will not shape itself to anything these eyes can recognize. Because the question for me was always whether that shape we see in our lives was there from the beginning or whether these random events are only called a pattern after the fact. Because otherwise we are nothing" (230). Most tellingly, she employs the Nietzschean metaphor of the coiner like that of the dream in *Blood Meridian:* "If fate is the law then is fate also subject to that law? At some point we cannot escape naming responsibility. It's in our nature. Sometimes I think we are all like that myopic coiner at his press, taking the blind slugs one by one from the tray, all of us bent so jealously at our work, determined that not even chaos be outside of our own making" (241).

Here she indicates that we attempt to make sense of the random events of our lives through the patterns inherent in language and controlled by the brain, calling them *fate* and identifying one event as the cause of another, when in fact we have forgotten in our drive for control that *all* language is metaphor, even that language that describes the laws of the universe. As honest as she is about language and how it works for power, an honesty similar to the judge's, and again an honesty semiotic systems must have about themselves, she is willing nonetheless to participate in that control if it serves her purpose.

Yet another feature of intertextuality appears in the text in an echo of Freudian/Kristevan ideas about the constraints placed on the individual by family structures and society in the development of language acquisition and symbolization. In describing these constraints, Kristeva hypothesizes that "certain semiotic articulations are transmitted through the biological code or physiological 'memory' and thus form the inborn bases of the symbolic function" ("Semiotics" 96). To expand, contemporary brain theory (cf. Damasio 111) accepts that certain innate regulatory circuits of the brain are engaged in the organism's survival and receive signals from the body about the goodness and badness of situations in order to assist survival. Because language is an efficacious means of participating in this assurance of survival, it too is related to this circuitry. However, in the development of the individual, the design of brain circuitries further depends upon the activities in which the individual is engaged (Damasio 111). Thus, nature *and* nurture play a significant part in the development of mind. This theory appears to underlie Pérez's discussion of the differences between the mind of the Anglo and that of the Mexican (192–95). He states that whereas he once believed that the difference had its origins in the Anglo life of privilege, he has come to see that it is a difference of mind. He describes the mind of the Anglo as looking "only where he wishes to see" (192), a suggestion of differences in semiotic processes identifying cause and consequence. If he is suggesting that the mind of the Anglo functions differently from that of the Mexican, then he must also be suggesting that in addition to the Anglo's experiences (the "life of privilege"), there must also be genetic differences transmitted to ensure survival. These differences operate to exclude certain experiences and focus only on those deemed necessary for the well-being of the organism ("only where he wishes to see"). Pérez also describes the attribution by the Anglo mind of abstract qualities such as good and evil to inanimate objects, yet another difference from the Mexican mind: "The Mexican does not believe that a car can be good or evil. If there is evil in the car he knows that to destroy the car is to accomplish nothing. Because he knows where good and evil have their home. The anglo thinks in his rare way that the Mexican is superstitious. But who is the one?" (194) Because of certain experiences, the Anglo mind, according to Pérez, has learned to identify certain objects as good and evil and to react to them accordingly, whereas the Mexican mind recognizes that the concepts of *good* and *evil* are created by the organism in its struggle for survival.

I have explored the semiotic foundation of *All the Pretty Horses* more fully elsewhere (see "Deceiving the Will to Truth"). Throughout the novel McCarthy works with how discourse is governed by desire or the need to dominate; therefore, any attempt to utter a truth free of desire or power is also driven by these two imperatives, which mask truth. In his discussion of this "will to truth," Michel Foucault posits that "in every society the production of discourse is at once controlled, selected, organized, and redistributed according to a certain number of procedures, whose role is to avert its powers and dangers, to cope with chance events, to evade its ponderous, awesome materiality" (216). In attempting to impose his own version of truth on the various discourse communities that John Grady Cole encounters, he becomes a victim of the language of those communities and is forced to realize the wisdom of the captain's statement, "We can make the truth here" (168), and also that of the *charros* at the ranch, "a man leaves much when he leaves his own country" (226).

At the end of the narrative, the understandings that John Grady

Cole has acquired about language and its functioning have made him an exile, like Alfonsa, in the country of his birth. When Rawlins asks him where his country is, he replies, "I dont know where it is. I dont know what happens to country" (299); that is, as Kristeva suggests, national values and national identity are no longer possible when one understands the nature of illusory truths. In accepting his role in the loss of Alejandra (291) and his failure of courage in the death of Jimmy Blevins (293), he appears to understand Alfonsa's distinction in valuing what is true above what is useful, knowledge without which it makes "little difference" whether one "lives at all" (240). But there is evidence, too, that he has begun, in the words of the hermit in *Blood Meridian* (19), to know his heart. As he stands over the unmarked grave of Abuela, he passes a benediction over her life, and then "for a moment he held out his hands as if to steady himself or as if to bless the ground there or perhaps as if to slow the world that was rushing away and seemed to care nothing for the old or the young or rich or poor or dark or pale or he or she. Nothing for their struggles, nothing for their names. Nothing for the living or the dead" (301). We will see that this gesture is to be repeated later in the blessing of the waters by the diva, a gesture that changes the way Billy Parham would see the world forever.

The features of intertextuality begun in the earlier novels with their examinations of the relationship of language and reality are continued and expanded in *The Crossing,* where McCarthy places his border world into both historical time and monumental or spatial time (Nietzsche and Kristeva). As with *All the Pretty Horses,* the narrative itself explores historical time, that is, a time in linear history and of national and sociocultural identity, but the variation of rhetorical types, the encounters with other narratives, places the reader in a spatial time outside of chronology and, once again, examines Nietzschean concepts about language. Because of the urgency of its historical setting, shortly before the release of nuclear power, *The Crossing* presents these concepts in an attempt to demystify language itself and to call for a different kind of time—monumental time— outside of sociocultural identities. Kristeva describes the need for this direction:

to demystify the identity of the symbolic bond itself, to demystify, therefore, the community of language as a universal and unifying tool, one which totalizes and equalizes. In order to bring out—along with the *singularity* of each person and, even more, along with the multiplicity of every person's possible identifications (with atoms, e.g., stretching from the family to the stars)—the *relativity of his/her symbolic as well as biological existence,* according to the variation in his/her specific symbolic capacities. And in order to emphasize the *responsibility* which all will immediately face of putting this fluidity into play against the threats of death which are unavoidable whenever an inside and an outside, a self and an other, one group and another, are constituted. (210)

The rhetorical form of the first part of the novel is the traditional tragic tale, epic in the sense that its logic appears to be causal. In the first part, in which Billy Parham offers food to the Indian, thereby *appearing* to contribute to the death of his family, and carries the she-wolf back to Mexico where, in trying to save her life, he becomes her unwilling executioner, the narrative explores the potential of all for *victim/executioner,* the extent of human responsibility in cause/consequence, and the questioning of a moral system based on intention. Are we to believe that because Billy responds to the Indian's demands, because he takes the only gun the family has, resulting in his family's death, he is responsible for their deaths? Are we to believe that because he takes the wolf to Mexico where he must become her executioner, he is responsible for her death? Or, when in a parallel action he takes Boyd to Mexico even though Boyd, according to Billy, cared little about the horses, that Billy is responsible for Boyd's death? In "The Free Spirit" Nietzsche questions the legitimacy of basing values in a moral system on intention: "The intention as the whole origin and prehistory of an action—almost to the present day this prejudice dominated moral praise, blame, judgment, and philosophy on earth" (44). Although in all of these cases Billy's intentions are honorable, using devotion as one of the standards of contemporary moral judgment, the consequences are disastrous. Yet was there anything in his experience that could have guided him otherwise? Probably not. The consequences of Billy's actions simply illustrate the delusions and emptiness of placing value in moral judgments on intentions. There-fore, in this narrative sequence causes do not necessarily lead to certain consequences, and although Billy feels regret at the conse-quences of his action at the end of the novel, he seems to have absorbed the statements of the *ganadero:*

> You do not know what things you set in motion. . . . No man can know. No prophet foresee. The consequences of an act are often quite different from what one would guess. You must be sure that the intention in your heart is large enough to contain all wrong disappointments. Do you see? Not everything has such a value. (202)

Billy at the beginning of his journey was unable to know all of the wrong turnings, and yet at the end of the novel he appears to have sorrow for his brother's death but no overwhelming sense of blame, inasmuch as he asserts, "I been more fortunate than most. There aint but one life worth livin and I was born to it" (420).

Yet another feature of intertextuality is apparent in one of the novel's key sections: a mock scholastic dialogue, or rather a monologue that is dialogical, in which a priest tells of his encounter with another man. Here, once again, Nietzschean concepts about language and human inability to know the natural world are presented, accompanied by the responses of religion to those concepts. This dialogue is no parody, however, because it challenges God and social law (Kristeva, "Word" 49). The priest first comes to the church because of the other man and finds there a story because "things separate from their stories have no meaning" (142): "The story on the other hand can never be lost from its place in the world for it is that place. And that is what was to be found here. The corrido. The tale. And like all corridos it ulti-mately told one story only, for there is only one to tell" (142). As he tells the story of the man who had suffered because of the loss of his child and had left the order of the world to live under the toppling dome (similar to Nietzsche's dome of concepts built on running water; "On Truth" 85) that has been destroyed by flooding (149), the priest explains that the people of Caborca place such importance on the dome "that they scarce speak of it at all" (150), and events are made "subject to its standing" (150). The man had come to that church to study God, and in his dreams, he peered into the place where God was busy "weaving the world" (149), an image much like Nietzsche's "web of concepts" (89). The priest describes how he argues against the man's heresy from "those high canonical principles to which he gave such latitude" (151). In this dialogical monologue, the story told by the priest, the priest assumes the position of third person in its telling, creating a dialogue framed by narrative, thus disputing any claim to ready presentation of truth (Kristeva, "Word" 51). In this correlational relationship, the observer/ hearer/ witness/ reader retains an autonomous viewpoint, for, as the priest tells Billy, "the lesson of a life can never be its own. Only the witness has power to take its measure. It is lived for the other only" (158), and again, "There is another who will hear what you never spoke" (158). And in the clearest statement of what we have been considering about the role of language in holding the individual apart from the other, the priest says to Billy, "To God every man is a heretic. The heretic's first act is to name his brother. So that he may step free of him" (158). In this passage, the priest identifies God as the interconnectedness of all things. The heretic's act then is to break free from that interconnectedness, in this case through language. Thus, we are all heretics. (For further expansion of these ideas, see my essay "*De los Herejes y Huérfanos:* The Sound and Sense of Cormac McCarthy's Border Fiction.")

Nonetheless, this is a *monologue,* and the words of the old man, the words that echo Nietzschean philosophy, are given to Billy from the memory of the priest, as are the words of Socrates given to us by Plato. Evidence exists that the memory may even be, in part, a fabrication as the priest moves back and forth from past to present in its telling. Ultimately this encounter is an example of witnessing—a consecration of the life of the old man through the memory of the priest. At the end of the book, Billy's statement that it has not been his experience that most of what one hears is right (418) is inclusive, lending further testimony to the idea that the witness/ hearer/ reader is to remain autonomous. Like John Grady Cole, Billy Parham is another kid faced with the truth about language, the judge. In the end, he appears to have begun to understand the truth about truth.

Additional Nietzschean concepts are explored in Billy's encounter with the blind man whose eyes have been sucked from his head by a German Huertista. The acts of three people, significantly those of the traditional family structure, a man, a woman, and a child, have been his salvation (284). The blind man describes a world whose light is "in men's eyes only for the world itself move[s] in eternal darkness and darkness [is] its true nature and true condition" and "in this darkness it turn[s] with perfect cohesion in all its parts but that there [is] naught there to see" (283). In his loss of memory of the seen world, he finds that "in the deepest dark of that loss that there also [is] a ground and there one must begin" (291), echoing Nietzsche's statement, "Only by forgetting this primitive world of metaphor can one live with any repose, security, and consistency" ("Truth and Lies" 86). That ground is his understanding of the distraction of the seen world and of the value of listening: "En este viaje el mundo visible es no mas que un distraimiento. Para los ciegos y para todos los hombres. Ultimamente sabemos que no podemos ver el buen Dios. Vamos escuchando. Me entiendes, joven? Debemos escuchar" (292) (In this journey the visible world is no more than a distraction. For the blind and for everyone. Finally we know that we cannot see the good God. Let's listen. Do you understand me, young one? We ought to listen). He has found this ground through his interaction with the three others. In a metaphorical tracing backward of the Freudian steps of language acquisition, from the child and the connectedness to the mother and the subsequent castration in identification of the other through language as the child becomes the man (Kristeva, "Revolution" 100–105), this man is drawn from the river by the other man, is nurtured by the woman's food and shelter, and comes to live with the child.

The Crossing, with its multiple voices of characters and concepts about language, assumes features of a carnivalesque novel. Following Mikhail Bakhtin in calling this kind of novel *polyphonic,* Kristeva suggests that such a novel, conscious of its being as sign, refuses dogma

("Word" 54). The form of the novel itself underscores the message of the text in opposition to tragic unity and causality/consequence, as does *The Crossing* in its episodic nature. But despite its features of carnivalesque, *The Crossing* does appear to carry a message. Its message seems to consist of those very words, "Debemos escuchar," and those words summarize other messages as well, both linguistic and semantic. The judge in *Blood Meridian* asks the kid if he has left witnesses (331), and the priest in *The Crossing* remains at the church to bear witness to the existence of the old man (158). This sanctity of hearing the narrative of others, narratives of their individual and created histories, offers to the other his or her individual worth. It is reverent acknowledgment of the existence of the other, for, as Kristeva explains, speech is humans and their activity (51). In Nietzschean philosophy, too, reason exists for this listening, because the best moral judgments are made from observing the experiences of others. If Billy Parham has gained nothing else from his experiences in *The Crossing*, he appears to understand the value of this witnessing, of holding the other in memory and of leaving witnesses. In an uncharacteristically long and self-revelatory response, he "jabbers" his own history to the other passer-through (419).

At the linguistic level, this listening can take meaning as well. Following Freud's drive theory as the foundation of all language, with the death drive as foremost among these, and following Mallarmé's "Le Mystère dans les lettres," Kristeva speaks of the possibility of the rhythms of language that underlie all discourse. Beginning with the *chora*, identified by Kristeva in Plato's *Timaeus* as the ruptures and kinetic rhythms that precede patterns of surface language—"evidence, verisimilitude, spatiality and temporality" ("Revolution" 94)—she follows Mallarmé in identifying this *semiotic motility* as feminine: "They [the critics] play their parts disinterestedly or for a minor gain: leaving our Lady and Patroness exposed to show her dehiscence or lacuna, with respect to certain dreams, as though this were the standard to which everything is reduced" (quoted in Kristeva, "Revolution" 97). Poetic language, aesthetic practices, the creation of the self's narrative, dreams, all allow for these rhythms to be heard and felt at a level below conscious meaning. Kristeva describes the necessity for intensifying these aesthetic practices to accomplish the demystification of unifying language and to emphasize the relativity of each person's existence ("Women's Time" 210). These aesthetic practices, she asserts, are the "modern reply to the eternal question of morality" (210).

Not only do the prose structures of McCarthy's fiction reflect these rhythms, but the diva of the traveling opera company in *The Crossing* symbolizes the Lady as well. As Billy observes her standing in the water, passing "one hand over the surface of the water as if to bless it" (220), he understands "that the world which had always been before him everywhere had been veiled from his sight" (220). Wearing the *mascara* and singing the stories of others, stories that exhibit human drives and that recognize the identity of the other without the drive accompanying the language of power, she bears witness to the rhythms and movements of humanity. Her words advise this same listening: "Listen to the corridos of the country" (230). Her gesture and her words, language very different from the language of the judge (the Law, the Father), suggest a receptivity, a caress, and remind the reader of the words of the priest at Caborca, "Every breath taken that does not bless is an affront" (158). Although Billy's words to Quijada about there being only one life worth living are the sum of his experiences, nonetheless they are a variation of the diva's words to him: "The shape of the road is the road. There is not some other road that wears that shape but only the one. And every voyage begun upon it will be completed. Whether horses are found or not" (230).

In the third novel of the trilogy, *Cities of the Plain*, the element of intertextuality almost disappears. The novel takes the form of a narrative chronicling the further adventures and death of the idealistic John Grady Cole and of the deep friendship of Cole and Billy Parham. Only in the epilogue do we learn that Billy continues to be a drifter, living into old age, and when the epilogue ends we sense that his life is almost over. The elements of philosophy that do appear in this work are said by the characters briefly and directly, but they continue many of the ideas presented in the earlier works. For example, Billy's words to John Grady reinforce the idea that World War II marked a change in human existence forever: "The war changed everthing. I dont think people even know it yet" (78). When John Grady asks how the war changed everything, Billy replies, "It just did. It aint the same no more. It never will be" (78).

In discussing the cause/consequence pattern of human thought that we have seen questioned particularly in *The Crossing,* the blind man suggests to John Grady the inability of humans to bring about consequences of their own will (195). Reminiscent of Alfonsa's image of puppets holding other puppets' strings in *All the Pretty Horses* (231), the blind man's words indicate a complicated maze of actions in which "each act in that maze is itself an enslavement for it voids every alternative and binds one ever more tightly into the constraints that make a life" (195). Later, Eduardo makes a similar statement to Billy about will: "In spite of whatever views you may hold everything that has come to pass has been the result of your friend's coveting of another man's property and his willful determination to convert that property to his own use without regard for the consequences. But of course this does not make the consequences go away" (240).

Even the ideas expressed in *All the Pretty Horses* about fundamental differences of thought between the Anglo and the Mexican mind appear again in the words of Eduardo to John Grady: "Your kind cannot bear that the world be ordinary. That it contain nothing save what stands before one. But the Mexican world is a world of adornment only and underneath it is very plain indeed. While your world . . . your world totters upon an unspoken labyrinth of questions" (253). Here again is a suggestion of differences in semiotic processes identifying cause and consequence.

In the epilogue, Billy, now an old man, meets a traveler who tells him a story of a dream. This storyteller's dream describes a traveler and begins a narrative about that traveler, but the story has no end. In the process of telling the story, the storyteller asserts that "it is the narrative that is the life of the dream while the events themselves are often interchangeable" (283). This dream-narrative serves as an exemplum for humans' use of language, demonstrating that it is the user of language who puts a cause/consequence pattern to what would otherwise be random events; therefore, the power of language lies in the motives of its users: "So the question of who is telling the story is very consiguiente [consequential]" (277). But the storyteller reminds

Billy of another way of using language, allowing the fellow passerby to be a "witness" to his story and listening with respect: "Do you love him, that man? Will you honor the path he has taken? Will you listen to his tale?" (289). This way with language is not devoid of power, but it does not risk as much, and it speaks of human dignity.

At the end of the epilogue a family takes Billy in, and we are led to assume that he is near the end of his life. The family offers him the respect of listening to his stories: "sometimes he and the children would sit at the kitchen table and he'd tell them about horses and cattle and the old days" (290). When Billy explains to Betty, the woman of the family, that he does not know why they are so kind to him ("I'm not what you think I am" [292]), she responds, "Well, Mr. Parham, I know who you are. And I do know why" (292). Like the story the title of the book alludes to, in which the angels of God visit Lot's family, Betty's response seems to suggest that each of us will be visited from time to time by another to whom we should offer respect, dignity, a bit of food, and the willingness to "listen to his tale."

If the Nietzschean revelations about the inadequacy of language to convey truth as presented by the characters throughout Cormac McCarthy's border fiction are to be believed, then they call into question the very revelations themselves, as honest semiotic systems must do. But if speech is *the* human activity, as Julia Kristeva asserts, then in that speech we may be able to hear beyond the imposed surface patterns to reveal the underlying rhythms and to glimpse their truths. As we listen to the stories of others, their *corridos,* we may find a way to use language less accompanied by desire and power. These stories, these aesthetic practices, become a way of avoiding the *victim/executioner* language of the judge in favor of language that recognizes the other without a goal of dominance. McCarthy may be guiding us to find there a way, in Kristeva's words, to "counter-balance the storage and uniformity of information by present-day mass media, data-bank systems and, in particular, modern communication technology" ("Women's Time" 210), language that "totalizes and equalizes" (210), a way to recognize the individual worth of the other without destruction and without further speeding up of the destruction of the natural world, the "darkening land, the world to come" (*All the Pretty Horses* 302).

Works Cited

Damasio, Antonio R. *Descartes' Error.* New York: Avon, 1994.

Foucault, Michel. *The Archaeology of Knowledge and The Discourse on Language.* Trans. A. M. Sheridan Smith and Rupert Swyer. New York: Pantheon Books, 1972.

Kristeva, Julia. "Revolution in Poetic Language." *The Kristeva Reader.* Trans. Margaret Waller. Ed. Toril Moi. New York: Columbia University Press, 1986. 89–136.

———. "Semiotics: A Critical Science and/or a Critique of Science." *The Kristeva Reader.* Trans. Sean Hand. Ed. Toril Moi. New York: Columbia University Press, 1986. 74–88.

———. "Women's Time." *The Kristeva Reader.* Trans. Alice Jardine and Harry Blake. Ed. Toril Moi. New York: Columbia University Press, 1986. 187–213.

———. "Word, Dialogue and Novel." *The Kristeva Reader.* Trans. Alice Jardine, Thomas Gora, and Leon S. Roudiez. Ed. Toril Moi. New York: Columbia University Press, 1986. 34–61.

McCarthy, Cormac. *All the Pretty Horses.* New York: Alfred A. Knopf, 1992.

———. *Blood Meridian.* New York: Random House, 1985.

———. *Cities of the Plain.* New York: Alfred A. Knopf, 1998.

———. *The Crossing.* New York: Alfred A. Knopf, 1994.

Nietzsche, Friedrich. "On Truth and Lies in a Nonmoral Sense." *Philosophy and Truth: Selections from Nietzsche's Notebooks of the Early 1870's.* Ed. and trans. Daniel Breazeale. Atlantic Highlands, N.J.: Humanities Press, 1979. 101–23.

———. "The Free Spirit." *Beyond Good and Evil.* Trans. Walter Kaufmann. New York: Vintage Books, 1966. 35–56.

Wallach, Rick. "Judge Holden, *Blood Meridian*'s Evil Archon." *Sacred Violence: A Reader's Companion to Cormac McCarthy.* Ed. Wade Hall and Rick Wallach. El Paso: Texas Western Press, 1995. 125–36.

Woodson, Linda Townley. "Deceiving the Will to Truth: The Semiotic Foundation of *All the Pretty Horses.*" *Sacred Violence: A Reader's Companion to Cormac McCarthy.* Ed. Wade Hall and Rick Wallach. El Paso: Texas Western Press, 1995. 149–54.

———. "*De los Herejes y Huérfanos*: The Sound and Sense of Cormac McCarthy's Border Fiction." *Myth, Legend, Dust.* Ed. Rick Wallach. Manchester: Manchester University Press, 2000. 201–8.

———. "'The Lighted Display Case': A Nietzschean Reading of Cormac McCarthy's Border Fiction." *Southern Quarterly* 38.4 (summer 2000): 48–60.

"Hallucinated Recollections"

Narrative as Spatialized Perception of History

in *The Orchard Keeper*

Matthew R. Horton

> *The tree was down and cut to lengths, the sections*
> *spread and jumbled over the grass.*

CORMAC McCarthy begins the first fragment of *The Orchard Keeper* with this condensed image of perceived history, giving shape to the passage of time, representing how human hindsight objectifies the passage of time. As a metaphor that illustrates the disintegration of historical continuity, the fallen tree, with its pieces still somehow reminiscent of a majestic coherence, signals McCarthy's use of disjunct episodes to narrate his novel. Even the syntax of the first line reflects a concern with the dissection and breakdown of order. The sentence, composed of sixteen words split down the middle with a comma, mimics the tension between two opposing forces. Whereas the first eight words adhere to iambic tetrameter, McCarthy subjects the second half to a metrical meltdown, initiated by the word "jumbled." This juxtaposition of rhythmic order and dissolution denies the potential for poetic balance, asserts the reality of collapse, and reinforces the elusive but inherent boundary between the two. Both the image and the language that creates it, therefore, draw the reader into a broken world of divisions and borders where fragmentation overwhelms holistic perception. Indeed, the tree has been sliced into segments that are "spread and jumbled," which anticipates the fractured surface and disordered sequence of the narrative to follow: the tree segments symbolize remnants of an untold story. To tell it, McCarthy abandons the ordered wholeness of the tree and chops it into smaller and more manageable wedges, which he intricately displaces and rearranges into stacks; consequently, he constructs a network of episodes that reshapes chronologically intact history.

If this initial metaphor for storytelling generates tension between coherence and disorder, it does so in part by bridging the apparent perceptual gap separating time and space. McCarthy projects a temporal concept (history) through a spatial lens (tree fragments) and so foregrounds distortion as an integral part of conveying historical perception. The fallen and fragmented tree represents the mind of man struggling to recollect and reassemble the past. Just as the scattered segments indicate that the tree has been fractured, so must the events and sensations of a story told about the past be extracts from the temporal order of sequential history. But McCarthy's style of storytelling, his narrative technique, goes beyond the idea of distortion as a consequence of limited memory. He deliberately warps conventional appearance, reveals multiple dimensions of perception, and jumbles the sequence of his narrative to simulate how man reconceives the past within memory. Thus, the aesthetic engine of storytelling gives birth to and is sustained by distortion, the predominant means by which McCarthy undermines the boundary between time and space and uncovers the structures that exist hidden within chronology.

As a result, the narration of *The Orchard Keeper* generates shapes that are difficult to see, and the reader must adopt the kind of vision that apprehends form, recognizes shifts in angles of perspective, tracks the intersections of plot lines, discovers patterns of imagery and theme, and synthesizes disjunct but simultaneous fragments of action. The need for these strategies suggests one of McCarthy's aesthetic kinships with modernism and the tradition of spatial form. James Joyce's *Ulysses* (1922), Virginia Woolf's *To the Lighthouse* (1927), and William Faulkner's *Absalom, Absalom!* (1936) demand a reading technique that can untangle and unfold their fragmented, self-regurgitating, and overlapping texts. In 1945, Joseph Frank used the term *spatial form* to propose that modern authors "intend the reader to apprehend their work spatially, in a moment of time, rather than as a sequence" (10). The "principle of reflexive reference," which Frank upholds as the dominant structural element in modern literature, suggests that the reader must suspend attention to the temporal sequence of narrative long enough to identify the spatial relationships between different units of meaning in the text (15).[1] Because he published *The Orchard Keeper* in 1965, it is historically erroneous to define McCarthy as a "modernist." However, his episodic narrative style and his simulation of thought processes and perceptual activity with syntax and form link him to the influences of that experimental period. The "spread and jumbled" sequence of *The Orchard Keeper* requires the reader to stand above the order of words and discern how McCarthy reshapes history. The tree fragments, chopped up and stacked away, eventually reveal a new structure that overturns the more conventional notions of historical perception.

But McCarthy takes his metaphor one step further to show how this spatial reorganization of history falters when faced with an age of anxious uncertainty. Forming a strange composite, the lower trunk of the tree has grown around part of an iron fence: "The stocky man laid aside the saw and he and the Negro took hold of the piece of fence and strained and grunted until they got the log turned over." They try every way they can to cut the trunk, but there is no angle that permits the saw blade to pass through. The young adult John Wesley Rattner watches the process and is intrigued by the apparent fusion of the tree and fence: "The young man came over to see. Here, said the man, look sideways here. See? He looked. All the way up here? he said. Yep, the man said. He took hold of the twisted wrought-iron, the mangled fragment of the fence, and shook it. It didn't shake." This fusion of incompatible materials produces an ambiguous metaphor: not only does the new industrial order violate the flux of nature, but time's relentless flow also swallows the pastoral dream of containing history, the desire for stasis. Though he cannot shake loose the piece of fence,

John Wesley makes no conspicuous attempt to discern why. In fact, with the "sideways" perception of the cutters and the strength of the composite, McCarthy shows that the infiltrated segment is immune to both philosophical and physical dissection. The man ironically claims that the fence has "growed all through the tree" and gives up trying to break up the segment any further: "We cain't cut no more on it. Damned old elum's bad enough on a saw" (3). The elm and iron have fused inextricably and, as a result, symbolize a transitional age in history defined by overlapping, interrelated, and clashing times. To separate those times, to slice through them in the same way as the rest of the tree, proves to be impossible.

McCarthy channels this impenetrable tension into his entire narrative design: to spatialize an inherently temporal art; to fragment and reorder the chronological path of history; to narrate a story as one would saw and stack wood—none of these entirely subverts the continuity of time. Certainly, a reader cannot recognize the patterns and shapes of a narrative without engaging in what Joseph Frank calls "the time-act of reading" (75). This perceptual duality complements the historical setting of *The Orchard Keeper*: a time of unsettling change in social order and values. Though the text is read in the order set upon the pages, the narrative, much like the tree, has been diced into disjunct episodes and rearranged so that the temporal order of the fictional world is somewhat fragmented and scrambled. At the same time, although the episodes appear to be in disarray, McCarthy manipulates their sequence to construct an intricate matrix of relationships. The tree-cutting scene at the beginning and John Wesley's return to his mother's grave at the end, both of which occur on the same day in 1948, frame the entire novel. Running through the four larger sections of the main narrative, which takes place in the 1930s and early 1940s and roughly follows the seasonal cycle,[2] are several prominent narrative threads. Roughly assigned to Kenneth Rattner, Marion Sylder, John Wesley Rattner, and Arthur Ownby, these threads run parallel to, intersect with, and thematically refer to each other. Within his frames and structures, however, McCarthy spins these threads discontinuously, interweaving episodes of varying lengths that confuse the sense of temporal cohesion and chronological order.

Several critics have suggested how narration in *The Orchard Keeper* indicates a spatial conception of history and a storytelling technique that foregrounds structure before chronology[3]; however, the aesthetic tension between coherence and dissolution in the novel remains relatively unexplored. The shape of the narrative as a whole attests to this tension: unpredictable episodic sequences of discontinuous threads put in some semblance of order by frames and recognizable sections. It inevitably generates confusion, but patterns gradually surface through thematic repetition and what David Paul Ragan terms "structural juxtaposition" (15). For instance, after the authorities interrogate Marion, John Wesley goes to visit him. A few pages later, a welfare agent questions Uncle Ather, and, shortly afterward, the boy visits him at the asylum. Beneath this connection, however, the ground slides, for the amount of time that elapses between the boy's two visits remains unknown. Only one event takes place in the narrative sequence between the visits: the mysterious owl attacks the cat. But there is no way to determine when this scene occurs in relation to the episodes contiguous to it. Across this obscure borderland, a distinct textual echo reverberates; however, McCarthy frustrates clarity of perception even as he establishes links or patterns of meaning. In fact, what he does allow his reader to see depends on the suspension of temporality he forces his reader to endure. The distortion of strict linear chronology into another shape continually reinforces the inherent tension between narrative space and time.

Specific moments in the text show that McCarthy distorts both form and time, and it is on this level that the reader most directly experiences a collapse of stable perception. Following the metaphor of the felled tree, the "history" begins with Kenneth Rattner, who is confronted with an image that illustrates the problem of vision:

He turned again. Far down the blazing strip of concrete a small shapeless mass had emerged and was struggling toward him. It loomed steadily, weaving and grotesque like something seen through bad glass, gained briefly the form and solidity of a pickup truck, whipped past and receded into the same liquid shape by which it came. (7)

McCarthy seems to suggest that his approaching narrative will not be easily recognized and will eventually dissolve into its initial shapelessness. His narrative reflects this process, gradually gaining form even as it resists absolute clarity, and finally threatening to run away, dissipate, as John Wesley struggles to connect with his past in the last scene of the novel. The young adult sees a similar image as he walks away from his decaying home:

> They swung by slowly, laboriously, as if under the weight of some singular and unreasonable gravity. The ruined and ragged mule, the wagon, the man . . . up the road they wobbled . . . shimmered in waves of heat rising from the road, dissolved in a pale and broken image. (244)

This time the vehicle represents an older age, creeps by in its decrepitude, and slowly moves away. These two passages ostensibly refer to one another and so provide another frame for the novel. But each also embodies how the passage of time, even the narrative itself, tends to defy coherence or containment in shape. As McCarthy attempts to rearrange the chronological sequence of his fictional world, the forms that materialize are always on the verge of disintegrating.

Stationary objects on a moving background or from the point of view of a character in motion provide another metaphor for this spatial-temporal distortion. The moon's reflection on the river, for example, looks to Marion like "hordes of luminous snakes racing" (32). In another scene, Marion loses control of his car and spins: "a streaming herd of trees swam past in the lights as if rushing headlong off the very rim of the earth and the store loomed again, glazed onto the green frieze, spinning past starkly white and in incredible elongation. And yet once more, trees and building in one long blur" (75). These images attest to the limits of perception when faced with an inseparable fusion of the static (spatial) and the kinetic (temporal). It is difficult to discern even the source of the distortion, whether it is a static object deformed by a moving frame or movement erroneously contained within a static frame. Spatializing history presents the same kind of dilemma: McCarthy must imagine where the dimensions meet and how they converge to produce distortion. When John Wesley goes to retrieve his mangled mink fur, the flooded creek is a "roily misshapen flume more like solid earth in motion than any liquid . . . each dip and riffle, eddy, glide, uncurling rope coil fixed and changeless" (176). Inversely, when John Wesley enters the creek, he is "standing with the thin brown wings of water flying over his shins with a slicing sound, standing so in an illusion of fantastic motion" (178). The constant flow of the water is rendered static but gives to a static body the properties of flux, a perceptual clash caused by the distorting superimposition of spatial and temporal dimensions.

But distortions of form are not his only preoccupation with small-scale eclipses of normal perception. McCarthy also distorts the passage of time by portraying a series of actions as if they occur in a sluggish or frozen temporal frame. A fragment from the scene in which Sylder and Rattner fight to the death illustrates this technique:

> They were like that for some few seconds, he sitting, the man standing, holding either end of the jack as if suspended in the act of passing it one to the other. Then Sylder stood, still in that somnambulant slow motion as if time itself were running down, and watched the man turn, seeming to labor not under water but in some more viscous fluid, torturous slow, and the jack itself falling down on an angle over the dying forces of gravity, leaving Sylder's own hand and bouncing slowly in the road while his leaden arm rose in a stiff arc and his fingers cocked like a cat's claws unsheathed and buried themselves in the cheesy neckflesh of the man who fled from him without apparent headway as in a nightmare. (38)

The disparity between the duration of the passage and the actions described creates what John Ditsky calls a "frieze of rigid violence," a scene in which "action is frozen in a stasis of reader attentiveness" (3). By emphasizing the position of the characters in relation to one another and conveying simultaneous activity, McCarthy spatializes the actions in this passage. He highlights each gesture long enough to make the progression of events seem more stroboscopic than fluid. However, he does not subvert linear time completely. The scene is disorienting in part because the reader still recognizes the passage of time, though it is diffused and slowed down by time-consuming details.

These small-scale glimpses of distortion, which reveal a dimension of reality that usually remains hidden from sight, set the stage for McCarthy's more sweeping narrative techniques in *The Orchard Keeper*. Section I progresses by switching back and forth between two seemingly unrelated threads that suddenly begin to converge and finally intersect. At an undesignated time but within a few hours, Kenneth Rattner hitchhikes his way north toward Red Branch and drinks in a roadhouse bar. Interspersed in the text are episodes about Marion Sylder, who is born in 1913, leaves Red Branch at age sixteen, and returns five years later to flaunt his wealth. Vaguely keeping the chronological order of each thread intact, McCarthy structurally mixes the two even as he keeps their storylines separate. He suspends the progression of any recognizable plot by stacking episodes from each thread that are too short to approach a crisis. As a result, the reader remains stuck in a perceptual limbo until the next chapter, when, in August 1934, Marion loses his job and drives off angrily. As he pulls into a roadhouse bar just short of the Atlanta city limits, a subtle sense of familiarity and repetition pricks the reader. Certain details of Rattner's arrival to Jim's Hot Spot, such as a "limegreen neon" sign and "an endless whirlpool of insects" in a "dome of yellow light" (15), reappear as Marion looks at the cars, which are "dimly lustrous in the neon ambience," and passes "through a fanfall of moths under the yellow doorlight" (32). Both see themselves strangely reflected in the bar mirror when they enter: Rattner is "surprised to see himself, silhouetted in the doorframe, poised nimbly atop a stack of glasses" (22), and Marion, "above the heads of the dancers," stares "hollow-eyed and sinister in the bar mirror" (32). The two men finally cross paths when Marion finds Rattner "sitting in his car as if conjured there simultaneously with the flick of light by the very act of opening the door" (33). It is an abrupt convergence that confirms how McCarthy has manipulated not only the time-act of reading but also fictional time: Marion's narrative catches up with Rattner's and has been closing in on it from the outset. This retroactively designates the time frame in which Rattner is returning to Red Branch and indicates that the movements from one thread to another before they converge necessitate movements backward and forward in time. Twenty-one years seem to pass in the duration of a few hours. However, from the vantage point of the present, as these threads move toward intersection and finally converge, history and narrative take on an extralinear shape. All of the events that lead Marion to the point of opening his car door seem to have occurred for the very purpose of doing so at that moment.

McCarthy pursues this line of development throughout the novel, always requiring the reader to look back from points of intersection to retrace the path taken to arrive there.[4] Preceding the moment when John Wesley meets Uncle Ather, to cite another example, there is a series of episodes from disparate threads of action on the same day: the latter scouts the snowy landscape while the former explores caves and skunk holes with Warn Pulliam and his friends. Sometimes McCarthy juggles three or four different strains in order to show how they converge and diverge and converge elsewhere, though maybe not all at once. Other times there is no convergence at all, when characters observe each other but never meet (Marion and Arthur Ownby) or cross paths with each other at different times (the cat and John Wesley). The former illustrates temporal coincidence, whereas the latter exemplifies a solely spatial intersection. One of the most surreal variations of narrative discontinuity occurs when Arthur Ownby falls unconscious in a rainstorm. McCarthy suspends the moment first by burning him "out of the near-darkness in antic configuration against the quick bloom of lightning" and then by switching to the present tense, as if to freeze time with the words "he is down" (172). As he lies there, six days pass in which the cat wanders the landscape and mangles the boy's mink fur, John Wesley finds the fur in the flooded river, and Marion's car quits while crossing the bridge into Knoxville. The last passage in the chapter returns to Ownby, who awakes in the rain and mud. With this sequence, McCarthy engineers another framing device, and, considering the suspension of time in the first passage, the narrative structure suggests that the other threads are somehow embedded in a dream of the unconscious Ownby. As a result, though there is no spatial-temporal convergence between him and the others, the six days seem pushed together into a few minutes. This variation of storytelling highlights another way the human mind reorders the sequence of events: memory often condenses the passage of time into smaller units. This essentially puts time in a different container, a different form, which is made possible by cutting it up and placing the pieces within the confines of the present.

The sequence in which John Wesley hears Marion crash into the creek, perhaps the most visually stunning variation of discontinuity and convergence, also mimics the distorting activity of memory. Conveying a reasonable transition from one place to another that occurs across the hiatus between two time frames, the scene illustrates how discontinuity in time does not always preclude continuity in space. Section II of the novel opens with Ownby watching the tower in the summer of 1940, six years after Marion dumps Rattner's corpse into the pit. A new thread begins, however, when McCarthy introduces John Wesley in the first weeks of September. At fourteen years old, he is anxious for winter to come: "He was pushing time now and he could feel it give" (65). The reader is left wondering why until two chapters later, when, "on the morning of the fifteenth of November," John Wesley sets his fur traps. Even after checking and resetting his traps for a week, he is at "the creek an hour before daylight in the morning with a flashlight" (87).

Interrupting this sequence, the chapter between captures Marion on a rainy night driving down the mountain. Although the time frame of this scene seems uncertain, the lightning glaring in "threatful illusions of proximity" recalls an earlier moment in the section (74). From his porch Ownby hears a crack and descries "the domed metal tank on the peak illuminated, quivering in a wild aureole of light" (58). That night he hears a car pass on the road (60). This temporal link not only dissolves the "illusion of proximity" between the driving scene and its two contiguous chapters but also prepares the way for McCarthy's imminent narrative experiment. Following the winter trapping scene, details such as "summer ivy" (88), "the counterpoint of crickets" (90), and "a handful of warm dust" (91) resurface in the narrative. Ownby walks in the moonlight, studying "the great silver ikon," and returns home to circumcise a dozen shotgun shells (93–94). The next chapter catches Marion loading whiskey into his trunk to take to Knoxville, when he hears at "four o'clock in the morning . . . the old man shoot the first hole in the tank" (96). This must happen on a morning following the night in the previous chapter, for Ownby has already heard "the long cry of tires on the curves . . . the sound of a motor racking the night" (91) when he prepares the shells. But it probably happens within a day or so and for sure in the midst of that summer as the whiskey is hidden in a "honeysuckle jungle" (97). Marion anxiously loads the rest of the whiskey and heads down the mountain.

Here the narrative once again shifts to November and to John Wesley exploring the "wet mudbanks" with his flashlight (98). He hears a "car on top of the mountain coming down, the exhaust rattling and the tires sounding on the switchbacks." Because Marion has just left the scene where the old man shoots the tank, it makes sense that this moment is a continuation of the previous scene. But the reader must remember that the previous scene occurs in the summer, whereas now the boy huddles down under the bridge, "wiggling his numb toes" and breathing "slowly into his cupped hands" (99). Negotiating two kinds of perception, McCarthy fuses in the reader's mind a sense of chronology with an awareness of an abrupt shift in time. He achieves this effect by juxtaposing two scenes that are, however far apart in time, contiguous in space. As a result, the convergence that follows is invested with a tricky form of distortion: while driving along the same path as usual, Marion is suddenly thrust into the time frame of John Wesley's narrative thread.[5] He hears tires screech again, "closer, and then the motor revving . . . and the explosive sound of the shift to high gear." The climax of the scene occurs when the car leaps through the trees and crashes into the creek (99). The abrupt end to his disastrous time travel and the silence afterward simulate the convergence and the order it brings, respectively: the finale of the sequence gives shape to the episodes leading up to it.

McCarthy's discontinuous narrative threads require the reader to discover order by way of hindsight: his use of distortion breaks down normal perception and raises up from beneath the rubble a new way of seeing. Indeed, shifting angles of vision play a large role in the way his narrative structure spatializes history. Part of the disorienting effect of narrative discontinuity results from sudden changes in perspective from one character to another. For instance, Marion hurries away when he sees Ownby shooting the tank, but it is John Wesley who hears his car come down the mountain. By shifting and mixing the vantage points from which the reader views the action, McCarthy demonstrates how time passes in several places and from several angles at once. Taking form through these shifts from thread to thread, history comes to be seen as layered, made up of events that do not merely exist on linear chains.

But McCarthy applies a similar technique even within certain threads, within isolated episodes. When Ownby goes outside to give Scout some biscuits, a strange shift occurs in the narrative voice, which has stayed with the former for several pages: "the hound bolted down the biscuits and looked up after him. The screendoor banged to, the square of light on the porch floor narrowed and went out with the click of the latch. The old man did not appear again" (58–59). Foreshadowing the moment when the old man is later forced to abandon him, this sad scene is viewed through Scout's "wrinkled and sorrowing eyes" (59). The next episode restores the original narrative perspective, leaving the hound outside for the night. When Marion takes John Wesley hunting, shifting perspectives help to convey their swift running and quick stops in the woods. Having stopped to listen for Lady's barking, Marion hears the boy "at his elbow, trying to breathe quietly, listening too hard" (119). Running again, the narrative follows Marion for a time ("He dropped into the gully, heard the beaded rush of sliding dirt as the boy followed") until he stops and the boy catches up. The narrative shifts to the boy when they move on: "The man paused for just a moment. . . . His back melted into the darkness again. The boy moved after him . . . following the sound of the brittle leaves. . . . Watch a log, the man called back to him. He jumped just in time, half stumbled over a windfall trunk" (120). Seeing both perspectives heightens the reader's awareness of both characters at once so that the scene captures the staggered motions and the simultaneity. On the sixth day of rainfall, Marion heads down to Mr. Eller's store for gas. The narrative stays with him as he drives there, obtains the gas key, goes outside to pump gas, and comes back in again to chat sarcastically about the forsaken kittens. When he leaves, the narrative eye remains in the store: "The storekeeper drummed his nails on the marble ledge of the cash register for a minute" (181). Once again, the next episode catches up to Marion driving to the orchard to load his whiskey.

All of these instances work in a way opposite to McCarthy's converging threads; that is, shifts in perspective within an episode suggest that two threads coexist in one, that a split occurs between them, and that they diverge. In the scenes with Ownby and Scout and with Marion and Mr. Eller, there is an intact thread that briefly joins another and then splits off again. In contrast, the hunting scene shows how two fused threads split apart, reconverge, break off again, and finally fuse once more. What matters in both cases is that the scene pulls the reader's eye in two directions at once. Although the shift may divert his focus from one character to another, the new angle of vision does not remove the first from his memory. Rather, the shift launches two different lines of action, and though the reader cannot observe both at once, the narrative makes it clear that time is passing in more than one place.

The problem of vision as it relates to the nonlinear dimensions of McCarthy's narrative endures throughout the novel. His storytelling technique disrupts not only the chronology of events but also the chronology of reading itself. Forcing the reader to look back and forth in order to see beyond the linear track of words, McCarthy uses Joseph Frank's aesthetic principle of "reflexive reference" (15), which proposes that the reader must recall several moments in the text at once to perceive the networks of connections that exist "independently of the time sequence of the narrative" (18). Certain recurring motifs emphasize the need for this kind of vision and accent McCarthy's historical concerns. Early in the novel, for example, the image of Rattner's bleeding leg anticipates how different plot lines will interact: "Blood trickled in three rivulets past the black smear his trouser had made, deltaed, rejoined; a thin line shot precipitously into his sock" (15). The kittens in Mr. Eller's store, "tottering aimlessly over the floor" (180), "lost . . . passing and repassing each other, unseeing" and "wailing . . . in broken chorus" (182), reflect the apparently random sequence of the episodes. These images not only provide condensed models of McCarthy's narrative technique but also refer to each other, associating both the wounded and the helpless, the wandering and the forsaken, with the disorienting structure of the novel. The latter image in particular emphasizes the problem of vision, linking it to the desperate suffering of spiritual crisis. Historically significant from a Christian point of view, the kittens' eyes are shown to be "closed and festered with mucus as if they might have been struck simultaneously with some biblical blight" (180). The plagues of old and the tribulations to come both ring through this passage.

Indeed, in *The Orchard Keeper,* the present time functions as kind of stage where relics of the past meet with predictions of the future. Archaeological artifacts from both the ancient and recent past are strewn across the landscape. The old man walks "past the sink where on a high bluff among trilobites and fishbones, shells of ossified crustaceans from an ancient sea, a great stone tusk jutted" (88). Later, Warn tells John Wesley in the cave that "they used to be cave-men hereabouts . . . pre-storic animals too. They's a tush over on the other side of the mountain stickin out of some rock what's long as your leg" (140). On a smaller scale, there seems to be a nascent geological preservation in the old man's neglected yard, which is littered with "barrel hoops, a broken axehead, fragments of chicken-wire, a chipped crock . . . small antiquated items impacted in the mud" (56). Likewise, after being exposed to rain and heat for seven months, the "caked and crusted" ash deposit left in the insecticide pit comes to resemble a miniature archaeological site:

> They sifted the ashes . . . and there found the chalked sticks and shards of bone . . . and the skull, worm-riddled, vermiculate with the tracery of them . . . the caried teeth rattling in their sockets . . . a zipper of brass, fused shapeless . . . They were there four hours, the two officers deferential before the coroner, dusting the pieces with their handkerchiefs and passing them on to him who placed them in a clean bag of white canvas. (234)

Whether withstanding thousands of years of decay or a few minutes of scorching heat, fragments of the past provide clues, however incomplete and distorted, for what has lived and what has occurred. Collecting them in a bag, puzzling over their origins, and perhaps reassembling them is similar to grappling with the past through memory. Once time has muddied the clarity of what has passed, one struggles tediously to extract events from the pool of experience, recognize them even in their fragmented form, and reorder them into a reasonable, though never fully accurate, sequence. Sometimes the empty spaces are filled by guesses that turn into falsehoods. The "idjit" Legwater epitomizes this tendency as he absurdly continues the dig, shoveling through the ashes for a "platmium plate" that in fact has never existed. His work is the desperate effort of a man who relentlessly searches for the one thing he cannot have: confirmation of the unknown.

McCarthy takes his concern with the processes behind archaeology a step further when he describes how the Green Fly Inn rapidly becomes an artifact: "[In the pit] it continued to burn, generating such heat that the hoard of glass beneath it ran molten and fused in a single sheet, shaped in ripples and flutings, encysted with crisp and blackened rubble, murrhined with bottlecaps. It is there yet, the last remnant of that landmark, flowing down the sharp fold of the valley like some imponderable archeological phenomenon" (48). An accelerated simulation of the passage of time, this image represents the mutations that usually occur over an "imponderable" duration of years. To whom does the voice belong that testifies to its perpetual existence? Has no one dug it up to study its fusions or tried to unravel its intricate complexity? One of Marion's flashbacks recalls a scene that happens as the flames die out:

> Gifford with a long pole poking steaming holes in the melt of glass. Gloop gloop. Vitreous tar. Damndest thing I ever seen. One brogan toe began to blister and blacken and a moment later he was hopping away snatching at his shoelaces. Goddamn. Whew. Leaning against a tree with his naked foot cradled in his hands like a hurt bird he dared a snicker with fierce eyes. (163)

Gifford's attempt is met with pain and frustration, just as Legwater's humorous curiosity in the ash pit turns him into a wasted survivor wandering in the ashen air of nuclear aftermath: "By nightfall he was a feathery gray effigy. . . . He spat gobs of streaky gray phlegm. Even the trees near the pit had begun to take on a pale and weathered look" (239). Indeed, both of these scenes metaphorically fuse apocalyptic and archaeological paradigms to unite the two extremes of the unknown; however, the burning, which points to one possible model for ultimate destruction, is strangely followed by the continued existence of the remains. Future doom becomes an event of the past as history recycles itself. As a result, the humor in these scenes is darkened by a serious undertone: the violence by which the past is born is bound to erupt again. Indeed, the reader should not take too lightly Warn's witty response to Boog's attempt to mimic an ancient age with his cedar fire ("This is the way the cave-men done it, Boog said") as the cave fills with smoke: "Cave-men be damned, we're fixin to get barbycued" (141). McCarthy telescopes history by connecting an ancient world that has been to an apocalyptic one that is yet to be. When the far reaches of time are unknown and the end seems to draw near, Warn's exclamation is an adequate response for the moment. He ironically offers universal advice: forget the past; take care of the present; prepare for the future.

Whatever the force of this warning, however, "forgetting the past" certainly does not thematically tie the novel together. With its convoluted structure and movements in time, McCarthy's narrative requires the past as an aesthetic engine. The reader is always having to look back from a particular place in the text to experience how the narrative forms new wholes from its broken episodes. The text repeatedly regurgitates itself as McCarthy continually resurrects the past in the present to convey how nearly impossible it is to separate them. This technique is most conspicuous when he simulates the processes of memory in his narrative form. Flashbacks appear all through *The Orchard Keeper*: McCarthy splits a particular narrative thread into two or more time frames and retells the past from the vantage point of the present. Consequently, there occurs a shift in a character's level of consciousness that causes a shift in the reader's perspective.

Sometimes the flashbacks are rather extended and virtually uninterrupted, as when John Wesley remembers meeting the girl (68–72), collecting bounty for the hawk and buying traps (77–85), and meeting Warn flying the "turkey buzzard" (133–34). Ownby recalls finding the corpse in a fairly long and continuous passage (52–54), but his flashbacks are more often short clips of memory that obscurely tell about his wife Ellen and her betrayal (153–56). Marion's flashbacks are all in such close proximity that, even though they intermittently describe isolated moments in time, they form an almost continuous sequence: being shot in the foot on a boat, seeing Gifford burn his foot in the molten glass of the Green Fly Inn, and seeing an owl in an abandoned church (161–64). Ultimately, the boundaries that keep the past out of the present are weak in this novel; they dissolve again and again, as McCarthy emphasizes the layeredness of reality and the nonlinear aspects of time.

Storytelling in *The Orchard Keeper* similarly infuses time frames from the past into the present. As stylized performances of intact memories, storytellers and their stories in the text come closest to embodying how perceiving history and composing narratives interact; moreover, performances, unlike flashbacks, require an audience to hear them, adding another layer to the idea of perception. Warn and Uncle Ather channel the past in this way, giving it another life but remolding it in such a way as to highlight the critical links in the sequence of events. Warn tells stories with a potent mixture of humor and latent gravity that makes them suitable for posterity. For instance, John Wesley's memory of meeting Warn is marked by the latter's story about how he becomes the caretaker of a "turkey buzzard":

> Been keepin him in the smokehouse, he said.
> Don't nobody care for you to keep him?
> Naw. The old lady set up a fuss but I told her I was goin to bring him in the house and learn him to set at table and that calmed her down some. Here, don't get too close or he'll puke on ye. He puked on Rock and Rock like to never got over it— stit won't have nothing to do with him. (134)

Having just pulled the vulture down from its leashed flight in the sky, Warn may seem cruel in his experimental treatment of it, but he is also portrayed as a sort of keeper, caring for the rejected: "He cain't get up lessen they's some wind. So when we get a little wind I gen'ly fly him some" (134). Later in the cave with Johnny Romines, he tells the story about blowing up the birds: "I remember we run out and you could see pieces of em strung all out in the yard and hangin off the trees. And feathers. God, I never seen the like of feathers. They was stit fallin next mornin" (141). Hyperbole characterizes the climax of the story, but this distortion enthralls his audience. John Wesley and the reader not only see the scene but also gain a sense of Warn's unique vision. McCarthy also uses storytelling to fill in gaps between discontinuous episodes. The reader sees the boys with the skunk but does not hear how they retrieve it until Warn tells Uncle Ather the story a few pages later (146). This suspension of linearity reflects how storytelling splices one section of time with another.

Warn also serves as a precursor to Uncle Ather: the former is a young man with flair but without the long-standing, exercised memory of the latter. The old man has told his tales of intrigue over and over again. His stories about the raccoon hunt, the "painter kit" he cares for after finding him in a blasted panther den, and the screech owl that is mistaken for a cat squall, all carry a tone of rehearsed familiarity. They seem part of the legend of Red Branch, the history known only to the privileged few and told only by those who care to preserve the simple values of a diminishing age. Uncle Ather displays "a benign look upon his face, composed in wisdom, old hierophant savoring a favorite truth" (148). When Warn entreats him to tell about the panthers, his tone suggests that he has heard the story before: "What about painters . . . was that a painter was hollerin around here one time?" With a "wise grin," Uncle Ather answers, "well now. . . . Shore, I remember that right well" (147). Relishing the chance to dramatize his memory, he not only magnifies his past but also passes it on to a younger generation to cherish and preserve. Enthralled and intrigued, John Wesley sparks another story with his curiosity: "was they really painters back then?" Uncle Ather has "already started" about the panther cub when Warn once again cues the old man: "Tell him about that'n . . . That'n you had" (150). Both are initiating John Wesley into a fellowship of sorts, which echoes the previous episode in the cave. The three of them sitting there sipping "muskydine wine" with the "solemnity of communicants" are like "troglodytes gathered in some firelit cave . . . their shadows, ponderous and bearlike upon the wall, weaved in unison" (150). Later when the boy visits Uncle Ather in the asylum, the old man's storytelling provides an avenue into prophecy, though not prophecy of the end: "I recollect one winter, I was jest a young feller, they wad'nt no winter. Not hardly a frost even. It was a sight in the world the things that growed. That was a seventh year seventh and you'll be old as me afore it comes again" (225). Uncle Ather gives his own version of spatializing history, as his memory of the past orders his anticipation for the future.

Shortly after this visit, John Wesley leaves Red Branch for seven years, which McCarthy leaves untold, and returns in 1948 to find his childhood home rotting and his mother's gravestone weathered. Providing a structural counterpart to this temporal jaunt, the text returns to the time frame in which it begins. What has happened since the tree-cutting passage? How much time has actually passed in McCarthy's fictional world? Between the two episodes set in 1948, he creates a highly stylized story about the past, but the span of years he covers does not correspond to the space of time within the frame. According to Mark Winchell, the "insidious design" of the narrative "extends beyond the form of the novel to the story being told" (295). But he misses the mark when he claims that McCarthy presents his story with a "paucity of narrative structure" (296). On the contrary, the novel is intricately structured in order to show how the story reorders events of the past. Furthermore, to emphasize that the story is told retrospectively, McCarthy frames it strictly within a relatively short period of time, between the scene where John Wesley talks to the tree-cutters and the scene in the cemetery where he touches his mother's gravestone: enough time passes for the narrator to look backward and reconstruct a spatialized history about changing values and social transformation.

The identity and attitude of this narrator present a more elusive puzzle. Whether it comes from an actual character or a collective narrative consciousness, the tone of the narrative voice has invited critical attention from several angles. John Grammer sees *The Orchard Keeper* as an "elegiac celebration of a vanishing pastoral realm . . . an older sort of pastoral community, nobly resisting but finally defeated by the gnostic will to deny history" (21, 23). Similarly, Vereen Bell calls it "an elegy commemorating a doomed way of life . . . a lament for the impermanence of human life" (10). But William Prather asserts more specifically that the framed portion of the novel comes from the mind of John Wesley, who, while sitting in the graveyard, fashions the narrative into its preserved form: he "recalls and pays tribute to the world of his boyhood." The young man rehearses a dutiful elegy that also "affords him the opportunity to reorder his past, a chance to recontextualize fragments of memory, an occasion to fill gaps in personal knowledge with passages of imagination and hallucination" (39–40). Certainly, the narrative strategies used in the novel embody this type of historical reflection, which distorts reality, compresses several lines of action into one narrative consciousness, and mixes the actual with the fictive. There is, furthermore, structural evidence to support the possibility that John Wesley is the psychological fountain for McCarthy's experiment in spatial form. John Wesley's flashbacks in the novel, for example, are more coherent, complete, and continuous than any other character's. Moreover, some of the most extended episodes in the narrative describe events that especially heighten his mental awareness: crossing paths with Marion after his crash, their lengthy hunting scene by the river, and returning the bounty for the dead hawk.

The possibility that McCarthy portrays the imaginative memory of John Wesley as a fragmented narrative illuminates the way in which the structure of the novel mimics perceptions of history. If, in fact, John Wesley narrates the framed portion of the novel, as a young man who looks back on his childhood and the circumstances that lead to his relationship with the old man and Marion, then realizing when he does so is critical to understanding what McCarthy achieves through this technique. When John Wesley returns to Red Branch, he first visits the old house that "was never his house anyway." There is a gap in the text as he walks away from the scene, and the next episode indicates a temporal leap as it begins with the word "evening" (244). He is now within the iron-fenced cemetery, where he notices the "wood-dust and chips, the white face of the stump pooling the last light out of the gathering dusk" (246). The first fragment of the novel, therefore, has already occurred when the last fragment begins. It seems plausible that he could rehearse the elegy in his mind some time after talking to the workers but before touching his mother's gravestone.

Several instances in the first and last framing sections of the novel, moreover, seem to inspire the young man to attempt to reconnect with a past that is slipping away. Outside his house, sitting beneath a tree, he sees a lamentable image of forgotten values: "Old dry leaves rattled frail and withered as old voices, trailed stiffly down . . . spun, curling ancient parchments on which no message at all appeared." When he walks away, an old wagon trundles by and dissolves in the heat, "a pale and broken image" (244). And finally, the workers in the cemetery, cutting the tree into sections and trying to loosen the fence from the trunk, compel John Wesley to reflect on the passage of time and historical transition. His episodic narrative models itself on the fragmented tree, starts with an image that resembles the broken-down wagon, and attempts, with a unique vision, to replace the lost voices of an earlier age sunk under by the encroachment of the new social order. If John Wesley does conjure the larger sections of the novel, then he succeeds the old man as a keeper of cherished values: he becomes a storyteller trying to save from oblivion some sacred remnant of a passing time.

It remains questionable, however, whether an elegiac tone can account for John Wesley's acquiescent departure at the close of the novel. Just after calling *The Orchard Keeper* an elegy, Vereen Bell embraces the novel's complexity by conceding that it is also "a meditation upon the irrelevance of the human in the impersonal scheme of things" (10). Other critics assert that John Wesley becomes exiled from the modern world, unable to reconcile his present metaphysical limbo with the memory of his childhood. Robert Jarrett argues that the "ending adds a new register of the anti-elegiac" (30), for John Wesley "repudiates his past" (31), and the narrator abandons "the elegy's essential consolation that the dead still live": "History, whether of the individual or of a culture such as the South, can indeed be narrated as only a wandering endless series with no limit other than death. We can observe a teleology in history if we wish, but we cannot control it. From the perspective of a current observer like John Wesley Rattner, history and the past are not a list of events and their causes; rather, historical names are 'myth, legend dust,' implying an absolute separation between the consciousness of the present survivors and the otherness of the dead acts of history" (33). David Ragan asserts that John Wesley's return to Red Branch is "noticeably lacking in nostalgia" (11) and that his "past condemns him to isolation in the modern world" (17). Although these two interpretations rightly ask us not to oversimplify the novel's reminiscent tone, both overlook how John Wesley at least *attempts* to discern how he fits into this uncertain stage of history. His view need not be ultimately elegiac in order to be nostalgic, nor does he need finally to embrace the past in order to have searched his memory for some definition of it.

Although McCarthy's narrative history borders on elegy at times, it also conveys the pain of loss, the violence of greed, and a lamentable disregard for the weak. If, at the end of the novel, John Wesley does repudiate the past recorded in his story, several instances suggest that he has been left no alternative. In the last scene before the abrupt shift back to 1948, Earl Legwater mercilessly kills Scout: Gifford turns and watches "the dog lurch forward, still holding up its head, slew sideways and fold up in the dust of the road" (242). When the old man is forced to abandon his old dog, McCarthy describes Scout as an "atavistic symbol or brute herald of all the questions ever pressed upon humanity and beyond understanding." The strange gesture of straining his head upward "to clear the folds above his milky eyes" at once seems to evoke pity and to assert the dignity of persistence and endurance under the weight of those elusive questions (205). Legwater rapes this dignity with empty cruelty when he shoots the hound. Likewise, when the officer arrests the old man, he slams the door on his walking cane: "in mutual defeat the door rocked open again as the cane cracked" (203). Being carved with "nosed moons, stars, fish of strange and pleistocene aspect" (46), the cane symbolizes the old man's communion with historical perpetuity. Thus, the destruction of the dog and the cane illustrate similar themes. Just as Scout holds his head up until he dies, the car door cannot close on the old man while his cane blocks the way. With harsh finality, however, Scout falls in the dust, and after the old man pulls in his cane "to examine the whiskers of wood standing up from the break," the door shuts "snugly" upon him (203).

John Wesley's retreat down the "western road" as the novel comes to a close is invested with the reality of death and the feeling of being cut off: "They are gone now. Fled, banished in death or exile, lost, undone. . . . No avatar, no scion, no vestige of that people remains. On the lips of the strange race that now dwells there their names are myth, legend, dust" (246). It seems that by leaving, John Wesley ultimately refuses to be part of that "strange race," for he can find no surviving connection with that past. His story ends abruptly with the death of Scout, and his visit to his mother's grave instills in him only the futility of trying to remember:

> He reached out and patted the stone softly, a gesture, as if perhaps to conjure up some image, evoke again some allegiance with a name, a place, hallucinated recollections in which faces merged inextricably, and yet true and fixed; touched it, a carved stone less real than the smell of woodsmoke or the taste of an old man's wine. And he no longer cared to tell which were things done and which dreamt. (245)

This acquiescence in the forces of forgetting and dissolution looks ahead to the words "lost" and "undone," but the passage suggests how the substance and form of John Wesley's imaginative memory coincides with the spatialized narrative that McCarthy constructs. Likewise, the story ends when John Wesley "no longer care[s] to tell." He loses the connection; the transmission is interrupted somehow. Or perhaps he merely gives up, becomes fed up with the trying, when he cannot find any sign that what has been will survive. The old man in his cell surrenders as well in response to an ignorant and patronizing welfare agent:

> He leaned back against the wall and passed one hand across his
> eyes as if to wipe away some image. Then he sat very
> still . . . restored to patience and a look of tried and inviolate
> sanctity . . . and the old man felt the circle of years closing, the
> final increment of the curve returning him again to the inchoate,
> the prismatic flux of sound and color wherein he had drifted
> once before and now beyond the world of men.[6] (222)

Likewise, the very last moments of the novel take the reader back to
the very first, for the young man walks "past the torn iron palings,"
through the gap in the cemetery fence left by the fallen tree (246). His
attempt to reorder his fragmented past, to tell a story that revitalizes
the initial harmony of the whole of what has occurred, is met with the
intrinsic barriers of history to human perception. Moreover, as he
considers where he stands in a changing world, the impenetrable
composite of the old and new orders resists his inquiry. The tree grows
around the fence, and the fence infiltrates the tree. That section of
history is removed, in a sense, by the telling of it, and John Wesley
finds a gap through which he can walk away.

Just as his narrative is framed by the duration of its telling,
contained by the opening and closing frames of the larger narrative
structure, so has John Wesley been contained by his memory of the
past, his desire to connect with the past. His retreat from his own
narrative indicates that, though he may not have fully overcome the
obstacles to making sense of history by reordering its sequence, he
does break through the barriers against moving ahead. However, the
perceptual tension with which the reader has struggled does not
release: McCarthy leaves his ambiguous treatment of man's relationship to the past and future somewhat unsettled. The new order, on one
hand, incarcerates the old man, depriving him of his familiar connection with natural cycles, silencing his stories, discontinuing his rituals.
On the other hand, John Wesley abandons not only his attempt to
succeed the old man as the keeper of tradition and humane values but
also whatever connections with the past he may have tried to establish. McCarthy demonstrates a similar duality in his relationship to the
literary past. Although he reveals his indebtedness to modernist narra-

tive techniques and their undeniable influence on his creative genius, he uses those techniques to venture away from modernist thought concerning history. Where modernist literature often seeks to mythologize the past and so seize it in its eternal significance, McCarthy, taking a more postmodern stance, presents history as an impenetrable mystery, something that must not be permitted to hinder the forward progress of time, the eternal dialectic between harmony and discord. Even in his first novel, he begins to move away from the setting of his early artistic development, from the traditions that shaped his artistic vision, toward the untamed and uncharted "western road" of *Blood Meridian* and the Border Trilogy.

Notes

1. Joseph Frank's assertions in *The Idea of Spatial Form* have not only invited theoretical objections but also inspired inquiry into its various aesthetic manifestations. For an opposing view, see Wendy Steiner, who claims that the idea of "spatial form" is an unsuccessful, metaphorical attempt to overcome "the space-time barrier" that separates the plastic and temporal arts (38). Frank Kermode agrees that "forms in time have almost negligible spatial aspect (the size of the book). Their interrelations had much better be studied by reference to our usual ways of relating past, present and future . . . than by the substitution of a counterfeit spatial for the temporal mode" (178). See W. J. T. Mitchell, "Spatial Form in Literature," for a more generous and comprehensive exploration of spatial form, and for a wide variety of approaches to the idea with a bibliography, see Smitten and Daghistany, eds., *Spatial Form in Narrative*.

2. To illustrate McCarthy's concern with historical context and designating certain events in the text with actual dates, I have compiled a basic timeline of the novel. Some of these events are directly designated by day or month. Others are known by indirect reference to another date.

   Section I

   > August 1913: Marion born (11, 29)
   > September 1929: Marion leaves for five years (11–12)
   > March 1934: Marion returns (13)
   > August 1934: Marion, now twenty-one, murders Rattner (32–40)
   > December 21, 1936: Green Fly Inn burns down (47)

   Section II

   > Summer 1940: old man in orchard remembers finding Rattner's corpse in 1934 (52)
   > August 1940: John Wesley finds the hawk and buys traps (77–85)
   > November 1940: John Wesley sets traps, meets Marion (85–87, 98–102)

   Section III

   > December 21, 1940: snow starts to fall some time after midnight; old man cuts seventh cedar; Warn and John Wesley retrieve the skunk; old man tells stories to the boys (131–33,137–39,143–57)
   > December 22, 1940: Rattner's corpse burns (157–58)

   Section IV

   > Spring 1941: Marion's car stalls (182–84); old man is arrested (201–5); Marion is incarcerated (209–15); cat is attacked by owl (216–17); old man is incarcerated (218–22); old man at the asylum (223–31); John Wesley returns the dollar (231–33)
   > May or June 1941: John Wesley leaves (235)
   > August 4, 1941: Rattner's remains found (235)

First and last framing sections

Fall 1948: visits home (243–44); talks to workers (3); touches gravestone (245); leaves through gap in fence and heads westward (246).

3. Walter Sullivan claims that the novel's action is a "tapestry woven by the infinite crossings and recrossings among the inhabitants of a small community" (721). According to William Schafer, McCarthy "interweaves several separate tales into a dense fiction," within which an "ineluctable fate brings a group of apparently disparate people together through small accidents and mischances" (105). Robert Jarrett argues more specifically that the narrative is "constructed of small, disconnected scenes that sketch seemingly unrelated settings and events in the lives of disparate characters." But the end of the novel shows how the "disparate lives" of Ownby, John Wesley, and Marion "interconnect historically and psychologically" (12). Vereen Bell cannot find this much coherence, for "the shifts from one point of view to another and from one story line to another are unpredictable, guided by no *apparent* logic" (italics mine). As a result, he too quickly asserts that "the story lines themselves are only tenuously connected to one another, and even then mainly by common theme rather than by character relationship or plot" (11). David Paul Ragan contends that the "fully controlled" episodic structure reflects "disintegrating cultural values" and requires the reader to "piece together a serviceable apprehension of shifting cultural norms through the calculated juxtaposition of characters and incidents" (10).

4. If a narrative map for *The Orchard Keeper* were meticulously drawn up and adequately annotated, it would illuminate more fully the complexity of McCarthy's narrative structure and his use of spatial form.

5. The repetitiveness of Marion's driving scenes offers another example of how narrative can illustrate the spatial realities of perception. We see Marion drive to several different places but all at different times; in other words, we never see the entire journey from the orchard to Knoxville as a continuous sequence. Under normal narrative conditions, the passage of time organizes movement through space, but McCarthy achieves an effect that reverses the relationship: space organizes time. We simply piece together a whole trip using the fragments McCarthy provides, after which we immediately see a whole trip for every fragment with which we begin.

6. The "circle of years" recalls Warn's leashed "turkey buzzard," flying in circles. Just as the former close in on the old man, the vulture's circles become narrower as Warn pulls him to the ground. John Wesley is curiously intrigued by the pet bird, and this memory may have something to do with the imagery used to describe the old man's surrender to the peace of oblivion.

Works Cited

Bell, Vereen M. *The Achievement of Cormac McCarthy*. Baton Rouge: Louisiana State University Press, 1988.

Ditsky, John. "Further Into Darkness: The Novels of Cormac McCarthy." *The Hollins Critic* 18 (April 1981): 1–11.

Frank, Joseph. *The Idea of Spatial Form*. New Brunswick, N.J.: Rutgers University Press, 1991.

Grammer, John. "A Thing Against Which Time Will Not Prevail: Pastoral and History in Cormac McCarthy's South." *Southern Quarterly* 30 (summer 1992): 19–30.

Jarrett, Robert J. *Cormac McCarthy*. New York: Twayne, 1997.

Kermode, Frank. *The Sense of an Ending*. Oxford: Oxford University Press, 1966.

McCarthy, Cormac. *The Orchard Keeper*. 1965. New York: Vintage International, 1993.

Mitchell, W. J. T. "Spatial Form in Literature: Toward a General Theory." *Critical Inquiry* 6 (spring 1980): 539–67.

Prather, William. "'Like something seen through bad glass': Narrative Strategies in *The Orchard Keeper*." *Myth, Legend, Dust: Critical Responses to Cormac McCarthy*. Ed. Rick Wallach. Manchester: Manchester University Press, 2000.

Ragan, David Paul. "Values and Structure in *The Orchard Keeper*." *Southern Quarterly* 30 (summer 1992): 10–18.

Schafer, William J. "Cormac McCarthy: The Hard Wage of Original Sin." *Appalachian Journal* 4 (winter 1977): 105–19.

Smitten, Jeffrey R., and Ann Daghistany, eds. *Spatial Form in Narrative*. Ithaca, N.Y.: Cornell University Press, 1981.

Steiner, Wendy. "The Temporal versus the Spatial Arts." *The Colors of Rhetoric*. Chicago: University of Chicago Press, 1982.

Sullivan, Walter. "Worlds Past and Future: A Christian and Several from the South." *Sewanee Review* 73 (autumn 1965): 719–26.

Winchell, Mark Royden. "Inner Dark: or, The Place of Cormac McCarthy." *Southern Review* 26 (spring 1990): 293–309.

Cormac McCarthy's Sense of an Ending

Serialized Narrative and Revision in *Cities of the Plain*

Robert L. Jarrett

> *You cant tell anybody anything, bud. Hell, it's really just*
> *a way of tellin yourself. And you can't even do that.*
> (*Cities of the Plain* 219)

HOWEVER compelling are the connections in theme, character, and technique between the first two volumes of Cormac McCarthy's Border Trilogy, no characters from *All the Pretty Horses* appear in *The Crossing*. Given this textual gap between the first two novels of the trilogy, *Cities of the Plain* invites two contradictory reading strategies: to read the novel as a self-enclosed narrative complete in its own right, or to read the novel as the final installment of a serialized work. All interpretations, to be sure, are troubled by such contradictory heuristic strategies and are torn between the opposed units of the sentence, paragraph, chapter, and entire narrative. But its serialization exposes to plain view the problematics of interpreting the Border Trilogy. Is there a superstructure of plot, theme, ideology, and language sufficient to join all three installments of the trilogy into a single narrative?

Published near the close of 1998, *Cities of the Plain* composes an ending, in several senses, to McCarthy's fiction. First, it is the final installment of the Border Trilogy; second, it is a revision of an earlier screenplay dating back to the early 1980s[1]; and third, it is a self-referential rewriting of the earlier novels of the trilogy and of his entire corpus. In comparison to the other novels of the trilogy, *Cities of the Plain* asserts its own priority over *All the Pretty Horses* and *The Crossing,* requiring their reinterpretation. Illuminated by the light of *Cities of the Plain,* my rereading attends less to these novels as autonomous texts and more to how the first two novels of the trilogy introduce, amplify, and revise aspects of narrative—language, character functions, motifs, and plots—that achieve full significance only in the trilogy's final novel.[2] *Cities of the Plain*'s dense, interlocking sequence of narrative modes acts as an exemplary meta-narrative. Obsessed with rearticulating and wrapping up the narrative threads of the earlier novels in the trilogy, it scrutinizes the act, the possibility, and the significance of postmodern narration.

The "wolf" section of *The Crossing,* published by *Esquire* under the title "The Wolf Trapper," is a matrix comprising three networks of intertexts: one intertext takes the form of a set of allusions to Faulkner and to the coming-of-age tale; another intertext gestures to the Victorian mode of the serialized novel; and the final intertext is McCarthy's own fiction, particularly the trilogy.[3] Read in isolation, the tale of Billy and the wolf is a classic coming-of-age tale. In her essay on the first novel of McCarthy's trilogy, Gail Moore Morrison reads *All the Pretty Horses* primarily within this thematic. Noting John Grady Cole's "expulsion from paradise," she comments, "By novel's end, when he returns to his own time and place and, briefly, to the now sold cattle ranch, John Grady's fall from innocence into experience encompasses sexual experience as well as betrayal in love and expulsion from paradise. . . . He left a boy and returns a man, but it is a poignant and sobering rite of passage that leaves him still adrift in time and space" (179). On its surface, "The Wolf Trapper" clearly reiterates this essential pattern. The story revises the conception of "coming of age" within *All the Pretty Horses,* while as the opening of *The Crossing* it acts as prologue to Billy's three journeys into Mexico.

Thus the *Esquire* excerpt presents *The Crossing* as a mass-market sequel to *All the Pretty Horses,* that rare combination of literary and popular fiction. In view of the remainder of the novel, it is not surprising that this "sequel" puzzled many reviewers and perhaps even more readers of *The Crossing.*

Significantly, the important matter of John Grady Cole's sexual initiation is omitted, both in *The Crossing* as a whole and more specifically in the tale of Billy and the wolf. The primary romance between the cowboy hero and Alejandra becomes secondary in the subplot of Boyd (a diminished Cole) and the peasant girl. Nell Sullivan has demonstrated in her reading of *The Crossing* how Billy himself functions as a kind of femininized double of his brother Boyd, most markedly in the iconography of his continual weeping over the bodies and graves of the wolf, his parents, his horses, and his brother Boyd (Sullivan 174). Nevertheless, as he releases the female wolf from the trap and departs on his quest to return her to Mexico, Billy temporarily acts according to dictates of a code of male "honor." Caught in the teeth of his trap, the female wolf enacts the doubled representation of the Other (the animal) and of the female as Other (Sullivan 171). Billy's motive acts out as an essential ambivalence, for until he and his wolf are captured in Mexico, the wolf is clearly depicted as being under his control (an analogue to the riding scenes in *All the Pretty Horses*); and in the wolf-baiting scene he claims and is interpreted by the *hacendado*'s son as attempting to reclaim the wolf as his "possession" (*Crossing* 117). Yet his ostensible quest is to free the wolf, to return the Other to her home, within a frontier Mexico that is the milieu of the Other.

As clearly as it rewrites *All the Pretty Horses,* "The Wolf Trapper" section of *The Crossing* revises Faulkner's *The Bear,* perhaps the purest combination in classic American fiction of the theme of the Fall with the masculine coming-of-age tale. The first three sections of *The Bear* construct Ike McCaslin's adolescent identity "outside" of society and "within" the wilderness. Like "The Wolf Trapper," these sections of *The Bear* were published as an autonomous short story in the *Saturday Evening Post,* as well as in the form of a longer version in *Go Down, Moses.* The latter version includes section IV, in which Ike discovers within the ledgers of Carothers McCaslin proof of his grand-father's miscegenation and disinheritance of his slave progeny. This final section of *The Bear* records, then, the deconstruction of Ike's identity "outside" society and the collapse of his sexual identity. In repudiating his paternal inheritance, Ike is self-neutered. Although variations of this oedipal structure are frequent in the American liter-ary tradition, several forms of this repudiation of the father or patri-mony reverberate through McCarthy's fiction, especially *Suttree* and John Wesley Rattner of *The Orchard Keeper.* Faulkner's McCaslin operates as a template in the genre of the Western for the cowboy's relation to the female. In vivid contrast to the romantic myth purveyed in fiction and the movies, many historians of the West have noted the economic exploitation and marginalization of cowboys as laborers. One effect of this marginalization was to make marriage nearly impos-sible, so that the cowboy becomes the eternal bachelor-adolescent. The opening pages of *Cities of the Plain* mirror this economic, social, and sexual reality most clearly in the adolescent antifeminism expressed in the cowboy's hostile jokes equating the fat whore with a bronco (*Cities of the Plain* 4). It is expressed secondarily in the skepticism Billy directs against John Grady's plans for marriage and life happily ever after in the abandoned adobe cabin on the McGovern range. The cowboys' jokes must be balanced against John Grady and Magdalena's love. Is the joke finally at the expense of the fat whore (never focalized in the novel) or on the cowboys—and especially on Billy, John Grady, and Eduardo?

In McCarthy's trilogy, all tales indeed are "one," nowhere more clearly than the manner in which *The Crossing* openly invokes its liter-ary history to complete the significance of the text. This dimension of the text becomes clearer when we look at the possible Jamesian donnée or origin of the novel in a piece of dialogue within the early 1980s screenplay of *Cities of the Plain*. In response to Cole's question whether he has seen a wolf, Billy reveals that his father had trapped wolves, primarily from Mexico, for the government in the 1920s and that he had "seen one in a trap one time. . . . Then I seen her down off the side of this cowtrail about thirty feet layin there just watchin us. . . . Hell, when I was a kid Apache indians used to come to the back door to ask for coffee or meal. I carried that wolf home dead across the pommel of my saddle and I wasn't but seven year old and I felt bad about it even then" (*Cities* screenplay 11–12).

The origins in *The Crossing*—the wolf episode, the Indian, Don Arnulfo the trapper, the ride into Mexico, and most importantly Billy as the cowboy of sentiment and guilt—are crystallized as narrative seeds within this speech of the screenplay, to be expanded and transformed in their revision.

As is the case of much of McCarthy's revision of Faulkner, the literary genealogy of "The Wolf Trapper" is unstable, subject to the dangers of critical overdetermination. In revising *The Bear*, *The Crossing* revises not only Faulkner's own revision of Twain but also later contemporary writers in this visionary line, especially Hemingway's *In Our Time* and Ellison's *Invisible Man*. Earlier than Faulkner, the motif of the expulsion from paradise is the central motif in *Huckleberry Finn*, both in the raft scenes when the King and the Duke encroach on Huck and Jim and in the novel's conclusion, when Huck is threatened with adoption by a new matriarch only to "light out for the Territory ahead of the rest." As evidence of Cole's maturation near the novel's close, Morrison alludes to much of the plot of *All the Pretty Horses* as a "rite of passage"; more specifically, she refers to a scene of the funeral of Cole's "abuela" or Mexican "grandmother," a relationship not of blood but of affiliation (300–301). In *All the Pretty Horses* and *Cities of the Plain* the Faulknerian taboo against miscegenation is violated in Cole's erotic relationship with first Alejandra, then Magdalena. And relationships, sexually and socially, retain the force of the taboo, as Rawlins and Billy reveal in their heated oppositions, culminating in Billy's curse "Goddamn whores," which ends the screenplay and nearly marks the end of the narrative proper in the novel (*Cities* 261). Rawlins notes this taboo in his comic racist fantasy that he has become Mexican after his blood infusion. In his brief discussion of *All the Pretty Horses*, José E. Limón addresses the issue, arguing that although McCarthy evokes the Western motifs of the ride into Mexico as well as the "forbidden" love between an Anglo cowboy and a Mexican woman, the novel nevertheless "offers a powerful social critique" of the racist attitudes embedded in the

Western, again through Cole's "filial relationship" with Luisa as his "abuela" (199). Cole honors her as part of a familial relationship that extends beyond race and blood. Luisa here acts as a maternal analogue to Faulkner's Sam Fathers, the affiliate father of Native American and African descent who reengenders Ike McCaslin by inducting him into the wilderness and thus ironically renders him incapable of confronting southern modernity. For readers familiar with McCarthy's early fiction, this material in the McCarthy trilogy complexly rehearses and revises the origins of the McCarthy novel in *The Orchard Keeper,* which establishes a similar paternal affiliation between John Wesley Rattner and, first, the hill-dweller Uncle Ather, then the whisky-runner Marion Sylder. The substitution of a south-western milieu and the more crucially radical matriarchal figure for the paternal figure in part may determine Cole's inability to reintegrate or reassimilate his exiled identity within the contemporary. Or perhaps it is merely that McCarthy abruptly ends his first novel "within" the graveyard where Rattner's mother is buried, thereby allowing us to infer Rattner's successful but temporary integration through memory with the historic past.

"The Wolf Trapper" segment of *The Crossing* re-presents McCarthy's own revision of the genre of the Western in *All the Pretty Horses* and anticipates *Cities of the Plain*'s complex rewriting of key elements of both novels. Despite the similarities in structure and hero that link both novels within the trilogy, Dianne Luce's reading of *The Crossing* identifies the foregrounding of shorter tales within the novel as one of the primary differences between it and *All the Pretty Horses.* Adroitly reading the symbol of the wolf's matrix against the linked tales of the novel, Luce argues that "*The Crossing* is indeed a matrix of inter-secting stories, partial or complete, often competing, with varying rela-tionships to truth, cutting across and interwoven with the apparently simple linearity of the road narrative of Billy's life" (196). Taking up these interpolated tales one by one, Luce concludes that they suggest "the human capability for narrative—not for language, which is another kind of artifact, but for formulating the tale that carries our past, gives meaning to our present, and right intention to our future— is our primary means of accessing and perhaps communicating the thing itself: the world which is a tale" (208). If I may reformulate this point, in the American visionary coming-of-age narrative, man's fall is primarily into apperception, a self-conscious interpretation of perception, in opposition to the wolf's "matrix" or direct sensory perception of the world. We recall in "Experience" Emerson's sardonic reformulation of his earlier poetics of American vision: "It is very unhappy, but too late to be helped, the discovery we have made, that we exist. That discovery is called the Fall of Man. Ever afterwards, we suspect our instruments. We have learned that we do not see directly, but mediately." To Luce, narrative functions in *The Crossing* as a primary compensation (if I may borrow another Emersonian term) for man's loss of this primary perception of the world. She identifies that fall into narrative as a mediation, specifically not into the prison house of language, a proviso that perhaps would satisfy the narratologist, although not a poststructuralist.

In several ways, this theme of the swerve from a direct experience of the world is recontexualized continually within McCarthy's trilogy. Alfonsa names the tragic narrative ground of the Border Trilogy in her memorable formulation, "between the wish and the thing the world lies waiting" (238). In the latter half of the nineteenth century, in strategies like Henry James's use of the focal character to dramatize that character's imaginative perception and interpretation of reality, realistic fiction abandons the naive attempt to represent the world in language directly. In McCarthy's postmodern fiction this shift away from direct experience of the world is enacted within the very form of the text itself, which shatters into discrete narrative away from the enclosure within meta-narrative (first the screenplay, then the Border Trilogy series title). The literary history of visionary narrative seeks to enclose the screenplay, which in turn seeks to enclose the Border Trilogy, which encloses each novel, which in turn contains a series of interpolated narratives, and so on. Another way to recontextualize this swerve away from directly recording Billy's experience in *The Crossing* and the trilogy is to see the issue as a postmodern version of revisionism. In the trilogy, McCarthy's characters "fall" into a series of self-conscious narrations that constitute their compulsive attempts to delineate the "meaning" of their lives through a self-interpretation that itself takes the form of a dialogic renarration of their experiences to a fictionalized witness. This fall of McCarthy's characters into narration ironically mirrors the tendency of McCarthy's narratives to re-present a thematic problem—the fall from innocent perception to narrated experience—inscribed earlier in American fiction before McCarthy. Although conventional narratology insists on the difference between primary and secondary narrative, privileging the former, it is this obsessive recreation of secondary narrative in the Border Trilogy that is primary, suggesting the awareness of the narrative itself of its postmodern, revisionary (but decidedly not diminished) status. In an issue of *New Literary History* devoted to revisionism as a general literary predicament, Jean-Pierre Mileur summarizes the matter thus: "in true oedipal fashion, revisionism contains a conservative element in that it always proceeds from and is defined by what is and has already been. . . . In literary matters, the canon—those works deemed worthy of interpretation and emulation—has served this limiting, conservative function" (197). In particular, the form of *In Our Time* exerts direct thematic and formal influence on McCarthy's trilogy. Like *The Bear* (itself a set of scenes that, taken together and with the other novellas, constitute *Go Down, Moses* as an experimental novel that exceeds its parts), Hemingway's text consists of apparently autonomous short stories "linked" by italicized excerpts from an anonymous war diary. This narrative form thus points back toward the serialized novel even while the excerpts and short fiction (and Hemingway's style itself) embody the decisive modernist device of the fragment.

Another link between the Border Trilogy and its visionary line is that all are works of historical fiction that position the hero at a point of great historical rupture or crisis—marked usually by war. Billy Parham is abandoned by social history at the end of his novel-biography when he is denied entrance into military service because of his bad heart. The Civil War, for example, marks the historical dividing line between paradise and the sacred for Twain and Faulkner, World War I for the early modernists, World War II for McCarthy's fiction (and perhaps Vietnam for his novelistic sensibility). All these works foreground the gap between society and nature. Ike's expulsion from paradise is, of course, directly marked by the death of the bear, the event that marks the triumph of civilization over McCaslin's wilderness-paradise. Within *The Crossing,* the murder of the wolf obviously plays the same symbolic function (or the murders of Magdalena and John Grady for their modern societies). Finally, all of these works burden an inadequate hero with the task of redeeming the American present through reenvisioning its past. Yet this redemptive vision is ironic, available only through epiphany. The hero's historical vision must remain tragically internalized. The inherited evil of the past (slavery, the European history of conquest in Hemingway, the Mexican Civil War, the murder of nature in the form of the wolf, Eduardo's dance) blocks the hero from projecting his redeemed vision into society and thus integrating the redeemed past with the present. No grace, not even the death of the hero, can compensate the present for its tragic fall into the evil of history. Faulkner attempted to articulate this point in *A Fable* and in *The Bear,* but McCarthy's articulation in *Cities of the Plain* is even clearer as we and Billy, as readers, play the role of Lot's frozen wife trapped within the motion of history, staring back at the trilogy and at Cole's ceremonial death.

Beyond stylistic force, it is primarily this sacrifice of vision that gains for the trilogy the "power" of the literary. The point is both clarified and ironized by a scene in *Cities of the Plain* that anticipates and parodies Cole's death. Billy parodies Cole's revenge for Magdalena, for Billy can only ineffectually defeat Tiburcio, here Eduardo's comic double:

> The thin blade of the knife snickered past his belt and he leapt back and raised up his arms. Tiburcio crouched and feinted with the knife before him.
>
> You little son of a bitch, said Billy. He hit the Mexican squarely in the mouth and the Mexican slammed back against the wall and sat down on the floor. . . . The old woman at the end of the hall was watching with her fingers in her teeth. Her eye closed and opened again in a huge and obscene wink. (*Cities* 237)

This mock-epic duel must be read before and against the text's tragic (or sentimental) climax in the duel between Cole and Eduardo. McCarthy's revisionary texts thus situate themselves beyond parody, for the primary narrative contains within itself its own duplication and self-parody, "obscenely"—or ironically—winking at the reader and at itself. For readers susceptible to the romance of *All the Pretty Horses,* the passage may seem obscene, as is perhaps all of *Cities of the Plain.* But I think McCarthy's trilogy as a whole makes it clear that the irony of history and temporality itself make this narrative and modern life itself profane, detached from the sacred. This essential desacralization is crystallized within the screenplay, in the form of the santo that is Magdalena's only possession. Cole enjoins her to "take nothing" when she escapes—and her escape is discovered when the one-eyed woman, Tiburcio's mother, realizes that the saint is gone. The futility of Cole's—or Magdalena's—death as sacrifice establishes the text's pathos, and the trilogy as a whole transforms from the mode of the heroic into the pathetic.[4]

REPETITION AND SERIALIZATION WITHIN THE BORDER TRILOGY

McCarthy's decision (or that of his publisher) to serialize the Border Trilogy borrows a marketing strategy of contemporary mass-market fiction while simultaneously gesturing back to the history of the novel. In the 1830s and 1840s, the commercial—and critical—success of Dickens's novels established serialization as a norm for the production and distribution of literary fiction. In this form of serialization, sections of the narrative were issued either separately or within magazines in monthly or weekly parts. After the release of the final number, the reader then could have the "parts" rebound as a book or, if demand warranted, the plates could be reprinted, bound, and sold by the publisher as an entire novel. The serialized novel thus functioned as a form of marketing for the literary magazines in which they were issued. Dickens's fiction was serialized both in separate parts, in *Bentley's Miscellany,* and in Dickens's own magazines *Household Words* and *All the Year Round.* Yet serialized fiction was also autonomous art; indeed, in Dickens's fiction both the monthly "part" and the novel as a whole act as artistic units.[5] In retrospect, Dickens's artistic triumph over the imaginative constraints of serial publication was unique: many Victorian novelists struggled under the psychological pressures of the monthly serial deadline.[6] Most submitted the complete manuscript of their novels to magazines, with the manuscript divided into roughly equivalent monthly parts by the publisher.

Driven by the modernist conception of the text as a self-enclosed unit, Henry James compulsively revised his fiction, driven by the desire to expunge its serial origins. Thereafter, serialization functioned largely as a mode of distribution that exhibits relatively small influence over the final form of contemporary literary fiction.[7] Serialization as a mode of publication survived primarily within mass-market genres, along with the paperback as a vehicle for the dissemination of mass-market fiction.[8]

Contemporary fiction typically employs serialization in two primary modes. In the novel series, a larger, loose, plot is formed out of the combination of discrete but interconnected novels. In John Updike's Rabbit novels, the cement joining the novels is the central character as reconceived by the author from early adulthood to middle and finally old age. As post–World War II American culture is transformed into a consumer and car culture, so Rabbit is transformed as a character to act as Updike's fictional mirror and critique of America. (John Cheever's *Wapshot Chronicles,* in similar fashion, revives the family chronicle, joining individual fictional biographies in the larger form of a fictionalized family history.) Another mode of serialization within postmodern fiction is exemplified by Kurt Vonnegut's practice of relatively "loose" sequels, in which a minor character in one novel makes brief appearances in subsequent novels (the hack writer Kilgore Trout is one example) or is featured, like Billy Pilgrim in *Slaughterhouse-Five,* as the central figure in another work. Figures in Faulkner similarly appear and reappear, with the significant distinction that Yoknapatawpha provides a mythos that firmly cements such characters within an organic community and history, whereas Vonnegut's characters aimlessly wander through time and space.

Vonnegut's Kilgore Trout, wandering from novel to novel with his ideas for absurd tales, exposes fiction as mere pulp, the arbitrary invention of a hack writer trapped within futile attempts at escape into his "pulp" imagination.

Cities of the Plain employs both contemporary and postmodern strategies of serialization even while the narrative seeks a provisional transcendence of both. As in the Rabbit series, the novel extends, in apparently naive fashion, the biographies of both cowboy protagonists, John Grady Cole and Billy Parham. In his reading of repetition in *All the Pretty Horses,* James Lilley concludes that "both the dueña and John Grady represent the possibility of another kind of paradoxical freedom" within the confines of a historical repetition "of the past toward the future" (284). *Cities of the Plain* makes frequent use of narrative repetition to remind readers of earlier scenes and motifs in the trilogy and establish itself as the concluding sequel, even as it uses the earlier screenplay as a kind of Dickensian number-plan for itself and for the trilogy as a whole. As we have seen, in ironic fashion these repetitions enact a form of self-parody, critiquing directly or obliquely the initial histories of the heroes in the first two novels. But this self-imitation does not function like Vonnegut's dismissal of his own fiction as pulp or the historical imagination as paranoia in Thomas Pynchon's novels. McCarthy's successive reworkings of the structure and materials of the pulp Western within the trilogy instead highlight the difference between his form of Western and pulp. In an earlier study of McCarthy (to discuss the use of the cowboy myth in the first two novels of the trilogy), I used the terms *pastiche* and *revisionary Western*: "The revisionary western revises the earlier tradition of the western in a postmodern fashion, reusing and parodying elements of the genre and of the historical record in order to critique the historical myth of our traditional narratives of the West" (Jarrett 69, 98–99). Unfortunately, "pastiche"—and to a lesser degree the term *revisionary*—appears to equate McCarthy with a complete repudiation of the Western or a satiric laughter that would dehistoricize the cowboy. Perhaps this incompatibility between the postmodern and history ultimately derives from the Enlightenment's struggle with myth, in which mythos was thrown out with the bathwater. Again, the problem strikes to the essence of the postmodern as the contemporary version of revisionism. Alluding to Ernst Behler's study of irony, Mileur helpfully clarifies the linkage: "Postmodernism registers in an ironic, self-reflexive fashion (that is, in a fashion made possible by self-reflexive irony) the paradoxical nature of modernity. Or, to get more specific, it registers the fact that the modernist projects of, for example, bringing about the end of metaphysics or romanticism, or of stabilizing and rationalizing the play of revisionism, cannot be assayed without being reappropriated to metaphysics, romanticism, or revisionism. Under such informed self-skepticism, postmodern literature—of whatever mode becomes at the same time its own theory or philosophy" (Mileur 200–201).

This definition helps to explain the self-aware manner in which McCarthy's fiction rewrites "Southern" and "Western" fiction. Suttree, within the novel of that name, enacts the allegorical role of the contemporary "southerner" (a term whose meaning is under ironic erasure by and after Faulkner) as Cole enacts the role of "cowboy." For example, we might turn to the cowboys' self-mockery in the memorable dog-roping scene in Cities of the Plain, in which the participants lasso dogs instead of cows while satirizing in Spanish their identity (perreros, or "dogboys"). Each novel of McCarthy's Border Trilogy, in similar fashion, ironically erases and revises its tradition and the previous novels within the series. Each novel becomes part of something like a mathematic series or function, meaningless in and of itself, pointing ironically to the more general formula or literary consciousness expressed by the series as a whole.

This revisionist strategy was built into the trilogy from its beginning, in that the screenplay containing the essential plot of Cities of the Plain was written long before the first two novels of the trilogy. The biographies of Cole and Parham in the first two novels thus are encapsulated in teleological fashion within Cities of the Plain, both end and source of those histories. This use of teleological repetition in Cities of the Plain renders the earlier novels considerably more complex through complex doublings of the hero: Billy acts as Cole's double, while Cole acts as a double of Billy's outlaw brother Boyd, both renamed as "bud" by Billy, who remains the archetypal older brother.[9] Eduardo, in his dandyism, prefigures the hacendado of *All the Pretty Horses* and, at the same time, doubles the *cuchillero* who gives Cole his initial wound in *All the Pretty Horses*. And, in his dialogue in the knife battle, whose essence exists in the screenplay, Eduardo prefigures the avuncular advice Pérez, the godfather of the prison, gives to Cole.

The seeds of Cole and Parham's wanderlust and their respective "invasions" of Mexico are nascent within the screenplay in the form of a speech by Travis to the other hunters gathered around the fire high in the Franklin Mountains.[10] Responding to Archer's warning that in Mexico "you could get killed down there about as quick as a minner can swim a dipper and I say you still can," Travis contradicts, "You could travel in that country back then. I know cause I done it. . . . I rode all over Chihuahua and a good part of Coahuila. . . . You could stop at some little estancia in the absolute dead center of nowhere and they'd take ye in like you was kin. You could see that the revolution hadnt done them no good. A lot of em had lost boys out of the family" (*Cities* screenplay 32–33).

In much of *All the Pretty Horses* and *The Crossing*, both cowboy heroes, John Grady Cole and Billy Parham, are in exile from modern society, wandering across the southwestern landscape. In the conclusion of each novel of the trilogy, the archetypal romantic hero John Grady and the sentimental Billy are picaros, wanderers existentially severed from their society by the loss of the two beloveds, Alejandra and Boyd (and perhaps a third beloved, Billy's wolf). By reversal, *Cities of the Plain* establishes itself as sequel: a few years after the close of *All the Pretty Horses,* both Billy and John Grady have found an improbable home (however temporary) on the McGovern ranch in far western Texas. The elliptical opening scene works to exclude those readers who begin *Cities of the Plain* innocent of its narrative past: "They stood in the doorway and stomped the rain from their boots and swung their hats." In the second paragraph, the narrator identifies Billy Parham by his first name ("Damned if I aint half drowned, Billy said") while an anonymous speaker first refers to John Grady by his satiric nickname, "the all-american cowboy," named later in the dialogue by an anonymous speaker: "John Grady you look like a goddamned wharf rat" (3). At some point in the decade after World War II, both men have become friends and coworkers on McGovern's ranch. To such readers, a more conventional opening with narrative exposition is unnecessary, while the needs of those readers unfamiliar with the earlier novels are ignored, hence their disorientation. At the same time, McCarthy's opening scene operates within familiar conventions of the Western, a whorehouse complete with randy cowboys and bawdy dialogue. This opening possibly alludes to the violent prelude to Clint Eastwood's *Unforgiven,* whose opening scene is also set in a whorehouse (here it is the whore who jokes at the expense of the cowboy, to her great cost). *Cities of the Plain* opens naturalistically, in stark contrast to the more lyrical and traditional expository openings of the first two novels.

The text of *Cities of the Plain* also asserts its status as the final installment of a serialized narrative by employing a variety of narrative repetitions of the first two novels in the trilogy. The most intriguing strategy through which *Cities of the Plain* attempts to reform all three novels into a larger single narrative is a type of narrative repetition in which events from the earlier novels are renarrated by Billy or often merely recalled by John Grady. Edwin T. Arnold notes, "What becomes clear in reading the complete trilogy is how thoroughly and complexly McCarthy uses repetition, not simply to retell the same story . . . but to create a deep resonance as each parallel story moves towards its inescapable conclusion" (232). John Grady renarrates within *Cities of the Plain* the narrative of *All the Pretty Horses.* In several scenes, he remembers his past in his dreams, watching his first horse in its stall through the night and reliving the night of his grandfather's funeral. The narrator significantly interrupts his reverie with the rare comment, "All his early dreams were the same. Something was afraid and he had come to comfort it" (*Cities* 204). This narrative gloss points to Cole's motives in attempting to marry Magdalena, to train the stallion, and to rescue the wild pup. Another motive for keeping the pup is revealing in that the pup apparently has stayed far back in the den, loyal to the dead runt, its brother: "Maybe he was with the one that died. John Grady held the dog up and looked into its small wrinkled face. I think I got me a dog, he said" (177).

In two more scenes, Cole himself renarrates *All the Pretty Horses*. In the first he speaks to Magdalena: "He told her about working for the hacendado at Cuatro Cienegas and about the man's daughter and the last time he saw her and about being in prison in Saltillo and about the scar on his face that he had promised to tell her about and never had" (*Cities* 205). His narrative not only takes on the role of courtship (revealing the lover's history to the beloved) but also replicates in structure an earlier passage in which Magdalena reveals her own sexual history to John Grady before his proposal: "She was from the State of Chiapas and she had been sold at the age of thirteen to settle a gambling debt" (139). It is not accidental that both narratives mimic the form of confession; as in Donne's "Sacrament," the two act as if only their love can redeem the profane world. Indeed, their lovers' conversations continually evoke the sacred, with Magdalena first confessing her inability to pray, in the "belief" that God would not hear her, then posing to Cole the theological question whether all sins can be forgiven (205, 206). Cole's answer that all sins save suicide may be forgiven reverberates ironically within the narrative, for both Magdalena's return to the White Lake after her subsequent epileptic fit and Cole's final return to duel with Eduardo can be construed as tacit suicides (it is only in offering no defense against Eduardo's killing blow that Cole is able to strike the killing blow, as is the case in his earlier contest with the cuchillero).

In a later conversation discussing whether John Grady will return to Mexico, Billy points to the equivalences between his own experiences in Mexico in *The Crossing* and Cole's in *All the Pretty Horses*:

> You think you'll ever go back there?
> Where?
> Mexico.
> I don't know. I'd like to. You?
> I don't think so. I think I'm done.
> I came out of there on the run. Ridin at night. Afraid to make a fire.
> Been shot. (*Cities* 217)

Billy does not need to hear Grady's tale, so he fills in the blanks by speaking for the boy, summarizing earlier conversations between the cowboys. As Cole's double, Billy has already experienced this tale several times within *The Crossing*. In response to Billy's question as to what he will do after the ranch closes—"we all may have to think of somethin"—John Grady displays his own historical naivete, unable to articulate any plan other than another retreat into Mexico (and back into history) as a vaquero: "I don't know what it would be Id think of" (217). Billy's warning—"everbody I ever knew that ever went back was goin after somethin. Or thought they was" (218)—is as much a literary criticism of Billy's own earlier motives for going into Mexico as a warning to the younger man. Billy here essentially foretells Eduardo's dissection of John Grady's erotic attraction to Magdalena. In this sense it is John Grady's lack of ironic sensibility and his imaginative failure to accept his historical belatedness that overdetermine his death, one that repeats his earlier duel in prison and Boyd's death. To be the authentic hero within postmodern narrative, the hero must ignore history and its critique of heroism as absurd. Like Private Ryan, the postmodern hero mechanically mimics the motions of a role from which he is ironically detached, aware of its absurdity. The same analysis may be made of Magdalena's motives in refusing the refuge from the White Lake offered by the woman near the end of the novel: "She said that she could come with her and live in her house where she lived with her children. . . . She said that she could not. She said that in three days' time the boy she loved would come to marry her" (211). Magdalena is depicted as walking robotically back to the brothel and her death.

At the end of *Cities of the Plain*, the concept of the double helps clarify why both heroes are necessary, Cole as a representation of the naive hero, Parham as the sentimental witness lost within postmodernity. The ending of *Cities of the Plain* presents a sequel or second ending to both novels and to both modes. For Cole remains the hero when *Cities of the Plain* is read as romance in the manner of *All the Pretty Horses*. His nostalgia, his inability to achieve distance from history, enable Cole to reenact compulsively his role in *All the Pretty Horses* as romantic hero and last cowboy. Set after World War II, this reenactment is depicted as a choice that defends his heroism against existential irony. His heroic nostalgia leads him to attempt to restore from the last century the small cabin homestead in the wild, complete with a wooden santo (199), resisting Billy Parham's doubts: "It's goin to be cold up here in the wintertime, pardner. . . . Cold and lonely" (180).

Throughout the trilogy, a series of scenes, characters, and symbols nevertheless evokes our ironic consciousness of the close of Western history through the close of the frontier, an event generally associated much earlier with Turner and the end of the previous century. In the new territories running from far southwestern Texas to the bootheel country of New Mexico and into the mountains of Mexico, this closure can be delayed until the period after World War II, a delay made possible by low population density and by the existence of open rangeland only newly made available for settlement.[11] Serving the symbolic function of invoking this belated frontier are the "old man" Sanders of the SK Bar ranch and the wolf of *The Crossing* (64–72, 164, 350–54), John Grady's dream of the Comanche trail in *All the Pretty Horses* (5, 25–26), and John Grady himself, the all-American cowboy. Most prominently, *Cities of the Plain* evokes this elegiac history in John Grady's conversation with the senile old man Johnson, a "waddy" who rode the trail to "Abilene in eighteen and eighty-five" when he "wasn't much more than a button" (125). In comparing McCarthy's West of *Blood Meridian* to Turner's vision, Neil Campbell demonstrates how McCarthy fills in the dark, undeveloped gaps in Turner's negative insights into frontier and its influence on society (220, 225). With the use of such archaic dialogue encapsulated within McCarthy's high-literary narrative style, *Cities of the Plain* inscribes its dual existence as Western history and postmodern novel. Suspending postmodern irony (the myth of the inaccessibility of history), the reader can double the sensibility of John Grady Cole: the past is indeed accessible, momentarily . . . yet only through the exercise of the imagination. In the army's intent to take the ranch by eminent domain, the novel anticipates its own conclusion and the end of the Western. This threat to annex the ranch's acreage for military usage is, of course, the equivalent of the sale of his grandfather's ranch by John Grady's mother and the murderous raid on the Parham ranch in *The Crossing*. It raises for all of McGovern's hands the question of where to go next:

> You don't want to leave Mac.
> I don't know. Not without some cause to.
> Loyal to the outfit.
> It aint just that. You need to find you a hole at some point. Hell, I'm twenty-eight years old. (19)

The humor, of course, is not that Billy Parham is old at twenty-eight but that he is old in terms of what he has seen of life and death in the events of *The Crossing*, older yet in his vocation, now sixty years out of date.

The reenactment and repetition of historical and literary roles are so numerous in *Cities of the Plain* that John Grady Cole anticipates his critics by raising the question of his own autonomy: "he thought about his life and how little of it he could ever have foreseen and he wondered for all his will and all his intent how much of it was his own doing" (*Cities* 207). Read thematically, this passage evokes the themes of fate and free will so central to the first two novels of the trilogy. Read psychoanalytically, the passage suggests the compulsive drives of McCarthy's artistic imagination, resembling a late form of the Hawthornian conflation of history and typology in which fictional biography works as emblematic regional history (Goodman Brown, Robin Molineux). In his distinctive short fiction, Hawthorne explores the formation of nationalism out of colonialism in terms of the repressive formation of ego and superego. McCarthy's historical fiction works in reverse, exposing the repression and marginalization of regional subcultures and lifestyles by the forces of modernization, questioning the hegemonic drive of the United States toward the status of economic and military world superpower. At the trilogy's end, we readers gaze from the range toward the symbolic figures of the opposed border cities of El Paso and Ciudad Juárez. The romantic cowboy has transformed into poor Billy, who has abandoned Mac, the range, and the cattle trail in order to be deposited unceremoniously under a freeway bridge, offering crackers to death (*Cities* 266–67).

The joking yet slightly pejorative nickname of the "all-American cowboy," by which his coworkers refer to John Grady, ironically restates the elegiac myth of the last cowboy from *All the Pretty Horses*. The nationalism of his new title exposes to satiric deflation Cole, his title, his nationality, and his erotic choices. In contrast to *All the Pretty Horses*, comparatively less of the narrative of *Cities of the Plain* is devoted to Cole as cowboy and horse-breaker. We see him at work from a distance, primarily filtered through the commentary and queries of his coworkers:

> What does he want with that owlheaded son of a bitch anyway? . . .
> What is that thing he's got on its head? . . .
> How many times did he get thowed?
> Is he supposed to be some sort of specialist in spoiled horses? (14)

Besides the dog-roping scenes, the scene most dramatically rendered is the one in which Cole, with a newly sprained ankle, disturbs the ranch's sleep with his bronco-riding (17–19).

Although it is a mistake to conflate Eduardo with McCarthy's narrator, Eduardo anticipates McCarthy and John Grady's most severe critics in his deconstruction of Cole and his nationalist form of Eros. Naming him first as suitor, insulting him as a "farmboy," Eduardo sneers:

> They drift down out of your leprous paradise seeking a thing now extinct among them. A thing for which perhaps they no longer even have a name. Being farmboys of course the first place they think to look is in a whore house. . . . In his dying perhaps the suitor will see that it was his hunger for mysteries that has undone him. Whores. Superstition. Finally death. For that is what has brought you here. . . . Your kind cannot bear that the world be ordinary. That it contain nothing save what stands before one. (249–53)

Love is superstition. The lesson, I suppose, is to accept the irony of history, that capitalist economics have defeated the agrarian, the Protestant over the Catholic, reality over myth, the postmodern or contemporary over history itself. John Grady's pathetic death and Eduardo's mockery seems the last word on the grand narrative of the romantic cowboy: Cole deflates into merely a "dead boy," whose "partly opened eyes beheld nothing at all" as Billy carries his body through the Juárez streets (261). Yet Eduardo's death by Cole's underhand blow can be read as a symbolic silencing of his interpretation both of Cole, Cole's love, and the narrative as a whole: "his jaw was nailed to his upper skull" (254). The narrator's interpretation of John Grady's death as providential is both evoked and denied: after Cole's body is blessed by watching schoolchildren, "all continued on to their appointed places which as some believe were chosen long ago even to the beginning of the world" (262). Cole's death rewrites his earlier duel in prison and is ambiguous in its significance, at the same time mythic, pathetic and anticlimactic. To close the trilogy, the narrative instead must complete the narrative of its archetypal witness, Billy Parham.

THE WITNESS AND THE DREAM OF HISTORY

In *Cities of the Plain* Billy Parham again is entrapped in the role of sentimental witness and narrator—narrator of his own past and passive witness of the close of John Grady's narrative. Billy, of course, is not the least of these narrators of a dead past. *Cities of the Plain* is filled with narratives of the dead frontier, like old man Johnson's tale of the stampede caused by a burning cat. Responding to Troy's eccentric and horrific tales of the Oldsmobile, the dead jackrabbits, and the loss of his horses after his return from World War II, Billy states: "I lost a horse in Mexico I was awful partial to . . . I'd had him since I was nine" (23). Out of context, this one-sentence précis of the plot of *The Crossing* almost seems a parody of the marketing summaries on jacket covers. Even within the context of the scene, Troy must interpret the remark merely as sympathy for the loss of his horse. To informed readers of *The Crossing*, Billy here enigmatically expresses his empathy with Troy's earlier tale of his dead brother (the two are returning from a brief pilgrimage to Troy's home in west Texas). Billy will renarrate *The Crossing* in more detail when Troy questions Parham's decision to help "a truckload of Mexicans" with a flat tire: "the worst day of my life was one time when I was seventeen years old and me and my bud—my brother—we was on the run and he was hurt and there was a truckload of Mexicans just about like them back yonder appeared out of nowhere and pulled our bacon out of the fire. . . . They didn't have no reason to stop for us" (36).

Billy's act reverberates complexly—as sympathy, as repayment, as commitment to an existential code (he can see "nothing but the dark of the road and the deep of the desert night" before he stops). His decision to stop and render aid might also be deconstructed as a form of magical thinking. That is, his repetition of the gesture of stopping for a stranger attempts to interpret history's significance through the repetition of an almost Wordsworthian spot of time that constructs his personal history. Through this repetition, the original event of Billy's quest for his horses and his flight within *The Crossing* loses original signifier and signified; the privileged significance of his narrative is now the guilty weight of his dead past, which will determine most of Billy's actions within *Cities of the Plain*. Hence his decision to render aid to the Mexicans; hence his brotherly behavior toward Cole, which seeks to reverse Boyd's abandonment of Billy. The trauma of the original events of *The Crossing* is signified by its renarration in *Cities of the Plain* even as the signification of the repeated event is condensed and changed. Such a reading of the map of Billy's actions loses its bearings by overlooking the significance of the moral dimensions of his actions as choice, however overdetermined or existential and absurd. Billy psychoanalyzes his compulsion and motives to stop—yet still chooses to stop and render aid. The same may be said, with diminished confidence, of John Grady Cole's choice to go to his death in his battle with Eduardo. *Cities of the Plain* is replete with compulsive narrators who, through renarrating their pasts, interpret and hence control the story of their past, before they go out in their world to repeat the structure of the past within their present.

Much of Billy's behavior within *Cities of the Plain* seems motivated by a paradoxical attempt to exorcise the trauma of his past through repetition and renarration. Billy's relationship to John Grady evolves as he moves from avuncular teaser to the role of confidant, advisor, prophet, and—finally—impotent witness of the boy's tragedy. This evolution uncannily repeats Billy's earlier relationship to his "bud" Boyd, his passive inability as witness to prevent Boyd's tragedy, and his ceremonial role as keeper of his brother's dead remains. Again retrieving and burying a boy's body at the end of *Cities of the Plain*, Billy is trapped in history's repetition. Nor can Billy be relieved of this compulsion to repeat and renarrate his life, either within his lived experience or, perhaps more disturbingly, within his dreams. Perhaps this exposes the hunger for authentic history and action within the postmodern, and no doubt this analysis could be applied, in allegoric fashion, to McCarthy's own drive to compulsively rewrite history through the Border Trilogy itself. History may return in the form of narrative dreams, to Billy and to us, but it is not merely a dream.

Achieving closure for a historical narrative built out of such structural repetitions is problematic; hence the necessity for the epilogue to *Cities of the Plain*. Near the close of the novel, both awake and asleep Billy enacts the role of novelist by renarrating *The Crossing* and his past: "He'd tell them about horses and cattle and the old days. Sometimes he'd tell them about Mexico. One night he dreamt that Boyd was in the room with him but he would not speak" (290–91). Billy's dreams of Boyd, his compulsion to revise and renarrate, are not mere parody; this form of historical fiction is a form of reverse divination. Calling out to his past, Billy reenacts within his imagination his roles first of witness, then of narrator of the dead past. To his sympathetic interlocutor-hostess he tells the tale of his long-dead brother:

> Boyd was your brother.
> Yes. He's been dead many a year.
> You still miss him though. . . .
> He was the best. We run off to Mexico together. When we was kids. When our folks died. We went down there to see about getting back some horses they'd stole. We was just kids. He was awful good with horses. I always liked to watch him

ride. Liked to watch him around horses. I'd give about anything
to see him one more time. (291)

However naive (and this stylistic invocation and revision of Huck's
naive voice is, I believe, both deliberate and controlled), Billy's desire
to see the past again is fulfilled in his dreams. And this wish is as much
applied to John Grady as to Boyd, signaling the collapse of both
heroes and the first two novels of the trilogy into a larger narrative
whose significance is more broadly determined.

Besides Billy's attempt to repossess his life through dream, the
epilogue primarily consists of an autonomous and gnomic dream-
parable about the relation between dream, history, and the present,
told to Billy by the Mexican hitchhiker. Stripped of context, the dream
might be taken for a hermeneutical debate by two critics of opposing
interpretive camps, Billy representing a speech-act interpreter from the
common-sense tradition of John Searle ("I think you just see
whatever's in front of you"), and the Mexican an eclectic combination
of theological and deconstructive hermeneutics. The Mexican skepti-
cally critiques the failure of his attempt to draw a map that realistically
represents his life's journey, but then suggests that his dream vision
succeeds in projecting the shape of this desire (269). If the dialogue
between Billy and the Mexican, in a southwestern parody of *Waiting
for Godot,* were not sufficiently absurd, the shift in genre from the
historical novel of the Border Trilogy to the futurist setting of the
epilogue after the millennium is as disorienting to the reader as the
dream is to dreamer or the tale of the dream to Billy.[12] Billy's interro-
gation enacts our own interrogations of McCarthy's text. So this
dream tale functions less as conclusion to the story of Billy and John
Grady and more as meta-narrative—a narrative about narrative that
undercuts and critiques the mixture of geography, historiography, and
biography that comprises the main narrative of the Border Trilogy.

In the Mexican's dream, McCarthy complicates the structure of his
many other dream narratives through two devices: first, the dream is
narrated as an interpolated tale rather than rendered in omniscient,
third-person narrative (as in the dream vision of *Suttree* or in Billy's
dream visions, many of which are reported in *The Crossing* and one

of which concludes *Cities of the Plain*). Second, as in the visionary narratives of Ezekiel and Revelations, the structure of the dream narrative is further complicated by being mirrored as a dream within a dream. The narrator tells of his dream of a traveler who himself dreams a narrative. This mirror structure replicates the structure of the "lucent dream" in which consciousness—or the ego—is made aware of the unconscious dreamwork. This is also the structure of the reader of literature—or of psychoanalysis. Through this device of the dream mirror, the dream's interpretation is rendered exceedingly problematic: "He slept and events took place which I will tell you of, but when was this? You can see the problem. Let us say that the events which took place were a dream of this man whose own reality remains conjectural. How assess the world of that conjectural mind? And what with him is sleep and what is waking? . . . Things need a ground to stand on" (272). In this dream, McCarthy strips the narrative grounding of realism from the Border Trilogy to move directly out of history within the imaginary or the visionary.

McCarthy's replication of the structure of psychoanalysis in this dream is enticing as a possible "ground" for the interpretation of the trilogy. The opposition between dreamer-narrator and dreamer-traveler replicates the relationship between audience and narrative and between the author-function and authorial imagination. Several parts of the dialogue between Billy and the Mexican suggest this relationship, with Billy in the role as reader-interpreter and the Mexican as problematic author unable to take control of "his" dream narrative:

> He [the dreamer] wished me to be his witness. But in dreams there can be no witness. You said as much yourself.
>
> It was just a dream. You dreamt him. You can make him do whatever you like.
>
> Where was he before I dreamt him. . . . Two worlds touch here. You think men have power to call forth what they will? Evoke a world, awake or sleeping? (284–85)

Speaking for a realist model for fiction, our narrator-dreamer becomes the spokesman for a form of predestination, as do Alfonsa in *All the*

Pretty Horses and the blind man of *The Crossing*: "Nor is this life of yours by which you set such store your doing, however you may choose to tell it" (285). Again the dreamer repudiates his naive attempt to represent his life by a map, instead of by narrative or dream, warning Billy that the "story of the world, which is all the world we know, does not exist outside of the instruments of its execution. Nor can those instruments exist outside of their own history. And so on. This life of yours is not a picture of the world" (287). History threatens to disintegrate into stories of the individual, as in Carlylean heroic history, with the postmodern proviso that dream, biography, history as a whole, and finally the historical novel itself is the unique dream-projection and construct solely of the individual's imagination. In its supreme instance, that individual is the author who acts as both witness and narrator of his own dream tale and whose dream world, through writing, intersects the dream world of the reader-witness.

The Mexican—and perhaps McCarthy's author—here verges on a postmodern transcendentalism. The identification between dreamer and dream, author and novel appears complete with the dreamer's request, directed simultaneously to the dream traveler, to John Grady, and self-referentially to McCarthy's almost-concluded trilogy as a whole: "Every man's death is a standing in for every other. . . . Do you love him, that man? Will you honor the path he has taken? Will you listen to his tale?" (289) The epilogue's ending is necessarily ambiguous in its response, depending on the response of Billy and of the trilogy's readers whose realities have momentarily intersected the dream narrative of the trilogy. The epilogue's end necessarily ironizes the narrator's request for interpretation by the witness. Just as Billy, the resistant reader, and his narrative is dismissed by his listening hostess, so the future audience of McCarthy's trilogy is dismissed from the narrative's dream-world by the narrator: "You go to sleep now" (292). In the final line of the dedication, "Turn the page," history and trilogy dissipate into *corrido,* bad dream, nursery rhyme, or the bedtime book, which all function primarily to lull us readers to sleep, away from the traumas of history.

Notes

1. Edwin Arnold was the first critic to read the Border Trilogy against the screenplay. Sketching the differences between an early film script of *Cities of the Plain* and the novel, he notes that much of the cowboy material exists in the script in at least nascent form, that the role of the blind maestro is significantly reduced, that Eduardo's character in the novel is significantly complicated with the addition of his love for Magdalena, and, finally, that the mature Billy Parham of *Cities of the Plain* is much closer to his characterization in the screenplay than in most of *The Crossing* (226–28).

2. Soon after the publication of *The Crossing,* I wrote in *Cormac McCarthy,* "As a series title, The Border Trilogy supersedes the titles of the individual narratives, implying a larger historical continuity or other essential link that presumably connects *All the Pretty Horses* to *The Crossing* as phases of a single, larger narrative" (Jarrett 97). This essay attempts to accomplish this promise, an act originally more of divination than criticism.

3. *Esquire*'s partial serialization of *The Crossing* begins with the novel's first paragraph and encompasses approximately the first sixty pages of the novel, half of its first section (McCarthy, "The Wolf Trapper," 95–104). More than a year earlier, *Esquire* also serialized the bronco-busting section of *All the Pretty Horses.*

4. In her essay on Faulkner and wilderness, Ursula Brumm links the sacrifice of the corporal of *A Fable* to Ike's repudiation of conquest and to Huck's repudiation of the maternal (Brumm 130–33). John Grady Cole is a complex revision of Faulkner's heroes and Huck, whose antifeminism is primarily projected into Billy. Cole chooses to fight Eduardo (unlike the corporal) and, through marriage, seeks to redeem Magdalena. To Eduardo she may be property, but not to John Grady; in the end, I do not think we are to read his final trips into Mexico as the intrusion of capitalist hegemony into Mexico, seeking possession of Magdalena. Eduardo takes the role of capitalist who apes the aristocrat, although Billy's conversation with the captain clarifies that Eduardo is only a middle manager: "He don't own the White Lake, does he? Eduardo" (244). The novel thus destabilizes the stereotypes of Mexico and American with which it appears to work.

5. The decisive moment in the development of Dickens's authority occurs in *The Pickwick Papers* around the fourth number when the monthly sketches of country life "evolve" from loosely related pieces into a novel centered on Pickwick's innocence in opposition to the fallen world. This evolution was made possible after the suicide of the original illustrator, Robert Seymour, when the Dickens author evolved from the sketch writer Boz into the authorial persona identified as the Inimitable Boz. McCarthy's early sketches and, to a lesser degree, *The Orchard Keeper* deserve scrutiny for the traces of a similar authorial development.

6. The view, proposed by Henry James and continued by G. K. Chesterton and the tradition of British criticism, of Dickens as a great comic improviser who lacked formal control of the novel was outmoded by the discovery of Dickens's detailed "number plans" for the novels from *Dombey and Son* on. See John Butt and

Kathleen Tillotson, *Dickens at Work*. For the publication of Dickens's number plans, see Harry Stone, *Dickens' Working Notes for His Novels*.

7. Henry James exemplifies the formal development away from periodic serialization toward a larger, unified conception of the novel as a whole in which the monthly parts collapse into the less significant chapters. William Stafford summarizes the publication history of his second novel: *Roderick Hudson* began serialization in twelve monthly installments before James had completed the manuscript. Although the first book edition contains only minor changes, in the second Macmillan edition James fractured the twelve monthly parts into twenty-four untitled chapters and rewrote passages extensively, a revision expanded in the New York Edition (1269–70). James would similarly amend the book version of *The American* from its serialized beginning (Stafford 1272). He would complain continually of corrupt serial editions of his work.

8. A few exemplary instances of serial narrative in science fiction that bridges the literary and pulp serials are Gene Wolfe's *Shadow and Claw* tetralogy, Kim Stanley Robinson's Mars trilogy, and William Gibson's early cyberpunk novels (linked by the presence of Sally Shears).

9. *Cities of the Plain* uses this locution several times: Billy says, "Me and my bud— my brother—we was on the run and he was hurt" (36) and later, referring to the dying Cole, "Bud, he said. Bud" (258). This renaming of the sacrificial hero surely alludes to Melville's sacrificial victim par excellence, Billy Budd. But in southwestern vernacular "bud" operates as an all-purpose term asserting a fraternal relationship between male friends, fathers and son, or brothers.

10. For discussions of Cole and Billy as figures of imperialist invasion, see Molly McBride's essay "From Mutilation to Penetration: Cycles of Conquest in *Blood Meridian* and *All the Pretty Horses*" and John Beck's unpublished conference paper "It wasn't the future that brought me back here": Borderline Nostalgia and Global Impact." Beck reads *Blood Meridian* within the context of the rhetoric of internationalist intervention in the Reagan and Bush administrations.

11. Even today, the drive off Interstate 10 north of Van Horn, Texas, into the Franklin Mountains demonstrates that this sense of Cole's historical belatedness is not reality but an imaginary and literary construct of a mass culture, itself as open to exposure as a fiction of the metroplex. The older economy and workers of the West persists, although in less pervasive form.

12. Both Stacey Peebles in "*Lo fantástico:* The Influence of Borges and Cortázar on the Epilogue of *Cities of the Plain*" and Edwin T. Arnold (242) note McCarthy's use of magical realism and evocation of Borges within the epilogue.

Works Cited

Arnold, Edwin. "The Last of the Trilogy: First Thoughts on *Cities of the Plain*." *Perspectives on Cormac McCarthy*. Rev. ed. Ed. Edwin T. Arnold and Dianne C. Luce. Jackson: University Press of Mississippi, 1999. 221–47.

Beck, John. "'It wasn't the future that brought me back here': Borderline Nostalgia and Global Impact." Paper presented at the Cormac McCarthy Society Conference, San Antonio, Texas, November 1999.

Brumm, Ursula. "Wilderness and Civilization: A Note on William Faulkner." In *William Faulkner: Three Decades of Criticism*. Ed. Frederick J. Hoffman and Olga W. Vickery. New York: Harcourt, Brace, 1963. 125–34.

Butt, John, and Kathleen Tillotson. *Dickens at Work*. Oxford: Oxford University Press, 1958.

Campbell, Neil. "Liberty Beyond Its Proper Bounds: Cormac McCarthy's History of the West in *Blood Meridian*." *Myth, Legend, Dust: Critical Responses to Cormac McCarthy*. Ed. Rick Wallach. Manchester: Manchester University Press, 2000. 217–26.

Jarrett, Robert. *Cormac McCarthy*. New York: Twayne, 1997.

Lilley, James D. "'The hands of yet other puppets': Figuring Freedom and Reading Repetition in *All the Pretty Horses*." *Myth, Legend, Dust: Critical Responses to Cormac McCarthy*. Ed. Rick Wallach. Manchester: Manchester University Press, 2000. 272–87.

Luce, Dianne C. "The Road and the Matrix: The World as Tale in *The Crossing*." *Perspectives on Cormac McCarthy*. Rev. ed. Ed. Edwin T. Arnold and Dianne C. Luce. Jackson: University Press of Mississippi, 1999. 195–220.

McBride, Molly. "From Mutilation to Penetration: Cycles of Conquest in *Blood Meridian* and *All the Pretty Horses*." *Southwestern American Literature* 25 (fall 1999): 24–34.

McCarthy, Cormac. *All the Pretty Horses*. New York: Alfred A. Knopf, 1992.

———. *Cities of the Plain*. New York: Alfred A. Knopf, 1998.

———. *Cities of the Plain*. Unpublished manuscript, Cormac McCarthy collection, Southwestern Writers collection, Albert B. Alkek Library, Southwest Texas State University, San Marcos, Texas.

———. *The Crossing*. New York: Alfred A. Knopf, 1994.

———. "The Wolf Trapper." *Esquire* (July 1993): 95–104.

Mileur, Jean-Pierre. "Revisionism, Irony, and the Mask of Sentiment." *New Literary History* 29 (1998): 197–233.

Morrison, Gail Moore. "*All the Pretty Horses*: John Grady Cole's Expulsion from Paradise." In *Perspectives on Cormac McCarthy*. Rev. ed. Ed. Edwin T. Arnold and Dianne C. Luce. Jackson: University Press of Mississippi, 1999. 175–94.

Peebles, Stacey. "*Lo fantástico:* The Influence of Borges and Cortázar on the Epilogue of *Cities of the Plain.*" *Southwestern American Literature* 25 (fall 1999): 105–9.

Stafford, William T. "Note on the Texts." *Henry James: Novels 1871–1880.* New York: Library of America, 1983. 1269–77.

Stone, Harry. *Dickens' Working Notes for His Novels.* Chicago: University of Chicago Press, 1987.

Sullivan, Nell. "Boys Will Be Boys and Girls Will Be Gone: The Circuit of Male Desire in Cormac McCarthy's Border Trilogy." *Southern Quarterly* 38 (spring 2000): 167–85.

INDEX

abject, 126
abjection, 8; characteristics, 126; formation of, 127–32; kid, 253–54; melancholia, 253–54; as primordial conflict,
   253; sacred power of horror, 136
Adventures of Huckleberry Finn, 107,
   121n. 6, 317, 339n. 4
African American lullaby, 147
African Americans, 154–56
afterlife, 175–76
agency, 2, 3, 108, 121n. 5
aggressivity, 250, 252
Agrarian tradition, 51–52, 54–55
agriculture, 51, 52, 61, 54–55, 62–65,
   71n. 11
Alejandra, 161
Alfonsa, 148–49, 272–73, 319
allegoresis: baroque, 261; concept of,
   241, 243
allegory: child imagery, 248–49; defined,
   241, 259; facticity of death, 243;
   functions, 243; melancholia, 258–60
All the Pretty Horses, God's role, 217;
   historical repetition, 324; language,
   271–72; Mexican representations,
   141–50; monumental time, 275;
   novelistic world, 40–41; romance,
   315; romantic ideals, 145–47, 149,
   150n. 5, 165–66; significance, 18;
   women, 126; women characters, 138
American nation, 114–20
amorality, 212, 270
Anglo versus Mexican minds, 273–74,
   282
anthropocentrism, 28–29, 32, 37, 83,
   217
antimyth, 89, 93, 95
Anzaldúa, Gloria, 156, 164
apocalyptic paradigm, 300
Appalachian fiction, 47–48
Appalachian Land Ownership Task
   Force, 62, 71n. 6
Arcadia, 84, 248, 249, 264n. 14

argonauts, 111–12
asocial point of view, 178
aspen leaf imagery, 256–57
atomic. *See* nuclear issues
atravesados (border crossers), 10, 154,
   157, 160, 164, 167
autonomy, 331

Bakhtin, Mikhail M., 38–39, 44n. 16,
   122n. 11; carnival, 279
Ballard, Lester, 171–92, 194n. 4, 195n.
   10, 196n. 24
barbed wire fence, 98
baroque: allegoresis, 261; defined, 241;
   vision, 255–56
The Bear (Faulkner), 315–16, 318, 320
bear themes, 89, 91–92, 109, 111; death
   as symbol, 208–9
beautiful versus sublime, 45n. 21
beauty, 177, 180, 181, 188, 195n. 16
benign violence, 200
Beowulf: described and analyzed,
   200–201; Grendel's rival double, 205;
   martial code, 203–4, 206; relationship
   to *Blood Meridian,* 199
Berry, Wendell, 51–52, 58, 60
Bible, 96, 239, 244, 283
Bierce, Ambrose, 143
biocentric view of nature, 221
Birth of Iron myth, 189–90
blacksmith, heedless, 189–90
blind man, 218, 279, 282
blood: as metaphor, 267–68;
   Mexicanness, 160; milk and, 133–35,
   138–39n. 8
*Blood Meridian, or, The Evening
   Redness in the West*: aesthetic
   function, 261; agency, 2; conflict of
   doubles, 205; epic resonance, 38;
   female characters, 125; gender, 7; lack
   of human implication, 33, language,
   270–71; martial code, 11; martial
   interregnum, 204; melancholy subtext,

343